THE POSITIVE THEORY OF CAPITAL

THE
POSITIVE THEORY OF CAPITAL

BY

EUGEN V. BÖHM-BAWERK

TRANSLATED WITH A PREFACE AND ANALYSIS

BY

WILLIAM SMART

BOOKS FOR LIBRARIES PRESS
FREEPORT, NEW YORK

First Published 1891
Reprinted 1971

INTERNATIONAL STANDARD BOOK NUMBER:
0-8369-6604-X

LIBRARY OF CONGRESS CATALOG CARD NUMBER:
70-175689

PRINTED IN THE UNITED STATES OF AMERICA
BY
NEW WORLD BOOK MANUFACTURING CO., INC.
HALLANDALE, FLORIDA 33009

TRANSLATOR'S PREFACE

In his *Geschichte und Kritik der Kapitalzins-Theorieen* (1884), which I translated in 1890 under the title of *Capital and Interest*, Professor Böhm-Bawerk, after passing in critical review the various opinions, practical and theoretical, held from the earliest times on the subject of interest, ended with the words: "On the foundation thus laid, I shall try to find for the vexed problem a solution which invents nothing and assumes nothing, but simply and truly attempts to deduce the phenomena of the formation of interest from the simplest natural and psychological principles of our science." *The Positive Theory of Capital*, published in Innsbruck in 1888, and here rendered into English, is the fulfilment of that promise.

The criticisms directed against the various theories of Interest in the former work may be briefly summarised as follows.

The Productivity theories—those which, more or less explicitly, attribute the existence of interest to the productive power of capital —are dismissed as confusing quantity of product with value of product, either in the way of tacitly assuming the identity of the two, or of failing to show any necessary connection between them. The problem of capital is a problem of surplus value, and value does not come from the side of production but from the side of consumption. Capital is productive, but interest is not its product.

The Use theories, which are a more or less scientific expansion of the familiar formula, "Interest is the price paid for the use of capital," are shown to base interest, which is notoriously an income obtained from all kinds of capital, on an analogy drawn from one special kind of capital, viz. durable goods. The idea that the *use* of capital is something distinct from the *using-up* of capital, and interest something different from the price of the principal, becomes untenable when the true economic nature of the "good" is understood as the sum of its material uses or services. If consumption is only a single exhaustive use, and use only a prolonged consumption, the payment for "use" of Capital must be included in the price of capital.

In the Abstinence theory, which makes interest a compensation,

made to the owner of capital, for his renunciation of immediate consumption, Böhm-Bawerk sees a confusion of the origin and accumulation of capital with the source and cause of interest. Abstinence
will account for the owner having a sum to lend, but it will not
account for that sum growing 3% larger in a year's time.

Lastly, the Socialist or Exploitation theory, which makes interest
simply a gain from exploited labour, is shown to be a theory which
could only arise on the negative basis of the unsatisfactory accounts
hitherto given, and on the positive basis of a mistaken value
theory. When an income obtained without work and without risk
was claimed as the reward of abstinence, and when all value was
ascribed to the action of material labourers, it was inevitable that
there should rise a reactionary theory proving that interest was
robbery. Thus the board was swept clean for the *Positive Theory*.

A translator who does his duty must pass the work he renders
through his own mind. The necessity this imposes on him of
understanding his author, and getting at his point of view, should
make him peculiarly sensitive to certain difficulties which are not
removed by simple translation. Modes of thought, arrangement,
manner of working, may remain foreign. A translator's preface,
then, is not without justification if it anticipates some of the questions that are sure to arise in the minds of readers more accustomed, perhaps, to English economics. Now as the main difficulty
of the present work is that alluded to by Professor Böhm-Bawerk
in his own Preface, that the strikingly simple outlines of his theory
are obscured by the very elaboration and completeness with which
it is worked out, perhaps the best service I can do is to give a
short direct summary of the main argument, expanding on one
or two points which seem to me to require commentary.

Economic science being based on an analysis of the industrial
life, the first question in a theory of capital is one of terminology :
What does the practical world mean, and what has it hitherto
meant, by the word Capital ? Here we find in common acceptance
not one but two conceptions, both based more or less on Adam
Smith's old distinction between National Capital and Individual
Capital. It is quite necessary for scientific progress that the
exact distinction between these two conceptions should be fully
recognised, but it would be useless to refuse the name to either of
them : the practical world would not follow us. On looking closer
at the two, however, we can see that one of the conceptions really
includes the other, and that the difficulty may be avoided by adding
an appropriate predicate to each. Taking as basis the old root
idea of " an interest-bearing sum of money," we may define
capital in its widest sense (or Acquisitive Capital), as the complex
of products destined to the Acquisition of goods. Under this, as
narrower category, we put the conception that came later in time.

but perhaps better deserves the name without predicate, that of Social or Productive Capital, comprising all products destined for the production of fresh wealth ; briefly, the compiex of Intermediate Products. Thus we happily preserve in both conceptions the popular idea of "income bearing": society as a whole can only obtain an income by "producing" new wealth, while the individual may "acquire" it as well by the transfer of old wealth.

By these definitions Land and Labour are excluded from capital. They have certain analogies, even close analogies, with it, but scientific accuracy is not gained by making definitions so wide as to conceal really discrepant elements. The definition of Social Capital also excludes the Maintenance of Labourers ; for, obviously, to include the direct and most obvious means of living would be to take away all possibility of distinguishing between capital and consumption wealth.

The subject, then, naturally divides itself into two parts :—Capital in the narrower, but more widely important, meaning of the Instrument of Production, and Capital as the Source of Income.

First, of the Instrument of Production. In the economical world man finds himself a being of infinite want, confronted with a universe full of potential wealth but with no tools except hands and brains to give him possession of it. Incapable of creating anything, he yet finds himself endowed with a power of moving things, which, as he masters the secrets of nature's working, gradually enables him to imprison, impress, or suspend the action of her powers, and so make her his servant. In various concrete ways he adapts or rearranges nature—never, of course, changing her laws or acting contrary to them, but varying the causal connection of natural processes in such a way that, to a large extent, he remakes the natural world to suit his purposes. Thus, between man and his natural environment there gradually grows up a third term, a machinery for the fuller satisfaction of man's life, and to this, in general terms, we give the name Capital. But, however the growth of wealth and industry disguise the fact, in all production of wealth there are only two original forces at work, nature's powers and man's powers. Human powers, as always limited, and as always put forth "at the cost of" brain or tissue, are all "economic"; but in the great treasury of natural forces there are some powers so universal in their scope and working that they do not enter into calculations of cost. As we say, using two phrases whose full significance we do not always realise, we do not "economise" the free gifts of nature—they "cost" us nothing; although they enter into the operations of all production, they do not enter into "economic" consideration. The original factors of production, then, are man and nature : the strictly economic factors of production are labour and those natural forces (called by metonymy Land) which are limited and capable of being monopolised. But Capital, however much credit it gets and deserves for its work in present-day production, is no independent factor alongside of these. In one aspect it may be called "stored-up labour," in another—and more truly—"natural force stored up by labour"; but in capital itself, alike in its origin and in its working, there is nothing that is not accounted for by the other two factors.

We say, in its origin and its working, and it is advisable to emphasise that these are distinct things. The origin of capital is due to two factors, Industry and Saving, both being indispensable. It should be noted, however, that what is saved is not capital but productive power. The primitive labourer works overtime, produces a surplus subsistence, and spends it in making tools : his saving is saving of strength to make tools. The modern worker produces a surplus over his subsistence : gives that over to banks and other agencies to be spent in building factories, erecting machinery, etc.: what is saved is the natural forces thus put in position to turn out consumption goods. But when we know the origin of capital, we have still to ask : What is the nature and character of the production carried on by means of capital? The answer may be put in the following way. The aim of production is essentially the making or procuring of a living. The animal finds a certain provision spontaneously offered it in nature; goes straight toward that provision; and never gets beyond it. Man, on the other hand, even in the simplest state, takes an indirect course. He allies natural with his own (still natural) forces; and he gets behind these natural forces, setting them against each other, or co-operating with each other in carrying out his instructions. He steals fire from heaven, and turns it against the gods. The end is always the consumption good—the good which exhausts itself in ministering to man's life in its higher and lower forms; the factors are always labour and nature; but the way in which the end is reached is here indirect, lengthy, and roundabout. From the rude spade, which the savage first uses as a medium between his bare hands and the fruits or roots he lives on, down to the many years' production process stretching between the sinking of the shaft for coal or iron and the flying shuttles turning out the cloth which finds its goal in covering bare backs, is simply an evolution of the roundabout method. The course of economic progress puts increasing intervals between preparatory and finishing labour, decreasing the stock by increasing the tools; and at every new stage labour embodies itself in further intermediate products or capital. The characteristic result is twofold. As we should expect from the accumulation and concentration of natural forces, this capitalist method is immensely productive as compared with direct or unassisted labour.

On the other side, however, is to be put the sacrifice of Time necessarily involved in the indirect process. The relation of these two sides must be carefully noted. As time plays a greater part in production—as the average period is extended—the absolute productiveness of the capitalist process increases, but the relative productiveness decreases. That is to say : when the process has reached a certain point, it becomes subject to a law of diminishing returns.

The function, then, of capital in production may be said to be that of allowing labour and natural powers to work out their economic effects in processes that take time, or the utilisation of natural forces in roundabout methods. Or, if we adopt the peculiarly modern view that man is the economic *Zielpunkt*, we may say that capital gives time to labour to avail itself of those powers of nature which become available only at a considerable sacrifice of time.

So much for the function of capital, and one is apt to jump to the conclusion that, having shown how capitalist industry produces a great quantity of *products* as compared with unassisted labour, the sole and sufficient origin of *interest* has been indicated. A little consideration will show that we are yet on the threshold of that inquiry. The concrete result—the *raison d'être*—of a factory is the mass of products it sends to market. These are the transformed shapes of raw and auxiliary materials, machinery generally, and labour ; and the price realised for them repays the outlay on materials, keeps up the machinery, and pays the wages—including all the wages of intellect. But beyond the repaying of all these costs it is a familiar fact that, in normal production, the prices realised leave a surplus. This surplus is not accounted for by profits, although often confused with them. Profit is either employer's wage (and is thus already included), or it is the chance of a happy conjuncture that allows a higher price to be obtained than is normal—which chance is continually being levelled down by competition. But this surplus is recognised as something due to the owner of capital without claim of personal work from him, and it is a surplus of value which competition cannot wipe out. In Böhm-Bawerk's former book, *Capital and Interest*, it was exhaustively proved that no theory had yet shown what capital does, or forbears from doing, that it should get this surplus under the name of interest. It is not a payment for the labour embodied in concrete capital, for that labour is presumably fully paid for—say, by the machine maker to his men and to himself—and does not warrant a further continuous payment. It is not a payment for the working of natural forces embodied in the machine, for the value of the machine consists in nothing else than in the working of these forces, and in the price is already paid all the forces that the machine will put forth and

b

mediate. And it is not wear and tear, nor is it insurance against risk, for in all normal undertakings these are provided for by separate replacement and insurance funds. For proof of these statements I must refer the reader to that book, or the brief summary of it in the preface. What must be emphasised here is that the explanation of capital as the Instrument of Production is exhausted when it is shown that it allows nature and labour to work out their effects in lengthy processes. The source of interest will not be found simply within the sphere of production, for the reason that interest is a problem of surplus value, and value takes us into the sphere of distribution. Thus we come to the next division of the present work, Capital as it appears in the sphere of Distribution, or Capital as the source of the income called Interest.

If we begin, as usual, by asking what business people understand by interest, we shall be told practically that a sum of money paid down now—say £100—will buy a greater sum—say £103 or £105—this day twelve months. Or if I owe £100 now for goods received, and do not pay the debt for a year, I have to add a certain amount under the title of interest.

The most obvious fact here is that the payment of interest has some very definite connection with the time when payment is made. This suggests the general question : What is the place and influence of time on the value of goods. And the answer is : It is an empirical fact of undoubted universality that present goods are valued more highly than future goods of like kind and amount.

For this three causes may be given. First, is the difference between the circumstances of want and the provision for want in present and in future. In any case, if want is pressing and provision is scarce, value is high. But the pressure of want in the present is always with us, while as regards provision in the future it is generally true *omne ignotum pro mirifico*. Thus present goods obtain a permanent importance from felt present wants, and future goods a permanent unimportance from anticipated future provision. Most men, accordingly,—people in immediate distress and beginners of all sorts being types—are willing to pledge their future for a really inadequate present sum. Second, is the general underestimate of the future, common to humanity, and traceable to want of imagination, defect of will, or feeling of life's uncertainty. Children and savages are typical of the improvidence which is more or less striking in all classes. It may be that this cause is not on the same level with the first, and tends to less importance with social progress. But, in the world as it is, it is certain that the things of the future are of less value to us simply because they are future. And, third, is the technical superiority of present goods. As we have already seen, in the hands of labour wealth increases enormously with the extension in time of the production process.

Goods available now have accordingly the promise and potency of being greatly multiplied in the future, while goods coming into our disposal only in the future must undergo another period of production before the same abundance is reaped. Of these three causes the first two are cumulative, the second alternative. The first group alone would account for a difference in value between present and future goods : the appearance of the latter makes the difference not only apparent but measurable.

If, then, from so many sides and classes—from the young who expect to be better off, from the rich and improvident who wish to enjoy the present, from the industrious who wish to add to their wealth ; that is to say, from probably the majority of mankind—there comes an underestimate of the future compared with the present, it is easily explained why, as a rule, present goods have a greater value than future goods of like kind and amount.

In this empirical and psychological fact, for the full treatment of which the reader is referred to Book V., our author finds the source of interest in its three principal forms.

The simplest case of interest is that in which it appears in the loan for consumption. Here we have a real and true *exchange* of a smaller amount of present money, or present goods, for a larger amount of future money or goods. The sum returned, "principal" plus interest, is the market valuation and *equivalent* of the "principal" lent. The apparent difference in value is simply due to our forgetting that £100 in our hands now is not the same thing as £100 a year hence. This Agio on present goods is interest. In other words, interest is a complementary part of the price ; a part equivalent of the "principal" lent.

In this simple case interest is more evidently the result of the first two causes just mentioned. Apart altogether from an organised system of production this agio would emerge, and has emerged, as something claimed by the saving from the unthrifty. But so long as there was no organic production, the circumstances of borrowers and lenders were too diverse and arbitrary to allow of a measured rate of interest. But when the third factor comes into play, time becomes a condition of surplus product, and interest becomes measurable in terms of time.

The second and principal form assumed, then, by interest is that in which it appears as part of the so-called "profit of undertaking." A capitalist employer hires land, buys raw and auxiliary materials, machinery, power, and labour. He sets these to co-operate in the making of a product. The product is the new shape taken on by all these productive goods, and we should naturally expect that the price obtained for it would exactly cover and reimburse the value of all the goods consumed in making it. But, as we know, after all ordinary costs are accounted for, the price obtained in normal economic circum-

stances shows a surplus of value. The explanation of the surplus is
that productive goods, while materially and physically present, are,
to economical consideration, future goods : that is to say, they are
products *in the making*. The wants to which they minister, and
from which alone they get their value, are future wants. On the
admitted ground of equivalence between costs and products, then,
the value of the means of production must be the same as the value
of the goods into which they pass. But these goods being in the
meantime future goods, and suffering from the discount which, as
we have seen, is made on all future goods, the value of means of
production must suffer the same discount. The undertaker intentionally turns his wealth into productive goods : that is to say, he
exchanges his money for raw materials, workshops, machinery,
labour. In the production process these ripen into present goods,
with the full value of present goods. The price he receives for
these recoups all his expenditure plus interest. Interest thus
proves itself, as before, the difference between the formerly future
and now present goods.

There is a third case of interest which has some features so puzzling as to demand separate consideration : this is the case of income
obtained from Durable Goods, usually called Hire or Lease, and, in
one case, Rent. The distinction between a perishable and a durable
good is that, while both are the sums of their respective uses or
services, the durable good is a sum extending over a period of time.
But on our theory the later services of such a good must have a less
value than the proximate services, and the total value of the good
will be a sum of diminishing amounts. The " capital value " of such
a good, then, will be to all appearance much less than the sum of the
values really obtained during its lifetime. Here, as in the former
cases, the services originally undervalued ripen to full present value
in the hands of the owner, and the difference between the past and
the present values, after providing for replacement of the good, is
Interest. Thus if the owner of capital throws his parent wealth
into the form of stone and lime, he possesses, in the durable shape
of a house, a sum of future uses discounted according to their
futurity. As each year passes one annual service is realised, and its
value is thrown off, while each service still to be realised is one year
nearer the present, and is thus one year more valuable. The house,
as now containing one rent less, is less valuable, and this loss falls to
be deducted from the gross return as wear and tear. But what is
lost, be it noted, is not one annual service estimated at present
value ; it is the *last* future service of which the good is still capable,
—for if all the services have moved up one step in value it is the
value of the last service that drops off. The difference between the
present service realised (gross rent) and the last service now deducted
(economic wear and tear) is the net return of interest. Thus,

again, we find that interest is the difference between the formerly future and now present goods. This somewhat difficult point is made clear from the concrete figures on pp. 342-345.

It will be seen that in this we have a theory, not only of durable consumption goods such as houses, and of durable productive goods such as machinery, factories, and fixed capital generally, but a theory which carries us beyond our formal definition of Capital into the sphere of Land. In land we have a durable good whose services will be rendered to generations unborn : the "last" service is, therefore, to the calculations of the present, nil : there is no economic wear and tear—no need of any fund for replacement—and the gross return suffers no deduction but is all interest. To put it concretely. A man buys land as he buys fixed capital ;—to get an interest from it. He buys its annual services or rents for a sum which represents the future services diminished in perspective. In other words the "capitalised value" is not an infinite number of years' rents but so many years' purchase. In his hands the future uses ripen into present : he gets the present value of what he bought as future value : as there is no wear and tear, nothing of this need be set aside for replacement : the whole gross rent is net interest. Ricardo, in pointing to the "original and indestructible powers of the soil" as the cause of rent, was right so far as his explanation indicated why the gross return was also the net, but wrong so far as it indicated that rent was due to the productiveness of this peculiar kind of durable good. The interest on a mine and the rent from land are essentially the same, although the one should wear out in thirty years while the other is "indestructible."

These are the simple outlines of the *Positive Theory*. By it all three kinds of interest are traced to the one identical source, the increasing value of what are, either naturally or economically, future goods, as they ripen into present goods. But when dealing with the principal form of interest, that in which it appears as part of the profit of undertaking, Dr. Böhm-Bawerk makes a long excursus into the relation of wealth to labour, which is not the least suggestive and valuable part of the work. As it suffers somewhat, however, from its position in the text, I shall take the liberty of putting it in my own way.

There are three markets in which the particular kind of "future goods" known as means of production are exchanged against finished present goods—practically against money : these are the Labour market, the Land market, and the market for Concrete Capital. Taking the Labour market as the most typical and the most difficult, its prominent features are these. On the one side are the Capitalist Undertakers. These are men presumably possessed of a surplus of wealth which they cannot advantageously use in their own consumption ; to them personally, therefore, the

present goods which constitute their surplus have *per se* no
advantage over future goods.   But in this surplus they have
the means of waiting over lengthy processes of production.   As
their wealth increases the average period of production is extended, and with every extension the absolute productiveness of
the process increases.   On the other side is the majority of the
population, the Wage-Earners.   Their circumstances, as a class, are
such that they cannot engage in any independent production that
takes time.   Even if they could, their production period would
necessarily be short, and in competition with the long process the
handicap would be too heavy.   It may be assumed, therefore,
that they will rather take service as "hands" than risk independent
production.

Evidently the big battalions are on the side of the capitalist,
and in regard to this particular kind of present good, Labour, it
seems to need no further demonstration that the price of it, namely
Wage, will always be less than that of product, and thus allow the
employer an interest.   This is, in general terms and in a more dispassionate way, the Socialist answer.   But, while admitting, as we
very well may, that there is enough and to spare of exploitation in
profit generally, the question is by no means so simple as Socialist
theory would have it.   If there is force on the one side there are
certain forces which work steadily on the other.   The Trade Unions
give the labourers a certain power of waiting, and tend to force
employers, as a class, to give up at least that portion of profit which
is pure exploitation.   Yet wage would not be explained if it were
shown to be, in many cases, the exploitation of profit!   The inter-
competition of capitalists, again, has surely been effective enough
of late decades to force the remuneration of capital towards an
economic—as distinguished from an exploitation—level.   If there
is no economic level of interest, why has it not been wiped out of
existence altogether?   The argument is one that Socialism itself
often uses; that, in some respects, the dependence of capital is as
absolute as that of labour.   It is necessary even for the *status
quo* of wealth that the capitalist should bury his surplus in the
fertile womb of earth, or in the living powers of man.

But in the present state of economic development there is no
question of mere preservation of wealth—there can scarcely be,
so long as the seed sown returns some thirty, some fifty, some
a hundred fold.   The motive of the capitalist undertaker is
certainly not preservation but increase.   He changes his wealth
into means of production in order that the value of the products
should be more than the value of the costs.   He is warranted by
experience in assuming that, *at the worst*, the price realised will
contain a certain minimum rate of interest; will, most probably,
contain also a good wage for himself as master workman; and that,

possibly, a happy conjuncture may give him a "profit" besides. (Of course I am speaking of the enlightened employer who knows that "wage," technically, is remuneration for work done, and does not claim as wage more than, say, the remuneration of a Prime Minister.) Where the employer and the capitalist are separate entities—as they always are to economic consideration—the motives also are distinct : the motive of the employer is wage and "profit"—using that ambiguous word in the loose meaning of gain beyond wage of superintendence and pure interest — while that of the capitalist is interest—with perhaps a chance of "profit." Now, as thus separated, the competition of capitals with each other becomes more intense ; for capital becomes a suppliant, not only to the labourer who demands the minimum wage, but to the class of employers who expect a perhaps extravagant "wage of superintendence," and a "profit" besides. In this state of sharpened competition the insufficiency of the exploitation theory becomes manifest to experience. We are forced to see that there is a level of interest which no amount of competition normally levels away, and we conclude that this is the economic level. Where the inter-competition of capitals is the fiercest, the owner of wealth has not to content himself with the mere preservation and re-creation of his wealth—much less pay a premium to labour for keeping it—but gets his minimum $2\frac{3}{4}\%$ or 3% of interest.

This explanation will be found if we turn from the question as between labourers and employers, and consider the larger question as between owners of present goods on the one side, and labourers and employers alike on the other. And here we come to Böhm-Bawerk's enunciation of a proposition which seems to me one of the most important in modern economics. It is that the supply of present goods, available in any community either as means of production to labourers or as subsistence to mere borrowers for consumption, is the sum of that community's existing wealth exclusive of land. No one nowadays hoards wealth, drawing on it as needed. Thanks to banking systems and facilities for invest-ment, nearly all wealth that is not actually being consumed by the owners is made available to supply this double demand. Disre-garding as before the demand for consumption, the effect of which is merely to lessen the amount of wealth available for productive borrowers—and remembering in passing that the agio on present goods is the joint result of these two collateral demands, we find this wealth confronting the demand of labour, transmitted through the employers for the means of subsistence during the production period. Now, thanks to well-known motives, wealth in normal circumstances increases faster than population. As it accumulates it becomes possible for the labourers to extend their processes. Seed-time and harvest become separated, not by months but by

years, and the amount of wealth in a community, as enabling labour
to bridge over the long time of growth, becomes visibly the condition of its average production period, and so of its average productiveness.   Thus to him that hath much much is given : the
rich nation is the heir of the economic promises.

From this it is not difficult to see that the value of means of
production must always lag behind that of finished products.   There
is always a demand for ampler means of living, and the condition
of obtaining ampler means is—time to extend the production process.   So long, then, as the wants of spiritual beings call for fuller
and finer satisfactions, and so long as the working life rises to
higher levels, so long will there be a premium put on the present
wealth which makes more ample wealth possible.   Thus we are
justified in saying that the demand for means of production will
always be greater than the supply, and interest, as the agio on such,
will appear in the price of products.

The superficial resemblance of this Subsistence Fund to the
generally discredited Wage Fund of the classical economists will
not mislead any one who enters into the heart of Böhm-Bawerk's
theory.   The difference between the two will be found in the few
pregnant sentences on pp. 419, 420.   In case of misunderstanding, however, two cautions may be given here.   One is that by
"means of subsistence" must be understood, not simply food, nor
even the common necessaries and comforts of life, but all that goes
to the maintenance of the workers, whatever their various levels of
comfort.   It is not a certain wage fund, provided arbitrarily by
capitalist employers, that is available for the simple "subsistence"
of the working classes : it is the entire wealth of the community
that is available for the maintenance of all classes of workers.   The
caution is much needed quite outside of this connection.   I am
persuaded that many people think they have determined the
"cost" and due reward of labour when they have found how many
weekly wages of 20s. are contained in the community's stock of
wealth.   The mischief that this idea does, in making people think
that a rise of wages is a social calamity, is, to my mind, very great.
To economic consideration, however, the line is a vanishing one
which divides Hodge's beer and bacon from Plugson's venison and
champagne.   Rightly considered, the prices of books, the stipends
of clergymen and teachers, the seats at theatres and concerts are
"expenses of subsistence," just as much as the labourers' bread and
cheese—unless we are to limit the category of "workers" to the
20s. a week class.

The other caution is that this wealth available for subsistence
does not consist exclusively of goods already in the finished state.
To put all wealth into this form, indeed, would be the greatest
possible waste.   What is required is, that the various means of

subsistence should be ready when wanted, and this involves that, at any given time, the wealth of a country consists of products at all stages of maturity.   To put it concretely :—At this moment the wheat is being sown that will feed human beings after next harvest, while the sapling is being planted that will not come to its full growth for a century to come : at the same moment, perhaps, the oak is being felled that began its growth a hundred years ago, and to-morrow the wood of it will enter into the framework of a threshing-machine which will extend its life-work over a score of harvests : sapling and tree, machine and wheat, are alike parts of that wealth which is available for the labourers' demand in its continuity.

Remembering these cautions we can see the full import of this conception.   It defines the true relation of wealth to labour in the following terms : The function of existing wealth is to subsist the workers during the interval between the beginning and the end of the social production period.   This strikes us as strange mainly because of the bourgeois idea that wealth is the end and goal of labour, and the more vicious idea that labour is a tax on life.   For certain purposes of economic study we may think of labour as the means, and consumption wealth as the end of production, but the economist falls into error whenever he forgets that economic life is an endless circle, where wealth, as subsistence, passes into muscle and brain, and muscle and brain pass into wealth again.   Even when we rise—as the economist may do—to wider conceptions, and point to man's full free life as the goal of economic effort, we ought to recognise that the working life which we lead, and should lead, is at once an end and a mean.   In working we live; and in working we produce wealth : this wealth, again, permits of freer work and fuller life.   In correspondence with this, the type of labourer is not the man who produces on one day to consume on the next, but the man who consumes during his work day—who consumes while he produces—and, moreover, whose consumption increases with his production.   The function of wealth, then, we say, is to support this working life, with its increasing claims, during its work.   Thus instead of making wealth the final cause of industry—as the economist in virtue of his professional bias is apt to do—or making it the beginning and limit of industry—as the Wage Fund theory tended to do—this conception places wealth in the centre as the maintenance of the working world during its rise to higher and higher levels of working life.   In other words, it puts the economic conception into line with the moral by making wealth simply the mean to the working life.

If, then, interest is so purely a natural phenomenon, why has it met with so much covert dislike, and so much scientific opposition ? There are at least three reasons.   First, the element on which all interest is based, namely time, has come to be a peculiarly important factor in modern production. All things come to him who waits, and, in economic life, this describes the capitalist. But this fact involves that the labouring classes who cannot wait, and cannot compete with the productiveness of lengthy processes, are put in a position of peculiar dependence : hence the possibility of exploitation of wage, of usurious rates of interest, of unjust rents. Second, from a moral point of view, there is much that is objectionable in the fact that interest allows certain classes to live without working and to make this possibility hereditary in their families. Third, in this income there is no ratio between gain and desert. Those who have little must accept Savings Bank interest for their hard-earned shillings ; those who have much have all the chances of bonds, mortgages, joint-stock investments and the like. All the same, so long as men do put a different valuation on present and future goods, interest cannot be prevented. Even a Socialist state could not prevent it : if by forcible means it were stopped between individuals, it would still obtain between commune and labourer. The state in this case would replace the capitalist, and "exploit" the worker in the same way— although, it may be hoped, with a clearer view to the wellbeing of the exploited—but no organisation could make interest into wage.

In Book VII. Dr. Böhm-Bawerk passes to the most difficult part of the subject, the Rate of Interest. Here, however, we shall find him using terms which are scarcely intelligible without some knowledge of the theory of value enunciated by Jevons and Menger, and now held practically as the fundamental doctrine of the Austrian school. The formulation of this theory, so far as was necessary to the theory of capital, occupies Books III. and IV. of the present work. It is not possible, unfortunately, in the short space at my disposal, to give anything like an easy account of this theory. I have already found difficulty enough in putting it into the compass of my own *Introduction to the Theory of Value*, and all I can hope to do here is, perhaps, to assist the reader who finds any difficulty in the text.

The essential points are as follows. Value is altogether based on utility, and the amount of value is determined, not by average, but by final or marginal utility. The subjective *value* of a good, as distinguished from its utility, lies in its being the indispensable condition of some satisfaction of want : the *amount* of value it obtains is determined by the last use to which it, or a similar good of the stock, is put in the then circumstances of want and provision for want. Thus the utility of a bushel of corn is given it by its power of supporting life : its value comes from the fact that it is so limited that some human want *depends* on it for satisfaction : the amount of its value is determined by the least use to which the bushel is economically put in the circumstances of the consumers on the one hand and the amount of the harvest on the other. Thus value has no absolute level; it is neither intrinsic nor relative to any personal or material average: it is always found in the relation of these two determinants of Want and Provision.

Price, or Exchange Value, again, is a superstructure on this subjective value, determined by the competition of buyers and sellers with each other and among themselves. Under a simple barter system each party in a market would put a subjective value on the goods changing hands, as having a direct bearing on his own wellbeing, and would base the amounts offered and asked on this valuation. With organised industry comes the money valuation, where the comparative use value of goods to people generally becomes reflected on a money scale, and it becomes more definite and intelligible to say a thing is worth so many shillings than to say it is worth so many other things which admit of direct valuation in terms of satisfaction of want. Buyers and sellers, then, come together in markets with a definite valuation in their minds of what the goods or the money is worth to them. Thanks to the differences in subjective scales, it is the interest of both parties, and it is possible for both parties, to get an advantage by the exchange, although their interests diverge in regard to the *amount* of advantage that each may get. In this competition the goods pass from the "most capable" sellers to the "most capable" buyers, and the price is fixed between the valuations of the two "marginal pairs," viz. the last buyer and seller and the first unsuccessful buyer and seller. The level, again, of these marginal pairs is determined by the relation of the wants of both parties to their economical provision. It must be added that, in an organised economy, "utility" becomes a more complex conception. In the case of a manufacturer the utility of raw material is not the personal uses to which he can put his own products, but the uses to which he, as a manufacturer, can put the raw material, and these, again, are determined by the wants of his customers. The direct *use* of a good is here replaced by the *employment* of the good, and the "most useful" is translated into the "best paying," or "most remunerative." And this emergence of the professional producer, who makes for the market and to whom his produce has really no subjective value, simplifies the calculation of the marginal pairs by eliminating the subjective valuations of the sellers, and determines the price at the valuation of the last buyer.

This law does not, as one would suppose, come into collision with the old law that value is determined by costs of production. The Law of Costs is one amply confirmed by experience as regards the great mass of articles produced under free competition. But this empirical law was never thought to determine the value of goods produced under any other conditions. The point on which it requires amending is that it should be expressed as a law

of equality between costs and products. The old theory not only
said that the value of goods tended to an equality with that of
the means of production, but went on to put the causal relation
exactly the wrong way about. As we have said, it is human want
that gives value to goods ; and that value is thrown back upon the
means of production without which the goods cannot come into
existence, and which are really the goods in a previous state of
existence. In developed economy it is true that there comes a
reflex influence from costs to products. If a group of means of
production is capable of making goods which for the moment have
different marginal utilities, the value that is transferred to the costs
is the value of the last or marginal product made from these costs.
In time, no doubt, competition forces this value again on to the
other products, thus giving the impression that the value comes
from the costs : but the fact is that the very value which these
costs have, came from their product—not, however, from this or
that particular product, but from the marginal one.

Now the immediate point of connection between the theory of
value and the theory of interest is that the problem of interest, in
all its manifestations, is nothing more than a problem of price, the
commodity bought and sold being—Present Goods. When, then,
we go on to the final question, the Amount or Rate of Interest,
what we have to remember is that here, as in price transactions
generally, we have a resultant of subjective valuations, and that the
determining elements we have to deal with are the extent and
intensity of the subjective valuations of buyers and sellers. We
have already seen what is the extent of this supply, and we know
the motives which weigh with the owners and determine its intensity.
The demand, again, comes from those who borrow to consume, and
those who borrow to produce. Of these two co-ordinate demands
we shall, as before, confine ourselves to the more important and more
difficult, and to its most important section, the Wage-Earners, refer-
ring the reader to Böhm-Bawerk's last two chapters for the other
sections. One way of looking at this demand would be to consider
it, not as a direct demand from the wage-earners, but as interpreted
and in certain definite ways modified by the undertakers. But it is
perhaps better to consider the undertaker as the owner of capital,
and take the question simply as one between Wage-Earners and
Capitalists. In the following argument, then, we assume that the
demand comes exclusively from labour, that the entire supply and
demand meet in one single market embracing the whole community,
and that all branches of production show the same scale of surplus
returns.

If wage were a fixed point—say determined at the subsistence
level, as the Iron Law assumes—the calculation of the rate of interest would be comparatively easy. Say that every added £100

of capital permitted simply a further extension of process. Every extension of process assures an extra product. But where capitalist industry is well developed, the increments of product at each extension diminish relatively to those preceding, and there comes a point where the increase of product does not balance the expense of extension. To put it in familiar terms : an employer making 10% on his own capital, and offered loans at 4%, may profitably extend his business by borrowing although at every extension he makes a smaller profit. But when the extension made possible by the last loan returns him only 4%, there is no inducement to extend further. In this case the rate of interest would be determined by the "last dose of capital" economically applied, to use Thünen's phrase.

But the great difficulty is that wage is not a fixed amount. The value of labour to the employer depends upon anticipated product, and that product depends on productiveness, and productiveness depends on length of process, and thus we have no fixed point from which to start. Böhm-Bawerk's solution is the following. The fixed point which we cannot get in wage is got in another way. As in the theory of money it is well known that any quantity of currency, small or great, will effect the necessary exchanges, so here the available quantity of present goods offered for sale will buy up the whole of the available labour. This is due to the circumstances already spoken of—the need of the labourers to hire themselves out, and of the capitalists to hire out their wealth. The few cases of unemployed labour and capital may be left out of account, as, obviously, it is only because of bad organisation that there are such. When the proportion of wealth and of labourers changes, all that is required is to contract or extend the production period. Granted this assumption, then,—that at any moment labour buys up the available "wage fund,"—the rate of interest is determined on the ordinary lines of the formation of price. The period will be extended till such time as the marginal employment of the unit of capital is reached ; that is, till the extra product gained by extension of process is outweighed by the diminishing productiveness of the process.

To put this difficult argument in a way perhaps more easy to grasp. Say that at any given moment there is a certain amount of wealth divided out among the wage-earners as subsistence. In any case there will be some agio on this wealth, and there will be an average production period. If now wealth increases faster than population—in Great Britain it increases more than twice as fast— there must be some disturbance of the equilibrium at present established. The new wealth will seek for employment, and find it— not, of course, in offering higher wages, for there is still nothing in increased wealth to increase product—but in extending processes. But as, presumably, we have now entered the stage of progress where extension of period gives decreasing surpluses, the return to this last employment of wealth will be less than before. This marginal employment will bring down interest generally : the rate will be determined by the last extension of the production period : wage will rise relatively to interest : and the equilibrium be found at a new level. If population increase, wealth and productiveness remaining constant, the converse will be the case : wage will fall and interest rise because the community is brought back to a production period where the absolute product is less, but the relative surplus, due to extension of process, is greater. If, lastly, productiveness increase, wealth and population remaining constant, the same phenomenon will take place, owing to the decreasing progression of surplus returns being for the moment checked.

Thus we can see that the three concrete factors which determine the marginal extension of process, and thereby the rate of interest, are the amount of the national Subsistence Fund, the numbers of the working Population provided for, and the degree of Productiveness reached in the industrial development. To quote our author's words, "interest will be high in proportion as the national subsistence fund is low, as the number of labourers employed by the same is great, and as the surplus returns connected with any further extension of the production period continue high, and *vice versâ*."

All this is in perfect harmony with the known facts of interest. It explains how as a country grows wealthy the rate of interest falls while wages rise ; how an increase of population without a corresponding increase of wealth has a tendency to raise the rate of interest and depress wages ; and, finally, how inventions which increase productiveness tend to raise the rate.

It is not within the scope of my task here to follow Böhm-Bawerk in gradually adding on the other elements required to make the picture true to the actualities of life, and to show that they make no material change in the principles laid down. Enough has been said to give the outlines of a theory which challenges attention, both by the originality of its ideas, and the thoroughness of its treatment.

My thanks are due, first of all, to Dr. Böhm-Bawerk, who has materially added to the value of this rendering of his work by giving it the stamp of his revision : to Professor Edward Caird, of Glasgow, and Professor M'Cormick, of Dundee, for many valuable suggestions and corrections : to Miss Christian Brown, of Paisley, who has again put me under heavy obligation by most carefully revising my proof-sheets . and to two other of my students who have spared me many weeks of thankless work by deciphering and rewriting my crabbed MS.

GLASGOW, *June* 1891.

AUTHOR'S PREFACE

IT has taken me longer than I expected to follow up the publication of my *Geschichte und Kritik der Kapitalzins-Theorieen* by the present work. The heavy part of *The Positive Theory of Capital* lies in the theory of Interest. In the other portions of the subject I was able, at least on the whole, to follow in the footsteps of previous theorists, but for the phenomena of interest I had to put forward an explanation which breaks entirely new ground.

I make this latter statement with some confidence. It is quite true that my explanation of interest rests on certain important ideas previously put forward by Jevons. But Jevons did not give them that special application which might have made them serviceable towards the explanation of interest —if they had been taken in connection with certain other lines of thought not then familiar to Jevons. Thus it is that, in his interest theory, Jevons remained under the spell of the old classical opinions, notwithstanding these new lights which came to him from another quarter and were applied to other ends. And, moreover, as the ideas common to both of us were not borrowed by me from Jevons, but discovered in entire independence—indeed long before I became acquainted with Jevons's writings—I feel bound to take on myself, for good or ill as events may prove, the entire and undivided responsibility for the interest theory now put forward.

As regards the way in which I have treated the subject, I may be allowed to make two remarks.

The method of statement adopted for the most part throughout this book is that which people generally—not without a suspicion of passing judgment on it—call " abstract."

All the same I contend that my theory does not contain one single feature which is not based on true empirical principles. There are various ways of being empirical. We may obtain the facts of experience which serve us as foundations from economic history, or we may gather them from statistics, or we may try to get them directly in our common daily life by simple informal observation. No one of these three methods has any monopoly: each of them has its separate and peculiar sphere. In the nature of things the historical and the statistical method treat the matter of experience in much ampler fashion, and gather it from wider fields of observation; but for that very reason they fail, on the whole, to seize any but the larger and more apparent facts: they put economic events, as it were, through a large sieve, where a great many delicate and unobtrusive, but, perhaps, more essential features of economic life, escape unnoticed. If, then, we would rescue these and make them objects of economic investigation— and for very many scientific problems we simply cannot do without taking cognisance of them—there is nothing for it but to have recourse to the comparatively narrow but always impressive personal observation of life.

Now I have endeavoured to make full use of all three methods of investigation. What help economic history and statistics could afford me in my task I have thankfully accepted and conscientiously made the most of, even where I have not explicitly mentioned the original materials with which I worked. But the matter thus obtained was not by a long way sufficient for my purposes. The theory of capital has to reckon with a number of facts which history and statistics have not recorded, partly because in their nature they could not, partly because attention has not hitherto been drawn to the importance of these facts. What, for instance, could history and statistics say about the question which is so important in the explanation of interest, as to whether there is in perishable goods an independent enduring use? How much, again, could we get from them as to the actual grounds on which are based the different subjective estimates of present and future goods? Or what have we learned—up till the present at least—as to the relation between the amount of the national subsistence fund and the average production period in a community? In matters like these one is obliged, for good or ill, to turn to other sources of information, and other paths of knowledge than those of history and statistics.

And if proof be needed that I was right in doing so, and that indeed it was impossible for me to do otherwise, I may appeal to witnesses whose authority, as regards this question, is beyond dispute, namely, the leaders and adherents of the "historical school" itself. For full thirty years the historical and statistical tendency has been the prevailing one in German economics. During the whole of this long period there has not been even an attempt to solve the great problem of interest by the tools of the historical method, although this problem has always occupied a front place in economical discussion. Perhaps the nearest attempt to a really historical treatment was that of Rodbertus, with his famous statement of the different forms under which, in various ages, the ruling economic classes have always drawn the better part of the product of the nation's labour to themselves. But, accurately speaking, Rodbertus, in these historic flights, aimed only at winning assent to his exploitation theory, while the characteristic feature of that theory is that it makes use from end to end of the abstract-deductive machinery of the classical school, the labour theory of Ricardo. Or to mention only the recognised leaders of the historical school;—Roscher has put together his interest theory out of elements taken partly from J. B. Say, partly from Senior —that is to say, altogether from "pre-historic" theory; while Knies, following Hermann, invents a theory of the "use" of goods, which not only has nothing in the world in common with history and statistics, but, as I at least believe, dispenses with any inductive foundation whatever, and is the result of simple speculation—and not even happy speculation.

If, then, the historical economists themselves, when brought face to face with the problem of capital, have not trusted to their peculiar method, and have taken to a kind of investigation generally foreign to them, I cannot be reproached if I take the same course as they do. I am free—at least I try to be free —from any onesidedness of method. In my opinion there is no one royal road of investigation: to my mind that way is good which leads to the goal of knowledge in the individual case. And sometimes that will be the one, sometimes the other method, according to the different nature of the individual problems that present themselves. In the present case I imagine that I have employed the method of research which was most suitable to the special nature of the theoretical problems of capital—abstract in form, but empirical in essence; and indeed, as seems to me, empirical in a truer sense than can be assigned to the investigations which the historical school has directed towards the same end.

The second remark I should like to make is this. The fundamental ideas of my interest theory are, I believe, unusually simple and natural. Had I been content to arrange these ideas in a more concise form, avoiding all casuistical matters of detail, I should have put forward a theory which, in small compass, would have produced the impression of being exceedingly simple, even verging on being self-evident. So far as power of carrying conviction goes, this would certainly have been an advantage, and, if I have forborne to seize that advantage, it was only after full consideration. The fact is that, in the theory of capital, there have been so many plausible views put forward and subsequently found false, that I must expect to find the public very critically disposed, and indeed must presume that my best and most careful readers will be the most critical. In these circumstances it appeared to me more important to make the structure of my theory secure than to make it easy and pleasant reading. Thus I decided to encumber my work with numerous demonstrations, details, exact figures, and so on, rather than leave room at critical points for doubts and misunderstandings.

In this direction one circumstance gave me particular trouble. In a theory of any range and any difficulty there are points which, by reason of some casuistical peculiarities or other, are not always quite easily explained, even when the general principle which will give their solution is already known; and, so long as those points are not distinctly traced back to the general principle, they stand like so many living objections to its correctness. As it happens, there are a good many such points in the two theories so closely connected;—that of value and that of capital. Now in the theory of value I had experienced how unexplained questions of this sort may stand seriously in the way and hinder the acceptance of the best grounded general theories,—for I am convinced that people have been so long prevented from getting right views on the nature and laws of value only because they stumbled at certain striking facts, which, to hasty consideration, seemed to contradict these views, while in truth they were only complicated cases requiring casuistical treatment. To save my theory of capital from a like fate I tried to anticipate objections of this sort, and remove them by suitable digressions. Naturally I did not deal with all conceivable objections, but only with those which seemed to me likely to crop up in the minds of critical readers, and which, at the same time, seemed difficult enough to warrant a special explanation : all the same it gave me occasion to go into more detail than was favourable to the fluent statement of my theory.

Thanks to all this I have arrived at a result as paradoxical as it is natural : that the very trouble which I took to clear difficulties out of the way has given my theory a certain appearance of difficulty. Unsuspicious of these hidden and dangerous rocks, many of my readers, I doubt not, would have sailed safely over them, while I, knowing them so well, and trying to steer a safe but laboured course, have made the journey long, difficult, and troublesome. I trust, however, that something may be put to my credit in this regard ; for, after all, no one could very well expect to arrive at the solution of a problem of such recognised difficulty except through earnest and laborious thinking. I may at any rate take this opportunity of asking one favour of my readers ;—that, if they have once read my theory with all its casuistical detail, they would go over it a second time omitting the detail. If in this way the leading ideas are put directly together again, and cleared of all superfluous elaboration, I venture to think that the theory will again produce that impression of simplicity and naturalness which is warranted by the simplicity of its constituent ideas ; an impression which I may have sacrificed to a critical precaution that was perhaps exaggerated, but was not altogether without justification.

This book was already well through the press when Carl Menger's *Contribution to the Theory of Capital* appeared in Conrad's *Jahrbücher* (vol. xvii. part ii.) I very much regret that it was then too late for me to make full use of that most interesting and suggestive work, and, in particular, that I could

not do more justice to its author in my critical notice of the
historical development of the conception of capital.   Unfortunately by the time it appeared the first part of my book,—that
which deals with the conception and nature of capital, and
touches most closely on this work of Menger,—was already
printed off.

For the same reason I could not notice the important work
of Wieser on *Natural Value,* which only came to my hands
during the printing of my last chapter.

E. BÖHM-BAWERK.

INNSBRUCK, *November* 1888.

ANALYTICAL TABLE OF CONTENTS

BOOK II

CAPITAL AS INSTRUMENT OF PRODUCTION

BOOK III

VALUE

BOOK IV

PRICE

TABLE OF CONTENTS* xxxv

Chapter VII. The Law of Costs. The law that price tends to equality with costs of production seems at first sight to contradict our law. But the concatenation is really the following. The consumers' subjective valuations for each class of commodity determine the consumers' demand. Against this stands supply of the particular commodity. The valuations of the marginal pairs determine its price. This price again determines the extent and intensity of the manufacturers' demand for raw material, and this material passes to the most capable buyers at the valuation of the last buyer. Thus it is the least remunerative employment (the market equivalent of the subjective marginal utility) that determines the value of the cost goods. What gives colour to the law of costs is the subsequent phenomenon, that the value thus given to cost goods by marginal product is then transmitted from these costs to products of originally higher marginal utility. Explanation of cases where the movement of price seems to be from costs to products, as in improvement of processes : increased supply changing the level of subjective valuations, and lowering the marginal utility. The symmetry between costs and products is disturbed by two causes—(1) general friction, (2) the lapse of time. This leads us to the consideration of the effect of differences of time on the valuation of goods

pp. 223—234

BOOK V

PRESENT AND FUTURE

Chapter I. Present and Future in Economic Life. Our general economic conduct has more reference to the future than we are always conscious of. Not feeling future sensations we yet anticipate and compare them, and the greater part of our wealth in the present consists of goods getting ready for the future. As future feelings are commensurable so are future goods, our basis of valuation being the marginal utility which they will bring us in the future. It should be noted, however, that the element of objective uncertainty in future goods has nothing to do with the phenomenon of interest : it is simply a premium against risk. Our fundamental principle, then, is, that present goods have a higher subjective value, and thus a higher price, than future goods of like kind and number. This is the resultant of the causes mentioned in the three following chapters

pp. 237—248

Chapter II. Differences in Want and Provision for Want. Here two cases are typical—(1) that of immediate distress, (2) where economical prospects for the future are hopeful. In these cases present goods are obviously valued more highly than future. Even where the future does not promise better provision than the present, the shilling in my pocket, as a durable good, avails for the present, for the future, and for any chance that may turn up meantime. The exceptions to this—as in some perishable goods —are insignificant . . . . pp. 249—252

BOOK VI

THE SOURCE OF INTEREST

BOOK VII

THE RATE OF INTEREST

of productiveness of the last extension ? If, *ceteris paribus*, subsistence increases, the same calculations as before show that equilibrium cannot be maintained without an extension of process, an increase of wage, and a fall of interest—the latter accounted for by the fact that men can only keep the increased wealth employed by extensions of process which involve decreased surpluses. If, on the other hand, subsistence falls, equilibrium demands contraction of processes, fall in wage, and rise in interest. If, again, population rise or fall we have the converse results. Lastly, if productiveness increase, *ceteris paribus*, interest will rise along with the surplus now yielded by the last extension. Thus we conclude that there are three decisive factors which affect the rate of interest, and this is confirmed by history and experience . . . pp. 395—402

Chapter IV. The Market for Capital in its Full Development. And now to give the features of actual life to our abstract scheme. It makes no difference to our argument that product and wage vary from employment to employment: the essential matter for interest is the relation between the two. Nor does it matter that in actual life the annual increment due to extensions of process varies from employment to employment: capital follows an isohypse of surplus returns, not of periods of production, but this does not alter the essential circumstances on which our law rests. Again, there are other demands besides that of the wage-earners—(A) that for consumption credit, completely co-ordinate with the other, (B) that of landowners who require subsistence proportioned to the length of their production processes, (C) that of capitalists themselves, although their claim on subsistence is effect and not cause of the agio. Lastly, we may enumerate the seven concrete factors in the interest rate
pp. 403—412

Chapter V. The Market for Capital in its Full Development (*continued*). To look now at the struggle between immediate consumption and accumulation. In good economical management present and future will be alike considered, and provision made that the present consumption shall not reduce the level of future enjoyment. Thus parent wealth should be saved, and even some portion of income. The two great deviations from economic conduct are due (1) to the perspective undervaluation of the future and (2) to the neglect of exact calculation of the future's claims. Differences between our theory and that of the Wage Fund. Finally, the actual market for capital is not one great undivided market, but a great number of part markets all communicating and arbitrating each other's prices. Conclusion . . . . pp. 413—424

INTRODUCTION

IN systems of Political Economy the word Capital and the theory of Capital are regularly met with in two distinct spheres; first, under Production, and, second, under Distribution. In the former case capital is represented as a factor or tool of production : as an instrument which men use to extort from nature the various forms of wealth unattainable by simple labour. In the latter case capital appears as a source of income or a rent fund; and we are shown how, in the division among the various members of society of that wealth which has been produced in common, capital acts like a magnet, drawing a portion of the national product to itself, and delivering it over to its owner: it appears, in a word, as the source of Interest.

When we are told that capital assists in the production of wealth, and then again that it assists in the obtaining of wealth for its owner, we are apt to jump to the conclusion that the two phenomena are intimately and essentially connected, and that the one is the immediate result of the other— that capital can bring wealth to its owner because capital assists in the production of wealth. As a fact, Political Economy has taken up this idea only too readily and too completely. Captivated by the deceptive symmetry that exists between the three great factors of production—Nature, Labour, Capital— and the three great branches of income—Rent, Wage, and Interest — the science, from Say's day till the present, has taught that these three branches of income are nothing else than the payment for the three factors of production, and that

B

Interest in particular is nothing else than the compensation which capital rèceives for its productive services when the product is divided out among society. Propounded by various interest theories in various forms this idea has found its most concise and, at the same time, its most naïve expression, in the well-known " Productivity theories "—those theories which explain interest directly as the natural fruit of a productive power peculiar to and resident in capital.[1]

In beginning the study of the theory of Capital, it cannot be too emphatically stated that this idea, simple and natural as it may appear, contains a prejudgment calculated to preclude unbiassed consideration of the problems of capital. If there were no other objection, the fact that the word capital is never used exactly in the same sense in the two spheres of phenomena must give us pause. True, all capital which serves as a tool of production is also capable of bearing interest, but the converse is not the case. A dwelling-house, a hired horse, a circulating library bear interest to their respective owners without having anything to do with the production of new wealth. If, in the sphere of distribution, the conception of capital thus embraces objects which are not capital in the sphere of production, this alone is sufficient to show that the bearing of interest cannot by itself be an indication of the productive power of capital. We have not to deal with *one* motive power transmitting itself to two different spheres ; not even with two groups of phenomena which have grown up so intimately connected that the explanation of the one is got fully and entirely through the explanation of the other ; but with two distinct classes of phenomena. Thus we have two distinct subjects, which give us material for two distinct scientific problems ; and finally, we have to seek for the solution of these problems by two distinct and separate roads. It so happens, however, that these really distinct problems are accidentally linked together by one name ; they are problems of Capital. It may be that, besides identity of name, we shall find many inner relations between the two series of phenomena and the two problems ;—our investigation shall decide that later. But such relations are yet to be discovered ; they must not be assumed ; and unless we would give up all idea

[1] See my *Capital and Interest*, 1890, p. 111.

of being unprejudiced in our quest and in our conclusions, we must begin the inquiry free from any preconceived opinion of a necessary identity, or even of an exact parallelism, between the productive efficiency of capital and its power of bearing interest.

Our division of the subject will correspond to this real independence of the two problems. In one part of the present work we shall take up the theory of Capital as a Tool of Production, and in another the theory of Interest. But we shall first devote a separate book to the attempt to obtain some insight into what Capital itself is, in conception and nature.

BOOK I

THE NATURE AND CONCEPTION OF CAPITAL

CHAPTER I

MAN AND NATURE

THERE is scarcely a system or a text-book of Political Economy which does not, at some point or other, bring in discussions of matters belonging to the physical sciences. Usually these are introduced in the chapter on Production. There we are taught that to create new goods does not mean to create new material, since matter is constant and cannot be increased. We learn what nature contributes to the work of production in the shape of materials and powers; what is done by the mechanical, what by the chemical, and what by the organic powers of nature; what importance climate, heat, moisture have on the development of production; on what physical and technical foundations the working of machinery rests; and many things of this sort.

To the principle of this custom no sensible person will object. It is the form in which, consciously or unconsciously, we pay homage to one of the weightiest principles of our knowledge, the unity of all science. Ever since Bacon we have recognised that no single branch of inquiry explains to the very end the facts with which it deals, but breaks off at some point or other, and passes on its facts to some sister science for further treatment, so that the total explanation is only given by the totality of all the sciences. Thus it is that if one would not set before his readers simply a collection of barren fragments, he must add to what is distinctively departmental at least so much as will connect it with the related sciences in the organic whole of human knowledge, and thus indicate the way in which the explanations begun by him may be concluded.

It would, however, be rather impertinent if we theorists were to think that such terminal truths—as we may appropriately call them—are added only for purposes of statement and for the good of our readers.   Rightly employed they are of much greater use to ourselves as scientific inquirers. They may be an effectual means of preventing us from lightly building our whole system, or parts of it, on air, and unintentionally maintaining in the name of Political Economy something which, in its assumptions or conclusions, is, physically or psychologically speaking, nonsense.   I must not be misunderstood however.   It is not in the least my meaning that Political Economy should assume a nature foreign to it, and become natural science or psychology; what I do mean is that it must never be in contradiction with these sciences. What is false in natural science or psychology is false in all and every science.   And to prevent us unwittingly running counter to certain fundamental truths, perhaps the best way is to put these truths explicitly in black and white before our eyes.

Now the subject with which we have to deal in this work is of such a nature that it very specially requires to be based on sound natural principles, and a very great deal may be lost by neglect of this.   I have therefore strong reasons for following the good old custom, and prefacing my theory by some fundamental truths that stretch over into the neighbouring sphere of the natural sciences.   I shall endeavour not to abuse the opportunity by inflicting a mass of learned scientific detail on the reader.   The few truths I mean to start with would indeed, in a professional classification, be put within the sphere of the natural sciences, but they are of so general a character that, practically, they are outside departmental limits, and belong to the commonwealth of knowledge   They are known and recognised by everybody, and, in one form or other, they have been expressed all along in our economic literature. There is really only one thing that, I should like to think, will distinguish my use of them : I shall try so to put them that they will not be mere paragraphs introducing the theory, but will remain present and living in the spirit of it.   Usually these excursuses into the domains of physics are placed in some corner of economical books rather for ornament than use.   In one chapter they are made much of ; in the next they are forgotten

and contradicted.   In what follows I shall try to avoid this
error, and wherever anything depends upon these fundamental
truths—which will very often be the case in a discussion on
capital—to keep unobtrusively but firmly in touch with them.
In this way, while there is no fear of our economical theory
obtaining the character of a theory of natural science, it will
not be one that runs counter to physical facts.

Men strive after happiness.   This is perhaps the most
general and, certainly, the most vague expression for a complex
of strivings, all of which have for object the bringing about
of such occurrences and conditions as we know and feel to be
pleasant, and the averting of those we know to be unpleasant.
Instead of " striving after happiness " we may use the expression " striving after self-preservation and self-development," or
" striving after the greatest possible furtherance of life "; or
we may, with equal propriety, use the words, " striving after
the most complete possible satisfaction of wants "; for the
expressions we are so familiar with in economic terminology,
" want " and " satisfaction of want," mean, in the last resort,
nothing else than, respectively, the unsatisfied craving of
man to be put under conditions he thinks desirable or more
desirable than those he has, and the successful obtaining of
such conditions.

The whole world, as we know it, is subject to the law of
cause and effect ; no effect can take place without sufficient
cause.   From this law man and his conditions have no exemption ; none of those beneficent changes of condition, which we
call " satisfactions of want," can come about otherwise than as
the effect of a sufficient cause ; every satisfaction presupposes
an adequate instrument of satisfaction.   The adequate instruments for the satisfaction of human wants, or—what is the
same thing—the causes of beneficent changes in human conditions, we call goods.[1]

The man who " wants " finds goods in different spheres of
the world in which he lives ; he finds them in the world of
persons as well as in the world of things.   For obvious reasons,
which need not be discussed here, we use the word " good " in
somewhat different ways in these two spheres.   On the one

[1] See Menger, *Grundsätze der Volkswirthschaftslehre*, p. 1.   Vienna, 1871.

we designate by the name of goods not the persons who
~~se~~ to us, but only the acts, the services, through which
_, are of use; on the other hand, we give the name to the
impersonal material shapes themselves, and call them Material
as opposed to Personal goods.

In what follows we have to do with material goods only.

Material goods are part of the external world; they are
natural things. As such they are, in constitution and action,
wholly and entirely natural products, and subject to natural
laws. The fact that men's goods are instruments towards the
personal ends of the "lord of creation" gives these goods no
kind of immunity from complete subordination to the natural
order, any more than man himself is able to emancipate the
natural side of his being from similar control. Material goods,
therefore, come into existence only as natural laws allow and
demand that a material shape, thus and not otherwise constituted, should come into existence. They pass out of existence if
a new combination of natural powers, working according to
natural laws, results of necessity in the dissolution of their
former material shape. They cannot exert the smallest effect,
be it useful, hurtful, or indifferent to men, unless the given
coincidence of materials and powers under natural laws produce this very effect and no other.

These seem peculiarly trifling propositions. They are
trifling enough to require no formal proof; indeed, no one
will seriously dispute them. But, simple and trifling as
they are, on certain tempting occasions these fundamental
truths have been lost sight of, and theories have been
put in circulation which implicitly contradict them. The
theorist, therefore, has good cause to emphasise them, and even
follow out their logical conclusions to a certain extent into
those departments where they have to do duty as, peculiarly,
the fundamental truths of economic theory. These departments are the function of goods and the origin of goods; in
other words, the theory of the Use of goods, and the theory
of the Production of goods.

The theory of the use of goods I have already gone into at
length in *Capital and Interest*.[1] I there showed that material

---

[1] P. 219 (German edition, p. 265). See also my *Rechte und Verhältnisse*, p.
51. Innsbruck, 1881.

goods are nothing else than such distinct forms of matter as admit of the natural powers residing in them being directed to human advantage. I showed how the " use " they afford is realised through concrete activities of these natural powers, and, therefore, by real forth putting of power. I showed how a use (*Gebrauch* or *Nutzung*) cannot be made of them otherwise than by taking the peculiar forms of the energy of the good at the proper moment, supplying the conditions necessary to render them available where they previously existed in an unavailable form, and then bringing these forms of energy into proper connection with that object in which the useful effect is to take place. On these considerations I based the conception of the " Material Services " (*Nutzleistungen*) which I believe to be the only one that corresponds with facts, and rejected certain shadowy ideas which connected the old theory of interest with the word " Uses " of goods. What remains for us here is, on the same lines, to lay down certain fundamental ideas as to the *origin* of material goods.

We have already said that the origin of natural goods lies entirely under the control of natural laws. No material good can come into existence except when a previous coincidence of materials and powers has made it necessary in physical law that exactly this form of matter should emerge. Looked at from the point of view of nature, the formation of goods is a purely natural process. Not so, however, from the point of view of man. Man has cause to lay emphasis on a distinction which is not visible from the purely physical standpoint. One great class of useful forms of matter comes into existence, without interference from man, as the product of favourable coincidences of matter and force—a product which, from the teleological human standpoint, we should call accidental. Thus originate fruitful islands in the courses of streams ; thus the grass on natural pastures and prairies ; thus berries and trees of the wood ; thus deposits of useful minerals. But though in this way accident does much for man it does not do nearly enough. In nature left to herself we have on a large scale what we should have on a small one if we wished to make a definite picture out of coloured bits of stone, and, instead of piecing the picture together deliberately, were to put the bits of stone into a kaleidoscope and wait till accident

shook the planless stones into the wished-for picture. Among
the infinite number of ways in which the working materials
and powers might combine there are, in the one case as in the
other, a countless number of possible effects, but only a few
favourable ones; and in the natural undisturbed course of
things these few turn up too seldom for man, with all his
wants, to rest content with them. Accordingly he interposes
another factor in the natural process, his own consciously
directed energies—he begins to produce the goods he
requires.

To "produce": what does this mean? It has been so
often said by economists that the creation of goods is not the
bringing into existence of materials that hitherto have not
existed—is not "creation" in the true sense of the word,—
but only a fashioning of imperishable matter into more
advantageous shapes, that it is quite unnecessary to say it
again. More accurate, but still exposed to misinterpretation,
is the expression that in production natural powers are the
servants of man, and are directed by him to his own advantage.
If this proposition be taken to mean that man in any case can
impose his sovereign will *in place of* natural laws, can at will
"bully" natural law into making a single exception at his
bidding, it is entirely erroneous. Whether the lord of creation
will it or no, not an atom of matter can, for a single moment
or by a hair's breadth, work otherwise than the unchangeable
laws of nature demand. Man's rôle in production is much
more modest. It consists simply in this—that he, himself a
part of the natural world, combines his personal powers with
the impersonal powers of nature, and combines them in such
a way that under natural law the co-operation results in a
definite, desired, material form. Thus, notwithstanding the
interference of man, the origin of goods remains purely a
natural process. The natural process is not disturbed by man
but completed, inasmuch as, by apt intervention of his own
natural powers, he supplies a condition which has hitherto
been wanting to the origination of a material good.

If we look more closely at the way in which man assists
natural processes, we find that his sole but ample contribution
consists in the moving of things. "Putting objects in motion"
is the idea which gives the key to all human production

and its results;—to all man's mastery over nature and its powers.[1] And this is so simply because the powers reside in the objects. Now when man by his physical powers—the power of moving things—is able to dictate *where* the object shall be, he obtains a control over the place at which a natural power may become effective; and this means broadly a control over the way and over the time in which it may become effective.

I say a control over the way in which a natural power may become effective. Of course a pound weight acts as a pound weight and never in any other way; whether it be a paper weight on a writing-table, or a counterpoise on a scale-beam, or whether it keep down the valve of a steam-engine, it never ceases to exert the force of gravitation with which its mass is endowed. But just because the expression of one and the same natural power always remains the same, results that are extraordinarily different may be obtained by getting it to work in different combinations—just as by adding like to unlike a different sum may be got every time. And so our pound weight, while in itself constantly acting with perfect uniformity, will, according to the different surroundings in which we place it, sometimes hold together a heap of papers on a writing-table, sometimes indicate the weight of another object, sometimes regulate the pressure of steam in the boiler.

Again I say a control over the time in which a natural power may become effective. This proposition, also, must not be taken too literally. It must not be imagined that natural powers work intermittently; that man can sometimes bring them to a standstill, sometimes set them working again. On the contrary, natural powers are always at work; a natural power not active would be a contradiction in · terms. But it is possible that several powers may be so combined that their activities may for a time mutually balance each other, and the resultant be rest—if not complete rest. still some movement so slight that, as regards human purposes, it may be neglected. When this is the case, before any new resultant can emerge that is of interest to man, there must be an entirely different combination of materials and powers. This suggests how man may get control of the point of time at which a definite resultant

[1] See Mill's *Principles*, i. 1. 2.

emerges. It is only necessary for him, by skilful use of his power to move objects, to provide the causes of the desired effect, all but one. So long as this one is not present the conditions are unfulfilled, and there cannot be the desired result. But when at the proper moment he adds the last condition, the movement hitherto held in leash, as it were, is suddenly set free, and the desired effect is obtained at the opportune time. Thus the sportsman moves powder and lead into the barrel of the gun; he shuts the breech; he raises the cock. Each of these things has for long possessed and expressed its peculiar powers. In the powder are present the molecular powers whose energy later on is to expel the shot from the barrel. The barrel now, as formerly, exerts its forces of cohesion and resistance. The trigger which is to let the cock smash down, strains and presses against the spring. Still the arrangement, the disposition of the collective powers, is such that the resultant of their mutual energies is rest. But the sportsman covers the wild fowl with the barrel: there is a slight pressure on the tongue, a little dislocation of the arrangements, and the shot flies.[1]

---

[1] If we were to carry our analysis of what man does in production a step further, we might appropriately distinguish three fundamental ways in which the producing man "moves things." The first is what, for want of a better name, we may call simple movements or changes of place—where men transport entire objects from one locality to another. Thus the miner brings the ore from the depths of the shaft to the upper air; the merchant takes his goods from the place where they are produced to the place where they are demanded and used. The second embraces those movements of parts of one and the same object whereby it experiences a change of form, as when nails are made from iron, statues from marble, pipes from clay, dials from ivory, combs from caoutchouc, tumblers from glass, furniture from wood. The third, and much the most common way, is where different objects are brought together in space to form combinations of matter. These combinations may be merely temporary, or they may be lasting. Instances of the one are where the stamp falls on the coin, the chisel chips at the marble, the carving tool is applied to the wood, the ore put into the furnace, the yarn into the loom, the paper under the printing press, the stuff under the shears, the plough through the clods. Instances of the other are where we build a house out of wood, stone, lime, iron, etc.; where we put together a watch out of wheels, springs, pendula, weights, stop-action and many other things; in fact in manufacture generally. I must warn the reader that this division into three fundamental forms neither has, nor is meant to have, the character of strict scientific classification. Indeed, these forms merge in many instances into one another. Temporary combinations, for instance, are very often half-way to changes of form, and what I have called a simple change

The same considerations which show us the kind of mastery man has over nature show us at the same time the measure and the narrow limits of his mastery. As we have seen, man has a certain power to make natural forces act where, when, and how he will; but this power he possesses only in so far as he can control the matter in which these forces reside. Now the masses of matter, and therefore the masses of inert resistance, which have to be overcome before our purposes are served, are often immense, while the physical force which is at our command is very modest and comparatively trifling. Often, on the other hand, the matter is too fine to be manipulated by our rude hand. Our interests often call for infinitely delicate rearrangements of infinitely small pieces, and how unsuited are our clumsy fingers to deal with molecules and atoms! How entirely incapable is the human hand of imitating even one of those wonderfully delicate cellular tissues which nature flings out in thousandfold, every day, in every plant and leaf! Thus human powers are doubly deficient; they are too slight as against the mass, too rude as against the structure of the matter which they have to subdue.

In those circumstances we should be very badly off for the wherewithal of production if we had not some real allies behind these doubly insufficient powers. One of these allies is the human mind. In investigating the causal relation of things we come to know the natural conditions under which the desired goods come into existence : we thus come to learn where human force can be applied with advantage and where not; and thus we are taught to avoid exertions which are barren and choose those which are profitable. Human power so directed is like a small but well-officered army, which makes up in mobility, cohesion, and energetic use of opportunity,

of place is at the same time, in a certain point of view, a material combination, a bringing together of the thing moved and the object (personal or impersonal) to which it is moved. This division, however, will make it easier to find our reckoning, and will prove too, if necessary, the correctness of the general characteristics which I have ascribed in the text to productive processes. I mean to say that it is easy to see that every productive activity which one can think of ranges itself under some one of these three fundamental forms, and to that extent it is proved that such an activity must, *a fortiori*, range itself also under the general formula given in the text, where we have described the nature and method of the production of material goods as the mastery of natural powers by means of putting objects in motion.

what it wants in numbers.   Another powerful ally in the struggle against nature is nature herself.   All that we are able to do in production would be wretchedly small were it not that, in the storehouse of nature, we find the means of dividing nature against herself and setting force against force.   But here we touch on a subject which is, in itself, too important, particularly as regards our inquiry, to admit of merely a passing mention.

CHAPTER II

THE NATURE OF CAPITAL

THE end and aim of all production is the making of things with which to satisfy our wants; that is to say, the making of goods for immediate consumption, or Consumption Goods.[1] The method of their production we have already looked at in a general way. We combine our own natural powers and natural powers of the external world in such a way that, under natural law, the desired material good must come into existence. But this is a very general description indeed of the matter, and looking at it closer there comes in sight an important distinction which we have not as yet considered. It has reference to the distance which lies between the expenditure of human labour in the combined production and the appearance of the desired good. We either put forth our labour just before the goal is reached, or we, intentionally, take a roundabout way. That is to say, we may put forth our labour in such a way that it at once completes the circle of conditions necessary for the emergence of the desired good, and thus the existence of the good *immediately* follows the expenditure of the labour; or we may associate our labour first with the more remote causes of the good, with the object of obtaining, not the desired good itself, but a proximate cause of the good; which cause, again, must be associated with other suitable

[1] Menger has suggestively called these Goods of the First Rank, classing all goods which go to their production as Goods of Higher Rank. It is unfortunate that we cannot use the literal English equivalent of the "*Genussgüter*," but, as next to it in convenience, I propose to use the expression Consumption Goods for what otherwise we should have to translate as Goods for Immediate Consumption. See Menger's *Grundsätze*, p. 8, and Böhm-Bawerk's *Rechte und Verhältnisse*, p. 101.—W. S.

C

materials and powers, till, finally,—perhaps through a considerable number of intermediate members,—the finished good, the instrument of human satisfaction, is obtained.

The nature and importance of this distinction will be best seen from a few examples; and, as these will, to a considerable extent, form a demonstration of what is really one of the most fundamental propositions in our theory, I must risk being tedious.

A peasant requires drinking water. The spring is some distance from his house. There are various ways in which he may supply his daily wants. First, he may go to the spring each time he is thirsty, and drink out of his hollowed hand. This is the most direct way; satisfaction follows immediately on exertion. But it is an inconvenient way, for our peasant has to take his way to the well as often as he is thirsty. And it is an insufficient way, for he can never collect and store any great quantity such as he requires for various other purposes. Second, he may take a log of wood, hollow it out into a kind of pail, and carry his day's supply from the spring to his cottage. The advantage is obvious, but it necessitates a roundabout way of considerable length. The man must spend, perhaps, a day in cutting out the pail; before doing so he must have felled a tree in the forest; to do this, again, he must have made an axe, and so on. But there is still a third way; instead of felling one tree he fells a number of trees, splits and hollows them, lays them end for end, and so constructs a runnel or rhone which brings a full head of water to his cottage. Here, obviously, between the expenditure of the labour and the obtaining of the water we have a very roundabout way, but, then, the result is ever so much greater. Our peasant needs no longer take his weary way from house to well with the heavy pail on his shoulder, and yet he has a constant and full supply of the freshest water at his very door.

Another example. I require stone for building a house. There is a rich vein of excellent sandstone in a neighbouring hill. How is it to be got out? First, I may work the loose stones back and forward with my bare fingers, and break off what can be broken off. This is the most direct, but also the least productive way. Second, I may take a piece of iron, make a hammer and chisel out of it, and use them on the hard stone—a roundabout way, which, of course, leads to a very much better result than the former. Third method—Having a hammer and chisel I use them to drill a hole in the rock; next I turn my attention to procuring charcoal, sulphur, and nitre, and mixing them in a powder, then I pour the powder into the hole, and the explosion that follows splits the stone into convenient pieces—still more of a roundabout way, but one which, as experience shows, is as much superior to the second way in result as the second was to the first.

Yet another example. I am short-sighted, and wish to have a pair of spectacles. For this I require ground and polished glasses, and a steel framework. But all that nature offers towards that end is silicious earth and iron ore. How am I to transform these into spectacles? Work as I may, it is as impossible for me to make spectacles directly out of silicious earth as it would be to make the steel frames out of iron ore. Here there is no immediate or direct method of production. There is nothing for it but to take the roundabout way, and, indeed, a very roundabout way. I must take silicious earth and fuel, and build furnaces for smelting the glass from the silicious earth; the glass thus obtained has to be carefully purified, worked, and cooled by a series of processes; finally, the glass thus prepared—again by means of ingenious instruments carefully constructed beforehand—is ground and polished into the lens fit for short-sighted eyes. Similarly, I must smelt the ore in the blast furnace, change the raw iron into steel, and make the frame therefrom—processes which cannot be carried through without a long series of tools and buildings that, on their part again, require great amounts of previous labour. Thus, by an exceedingly roundabout way, the end is attained.

The lesson to be drawn from all these examples alike is obvious. It is—that a greater result is obtained by producing goods in roundabout ways than by producing them directly. Where a good can be produced in either way, we have the fact that, by the indirect way, a greater product can be got with equal labour, or the same product with less labour. But, beyond this, the superiority of the indirect way manifests itself in being the only way in which certain goods can be obtained; if I might say so, it is so much the better that it is often the only way!

That roundabout methods lead to greater results than direct methods is one of the most important and fundamental propositions in the whole theory of production. It must be emphatically stated that the only basis of this proposition is the experience of practical life. Economic theory does not and cannot show *a priori* that it must be so; but the unanimous experience of all the technique of production says that it is so. And this is sufficient; all the more that the facts of experience which tell us this are commonplace and familiar to everybody. But *why* is it so? The economist might quite well decline to answer this question. For the fact that a greater product is obtained by methods of production that begin far back is essentially a purely technical fact, and to explain questions of technique does not fall within the economist's sphere. For instance, that tropical lands are more fruitful than the polar zone; that the alloy of which coins is made stands more wear and tear than pure metal; that a railroad is better for transport than an ordinary turnpike road;—all these are matters of fact with which the economist reckons, but which his science does not call on him to explain. But this is exactly one of those cases where, in the economist's own interest—the interest he has in limiting and defining his own task—it is exceedingly desirable to go beyond the specific economic sphere. If the sober physical truth is once made clear, political economy cannot indulge in any fancies or fictions about it; and, in such questions, political economy has never been behind in the desire and the attempt to substitute its own imaginings! Although, then, this law is already sufficiently accredited by experience, I attach particular value to explaining its cause, and, after what has been said as to the nature of production, this should not be very difficult.

In the last resort all our productive efforts amount to shiftings and combinations of matter. We must know how to bring together the right forms of matter at the right moment, in order that from those associated forces the desired result, the product wanted, may follow. But, as we saw, the natural forms of matter are often so infinitely large, often so infinitely fine, that human hands are too weak or too coarse to control them. We are as powerless to overcome the cohesion of the wall of rock when we want building stone as we are, from carbon, nitrogen, hydrogen, oxygen, phosphor, potash, etc., to put together a single grain of wheat. But there are other powers which can easily do what is denied to us, and these are the powers of nature. There are natural powers which far exceed the possibilities of human power in greatness, and there are other natural powers in the microscopic world which can make combinations that put our clumsy fingers to shame. If we can succeed in making those forces our allies in the work of production, the limits of human possibility will be infinitely extended. And this we have done.

The condition of our success is, that we are able to control the materials on which the power that helps us depends, more easily than the materials which are to be transformed into the desired good. Happily this condition can be very often complied with. Our weak yielding hand cannot overcome the cohesion of the rock, but the hard wedge of iron can; the wedge and the hammer to drive it we can happily master with little trouble. We cannot gather the atoms of phosphorus and potash out of the ground, and the atoms of carbon and oxygen out of the atmospheric air, and put them together in the shape of the corn of wheat; but the organic chemical powers of the seed can put this magical process in motion, while we on our part can very easily bury the seed in the place of its secret working, the bosom of the earth. Often, of course, we are not able directly to master the form of matter on which the friendly power depends, but in the same way as we would like it to help us, do we help ourselves against it; we try to secure the alliance of a second natural power which brings the form of matter that bears the first power under our control. We wish to bring the well water into the house. Wooden rhones would force it to obey our will, and take the path we prescribe, but our hands have not the power to make the forest trees into rhones. We have not far to look, however, for an expedient. We ask the help of a second ally in the axe and the gouge; their assistance gives us the rhones; then the rhones bring us the water. And what in this illustration is done through the mediation of two or three members may be done, with equal or greater result, through five, ten, or twenty members. Just as we control and guide the immediate matter of which the good is composed by one friendly power; and that power by a second, so can we control and guide the second by a third, the third by a fourth, this, again, by a fifth, and so on,—always going back to more remote causes of the final result—till in the series we come at last to one cause which we can control conveniently by our own natural powers. This is the true importance which attaches to our entering on roundabout ways of production, and this is the reason of the result associated with them : every roundabout way means the enlisting in our service of a power which is stronger or more cunning than the human hand ; every extension of the roundabout way means an addition to the powers which enter into the service of man, and the shifting of some portion of the burden of production from the scarce and costly labour of human beings to the prodigal powers of nature.

And now we may put into words an idea which has long waited for expression, and must certainly have occurred to the reader ; the kind of production which works in these wise circuitous methods is nothing else than what economists call Capitalist Production, as opposed to that production which goes directly at its object, as the Germans say, "*mit der nackten Faust.*"[1] And Capital is nothing but the complex of intermediate products which appear on the several stages of the roundabout journey.

It is in this way I interpret the most important fundamental conception in the theory of capital, and I should be very glad to stop here. But, like so many another conception in the theory of capital, this conception of capital itself has become a veritable apple of discord to the theorists. A perfectly amazing number of divergent interpretations here confront each other, and block the approach to the theory of capital with one of the most vexatious controversies in which our science could be involved. This uncertainty as to the conception of capital, bad enough in itself, becomes worse in proportion as Capital gives modern science new questions to consider and discuss. It is certainly very unfortunate when a

---

[1] The expression Capitalist Production is generally used in one of two senses. It designates either a production which avails itself of the assistance of concrete capital (raw materials, tools, machinery, etc.), or a production carried on for the behoof and under the control of private capitalist undertakers. The one is not by any means coincident with the other. I always use the expression in the former of these two meanings.

science already earnestly, even acrimoniously engaged on the solution of questions which affect society to its depths,— questions which all the world knows, ponders, and discusses as the great "problems of capital,"—is struck, as it were, by a second confusion of tongues, and becomes involved in an endless wrangle as to what kind of thing it is that properly is called Capital! Such a controversy at such a point is more than embarrassing; it is a calamity; and has been found so in the history of Political Economy. Almost every year there appears some new attempt to settle the disputed conception, but, unfortunately, no authoritative result has as yet followed these attempts.[1] On the contrary, many of them have only served to put more combatants in the field and furnish more matter to the dispute.

I confess that, to me, the settlement of the real problems connected with the name of capital seems more important, and certainly is more attractive, than the cataloguing of controversies as to the proper use of the word. All the same the fact remains that the confusion about the name has brought a great amount of confusion into the matter; and, again, it might be open to misconstruction—and not without reason,— if the author of a somewhat comprehensive work on capital were to pass over the discussion of what is certainly the most noisy, if not the most weighty controversy about capital. On these two accounts I feel obliged again to tread the heated path of controversy, in the hope that impartial and sober inquiry into the matter in dispute may succeed in ending it.

---

[1] Looking back over the last few years only, I can recall, as coming in quick succession, the researches of Knies (*Das Geld*, Berlin, 1873, pp. 1-56); of Cossa (*La Nozione del Capitale*, 1874, published in the *Saggi di Economia Politica*, Milan, 1878); of Ricca-Salerno (*Sulla Teoria del Capitale*, Milan, 1877); of Umpfenbach (*Das Kapital in seiner Kulturbedeutung*, Würzburg, 1879); of Kühnast (*Ueber den rechtlichen Begriff des Kapitales* in *Beiträge zur Erläuterung des Deutschen Rechtes*, 1884); of Supino (*Il Capitale nell' Organismo Economico e nell' Economia Politica*, Milan, 1886). Meanwhile we have the well-known works of Rodbertus and Marx, both bearing the title *Das Capital*, and again the elaborate statements in the more comprehensive systems, particularly those of Wagner (*Grundlegung*, second edition, 1879, p. 36); of Kleinwächter (Schönberg's *Handbuch*, first edition, p. 170; second edition, p. 206); and of Cohn (*Grundlegung der Nationalökonomie*, Stuttgart, 1885, § 145-147).

CHAPTER III

IT will be most convenient to open the discussion by a historical survey of the development of the conception.[1]

Originally the word Capital (*Capitale* from *Caput*) was used to signify the Principal of a money loan (*Capitalis pars debiti*) in opposition to the Interest. This usage already foreshadowed in the Greek formation κεφάλαιον, became firmly established in mediæval Latin, and appears to have remained the prevailing one for a very long time, even pretty far down in the new era.[2] Here, therefore, Capital meant the same thing as "an interest-bearing sum of money."

In the meantime the disputes which had arisen over the legitimacy or illegitimacy of loan interest brought about an essential deepening and widening of the conception.[3] It had become apparent that the interest-bearing power of "barren" money was at bottom a borrowed one—borrowed from the productive power of things that the money could buy. Money only gave the exchange form—to a certain extent the outward garb—in which the interest-bearing things passed from hand to hand. The true "stock" or parent stem which bore interest was not money but the goods that were got for it. In these circumstances the obvious course was so to change the conception that, besides embracing the representative

---

[1] See on this subject Knies, *Das Geld*, Berlin, 1873, p. 6 (second edition, p. 24); Ricca-Salerno, *Sulla Teoria del Capitale*, 1877, chap. ii. ; and Schönberg's *Handbuch*, second edition, vol. i. p. 206.

[2] The English word "Cattle," as Knies (p. 7) has rightly remarked, has nothing in common derivatively with our conception.

[3] *Capital and Interest*, book i. chaps. ii. and iii.

thing, money, it would embrace the represented thing, goods.
And, indeed, popular language seems to have made this change
before science did.   At least, as early as the year 1678, in a
glossary of that year, besides the meaning of a sum of money
there appears this further interpretation of the word capital,
" *Capitale dicitur bonum omne quod possidetur.*" [1]   But science
was not long behind in sanctioning the adoption of the conception.   We find it substantially in Hume in his essay on
Interest, when he shows that the rate of interest altogether
depends, not on the amount of money, but on the amount of
riches or stocks available; the only thing wanting is that
he should have formally called these riches or stocks " real
capitals."   This formal change was finally made by Turgot:
" Whoever," he says in his *Réflexions sur la Formation et la
Distribution des Richesses*, " gets possession of more goods in a
year than he requires to use, can lay past the surplus and
accumulate it.   These accumulated goods are what people call
Capital. . . . It is absolutely the same whether this sum of
goods, or this Capital, consists of a mass of metal, or of other
things, since money represents every kind of goods, just as, on
the other side, all other kinds of goods represent money."
Thus Turgot gave the second reading in historical succession
to the conception of capital.

It was very soon superseded by a third.   For when Turgot
designated all saved goods indiscriminately as Capital, he
seemed to have gone too far in broadening the conception.
To replace the word " money " in the definition by the word
" goods " only reflected, indeed, the more thorough grasp which
was now taken of the subject.   But to give the name of
Capital, without any further discrimination, to stocks of
goods, was to give up, without sufficient reason, the second
feature in the old conception,— the reference that capital
had to a capability of yielding interest, to an acquisition of
goods.   To that extent Turgot's conception of capital was
only in part a development born of the time: in part it
was an entirely new reading of the term ; a reading
which, at the same time, exposed him to the charge that,
without due cause, he had neglected the very suggestive

---

[1] Glossarium of Dufresne du Cange, quoted by Umpfenbach, *Das Kapital in
seiner Kulturbedeutung*, Würzburg, 1879, p. 32.

differences there are between goods and goods.   It was no
less a man than Adam Smith who changed and rectified
Turgot's definition.   The "saved" stocks, he said, must be
distinguished as containing two parts.[1]   One portion is
destined for immediate consumption, and gives off no kind of
income ; the other portion is destined to bring in an income to
its owner, and this part alone rightly bears the name of
Capital.

With this distinction, however, Adam Smith connected
another consideration, which was destined to have very serious
consequences on the development of the conception.   He
remarked that his use of the term was applicable as well
to the case of individuals as to that of a whole community ;
only, with this shifting of the standpoint, the group of things
embraced by the conception was also somewhat changed.
Individuals, that is to say, can make a gain, not only by the
production of goods, but also by lending to other individuals
for a consideration goods which are destined in themselves to
immediate consumption, such as houses, masquerade dresses,
furniture, etc.   But the community, as a whole, cannot enrich
itself otherwise than by the production of new goods.   For
the community, then, the conception of "means of acquisition" coincides with the otherwise narrower conception of
"means of production."   In harmony with this the conception
of capital, from the point of view of the community, must be
limited to a complex of the means of production.   It is worth
our while to put more exactly before us the bearing of this
insignificant remark—which, by the way, in Adam Smith is
put more unpretentiously, and much less sharply, than in the
abstract which I have given of his meaning.

First of all, this was the beginning of the division of
capital into two independent conceptions — the conceptions
afterwards distinguished as National Capital and Individual
Capital.   Or, to indicate the relation still more exactly, the
parent conception of capital as a stock of goods yielding
income lived on under the designation of "private capital,"
but, under the name of "national capital," it sent out an
offshoot which quickly grew to independent importance ; soon,
indeed, to greater importance than the parent conception

[1] *Wealth of Nations*, book ii. chap. i.

itself. It was immediately recognised that a very notable importance as regards production attached to that class of goods which people now began to call capital *par excellence*; and this became the occasion of a great many profitable applications of the new conception to the theory of production. Thus we find the national conception in a short time taking its place as one of the chief fundamental conceptions of that theory, and engaged in those very important problems that are now associated with its name. In the triad, Land, Labour, and Capital, we find the new conception giving its name to one of the three great sources of wealth, or, as it was put later, to one of the three factors of production.

But all the time, in virtue of the old parent conception— that known later as Private Capital—the term capital remained connected with the phenomenon of interest, which belonged to the theory of distribution or income. Thus, from that time onward appeared the peculiar phenomenon which was to be the source of so many errors and complications, that two series of fundamentally different phenomena and fundamentally different problems were treated under the same name. Capital, as National Capital, became the central figure of the weightiest problems of Production; as Private Capital, of the fundamentally distinct problem of Interest.

In view of this it becomes of consequence to state clearly that Adam Smith's two varieties of the conception of capital are, properly, two entirely independent conceptions, resting substantially on quite different foundations, and only connected externally by a very loose bond. As chance, however, would have it, it was just this secondary and external relation that caused the name to be given to the younger conception, and brought about the identity of name between the two. The centre of gravity of the conception of private capital, as has been pointed out, lies in the acquisition of interest, in the characteristic of being a source of income: the centre of gravity of the conception of national capital, on the other hand, lies in production, in the characteristic of being a tool of production; and the loose bond that connects them is the accidental circumstance that the goods of which men make use in production are the same goods as are the source of profit and interest to a people considered as a whole, and are, therefore, capital in the original sense. Now this latter reference to income gave the national conception of capital its name, but it was very far from giving it its living substance. This was found so exclusively in the relation to production that, in a short time, the formal definition of capital was based upon that relation alone. It was defined as a complex of "produced means of production," and such like, and in the end it scarcely caused any misgiving when, on closer consideration, the produced means of production seemed never to be quite identical with those stocks which constitute the income-bearing capital of a people. For there can be no question that communities obtain income from consumption goods loaned to other countries against interest. When this incongruity was expressly noted, and yet, notwithstanding, national capital was quietly defined as a complex of means of production, it amounted to a practical and emphatic recognition of the fact that people were interested in capital solely on account of its relations to production, and not at all on account of its accidental characteristic of being the source of interest to the community. To put it shortly : in National Capital the characteristic of being the national source of interest came to the front only for a moment, but this moment was long enough to attach the name of "capital" to it. Scarcely was this done when the centre of gravity was shifted, and placed in its relation to production, and since then National Capital has been looked on as an independent conception, substantially quite foreign to its namesake, Private Capital.

Clearly as the historian of economic theory may now distinguish between these conceptions as developed, the distinction was not seen at the time, nor for long afterwards. With Adam Smith himself the whole matter lies, I might say, in embryo. His ideas were so far from being fixed that he could occasionally ascribe to them meanings which were quite distinct from and did not at all fit in with the fundamental conception. An instance of this is his extension of the national conception to all sorts of personal properties, talents, skill, etc.,—which seem a little out of place as elements of a "stock," and which, like spirits rashly conjured, banished peace for many a long day from the theory of capital. This, however, is an episode of only secondary importance. The prin-

cipal point is that the followers of Adam Smith not only failed
to get rid of the confusion in which he had left the conception
of capital, but, on the contrary, positively put their seal to
one of its worst mistakes.　They did not notice that, in what
Adam Smith and they themselves called " capital," there were
two fundamentally distinct conceptions; they considered the
capital of which they spoke in the theory of production as
identical with the capital which bears interest.　As we know,
Adam Smith had already noticed that there was a certain
difference in the meanings usually given to the word capital, and
that, for instance, rented houses, hired furniture, or masquerade
dresses were capital in one sense and not in another, and his
followers had not failed to loyally transmit the remark.　But
obviously they attached no importance to it,—what was the
use of making a fuss about a distinction which referred only
to a few hired fancy dresses and such like?—and held fast by
their conception of capital, the factor of production being
capital, the source of interest.　And now one confusion
resulted in another.　Before, it was the conceptions that were
mixed; now, it was the phenomena and the problems.　Capital
produces, and it bears interest.　What more natural than to
say shortly;—it bears interest *because* it produces.　And thus,
introduced and made possible by the confusion in the conception of capital, originated that naïve and one-sided theory of
the Productivity of capital which, from Say's days to our own,
has held, and still, in some measure, holds economic science
under its baneful influences.　The Socialist or semi-socialist
writers of our time were the first to face in earnest the confusion of conceptions by distinguishing capital into " pure
economic capital," and capital as a " historico-legal category." [1]
This distinction, as we shall see, did not indeed hit the nail
on the head; but it was at least a distinction which, of
necessity, finally distinguished between the object of the production problem and the object of the interest problem, and
thus paved the way for an advance in the treatment of the
still viciously confused problems.　But this is to anticipate
the course of development : to resume the methodical narrative
we must go back to Adam Smith.

　　It may be said that Adam Smith's fundamental conception

---

[1] Rodbertus, *passim* ; Wagner, *Grundlegung*, second edition, p. 39.

was never afterwards quite neglected; the relation of capital
to acquisition and to production, which in opposition to Turgot
he had again imported into the conception, has, in some form or
other, been retained by all later writers. On the other hand,
it very soon became manifest that, within the common fundamental conception, there was a surprising amount of latitude
for different readings of it, and, as it chanced, there were certain
circumstances which very much favoured the taking advantage
of this latitude. First of all, economists fell heir not only
to the fundamental conception, but to the seed of ambiguity
which Adam Smith had planted in it. This seed now burst
into full life. Almost everybody, entangled in the confusion
we have just described, thought that " Capital " must be defined
by *one* uniting conception. But the one party, and indeed
the majority, thought more about the instruments of production, while the other thought more about the source of income ;
and thus they attached to capital the characteristics of two
different conceptions. This was one fruitful cause of divergent
definitions, but there was another still more fruitful. Whether
the theoretical conception of capital was made to include productive instruments only, or whether, more liberally, it was made
to embrace acquisitive instruments as well, in any case there
are many different kinds both of productive and of acquisitive
instruments. Now, in proportion as economists discovered
more similarities or more contrasts between the various groups
of goods which serve for production and for acquisition,
they considered it appropriate to group together, under the
conception which they called capital, sometimes all acquisitive
or all productive instruments without exception, sometimes only
a certain circle of the same. And this circle again, according
to the tendencies of the writer, might be larger or smaller ;
sometimes of moderate dimensions, and sometimes, again, very
closely limited. It may be said, indeed, that of all combinations and permutations which were logically and mathematically
conceivable, economical science in this case was not spared
one.

Without attempting either to give a complete tale of these,
or to keep to the chronological order, I shall shortly collocate
the more important of them.

Numerous writers define capital as a group of " products

that serve towards production," or as groups of "produced means of production." This conception, which is expressly based on the relation of capital to production, excludes, on the one hand, land (as not produced) and, on the other hand, all goods that serve for immediate satisfaction of wants. This conception I have followed in defining capital as a group of Intermediate Products. In so far as it is not so much an alteration as a more distinct formulation of Adam Smith's (national) conception, I do not reckon it an independent variation.

The variation which Hermann, however, has given must be considered an independent one, and is the fourth reading in arithmetical order given to the conception. He goes back to capital as the source of income, and makes this the object of his definition : Capital, he says, is "every durable foundation of a utility (*Nutzung*) which has exchange value." [1] In opposition to the last definition this one includes under the conception of Capital all land, and besides embraces such consumption goods as are durable, like furniture, houses, etc., even if they are personally used by the owners.

A fifth variation is given by Menger. He defines capital as such groups of economic goods of higher rank (productive goods) as are now available to us for future periods.[2] This definition is, in one way narrower, in another, wider than Hermann's. It excludes durable consumption-goods ("goods of the first rank"), but it is wide enough to take in the productive services of labour,[3] which Hermann had not reckoned as capital.

A sixth variation comes from Kleinwächter. He finds it a characteristic mark of capital that it *lightens* the toil of acquisition or productive labour. Now this characteristic appears to him not to belong to all means of production, but only to one category of these, the tools of production, while the matter or materials of production are absolutely passive during the whole production process ; they are worked up or used up but give no assistance in working. "Logically,"

---

[1] *Staatswirthschaftliche Untersuchungen*, Munich, 1832, p. 59, and similarly in the second edition of 1874, p. 111. On p. 56 he expressly calls capital " Wealth which brings in income."

[2] *Grundsätze*, Vienna, 1871, p. 130.

[3] See Mataja, *Der Unternehmergewinn*, 1884, p. 180.

therefore, " the conception of capital should be limited to tools of production." [1]

A seventh interpretation has Jevons for its author. It runs parallel to a certain extent with the foregoing. That is to say, Jevons also considers it proved that by capital is to be understood "wealth employed to facilitate production." [2] But he finds this characteristic in quite another group of concrete goods from that of Kleinwächter. "The single and all-important function of capital," he says, "is to enable the labourer to await the result of any long lasting work—to put an interval between the beginning and the end of an enterprise." Capital, then, "consists merely in the aggregate of those commodities which are required for sustaining labourers of any kind or class engaged in work. A stock of food is the main element of capital; but supplies of clothes, furniture, and all the other articles in common daily use are also necessary parts of capital." The true and only capital thus, according to Jevons, is the sustenance of the labourers. [3]

Marx arrived at an eighth reading of the conception. As every one knows he sees in interest a profit got by the capitalist at the expense of the wage-earner. This element of exploitation seems to him so important that he brings it in to the conception of capital as a constitutive feature of it: he conceives of capital as only those productive instruments which, in the hand of the capitalists, serve as "instruments for the exploitation and enslaving of the labourer." The same things in the possession of the labourer, on the other hand, are not capital. [4]

A ninth variation we owe to the distinguished critic of the theory of capital, Karl Knies. It originates in a well-meant attempt to settle the terribly tangled controversy to the satisfaction of everybody. To this end Knies endeavours to construct a conception of capital which will be so wide that the most important of the contending interpretations may find room in it beside each other. The uniting element in the conception he imagines he finds in the devotion of goods to

[1] *Grundlagen und Ziele des sog. wissenschaftlichen Sozialismus*, 1885, p. 184.

[2] *Theory of Political Economy*, second edition, London, 1879, p. 242.

[3] *Ibid.* p. 242, and very emphatically p. 264 : "The capital is not the railway, but the food of those who made the railway."

[4] *Das Kapital*, vol. i., second edition, p. 796 (first edition, p. 747). See also Knies, *Das Geld*, first edition, p. 53.

the service of the future.   Accordingly he defines the capital
of a community as "its available stock of goods (whether for
consumption, acquisition, or production) which may be applied to
satisfying wants in the future." [1]   This definition does, as a fact,
afford room both for Turgot's "saved stocks of goods" and for
the "produced means of production" of Adam Smith's school,
as also for all goods embraced in Hermann's definition as
affording the foundation of a durable—and therefore a conspicuously future—utility.

Quite by itself stands the tenth interpretation, that of
L. Walras.   He divides all economic goods into "capital" and
"income" (*revenu*).   All kinds of goods, irrespective of their
destination, which can be used more than once—that is, all
durable goods—he calls capital; while all perishable goods are
income.   Going into details he mentions the following as
capital:—Land (*capitaux fonciers*), persons (*capitaux personnels*),
and movable durable goods (*capitaux proprement dits* or *capitaux
mobiliers*), while he considers food, the raw materials of industrial production, fuel and the like, as income.[2]

If the interpretations just mentioned are divided in
opinion as to the goods which should be designated capital,
they are, at any rate, all agreed that it is *goods* that are to bear
that name.   But, finally, an eleventh reading of the conception
calls this in question, and, instead of making capital a real
concrete quantity, distils out, as it were, some kind of abstraction as the essence of capital.   Thus M'Leod, who sometimes
recurs to a favourite metaphor of earlier writers and defines
capital as a "stock of accumulated labour," sometimes goes
still deeper in abstraction and defines it as "purchasing power"
or "circulating power."   These phrases are not meant as illustrations, but explanations given in full earnest; he gives us to
understand this in the most emphatic way by saying, in one
place, that the application of the word capital to goods is a
simple metaphor, and on another occasion, in so many words,

[1] *Das Geld*, first edition, p. 47. In the second edition (1885) the same conception is on the whole retained, but often formulated in a less exact manner.
Accordingly, where I do not explicitly mention the contrary, I quote from the
more distinct formulation of the first edition.

[2] *Éléments d'Économie Politique Pure*, Lausanne, 1874, p. 213. Launhardt
(*Mathematische Begründung der Volkswirthschaftslehre*, Leipsic, 1885, § 2) has
closely followed Walras.

that capital does not represent goods in any way whatever.[1] Quite recently too we have a strikingly similar conception in the suggestive work of a juristic writer, Kühnast. He also tells us emphatically that capital is of an immaterial nature, and does not consist of material objects at all—of goods themselves, that is to say—but only of their value. "Capital is . . . the value of the productive power contained in material goods . . . or a complex of productive material values." [2]

Numerous as are these various readings of the conception, our list does not by any means exhaust the divisions and sub-divisions that might be given. In addition to the above inter-pretations which differ in form—which are, that is, different definitions—there may be complete unanimity as to the formula of the definition, and yet a good deal of disagreement as to the essence of it. This might happen where a word employed in all the definitions as characteristic and distinctive was not used in all of them in the same sense. Not to speak of less important instances, there are two characteristic terms which, as capable of different readings, involve materially different interpretations of the conception of capital. One of these is the word " good." Of the many economists who were agreed in defining capital as a stock or group of goods, some, taking the word in its narrower sense, thought only of a supply of material goods; some, extending it to immaterial objects, thought of things like the state, peace, law, national honour, virtue; [3] some again, under the same term, included useful personal properties and powers; [4] while others took man himself into the conception.[5] A similar ambiguity has attended the use of the characteristic term " means of produc-tion," or simply " production." While some economists, and

---

[1] " It does not represent commodities in any way whatever, but only the power its owner has of purchasing what he wants" (*Elements of Political Economy*, 1858, pp. 66 and 69).

[2] "Ueber den rechtlichen Begriff des Kapitals," in the *Beiträge zur Erläuterung des Deutschen Rechtes*, 1884, p. 356 ; and particularly pp. 385-387.

[3] See also Knies, *Das Geld*, p. 17 (second edition, p. 38).

[4] Thus occasionally Adam Smith, J. B. Say,. and others.

[5] Thus Canard : " The fundamental wealth of one who pursues an art or a handicraft is his own person" ; and later, M'Culloch (*Principles of Political Economy*, 1825, p. 319) : " A labourer is himself a part of the national capital." Elsewhere he explains the wage of labour as an interest on capital of the "machine called man."

those the majority, understood by production simply a producing of materials for the satisfaction of human want, others included the producing of what they called "inward goods," the creation of satisfactory conditions for and in the human person. The consequence of this was that the significant term "means of production" lost every possible limitation, and that even goods for immediate enjoyment were received into the conception of capital on the ground of being instrumental in producing the "inward goods" of content, health, culture, etc. The greatest sinner in this respect is Roscher. He first defines capital to be "every product which is dedicated to further production," but then divides this general conception into "Productive capital" and "Use capital," according as these products affect the production of material goods or "the production of personal goods or useful relations."[1] Thus, notwithstanding the difference in definition, his conception of capital practically comes very near to that of Turgot.

[1] *Grundlagen der Nationalökonomie*, § 42.

CHAPTER IV

THE TRUE CONCEPTION OF CAPITAL

POLITICAL economists have not, as a rule, been noted for the unanimity of their definitions. But here the differences in the interpretation of the conception are so excessive as to suggest that there may be something quite peculiar about the object of dispute. I think Knies has quite correctly estimated the peculiar position of the case when he says that "there is something else in it than an ordinary scientific dispute as to whether a particular definition is happy or unfortunate, or, indeed, true or false."[1] It is not the definition that is the matter of dispute, but the thing defined; or, as I should prefer to say, the terminology. The material difference in the definitions is not so much that the one thing to be defined appears to each one in a different light, as that each one is defining an entirely different thing; and thus definitions that are really incompatible come within the same ring-fence, because each one claims the expression Capital for the object he is defining.

It is clear that, while this circumstance may explain the striking divergence of opinions, it makes it, unfortunately, more difficult to decide between them. For in questions of nomenclature there is, strictly speaking, neither right nor wrong. There is, therefore, nothing to compel conviction; there is only an appeal to a greater or less appropriateness; and people may, to a considerable extent, remain of different opinions as to the appropriateness. All the same it is clear that our controversy must be settled. It is impossible that economic science can for all time allow its representatives liberty to call

[1] *Das Geld*, p. 5.

ten or eleven fundamentally different things by the same name. Political Economy requires clear thinking, and for that the prerequisites are clear ideas and clear speech. We must come to an agreement, and it will be come to exactly as men have agreed and continue to agree over the innumerable disputes to which the nomenclature of the descriptive natural sciences, zoology, botany, mineralogy, geography, continually gives rise. The majority unite, and slowly but surely leave the dissentients and pass to the order of the day.

But on which of the numerous readings of our conception of capital can we hope to unite unprejudiced persons? To my mind, if we have once realised the nature of the controversy as pre-eminently one of terminology, we shall not find it so difficult to decide as the amount of confusion up till now might lead one to suppose. Happily there cannot be much doubt as to certain leading principles that have to be observed in questions of terminology; if these are impartially acted upon, the great majority of the competing definitions will be definitely thrown out, and there will not remain more than two or three between which there need be any real hesitation. And, even in this short leet, the arguments of appropriateness which must decide are so unequally distributed that, though we may not be able actually to force a universal acceptance of one definite conception—as it is, after all, only appropriateness that must guide us,—yet we may confidently look for the voluntary adhesion of a vast majority.

The leading principles we have to observe seem to me to be as follows. First, and chiefly, it is quite clear that our reading of the conception must be logically unassailable; that is to say, it must not contradict itself, and it must apply to the object which it proposes to define. Then, we must not be spendthrift in our terminology; that is to say, we must not attach the name capital to, and make it synonymous with, a conception that already has a name, while other suggestive conceptions, to which naturally the word would equally well apply, have to do without any name. Thirdly, the conception we adopt must be scientifically important and scientifically useful. Lastly, and not least, unless an alteration be urgently demanded on some grounds of logic or appropriateness, the name of capital must be left to that conception for which it has been longest and most generally used.   Or, to put it in a more roundabout way : as things are at present, everybody treats of the most weighty theoretical and social problems under the general name of " problems of capital " : that being so, the word capital, wherever possible, should be so used as to spare us the aggravated difficulties that will attend the great controverted questions of the day if we rebaptize their terms.

In view of these rules I would suggest the following as the most adequate solution of the controversy.

Capital in general we shall call a group of Products which serve as means to the Acquisition of Goods.   Under this general conception we shall put that of Social Capital as narrower conception.   Social Capital we shall call a group of products, which serve as means to the socio-economical Acquisition of Goods ; or, as this acquisition is only possible through production, we shall call it a group of products destined to serve towards further production ; or, briefly, a group of Intermediate Products.   Synonymous with the wider of the two conceptions, the term Acquisitive Capital may be very suitably used, or, less suitably but more in accordance with usage the term Private Capital.   Social Capital again, the narrower of the two conceptions, may be well and concisely called Productive Capital.   The following are my reasons for this classification.

Capital in its wider sense, and capital in its narrower sense, both mark out categories which, economically, are of the highest importance.   " Products which serve to acquisitive ends " possess a pre-eminent importance for the theory of income as being the source of interest ; while the " intermediate products " possess at least as great an importance for the theory of production.   The distinction between production from hand to mouth and production which employs roundabout and fruitful methods, is so fundamental that it is eminently desirable that a special conception should be coined for the latter.   This is done—if not, as we shall see, in the only possible way, yet in a way that is not inappropriate—in grouping together, under the conception of capital, the " intermediate products " which come into existence in the course of this roundabout production.

Again, the solution suggested is the most conservative one.

Without laying any particular weight on the fact that the historical origin of the word Capital[1] indicates a relation to an acquisition or a gain, and that our reading remains true to this, it preserves the double relation—the relation to acquisition of interest on the one side, and to production on the other—which was imported into the conception of capital by Adam Smith, and since his time has been adopted in scientific usage. It is no inconsiderable advantage, then, that we do not require to create a majority in its favour by a revolution in terminology; the majority is already with us, and the conception may easily be carried unanimously if we add some new unbiassed members. Here, too, it is worthy of particular attention that those writers who have occupied themselves professedly and most profoundly with the investigation of the conception of capital and its problems, have ended, almost without exception, by adopting exactly the same conception, or at least one which comes very close to it.[2]

Connected with this is the further advantage, that we avoid a puzzling change of name for the two classes of problems which

[1] See above, p. 24.

[2] Cossa (*La Nozione del Capitale*), *Saggi di Ec. Pol.*, p. 157, has the definition: "Capitale è un prodotto impiegato nella produzione." Ricca-Salerno (*Sulla Teoria del Capitale*, 1877, p. 51) says: "Il capitale è ricchezza prodotta applicata alla produzione." Rodbertus, whose opinion I am inclined to put particularly high, because, although not altogether happy in his solution of the problems of capital, he had an insight into its essence such as scarcely any one before him had, explains (*Das Kapital*, p. 234, also *Zur Beleuchtung der soz. Frage*, p. 98) that "Capital (materials and tools) is product which serves for still further production." A. Wagner, also, who has done good service in the theory of capital (*Grundlegung*, second edition, p. 38), calls capital a "Stock of economical goods, which serve as instruments to the making or acquiring of new economical goods." In the most recent Italian monograph on capital, Supino (*Il Capitale nell' Organismo Economico e nell' Economia Politica*, 1886, pp. 9 and 17) defines capital again as "Il prodotto del lavoro passato che serve a produzione successiva," or as "ricchezza impiegata produttivamente allo scopo di ricavarne un profitto." Of other prominent modern writers may be mentioned Pierson (*Leerboek der Staathuishoudkunde*, Haarlem, 1884, p. 157); Schönberg (*Handbuch*, second edition, p. 209), "Capital is a material means of production obtained by human labour, which, employed as such, is destined to give a return to its owner"; E. Sax (*Grundlegung der theoretischen Staatswirthschaft*, pp. 115, 315, 323, etc.) Of recent French writers on the subject Gide (*Principes d'Économie Politique*, Paris, 1884) recognises the two varieties in the conception of capital with a clearness rare even in French literature, and distinguishes them as "capitaux simplement lucratifs" and "capitaux productifs." "Les premiers," he says, "sont ceux que rapportent un revenu à une personne;

are both treated of now under the name of problems of capital.
The popular name is retained both for the "factor of production" and for the "source of interest." And finally, it seems
to me no small advantage that, notwithstanding the material
difference there is between capital the factor of production,
and capital the source of interest, it is not necessary in our
reading of it to make two conceptions of capital that are
entirely foreign to one another, and have nothing more in
common than cat has with category. Our two conceptions
have just enough in common to allow of their being formally
coupled under one common definition, and then distinguished
as narrower and wider conceptions. True, their connection is
not an intimate one, and in the light of what has been said
it cannot be so; it rests simply on the accidental circumstance
that, for society as a whole, which cannot acquire except
through producing, the goods which constitute the produced
means of *acquisition* (capital in the wider sense) coincide with
the goods which constitute the produced means of *production*
(capital in the narrower sense, or Social Capital). It will be
noted that I use the phrase Social Capital, and not the common
expression National Capital. I do so for this reason, that, for
a limited community, the means of acquisition embrace not
only productive goods but consumption goods lent to foreign
countries. Those who hold by the conception of National
Capital, then, must either take in the above-named consumption goods along with productive goods, thereby arriving at a

les seconds sont ceux qui produisent une richesse nouvelle dans le pays" (p.
148). His only failure is that he would recognise productive capitals alone as
"true" capitals.

    In English literature our conception of capital (without, of course, any clear
distinction being kept between its two varieties) is almost exclusively the prevailing one ; this is so well known that I may spare quotations. Generally speaking,
it is very significant of the state of "public opinion" in the matter that not
long ago Kleinwächter (Schönberg's *Handbuch*, second edition, p. 210) could
explain "Common usage in political economy to-day considers it an essential
characteristic of capital that it is a material means of production." The only
difference of opinion is as to whether land should be reckoned as cápital or not.
Finally, I think I may venture to express the opinion that even the fore-
most representative of a rival definition, Knies, is in opposition to us more in
form than in matter. It is he at any rate who has, in a masterly manner,
developed the idea—the really important one in our statement of the conception—that, in defining capital, we must define that which is the object of those
problems that "have appeared on the scene under the name of capital" (*Das
Geld*, p. 19).

very uninteresting conception indeed; or if they mean to confine it to productive goods only, they must build their national conception on a quite independent basis, and break off all logical connection with the other conception,—which would at any rate be a doubtful policy. Our "Social Capital" avoids both these difficulties.

CHAPTER V

THE COMPETING CONCEPTIONS OF CAPITAL

AND now we may review the other conceptions of capital already mentioned, and see if any of them can better satisfy scientific requirements.

The conception which seems to me to come nearest to ours is that suggestive one which may be most concisely called the "National Subsistence Fund," and which very much coincides with Turgot's "Saved Stocks of Goods." This conception embraces all material goods with the exception of land. Later on we shall have to make ourselves very accurately acquainted with it, and to avoid repetition I refrain from going farther into it here. I shall only say this much. The conception of the national subsistence fund is, like our own, a conception of great scientific suggestiveness, and is so as regards those very problems which connect themselves with the word capital. In particular, as being so much in touch with the phenomenon of capitalist production (production carried on in lengthy processes and roundabout methods), it is even more happy than our conception of the Intermediate Products. The latter, indeed, embraces all those goods which come into existence *during* the production process, the goods which carry it on and help to complete it; but it does not embrace the initial fund of consumption goods needed to commence the process. It therefore leaves out the first link in the chain, which is a very important one, while the conception of the Subsistence Fund, as I understand it, embraces the entire group of goods by means of which the capitalist process is begun and carried through.

Notwithstanding the importance of this conception in the

theory of capital, I put it second to the other for the following reasons.   First, on account of the difficulty of sharply dividing between those funds of subsistence which serve for acquisition and production, and those which stand outside of any relation to acquisition and consequently have nothing at all to do with the scientific problem of capital.[1]   Second, that in any case the conception of "intermediate products" is so conspicuously important, that it is scarcely less worthy of being indicated and emphasised by the name of capital, than is the conception of the "national subsistence fund."   Third, that, as compared with the latter, the "intermediate products" appear to me to have in their favour the distinct and also the decisive advantage of being already familiar expressions.   Capital, the factor of production, cannot again be left without a name, and for that reason the conception of "national subsistence fund" must come second.

Next in importance comes Roscher's conception.   It is due as much to the high scientific position of this writer as to the widely spread acceptance of his doctrine that we should go more fully into the definition he gives of capital.   Unfortunately, I am bound to say that it seems to me anything but happy.   In the form of it Roscher appears to come very near to the same conception as lies at the basis of our definition, in claiming the designation capital for "every product saved for further production."[2] But in the very next lines, when enumerating the elements of a community's capital, he veers round to Turgot's conception, and includes dwelling-houses, "utensils of personal service,"

---

[1] I do not care to waste more words than necessary here on things which will become clear of themselves as we go on, but I may make one remark.   For reasons that Rodbertus (*Das Kapital*, p. 301) has seen through tolerably correctly, and which will be fully explained later, it is by no means my meaning to emphasise only the subsistence advanced to productive labourers, and reckon it capital. Either the conception of capital is limited to goods which serve *immediately* in production, and therefore to productive goods proper,—in which case means of subsistence in general, and also the means of subsistence of labourers, have no share.   Or, besides "intermediate products," such finished consumption goods are taken into the conception as serve indirectly by their existence to production,—in which case, as will be shown in the proper place, certain advances of subsistence given to landowners and capitalists must be included.   But then we are at once met with the difficulty suggested in the text of fixing definitely, when the advances of subsistence, given to people who do not themselves produce, are of indirect assistance to production, and when they occupy no relation to it.

[2] *Grundlagen der Nationalökonomie*, § 42.

and, in short, goods for immediate consumption.   This vacillation is due to the fact that Roscher gives an unusually wide interpretation to the conception of "product" and "means of production."   He looks upon every satisfaction of a real want as the production of a "personal good,"[1] and this causes him to recognise everything that serves to the satisfaction of human want (that is, simply, all goods) as means of production. Any unbiassed person can see how unfortunate this is.   Without due cause it obliterates the very important opposition that exists between the production of goods which satisfy want, and their consumption.   It christens, for example, the idler as a zealous producer, always thinking how he may produce the personal goods of satiety, of ease, of contentment, and so on. It leads, moreover, to a lamentable waste of terminology. When the conception "means of production" is made synonymous with the conception "good," there is no name left for the true instrument of production.   But the latter, as a highly important economic category, must be kept prominent and distinct from goods for immediate consumption, and so we fall from one confusion and ambiguity of terminology into another. This shows itself most significantly in Roscher's own conception. He feels the very sensible need of distinguishing, inside his conception of capital, those goods which serve to the production of "material goods" from those other goods which serve simply to the production of "personal goods," and he does this by designating the former as "productive capitals" and the latter as "use-capitals."   This expression is doubly unfortunate. First, in putting "use-capitals" in opposition to "productive capitals," the capacity of being means of production is implicitly refused to "use-capitals"; while they found admittance to the conception of capital only on the ground of this very capacity, viz. as "products saved for further production." And second, the same word "productive" is made to serve in the one breath as the predicate which binds together all capitals, and as the predicate which divides capital into two. Could any terminology be more unfortunate ?[2]

     But Roscher's definition of capital is not only inappropriate; it is, in my opinion, logically unsound, inasmuch as it

---

[1] *Grundlagen der Nationalökonomie*, § 211.
[2] See also the acute criticism of Knies, *Das Geld*, p. 46.

does not cover those things which Roscher means it to define. After he has christened all goods productive instruments, it might be thought that he would consider the totality of goods as capital, with the exception of land.   The definition of " products saved for further production "—if the production of personal goods be included—seems to apply to them all.   That, however, is not Roscher's meaning.   From his enumeration of the elements of a community's capital, as well as from an expression used in § 43, where he puts the use-capital in opposition to objects of use which are not capital, it follows that, of consumption goods he will reckon as capital only those which are durable, such as houses, furniture, etc., and not those which are perishable (with the exception of the means of subsistence of productive labourers).   He justifies this by saying :—" On the other hand, the sharp line of division between the Use-Capital and those objects of consumption which are not capital rests, in conformity with our definition of capital, on the fact that the latter are not only more speedily consumed, but are always meant to be consumed ; whereas, in the case of the former, the consumption is only the inevitable and the reverse side of the use."   These words cannot very well mean anything but that the speedy intentional consumption of goods is the direct opposite of " saving," so that one characteristic demanded by Roscher's definition is not present in perishable consumption goods.   Suppose this granted, is the same defect not inherent in the perishable raw materials and auxiliary materials of production as in the means of subsistence of the productive labourers, which Roscher has expressly enumerated among the elements of the community's capital ?   Is not " the coal at the forge," the " gunpowder in the chase and in blasting operations," the bread in the worker's mouth, quickly and intentionally consumed ?   It is either, or——! Either speedy and intentional consumption is the opposite of " saving," and takes away from such goods the property of being capital, in which case Roscher must also exclude the perishable raw and auxiliary materials of production and the maintenance of the producers ; or speedy consumption is not a ground of exclusion from the conception of capital, in which case the perishable means of " production of personal goods " cannot be refused admittance to the conception.   Roscher's definition therefore fits either a wider or a narrower circle of things, but never exactly that circle which he meant to define as capital.[1]

The conception of capital most closely allied to this—in so far as it also enumerates consumption goods along with acquisitive instruments—is that laid down by Knies. It is based on an idea which, from the point of theory, is as interesting as it is important. All the same, I think that, on closer examination, it will not be preferred to ours.

Knies defines as capital "that complex of goods available to a community which may be applied to the satisfaction of want *in the future*." This definition, as we can easily see, agrees almost word for word with that of another conspicuously important and fundamental conception. If we leave out the words "in the future," it takes in all the goods in a community available for the satisfaction of want, and that is an amount which most writers are in the habit of calling the "wealth" (*Vermögen*) of the community. If, like Knies,[2] we emphasise the fact that wealth embraces only the *net* amount of goods after deduction of debts, we may perhaps call that amount the community's "gross property"[3] (*Guterbesitz*). In any case we have in this to deal with an independent amount bearing an independent name, with which "capital" neither coincides nor should coincide.

Now from this amount Knies would distinguish his conception of capital by adding the words "in the future." Do these words really convey a distinction? In my opinion they do not; at least, if we strictly give them the meaning they naturally have. It is an attribute of all wealth without exception that it is used for the satisfaction of wants in the future. All accumulation of wealth is based on provision for

---

[1] In latest editions Roscher, evidently under the influence of what Knies has said on the subject, formally widens his definition of capital to some extent by an addition. It now runs: "Every product which is destined to further economical production (even to systematic later use) we call capital." This addition, however, does not materially widen the conception, as Roscher, independent of this, has already included *every* use—therefore every "systematic later use"—in the production of (material or personal) goods.

[2] *Das Geld*, pp. 83 and 92.

[3] For the community as a whole, moreover, which, naturally, has neither claims nor debts, its material property, according to Knies's definition, completely coincides with its wealth.

future requirements. Every atom of wealth in my possession at this moment has been acquired at a previous point of time with the view of being spent at a future point of time. That point of time may not be far away; it may, perhaps, be the next day, or the next hour; but certainly it is still in the future. If, therefore, we take the word "future" in its strict sense, Knies's formula has obviously defined not only Capital but Wealth; and his conception of capital coincides with the ordinary conception of wealth.

If Knies had actually contemplated this, it would not be difficult to pronounce upon his conception of capital. We should have to accuse him of waste of terminology. It would evidently be a highly inappropriate duplication of terms to use the word capital as a synonymous expression for the familiar conception which already bears the name of wealth, while other weighty conceptions--as, for instance, certain groups of acquisitive instruments—have no name.[1] But Knies had no thought of any such identification. Indeed, he repeatedly and emphatically says that his conception embraces only a part of the total possession of goods, and he opposes to it, as the second member of his division, those goods that serve for the satisfaction of "current present want." This classification obviously assumes that the word "present" is not to be taken altogether literally. For if by the "present" were to be understood strictly that point of time which divides the past from the future, the goods which entered into employment in that moment of time would, of course, represent so insignificant an amount that it would not be worth while to speak of them, to say nothing of basing a scientific classification and a new conception on their short lease of life. If the second member of Knies's classification is to be anything at all, the "present" must be extended from a point of time to a period of time, and this, naturally, can only be done at the expense of the future. By the "present" we must understand a period of time which goes beyond the narrow limits of the fleeting moment, and takes in some part, large or small, of the immediate or near future.

Now, while it would be pedantic to say that such a

---

[1] Knies himself has pronounced this opinion in saying (*Das Geld*, p. 22) that no one would claim that "capital is identical with economic goods."

deviation from strict literal exactness is inadmissible, it seems
to me unfortunate if a scientific conception can only hold its
own by allowing its most important, indeed its only characteristic feature, to be used in a loose sense; all the more so that
Knies, in order to guard his conception of capital from merging
into that of wealth, should have made the distinction between
present and future into a sharp opposition.   It is not too
much to say that his conception of capital lives by the opposition between present and future, and this opposition must lose
its strength whenever, and so far as, goods devoted to the
service of a near future, but all the same a future, find their
place not on the side of capital devoted to the future, but on
the other !

But to look further: if we add a portion of the future to
the present, how far is this addition to go ?   Is it to be the
next hour, or the next day, or is it to be a longer period—say
the current month or the economic year ?   This seems to me
rather an important point to determine, but Knies himself has
not said anything about it.   If, in his place, we consider the
different possibilities, it is easy to see that the addition of a
short period, an hour or a day, does not secure the end contemplated.   The amount of goods that a people consumes in a
day is $\frac{1}{365}$ of its income, and is a much smaller fraction of its
wealth.   Now, very few people would think it appropriate to
separate off a thousandth part from the total amount of goods
which form the total wealth of a community in order to put
the remaining $\frac{999}{1000}$ together under one independent conception
—particularly when that thousandth part is not divided off
from the principal sum by a clear and well-marked opposition,
but only by a conventional and somewhat metaphorical reading
of the word " present."   To put it shortly: a conception of
capital which embraces roughly $\frac{999}{1000}$ of the conception of
wealth comes too close to the conception of wealth to have
any scientific significance.

But if we add a longer period of time, say a month, we
encounter new difficulties.   Owing to this altered reading we
shall now deduct from the conception of capital all goods that
are destined to be consumed in the ordinary purposes of life
during the current month.   Good.   But it is possible that I
may make a profit out of these very goods previous to their

consumption and without prejudice to it.   For instance, a sum of money which I intend to dispose of finally on the fifteenth of the current month, I may lodge with a bank as an interest-bearing deposit from the first to the fifteenth, against a deposit receipt, or I may put it into open account. What then?   Does this interest-bearing money belong to capital or does it not?   Whatever the answer, we do not avoid serious difficulties.   If we answer it in the affirmative, we lay ourselves open to the charge of being illogical; for, by hypothesis, the whole of the current month is a widened present.   But if we answer it in the negative, we first put ourselves in a position of flagrant contradiction with firmly-established usage; then we commit ourselves to the strange doctrine that a thing which undoubtedly bears interest is not capital; and, finally, we give up what formed the strongest recommendation of Knies's conception—its purpose of reconciliation.   This conception of capital has been put forward by Knies with the express intention of uniting under it, as a higher and broader unity, all former and competing conceptions. In it Turgot's "stocks of goods," and Adam Smith's "complex of acquisitive instruments," and Hermann's "goods of durable use" were to find ample room beside each other.   But this mission of reconciliation, and with it the *raison d'être* of Knies's theory, disappears the moment that any one acquisitive instrument is denied recognition as capital—especially interest-bearing money, the first parent of the conception.[1]

In whatever way, then, it is looked at, we get no clear satisfaction from Knies's conception.   But, to be just to Knies, I must recognise emphatically that there is a deep and significant idea at the root of it, and that if his conception fails of its end it is only because of external defects, or, if I might say so, defects that belong to the technique of conception.   As a fact their destination to the service of the future is a peculiarly important characteristic of the goods we call capital, indeed, a characteristic which gives us the key to the most important problems connected with the subject.   Only it is not exactly the distinguishing characteristic, but one that capital shares

---

[1] It needs no showing that the group of short-dated money claims, although the most obvious, is by no means the only example that might be given in proof of the objection urged in the text.

with several other classes of goods which we have good reasons
for not reckoning as capital; and for that reason—but only
for that reason—it is not fitted to act as the constitutive and
distinctive feature on which to base our definition.[1]

The conceptions of capital hitherto mentioned are distinguished, as a whole, from our conception in that they include
consumption goods as well as acquisitive instruments.   We
come now to certain conceptions that agree with ours in
reserving the name of capital for a complex of acquisitive
instruments, but differ from it, and from each other, as to
what this complex includes.

The widest of these would simply include under capital all
acquisitive instruments — not only material but personal.
Under different names it counts labour as capital.   Many
conceive of the *work* of the labourer as capital; others, of his
labour power;[2] others, again, of the entire *person of the labourer*.[3]
In itself of course there is nothing in the world to prevent the
totality of things which serve in acquisition from being
grouped together under one uniting conception, and called by
one common name.   This has already been done substantially
in the conception and under the title of "acquisitive instruments," or "productive goods," or "goods of higher rank."
But it is an entirely different question whether one is justified
in claiming the name of "capital" for such a conception.   I
should say with all possible emphasis that one is not.   First
of all, if the title is given to the totality of all acquisitive
instruments, it can only be at the cost of refusing it to any
narrower group of acquisitive instruments which likewise
claims it.   Now the former conception is already sufficiently
known by the above-mentioned names, while the narrower and

---

[1] Among others Ricca-Salerno (*Sulla Teoria del Capitale*, Milan, 1877, p. 58)
and lately Emil Sax (*Grundlegung der theoretischen Staatswirthschaft*, p. 310)
have criticised Knies on this point.   Sax's criticism of the weaknesses of Knies's
conception is both trenchant and substantially correct, but he does not recognise
the kernel of truth that is in it, and ends by a judgment which, on the whole, is
rather rudely expressed.

[2] For instance, Adam Smith, ii. 1 ; Umpfenbach, *Das Kapital in seiner Kulturbedeutung*, 1879, p. 19 ; Say, *Cours Complet*, part i. chap. x.

[3] Thus Say, *Cours Complet*, part i. chap. xiii. ; M'Culloch, *Principles*, first
edition, p. 319 ; fifth edition, p. 294 ; Walras, *Éléments d'Économie Politique*,
p. 217.

rival conception is very important and has no other name but capital. Even were the question, then, in other respects an entirely open one, we should, on the ground of economy of terms, decide against the use of the word capital for the totality of acquisitive instruments. But it is not an open question; it is already prejudiced by universal usage. In political economy and in practical life generally we have long been accustomed to treat of certain great social problems as problems of capital, and in doing so we have had in our minds, not a conception which embraced labour, but a conception that opposed capital to labour. Capital and Labour, Capitalism and Socialism, Interest on capital and Wages of labour, are certainly not harmless synonyms; they express the strongest conceivable social and economical contrasts.

Now what would be the consequence if people began all at once to call labour capital? In the most favourable circumstances it would be an innovation in terminology with little to recommend it. If all the world were to adapt itself to the innovation, and were to do so in full consciousness that it was an innovation in terminology and nothing more, it might remain perfectly clear that, in putting under one common name the real differences that separate labour from what has hitherto been called capital, these differences are not in the least reconciled. As before, everybody would notice these differences, and work without bias at the social problems to which they give rise. Economic theory would not then suffer any material injury beyond the inconvenience of having no name for the chief object of such inquiries; for, of course, from the moment that labour is reckoned capital we must cease to give the name of capital to its social opposite.

This, I say, might be the result in the most favourable circumstances; unfortunately such a result is most unlikely. It is much more probable that the blending of the names would bring confusion into the matter. We need not deceive ourselves on this point; names and catchwords always exert an immense influence over us. Most of us are very fond of slurring over inconvenient contradictions and smoothing down thorny problems. How could one resist the tempting opportunity which the new meaning of the word capital would offer? Between Capital and Labour, as these words were used formerly, there was discord, contrast, conflict. Now one single happy word unites all contrasts; what we thought opposites are really homogeneous; labour is capital; wage and interest are at bottom one!

The reader will perhaps think it a mere jest to put such words in the mouth of serious thinkers. Economic literature, unfortunately, witnesses to the earnest of it, as we see in the case of those writers who conceived the unlucky idea of rebaptizing labour as capital. There is first M'Culloch. He represents the labourer as a piece of fixed capital, as a kind of machine. When he has thus torn down the partition wall between capital and labour he immediately goes on to the logical conclusion, and abolishes the distinction between Interest and Wage. To him they are homogeneous; but— and it is as significant as it is ridiculous—he does not very well know whether he should explain interest by wage, or wage by interest. He gets out of the difficulty by explaining each by the other. He first sets forth, at great length, how interest is essentially nothing else than the wage for "previously accumulated labour," and then he tries to make the nature of wage clearer by explaining it as a profit of capital— "the common and ordinary rate of profit on his capital, exclusive of a sum to replace its wear and tear, earned by the machine called man."[1] It does not seem to have occurred to him that a see-saw like this does not really explain either of the phenomena.

M'Culloch's ill-digested doctrines have nearly fallen into well-deserved oblivion. But if I am not mistaken, we are threatened with a resurrection of them in changed form. Quite lately we have had a number of views, closely related to the foregoing, put forward with that suddenness and abundance which is at all times a sign that the idea is, so to speak, in the air, and promises to be fashionable. We are told almost simultaneously, and in almost the same words, by Weiss, by Dargun, and by Ofner, that every labourer represents a capital equal to the cost of his upbringing—say, a thousand thalers for the unskilled, or three thousand thalers for the skilled labourer. Or, on another method of valuation, we are taught that the labourer is equal to the capitalised net return of his

[1] See my *Capital and Interest*, p. 99.

year's labour. His wage, therefore, is peculiarly a kind of hire
of capital, and must, like every other hire, contain at least the
three following elements : (1) The replacement of the cost of
necessary upkeep of the human machine, calculated at the
minimum of existence; (2) a quota for amortisation, in pre-
miums of assurance against old age; and (3) a net interest
calculated on the capital value of the human machine at the
ordinary interest rate.[1]

All honour to the motives which have given rise to this
theory. It is devised in the interests of the poor, and for
the reconciliation of all classes. Between the iron law of
wages which takes away all hope from the worker of earning
anything but bare necessaries, and the socialist theory which
promises the labourers everything, and the propertied classes
nothing, it steers a middle course; it leaves the owner of
material capital his hard contested interest, but would have him
share it with the owner of personal capital. Thus the joint
capitalism of the worker becomes on this theory the magic
formula that is to be followed by the golden fruits of reconciliation and humanity. The pity is that it is only a formula ; a
parade of words with no soul of truth in it. Very few people
would deny that, in certain points, there is a real analogy between
a worker, the cost of whose education and training in production has been advanced to him, and a piece of capital. But
how deep does this analogy go ? On occasions when we wish to
make use of it in making comparisons that are really instructive,
or when nothing depends on scientific exactitude, the analogy
goes deep enough to permit of using a figure of speech and
calling the labourer a "capital," just as capital also is often spoken
of figuratively as " previous labour " or " stored-up labour." But
the analogy does not hold right through, and in particular it
fails as regards wage and interest. That capital yields a profit or
gain, rests on a quite peculiar ground—a ground that does not
obtain in the case of labour, or does so very exceptionally. I
hope to establish this with perfect clearness when we come to

---

[1] Fr. Albert Maria Weiss, Ord.-Priester, *Die Gesetze der Berechnung von
Kapitalzins und Arbeitslohn*, Freiburg, 1883. Quoted by Schäffle in *Tübinger
Zeitschrift*, vol. xli. p. 225. Dargun, *Arbeitskapital und Normalerwerb,
Tübinger Zeitschrift*, vol. xl. p. 514, and specially pp. 530-535. Ofner, *Ueber
das Rechtsprincip des Arbeitslohnes nach herrschendem System, Juristische Blätter*,
1884, Nos. 3 and 4. Engel, *Der Werth des Menschen*, 1883.

the theory of interest, but this much I may say meantime,—
that a man must have curiously shifted his point of view if
he thinks to make the essential nature of wage more intelligible
by supporting it on the phenomenon of interest.   Of the two
phenomena, that of wage is by far the more simple and self-
explanatory.   One man gives the valuable good called labour,
and another man gives him a price for it.   Anything simpler
cannot well be imagined.   But the fact that capital yields
an interest is much less easy to understand.   Witness the
many theories we had to discuss in *Capital and Interest*,
none of which were ever able to state satisfactorily the
essence of that phenomenon.   To think of explaining the
simple facts of wage by reading into them the much more
involved and obscure facts of interest, is really to explain the
church by the steeple.   Moreover, the value of these forced
interpretations receives a vivid illustration in the fact that,
as we have seen, numerous writers are at the same time striving
to get at a better understanding of the nature of interest by
expounding it as a peculiar kind of wage.   Where then the
one sees the riddle, the other sees the solution.   What an
amount of vagueness as to the nature of the problems waiting
solution is involuntarily betrayed in all this.[1]

   To sum up.   The inclusion of labour in the conception of
capital would be, in the most favourable circumstances, inappropriate ; in the more unfavourable, which unfortunately have
been the real circumstances, it has been pernicious, calculated
to perpetuate the confusion of terminology, to open door after
door to false analogies, and to obscure and prevent clearness of
thought in those very questions which are at once the most
difficult and the most important in the social science of to-day.
We shall therefore decide very emphatically and, I hope,
unanimously, to exclude personal means of acquisition from
the conception of Capital.[2]

---

   [1] It is very significant that none of the authors who explain wage by interest
makes any attempt to explain interest itself.   They simply accept it as a given
fact—with the exception of M'Culloch, who, with amazing *naïveté*, repeats the
trick again in the opposite way, and explains interest by wage.   It is very
gratifying to me to note that Schäffle holds himself aloof from the theories just
criticised, although his social and political tendencies must certainly lie in their
direction (*Tübinger Zeitschrift*, vol. xli. p. 225).
   [2] See also Schmoller, whose conclusions agree with mine (*Lehre vom Ein-*

The next stage of the controversy brings us to the question whether we are to give the name of capital only to the *products of labour* that serve for acquisition, the "previous stored up labour," or are to include land. Both views claim for the name of capital a really important and fruitful conception. As contrasted with labour, land has so much in common with the "produced" acquisitive instruments of material nature that a union of them under one conception has good justification. So, too, the income which flows from the two kinds of acquisitive instruments has, in many essential respects, the same nature, and this likewise favours the uniting of them in one conception. On the other hand, in many essential respects land and capital take different ways. The former is immovable; the latter, for the most part, movable. The former is a gift of nature ; the latter, a result of labour. The former cannot be increased, the latter can be. The landowner has a social and economical position essentially different from that of the capitalist; property in land is justified on essentially different grounds from property in movables. Land is the special object of a kind of production which is economically distinguished by many important peculiarities. Income from land, while subject to many laws in common with income from capital, obeys many distinct laws of its own—land rent, for instance, rising with economical development, while interest falls. On all these considerations, the number of which might easily be increased,[1] it is most convenient to keep land quite distinct from the other kinds of productive wealth.

kommen in ihrem Zusammenhang mit den Grundprincipien der Steuerlehre, Tübinger Zeitschrift, 1863, p. 24) ; Knies, *Das Geld,* pp. 15-22 ; Ricca-Salerno, as before, p. 28 ; and Cossa, *La Nozione del Capitale,* in the *Saggi di Ec. Pol.,* 1878, p. 163. What Cossa says against the passion for immoderately widening the conception of capital is well worth noting. He is remarking that one very often feels the want of an expression which would indicate without ambiguity just those products which serve immediately for production, and he continues :—" Se il concetto del capitale si allarga di troppo, comprendendovi altri prodotti, o altri fattori della produzione, esso o sfuma del tutto, o non ha più la sua ragione di essere. Si contruisce, per dir la cosa in altro modo, uno strumento od imperfetto o superfluo, il quale o non serve punto, o non serve bene. E tali categorie debbonsi senz' altro espellere, e non già moltiplicare nelle investigazionieconomiche, se non vogliamo che la scienza si isterilisca in polemiche oziose e puramente nominali," p. 168.

[1] See Knies, *Das Geld,* p. 33 ; Schönberg, *Handbuch,* second edition, vol. i. p. 210 ; Roscher, *Grundlagen,* § 42, note 1.

Thus the two competing conceptions are fairly well balanced in importance and suggestiveness, and if these properties were the only things to look to in deciding our controversy the decision might really be left very much to individual choice. If, however, we go on to compare the two in the light of the other rules we have laid down as regulating appropriate terminology, we find several points in which the "complex of produced acquisitive instruments" has a definite advantage over its competitor. The first is that of economy of terms. If we apply the word capital to *all* the material means of acquisition, then the narrower of the competing conceptions, and the branch of income that corresponds to it, remain, notwithstanding their importance, without any name at all. When we have disposed of the words capital and rent of capital otherwise, we have no correspondingly simple name, either for the group of produced acquisitive instruments, or for the income that comes from them. On the other hand, we avoid any such confusion of terminology by giving the name capital to the produced acquisitive instruments. The totality of all material acquisitive instruments may then, well and simply, be called "acquisitive wealth," and all income flowing from it may, on Rodbertus's precedent, be called Rent with its convenient subdivisions of land rent and capital rent.

The limitation of capital to "produced means of acquisition" has another advantage in being in accord with popular usage. Both scientific and popular language tell us unmistakably that they do not put land under capital, but oppose the two. The genius of our language plainly distinguishes between landowner and capitalist. No one will say that a nation that has an abundance of fruitful soil is possessed of great capital on that account. The name of interest is never applied by people generally to the income from land, and in scientific literature it is so applied only by an insignificant minority. And in the discussion of the great social problems, property in land and property in capital are generally attacked and defended by quite distinct people and by quite distinct methods. If we sum up all that has been said, the conclusion seems to be that while, for reasons repeatedly given, there can be no idea of an absolutely convincing argument, there is still a considerable balance in favour of defining capital as the "produced means of acquisition," and against the inclusion of land.

Finally, such conceptions as would limit capital still more severely, may, I think, be easily and decidedly refuted. Kleinwächter would distinguish between the materials and the tools of production, and reckon only the latter as capital, on the ground that in production it is only the tools that actively co-operate and assist us, the materials of production being purely passive.[1] But this assumption is not correct. The function of materials of production is not simply to serve as a "dead and plastic mass"; by means of the natural powers residing in them these materials take a share in the work of production which is, indeed, less prominent, but is, essentially, no less active. Kleinwächter's view is, by his own confession, incorrect from the point of physical science,[2] and as we have here to do with a question of productive technique, where political economy must take its stand on natural science, it is incorrect from the point of economics.

Marx, again, would confine the conception of capital to those productive instruments which are to be found in the hands of persons other than the labourers themselves, and are used to exploit the labourers. With him, therefore, capital is the same thing as "means of exploitation." This distinction would be quite an important and suggestive one if the Exploitation theory itself were correct. But since, as has been shown in my former work,[3] it is not, the justification of the distinction based on that theory falls with it.

Jevons's notion of capital is that of "the aggregate of those commodities which are required for sustaining labourers of any kind or class engaged in work"; "the wages of labour either in its transitory form of money, or its real form of food and other necessaries of life."[4] If this were correct, every land would be rich in capital in proportion as its wages were high and its means of subsistence cheap. An African tribe that has neither industry, nor machinery, nor factories, nor railways, but lives under a tropical sun, where the necessaries of life are

---

[1] *Die Grundlagen und Ziele des sog. wissenschaftlichen Sozialismus*, Innsbruck, 1885, p. 185.

[2] "In the strict physical sense, of course, this is not correct" (p. 192).

[3] *Capital and Interest*, book vi. p. 313.

[4] *Theory of Political Economy*, second edition, pp. 242, 263.

poured forth without stint, would be the richest in capital!
Obviously, of course, the idea that Jevons had in his mind
was a perfectly correct one, but the expression he gave it was
unfortunate.   He confused a condition of the formation of
capital with capital itself.   The way of capitalist production is
long and roundabout, and man cannot enter upon it unless he
is provided with the means of subsistence for the time that
must intervene before he reaps the return.   But it is not the
means of subsistence, and, in particular, it is not the means of
subsistence *alone*, that constitutes capital.   Capital only comes
into existence when man actually enters upon the profitable
roundabout journey that the means of subsistence have made
possible ; when he builds machines, tools, railways, factories,
raises raw materials, and so on.   However abundant the
means of subsistence were, if the workers were to consume
them in living from hand to mouth, the community would
evidently never accumulate capital at all.

Finally, there remain those conceptions which see in
capital not a complex of goods, but an abstract quantity
hovering over goods, as it were ; as, for instance, Kühnast's
" sum of value," or M'Leod's " circulating power."   I have,
generally speaking, a very poor opinion of such idealisations
of economic conceptions.   They are usually cheap expedients
for getting round difficulties.   If in any difficult subject there
occurs some troublesome, angular kind of conception that
corresponds with real life and will not fit in to the particular
line of explanation, there are always certain theorists ready to
disembody it, whereby, of course, it loses its unmannerly
angles and edges, but, at the same time, its strength and
truth.   It becomes a phrase and leads to phrases.   We have
an instance of this here.   If we were to take the sponsors
of those definitions at their word, and ask them whether they
would seriously say that an immaterial sum of value or
circulating power can grind corn, or spin yarn, or plough up
land, or carry a load ; or whether it is not the case that these
good things are done by the common material goods called
mills, looms, ploughs, locomotives, they would be very much
perplexed.   For, asking at their own consciousness, they could
scarcely deny that, under the name capital, they have always
and peculiarly thought of that something which helps man to

work in his production; and the rude materiality of this something agrees but ill with the high-sounding abstract definition
of " sum of value " or "circulating power." It is very significant, as regards this group of definitions of capital, that their
origin may be traced to a slipshod expression of a writer who
was always too careless about the way in which he stated his
conceptions—J. B. Say.   Say first—and quite correctly—
gives the name of capital to certain results of labour that
serve as tools to further production, such as Seed, Dye-stuffs,
Wool, Tools, Machines, Buildings, Cattle, etc., and calls their
total value Capital Value. Later on he makes the remark
that a capital value may take very different forms, such as
money, houses, utensils, commodities, etc., and this gives him
occasion to call " this value a *capital*, so soon as it is contained
in objects, whatever they be, which are destined to productive
activity." [1] Evidently a careless and contradictory expression,
which, however, his economical disciples made the basis of a
serious theory ! [2]

Thus, of all the many readings of the conception of capital,
there is only one left on the field,—only one, of which it can be
said that it has stood all the tests. It is that which, by capital,
understands an aggregate of products destined, not for immediate consumption or use, but to serve as means of acquisition.
It is a conception which meets all our logical and terminological requirements. Logically it is unassailable, and it is
suggestive; so suggestive that it distances the most of its
competitors, and is distanced by none of them. And,
terminologically, its investiture with the title of capital
best economises our terms, and agrees with that usage which

---

[1] *Cours Complet*, part i. chap. viii. It may be added that Say, in this and
other passages formerly quoted, gives no less than four contradictory readings of
the conception of capital.   In one place, chapter viii., he explains it as *products*
of labour which serve towards production ; and in the same chapter he speaks of
it as the *value* of these products. In chapter x. (see above, p. 50) he makes it
the *talents and skill* of the labourers ; and in chapter xiii., again, the *persons* of
the labourers !

[2] That theories of such doubtful value should commend themselves to the
recognition of eminent jurists like Kühnast may, perhaps, be explained by pointing out that jurists, as having to deal in their systems, to a very great extent,
with abstract persons and objects, have, generally, a strong tendency to hypos-
tatize conceptions ; a practice which may be quite suitable for their special field
of investigation, but is certainly misapplied in political economy.

has taken most general and firm root in economics and in popular speech.   Finally, it is the conception which most exactly coincides with the object of those great social problems of our time which people are in the habit of discussing as problems of capital.   In its one division, as " Social Capital," it indicates the third instrument of economical production in the triad of Nature, Labour, and Capital; and in its other division, as " Private Capital," it indicates the third source of the economical acquisition of goods by individuals in the triad Rent of land, Wage of labour, Interest on capital.   If, then, unbiassed people are ever to agree on a conception of capital, we may expect that this will be the one chosen.

CHAPTER VI

SOCIAL AND PRIVATE CAPITAL

A FEW remarks still remain to be made on the relation in which the two divisions of our conception, Social (or Productive) Capital, and Private (or Acquisitive) Capital,[1] stand to one another. When enumerating and reviewing the various theories, I have already expressed my views generally on this point, and may here shortly sum them up. Private Capital, as we now call it, is the parent conception. It is not so much a branch, or a subdivision of the general conception of capital, as the conception itself. The conception of National Capital, or, more correctly, Social Capital, has detached itself from the other, in the historical development of theory, as a narrower conception. Substantially it is a quite independent conception. In every essential respect (in definition. in scientific employment, and in scope) it stands on entirely independent principles. It is bound up with the conception of Private Capital only by the external and subordinate circumstance, that the aggregate of its " intermediate products " happens to coincide in extent with the aggregate of those products which are the source of income to society as a whole, —those products which constitute capital in the older sense.

[1] As I have already remarked on p. 38 I consider the terms in brackets, Productive and Acquisitive Capital, as essentially the more appropriate. But since Rodbertus and Wagner the terms National and Private capital have been used almost universally, and as I consider it conducive to the final settlement of this jumble of terminology not to disturb names that are fast rooted in common usage, unless there is some quite overwhelming reason for doing so, I content myself with making the one change—which seems to me in any case indispensable—of the term "National" into the term " Social " capital.

But through a historical accident it is this subordinate feature that has had most to do with the naming of the new conception; and thus it also bears, and will perhaps continue to bear, the name capital.   And this circumstance, so long as the whole relation was not clearly understood, led to the lamentable tangle so often spoken of, that not only the conceptions themselves, thus similarly named, but the fundamentally distinct problems connected with them, were confused and interchanged.

This unfortunate confusion of the problems was first attacked, so far as I know, by Rodbertus, and his efforts were seconded with peculiar clearness by Adolf Wagner.   In the course of this a new interpretation was given to the distinction between National and Private capital, which is highly interesting in itself, and which, at the same time, has been accepted so quickly and over so wide an area that I feel bound to take up a definite position towards it.   Wagner, like Rodbertus before him,[1] makes a distinction between capital as a " purely economic category," and capital " in the historico-legal sense," or *property* in capital.   " Capital as a purely economic category, considered apart from the legal relations which obtain as regards property in capital, is a store of those economic goods,—natural goods, —which serve as technical instruments to produce new goods to a community ; it is a store of productive instruments; it is National capital (or a portion of such).   Capital in the historico-legal sense, or property in capital, is that portion of a person's wealth which may serve him as a means of obtaining an income (Rent, Interest), and which, therefore, is owned by him to this end ; it is a Rent Fund, or Private Capital."[2] In this the distinction between National capital and Private capital is narrowed down to the distinction between a natural store of goods on the one hand, and the legal rights which private individuals have over that natural store on the other.

I am far from denying the very great importance and usefulness of this new distinction.   Its appearance was an event

[1] See particularly *Zur Erklärung und Abhilfe der heutigen Kreditnoth des Grundbesitzes*, second edition, vol. i. p. 90, vol. ii. p. 286, where *das reale Kapital*, as consisting of the natural objects of capital, is sharply opposed to *Kapitalbesitz*, or property in capital.   Similarly *Das Kapital*, pp. 304, 313, and *passim*.

[2] Wagner, *Grundlegung*, second edition, p. 39.

of the first rank in economic criticism, and it has done good and
laudable service in clearly stating the fundamentally distinct
problems associated with the one name of capital. Without
it, certainly, the far-reaching consequences of the other distinction, that between Social and Private Capital, would never
have been noticed.   One thing, however, I cannot allow.   It
does not exhaust the meaning of this latter distinction, and,
consequently, it is not exactly fitted to take its place.   The
categories of Social Capital and Private Capital on the one
hand, and of Natural Capital and Property in Capital on the
other, do not coincide, either in compass or in content, so as
to allow us simply to explain or replace the former by the
latter.   They are rather independent categories, each of them
resting on a different basis of distinction.   Social Capital
and Private Capital are not distinguished from each other
simply as a natural store of goods and property in these goods ;
they represent two distinct *natural stores of goods.*   Social
Capital embraces only the means of production ; Private Capital
embraces also certain consumption goods.   These distinct
natural quantities or stores of goods, further, exert distinct
economic functions.   And if to these we add the further
distinction that Social Capital is a category independent of
any regulations of positive law,—is, that is to say, a purely
economic category,— while all capital as Source of Income
presupposes an owner, and therefore a right of ownership
founded on history and law, then this is only one distinction
out of many, and that not the peculiar and essential distinction.
For if we were to drop the two former distinctions, and draw
our dividing line according to the absence or presence of
historico-legal claims of ownership, we should find that the
division had made some very considerable changes in the
constitution of the members.   In the first branch, indeed, we
should have as before Social Capital, the natural means of
production.   But in the second branch we should have only
the *same* means of production now looked at as private
property and as source of rent, and we should not have
those consumption goods, such as dwelling-houses, libraries,
etc., which serve as sources of rent.   To cover these latter,
and so fill out the compass of private capital to its true
extent, we must set against the natural means of production

not only private claims based on history and law, but also another natural store of goods that is still more extensive.

Perhaps the peculiar inappropriateness of confusing these two distinctions may be most strikingly shown by taking an exactly analogous example. If one were asked to characterise the distinction between the two conceptions " producing " and " exchanging," and were to answer that production is a purely economic category, whilst exchange, as presupposing the existence of private property, is a historico-legal phenomenon, the answer would scarcely be taken as sufficient. We should certainly have the impression that it gave us *a* distinction but not the distinction between producing and exchanging. For the essence of exchanging obviously does not consist in its being a " historico-legal category." It is also a very important economic category ; indeed, it is just such another as producing ; and one who would explain both conceptions must, at once and before anything else, establish the distinction between the *economic* nature of the two. And, similarly, in this opposition between " purely economic " and " historico-legal " categories, *a* distinction is put forward—and a very important distinction,—but not the characteristic distinction between Social and Private Capital.

Let me say once more that I consider the distinction made by Rodbertus and Wagner between natural capital and property in capital a very important one indeed, and one which, in any case, must *also* be drawn. What I want to point out is, that it should not be confused with the distinction between social and private capital, which rests on an entirely different basis ; and the definition of social and private capital should not be based on characteristics borrowed from another and totally different distinction.

The example of Rodbertus himself is the best proof that this is not simply a quarrel about formulas. His one-sided conception led him directly into a false theory of interest. In his view the essence of private capital consisted in the historico-legal circumstances of force that were connected with it ; and he was thus logically committed to explain the interest on private capital simply and solely from the existence of those circumstances. Interest to him was robbery ; a profit which the owners of capital squeezed out of the labourers in virtue of the brute strength which their exclusive property in the means of production gave them.[1]

If, on the other hand, Rodbertus had attended to the peculiarly economic side of the matter, he would have found that that other natural complex of goods, called private capital, has exerted and continues to exert a peculiar economic function quite equally with social capital ; and, further, he would have found that it is simply as the natural fruit of this economical element that interest originates. Thus he would have found that interest is not purely a growth of history and law, but an original *economic* growth, the emergence of which is, to a certain extent, independent of the form which history and law have given it. This will be shown with sufficient clearness, I trust, in the investigations into the origin of interest which follow.

Before concluding this chapter there is still one question to be put : What in the concrete are the groups of goods that constitute Social capital, and what Private capital ?   The answer to this should, by rights, follow from the very definition of the two conceptions. But peculiar circumstances have led to disputes not only as to the correct definition, but even as to the compass which was to be allowed to each conception in conformity with the accepted definition. It is well, therefore, to be quite clear on this point.

Social Capital, as an aggregate of products destined to serve for further production, covers—

1. Productive improvements, arrangements and dispositions of land, so far as these preserve an independent character, such as dams, drains, fences, etc. So far, however, as they are completely incorporated with the land, they are to be kept separate from capital for the same reasons which made us keep land itself separate from capital.[2]

2. Productive buildings of all sorts—workshops, factories, sheds, steadings, shops, streets, railways, and so on. Dwelling-

---

[1] See my criticism of this theory in *Capital and Interest*, p. 337.

[2] I may be accused of want of logic here on the ground that such improvements are always products which serve towards further production, and therefore come under our definition of capital. The criticism is correct as to the letter, but wrong as to the spirit. A stay propped up against a tree is certainly not the tree itself but an outside body. But who would still call it an outside body if after some years it had grown inseparable from the tree ?

houses, however, and other kinds of buildings, such as serve immediately for any purpose of enjoyment or education or culture, *e.g.* theatres, schools, churches, law courts, do not come under Capital.

3. Tools, machines, and other kinds of productive utensils.

4. Useful animals and beasts of burden employed in production.

5. The raw and auxiliary materials of production.

6. Finished consumption goods in the hands of producers and merchants as (warehouse) stock.

7. Money.

At the first glance the two latter categories may be called in question.   Consumption goods as found in warehouses are, to all appearance, no longer "intermediate products," but "finished goods," and Money is not a tool of production but a tool of exchange.   Still, I think it correct to put both conceptions under capital.   They both serve to complete a roundabout way of production.   When, in order to take advantage of more favourable conditions, goods are produced, or caused to be produced, at a different place from where they are demanded, it is nothing else than a peculiar kind of roundabout process. The consequence then is—and it is here that the "round-aboutness," which is to be understood literally in this case, comes in—that, after the product is technically finished, it must be conveyed to the place where it is demanded.   All this is done very often inside the narrow limits of an isolated economy ; the peasant must bring his harvested grain from the field, his felled wood from the forest.   But it is done, on an immensely greater scale, in the wider field of social production and divided labour.   Just as the peasant may raise his crop a quarter of an hour's distance from his house, or cut his wood an hour's distance off, because in this way he can best utilise the conditions of production, so for good reasons it is quite common in organised and divided industry to obtain the objects of our demand from other people's workshops, indeed often from other places, other lands, other continents; and then, naturally, in the end we have to provide their means of conveyance.   In the one case as in the other the conveyance forms the last act of production, and before this last act is finished we cannot properly say that the products are ready for human consumption.   So, just as everybody would include among instruments of production and capital the horse and cart which assist the peasant in carrying in his grain and wood, must we reckon as capital the objects and apparatus of that more extensive "leading in" of the national harvest—the conveyed products, the streets, rails, ships, and the commercial tool money.   It may be noted, besides, that those commercial roundabout ways, arising out of the division and organisation of labour, rank, as regards the advantage they confer, along with the other technical roundabout ways.   They are as profitable as, or even more profitable than, any of the capitalist methods of production to which the most famous technical inventions have led.

These seven categories exhaust, in my opinion, the group of things which constitute Social Capital.   It goes without saying that economists who take another view of the conception of capital add other categories, such as land, durable consumption goods, the person of the labourer, and so on, and this needs no further elucidation here.   It is surprising, however, to find writers, who take exactly the same view of the conception as we do, proposing to add certain other categories.

Most surprising of all in this connection is the unanimity with which economists, from the earlier English writers down to Adolf Wagner,[1] put the *maintenance of productive labourers* under social capital.   Certainly the real wages of the labourers —the articles of food, clothing, fuel, lighting etc., which the labourers use—are, from the standpoint of the undertaker who advances them, his *private* capital.   But it is just as clear in my opinion that, from the standpoint of the whole community, these objects cannot be counted capital if capital is defined as a complex of means of production.   The conception of "means of production" should and does form an antithesis to the conception "means of consumption."   There cannot be the slightest doubt as to the meaning of this antithesis, and just as little can there be as to the fact that the workers' subsistence is the immediate instrument to the satisfaction of their wants, and that labourers are men and members of society.   But if this is so, it seems to me absolutely proved

[1] *Grundlegung*, second edition, pp. 39, 43.

that the maintenance of the labourer must be classed along with wealth destined for consumption and for the immediate satisfaction of the wants of society, and not with the means of production or capital.   It could only be otherwise if the labourers were to be looked upon, not as members of the civil society in whose interest industry and commerce are carried on, but as material machines of labour.   Then, but only then, the maintenance of the labourers would, as a matter of course, fall under the same category as the feeding of beasts of burden and the stoking of furnaces; it would be a means of production, or capital.   The idea, however, scarcely needs refutation.

It may be pointed out, however, that productive labourers are not simply consuming subjects, but are also active economical instruments; and that, consequently, the subsistence which does directly serve for the maintenance and furtherance of their life indirectly serves towards the further production of goods.   But in this case a simple indirect relation to production is not sufficient.   For it is easy to see that the distinction between means of production and means of consumption has a meaning only if it refers to the *immediate* destination of goods.   If we were to take notice of their indirect or mediate destination we should require to put all goods without exception under the category of means of consumption, since even the means of production serve indirectly to the satisfaction of human wants.   Then this raises another difficulty.   The division of goods into goods for consumption and goods for production is intended to be a real division; it should be based on an opposition.   Now it is impossible to deny that the food which the labourer consumes serves for the immediate satisfaction of the wants of a member of the community; that is, it corresponds entirely to the definition of a consumption good.   How then could we class a thing which has all the properties of *one* category under the category opposed to it?   Thus, as is so often the case, the laboured explanation leads us into a net of confusion, and the simplest is the truest.   The goods with which the working members of the community feed, heat, and clothe themselves, are goods for immediate consumption, not means of production.

That, in face of arguments so obvious, the opposed doctrine should be held so universally and so tenaciously is a phenomenon scarcely intelligible at first sight, but easily explained when we inquire more closely into the circumstances of the case.   Two powerful factors, I think, co-operated towards it. One was historical tradition, which, in this case, was very strong and deep-rooted.   It should not be forgotten that the inclusion of the labourers' maintenance into the conception of capital came at a time when the conception itself was not yet clearly defined, and when, in particular, Private capital, to which the labourers' maintenance in any case belongs, was not yet sharply divided off from Social capital, to which it does not belong.   This was assisted by the peculiar view, dominant for a long time, that the function of capital was the " putting of labour in motion "—a function which the labourers' maintenance conspicuously realised.   It was assisted, moreover, by the famous Wage Fund theory.   That theory made the rate of wages depend chiefly on the proportion between the number of labourers and the amount of the Wage Fund; that is, the amount of capital destined for the support and payment of the labourers—an idea which helped to connect the means of subsistence still more closely with the conception of capital.   And, finally, another impulse in the same direction may have been given by the frequently and justly criticised tendency of the English school to look upon the labourer as a machine of production, and to consider his wage simply as an element of the costs of production—a deduction from the national income and not a part of it.[1]

Resting on such a wide basis of support, the proposition that the maintenance of productive labourers forms an element in Social capital worked its way by degrees so firmly into the scientific consciousness, that it was considered by many as an axiom quite above discussion; and in the end it was able to maintain its position on the strength of its own authority, even after the ground had really been taken from under it by the discovery of the distinction between Private and Social capital, and by the definition of the latter as an aggregate of means of production.

The second factor has had even more effect than the weight of historical tradition; and not only has it co-operated in the past in the creation of these traditions, but it still

[1] See Schmoller, *Tübinger Zeitschrift*, vol. xix. (1863), pp. 10, 25.

asserts its living influence.   That factor was, if I am not very much mistaken, the conscious or unconscious inclination towards another reading of the conception of capital than that recognised in what we may call the official definition.   Economists have stood, and still stand, in hesitation between those two conceptions which have the most numerous and suggestive relations to the problems of capital—the conception of " produced means of production " and the conception of "national subsistence fund." [1]   In the official definition, it is true, the preference was finally given to the " produced means of production"; but economists, quite rightly feeling that the "national subsistence fund" had also something to do with the theory of capital, could not quite give up this conception.   And thus they put together a hybrid conception, adding to the Means of Production proper, which had the stamp of the official definition, a portion of the Subsistence Fund conception, in the maintenance of productive labourers. Of course a classification like this, which is nothing else than the result of uncertainty and compromise, cannot be satisfactory.   Economic theory must make decisive choice between the two competing conceptions, and, however the choice turns out, the conception will be limited and determined otherwise than it is by the writers now being criticised.   Either we shall decide for that conception which makes capital an aggregate of Intermediate Products—and this choice, for reasons of appropriate terminology already stated, I consider the happier one—and in this case the labourers' maintenance falls outside the conception; or we shall give the name capital to the Subsistence Fund which makes the roundabout way of production possible, and then, as will be shown later,[2] not only must the means of subsistence of the productive labourers be reckoned as capital, but also the subsistence of the capitalists and landowners, as standing in exactly the same indirect relation to the adoption of "capitalist" methods of production.   If all this cannot justify, it may at least explain the phenomenon, otherwise almost incomprehensible, that, in flat contradiction to the official definition of capital, people continue to add to it the maintenance of the labourers; and

[1] See above, p. 42.
[2] See also above, p. 43, note 1.

perhaps the exposure of this origin may help to put an end to the curious habit.[1]

Another category which seems to me wrongly placed among the constituents of Social capital is the so-called "incorporeal capitals," such as debts and other kinds of claims, goodwill of businesses, the state, etc. These things are not capital, because they are not real goods. They are, as I have shown at length in another place,[2] nothing but representative words or collective names for a sum of real goods, which may be capital, or may not. If they are, then they are already contained in our seven categories; if they are not, we should not, of course, open a special category for them.

Finally, Private capital consists of the following :—

1. All goods which form Social capital.

2. Those consumption goods which their owners do not use for themselves, but employ by exchange (sale, hire, loan) in the acquisition of other goods, *e.g.* let-houses, lending-libraries, means of subsistence advanced by undertakers to their labourers, and many others.

---

[1] The case is exactly the same with the notorious Wage Fund theory. In it also I see a misbegotten fruit of an idea which is quite right in itself. It is, as we shall see later, a very unsuccessful attempt to express certain relations that really do exist between the national subsistence fund on the one hand, and the height of wage and interest on the other. Against the inclusion of the labourers' means of subsistence in national capital Rodbertus has expressed himself in a quite classical style, *Das Kapital*, p. 294, and before that in his *Zur Erkenntniss unser. staatsw. Zustände*, theorem i. Very clear and convincing, too, is Gide, *Principes d'Économie Politique*, Paris, 1884, p. 150. See also Sax, *Grundlegung*, p. 324, note.

[2] *Rechte und Verhältnisse vom Standpunkte der volks. Güterlehre*, 1881, *passim.* Since then, see H. Dietzel (*Der Ausgangspunkt der Socialwirthschaftslehre und ihr Grundbegriff*, in the *Tübinger Zeitschrift*, 1883, p. 78), and Sax (*Grundlegung*, pp. 39, 199), who surely goes too far in excluding personal service from the conception of goods. Neumann, on the other hand (Schönberg's *Handbuch*, second edition, p. 151), remains firm in recognising rights and relations as real goods on grounds which do not commend themselves to me as at all convincing. On one single point I feel myself bound to reply. In my definition of the conception of goods, Neumann "does not find" the lines sufficiently distinctly drawn, and quotes, in a tone of irony, a number of expressions which, taken by themselves, certainly do not draw any distinct line (*ibid.* note 41). But Neumann can only have read portions of the work he objects to, or read it very hurriedly. Otherwise it would not have escaped him that the expressions he quotes stand at the end of a chapter (*Rechte*, p. 29), and that the beginning and middle of that chapter (p. 13 onwards) are devoted to what he "does not find," and that, obviously, the later expressions are to be taken and understood along with what goes immediately before.

Many writers add certain " relations," patents,[1] trade connection,[2] legal claims.[3] These, of course, on the same grounds of theory as above, I must reject as constituting an independent category of capital.

And now, after this very lengthy introduction, which can only be excused by the singular confusion in which we found the theory, we may turn from the conceptions to the problems which are associated with them. In the book which follows we shall work out the theory of the conception we had to glance at in the two first chapters of the present book ; the theory of capital as Instrument of Production, or the theory of Social Capital.[4]

---

[1] Wagner, *Grundlegung,* second edition, p. 42.

[2] Roscher, *Grundlagen,* eighteenth edition, § 42.

[3] Hermann, *Staats. Untersuchungen,* second edition, p. 122.

[4] The careful reader will, without doubt, have remarked that the statement as to the nature of capital given in the second chapter, relates solely to Social economic capital. For obvious reasons I did not wish to mix up the dogmatic statement with the terminological and critical discussion which, I am afraid, has been terribly prolix. And, for reasons as obvious, I did not wish to commence this discussion without having, at least partially, put before my readers the object to which the discussion refers. I therefore made use, for the time being, of the word Capital without any of the clauses and additions which would at once have necessitated the tedious terminological discussions I wished at the time to avoid. The more exact explanations which follow will prevent any misunderstanding to which this may, perhaps, have given rise.

BOOK II

CAPITAL AS INSTRUMENT OF PRODUCTION

CHAPTER I

INTRODUCTORY

IN expounding the theory of capital as Instrument or Tool or Means of Production we have to describe and explain the emergence and effects of capital in the economic production of goods. What we have to say on this matter groups itself round two questions: How does capital originate? and what is the nature of its productive work? The first question has to do with the theory of the formation or accumulation of capital; the second, with the productive function of capital.

The reader who has waded with us through the dozen theories and dozen definitions of capital will scarcely be surprised at meeting a similar divergence of opinion on the question we have now to consider. Of course there is no dispute about the fact that capital is, in the highest degree, useful to production. But I am much afraid that this is the only proposition on which our economists are quite agreed. So soon as the further question is asked: In what does this usefulness consist, or what character does the co-operation of capital in itself bear?—agreement is at an end. One finds the utility of capital in putting labour in motion;[1] another, in saving or supplanting labour;[2] a third, in performing labour;[3] a fourth praises it as giving man the mastery over the powers of nature;[4] and a fifth, as enabling the labourer to "put an interval between the beginning and the end of an

---

[1] Adam Smith, book ii. chap v.

[2] Lauderdale, *Enquiry*, p. 161, *passim*.

[3] Lauderdale, *ibid*. So also J. B. Say, "Il faut, pour ainsi dire, que les capitaux travaillent de concert avec l'industrie" (*Traité*, i. 3).

[4] Strasburger, Hildebrand's *Jahrbücher*, vol. xvii. (1871), p. 325 ; and Carey.

enterprise."[1]　Some, like Lauderdale, see in it an independent, original factor of production along with land and labour; others, like Gide, call it an independent but still merely derivative factor.　Kleinwächter looks on it simply as a "condition"; Carey, again, as an "instrument" or "tool" of production.　Indeed, our theorists cannot even agree as to the way in which that useful auxiliary of production comes into existence.　If we ask the question concretely : How is a plane, or a plough, or a steam-engine made ?—they would probably be able, with perfect certainty, to give minute information as to how those concrete portions of capital come into existence. But whenever they have to generalise what they have observed, they divide into hostile camps.　Capital originates in saving, says one; no, says another, it must be produced; while a third proclaims that it originates in the two together.

It is a much greater cause for wonder that economists came to no agreement in these and similar questions than that they remained apart in their theories of interest.　The task here was quite different, and essentially easier.　In the interest theory the difficulty is to give the proper *explanation* of facts which are really much entangled, while here there is almost nothing to do but to *describe* the facts correctly ; and facts, moreover, with which everybody is quite familiar.　As we have said, every one knows how a plane or a steam-engine comes into existence.　Similarly every one has a sufficiently exact idea what and how a plane, a machine, a plough, a raw material, does in production.　It was only necessary to leave out everything peculiar in those cases, and to describe in appropriate words everything universal and typical in them, and the theory of the formation and function of capital would almost have been written.

The reason why economists failed in this simple task was that they did not allow the facts to speak for themselves. Instead of simply describing them as they were, explanations were read into them and added to them ; one feature was pushed into the foreground, another kept in the background, a third was quite overlooked, while perhaps a fourth was entirely absent, but was read into them.　When every man had thus imported his own particular views bodily into the

[1] Jevons, *Theory of Political Economy*, second edition, 1879, p. 243.

facts, it was, of course, no wonder that everybody got something different out of them.

To my mind the most important duty of the theorist in such a case is to avoid the faults we have just condemned. To make certain of this we shall make a clear distinction, even in outward form, between the statement of the facts and the interpretation of them. The next chapter, therefore, will delineate and describe the process of capitalist production. When a solid basis of fact has thus been obtained, the interpretation and construction will follow in the chapters on the productive function of capital, and on the theory of the formation of capital.[1]

---

[1] In economic literature the clearest views as to the nature of capitalist production are, in my opinion, to be found in Rodbertus, Jevons, and Carl Menger. The works of Rodbertus, where they are not directly disfigured by the influences of his one-sided Socialist standpoint, are of quite classical accuracy and clearness. Unfortunately there are certain features which very sensibly mar what he has said. This is true in particular of his omission to notice the share which the valuable natural powers take in production, and the influence of time — two things which, obviously, could not easily be fitted into the "exploitation" theory he maintained so vigorously, and so were suppressed. We shall see this more fully later on. Carl Menger, again, by his arrangement of goods according to "rank" (*Grundsätze*, p. 7), and his statement of the laws which connect together goods of various ranks, has given at once a brilliant proof of his clear insight into the developed phenomena of production, and an invaluable tool to the hands of succeeding investigators.

CHAPTER II

WE have already sketched, in its most general outlines, the process of capitalist production.[1] There are certain features of it which now require more exact treatment. I shall briefly recapitulate, interpolating what remains to be said as we go along.

All human production aims at the obtaining of goods for consumption. These consumption goods are dependent for their existence on physical conditions, and are subject to natural laws. To obtain them, as we have seen, we must seek to bring about such combinations of active forces as will result in the desired object. Thus we get a product which has come into existence under natural law and continues to exist under natural law. Now look a little more closely at the nature of the power which man can employ towards these productive combinations. It is made up of two components very dissimilar in amount—first, an enormous mass of powers which the natural world exerts spontaneously year out year in; and second, the much more limited natural powers which reside in the human organism.

The natural world, in midst of which man lives, is endowed with a vast number of forces which are never for a moment idle. Gravitation holds this ball of earth together; keeps all things fast to its surface; makes the rain fall to earth, and rolls streams and rivers to the sea; governs the ebb and flood of the tides; works unceasingly at every point of the earth's crust as stress, weight, pressure. The sun sends our earth light and heat, and thereby develops an

[1] Book i. chap. ii.

infinity of mechanical and chemical processes, of which vegeta-
tion particularly attracts our attention, both by its mysterious
magic and by its enormous importance for the human race.
Uncounted and countless again are the molecular, electric, and
chemical effects and counter-effects which every atom of
matter exerts without intermission on its neighbours.   The
total of those energies which nature pours forth in ceaseless
stream, without help from man, we may look upon as one
branch of the productive endowment of humanity ; and this
extremely valuable branch we shall call man's natural endowment.   It is an infinite treasure-house from which the producing man may draw as much as he will and can.   As yet
it is only the very smallest part of this treasure that has
been touched.   As yet by far the greater portion of the
energies of nature pass away in combinations which, from the
human teleological standpoint, seem useless or even harmful.
The resistless rise and fall of the tide, the rush of rivers and
waterfalls, the atmospheric movements, the giant forces of
electricity, magnetism, and gravitation slumbering in our
earth, are powers turned to human account only to a very
small extent.   Others again, such as the vegetative powers of
land, have been utilised to a greater, but still very far from
complete extent.   The steady advancement in agricultural
science not only leads us to expect a constantly increasing
amount of utility from the land, but makes us suspect that the
possibility of such advance is still far from being exhausted.

Now, as we have seen, the way in which we get command
of these natural treasures is through the other branch of our
productive endowment, our own personal powers.   We put
forth our labour in all kinds of wise combinations with natural
processes.   Thus all that we get in production is the result of
two, and only two, elementary productive powers—Nature and
Labour.   This is one of the most certain ideas in the theory
of production.   Man finds ready to hand an abundance of
natural processes, and allies his own powers with them.   What
nature by herself does, and what man does along with her—
these form the double source from which all our goods come,
and the only source from which they can come.   There is no
place for any third primary source.

These two elements, then, *technically* do everything in the

work of production. But, *economically*, a further and very
suggestive limitation must be drawn. Of the vast natural
endowment which serves as foundation for man's productive
combinations, one portion particularly claims the interest of
economics, and that is, those useful things offered by nature
only in limited amount. In nature, indeed, there is no lack
either of materials or powers; carbon and nitrogen, oxygen
and hydrogen—generally speaking, most of the "elements"—are
per se not more scarce than are electrical, magnetic, chemical,
and gravitation forces. But certain spontaneous combinations of these elements that are peculiarly well adapted to
human want may be, relatively, scarce; such, for example, as
useful plants and minerals, water for driving power, fertile
land, etc. These limited gifts and energies of the natural world
obtain for us a peculiar *economic* importance. It would be
foolish not to economise them. Technical elements of production which we may have in any quantity, like atmospheric air
or water or sunlight, we may employ or waste as we please
without suffering loss in our productive returns. But the
limited technical elements must be treated with consideration,
must be saved, must be fully utilised. In a word, within the
technical natural endowment, as a wider circle, they form the
specifically *economic* natural endowment of man. Since all, or
at least almost all, limited gifts and energies of nature are connected with land, we may, without much danger, take Land,
with its activities or uses, as the representative of this economic
natural endowment.[1]

To the uses of land the exertions of labour form the
counterpart. Labour has almost entirely an economical character. This is due partly to the fact that physical strength is
given us in such scanty measure, as compared with the very
extensive claims put forward by human needs, that even the
most assiduous exertions of labour power cannot fully satisfy
our desire for goods, not to speak of supplying them in superfluity; partly to the fact that the exercise of our powers is
usually attended by the painful feeling of distress and fatigue

[1] Where population is scanty, of course, it is possible that land, or at least
certain of the uses of land, such as the growing of timber, may be free goods, as
obtainable in any quantity. But in modern communities, to which naturally I
refer by preference in this statement, the uses of land—with the exception of
waste land or desert—are entirely economic goods.

—at least when carried beyond a certain point,[1]—and the feeling warns us to economise our labour.

Nature and Labour are, then, the technical elements of production; Uses of Land and Labour are the economic elements. These latter are the talents which the producing man puts out at usury with nature, with her great fruitful soil and infinite store of force. They are the only powers that require economic treatment, inasmuch as the co-operation of the free natural powers, which, technically, is also indispensable, is given without question and without cost. It is only the man who has command over the requisite uses of land and services of labour who receives the desired economic product; the man who has not these must do without the product; the man who owns a double allowance or a half allowance of them will—if the technique of production remain the same—receive double or half the product. In production, therefore, they are the only powers with which the economic community has any concern, and with which it has to reckon. In short, land and labour—or, more accurately, uses of land and services of labour—are the primary economic productive powers.[2]

Now in what way does man use these original productive powers? In answering this question we turn back for a little into familiar paths.

To construct goods for human consumption out of these productive elements man may take one of two ways. He may combine the economical productive powers with one another,—or with activities of free natural powers,—in such a way that the desired good immediately emerges as result of the combination;

---

[1] On the common experience that "as labour is prolonged the effort becomes, as a general rule, more and more painful," see Jevons, *Theory of Political Economy*, second edition, p. 185; and Gossen, *Entwicklung der Gesetze des menschlichen Verkehrs*, 1854.

[2] This is the state of the case, as I believe, expressed with perfect clearness in the facts, and this is what Rodbertus profoundly misunderstood when he maintained, and repeated with emphasis, that labour is the sole original power with which human economy has anything to do, and drew from that the conclusion that all goods, economically, are to be conceived of as products of labour alone (*Zur Erkenntniss unserer staats. Zustände*, theorem i.; *Zur Erklärung*, second edition, p. 160; *Zur Beleuchtung*, p. 69). If to-day we allow a fruitful field to lie fallow, or a mine or water power to remain unexploited; if, in short, we do not act economically with valuable uses of land, we act as directly against our economic wellbeing as when we throw away labour uneconomically.

as when he gathers shellfish on the shore.   Or he may take a roundabout way, and, with the element at his command, may make, first, another good, and then, with its assistance, the good he wishes; as, for instance, when he makes a boat and net and takes to fishing systematically.   We already know that the former method is identical with what the Germans call *kapitallos* production, the latter with capitalist production; and that the intermediate products, which come into existence in the course of the indirect methods, represent economic social capital.

The adoption of capitalist methods of production is followed by two consequences, equally characteristic and significant. One is an advantage, the other a disadvantage.   The advantage we have already looked at; it consists in the greater technical productiveness of those methods.   With an equal expenditure of primary productive powers [1] (that is to say, labour and valuable natural powers) more or better goods can be produced by a wisely chosen capitalist process than could be by direct unassisted production.   This proposition, which is quite convincingly accredited by daily experience, we illustrated and tried to explain in the second chapter of Book I. by a number of examples.   We found the explanation to be that, when roundabout methods are skilfully chosen, new allies are obtained from the immense stores of natural powers, and their activity is enlisted in the work of production.   It is this well-known fact that is usually indicated by the term "productivity of capital."   This name, however, imports into the facts a particular interpretation, the correctness of which has yet to be examined in the next chapter.

The disadvantage connected with the capitalist method of production is its sacrifice of time.   The roundabout ways of capital are fruitful but long; they procure us more or better consumption goods, but only at a later period of time.   This proposition, no less than the former, is one of the ground pillars of the theory of capital.   We shall see later on that the very function of capital, as a means of appropriation or source of interest, to a great extent rests upon it.   I must,

---

[1] "Primary productive powers" is the more correct expression, which we must now employ instead of the partial expression "labour" used by me in the second chapter of Book I. in order to avoid tedious explanations.

therefore, guard it against any misunderstanding by the two following remarks.

In the first place, it may very well happen, in an exceptional case, that an indirect method of production is not only better but speedier. A man wishing to gather apples from a high tree will evidently attain his purpose sooner by first cutting a stick from another tree, and using it to knock down the apples, than by climbing the tree and trying to break off the apples one by one with his hand. But this is not the rule. In the overwhelming majority of cases we must tread the roundabout ways of capitalist production under technical conditions of such a nature that we have to wait, and often for a very long time, before we get the ripe final product. Instead of giving examples which must occur of themselves to every reader, I would rather draw attention to the fact that, in the loss of time which is, as a rule, bound up with the capitalist process, lies the sole ground of that much-talked-of and much-deplored dependence of labourer on capitalist. If capitalist production led as quickly from the hand to the mouth as unskilled direct production does, there would be nothing to hinder the workers carrying on such roundabout methods from beginning to end on their own account. They would still be dependent on the landowners, who could prevent them from access to the land which at the outset they require, but they would not be dependent on the capitalists. It is only because the labourers cannot wait till the roundabout process— which begins with the obtaining of raw materials and making of tools—delivers up its products ready for consumption, that they become economically dependent on the capitalists who already hold in their possession what we have called " intermediate products." [1]

[1] It is very characteristic that Rodbertus, when describing the economical effects of adopting roundabout ways of production, chooses his illustration just out of that minority of cases where the roundabout way is the quicker (*Das Kapital*, p. 236). The consequence is that, on this and other occasions, he leaves in the shade all the *economical* elements which form the basis of the phenomenon of interest—and of these the most notable is the loss of time connected with the carrying through of productive methods—and, taking a very one-sided view, lays the origin of rent at the door of the existing circumstances of private right (*e.g.* p. 310). But private rights in capital would not, by themselves, do any harm to the labourers, and it would be very easy for them to avoid the toll-bars which the capitalists have erected, if the fatal lapse of time between beginning and end of the lengthy capitalist process did not make it impossible for labourers to adopt similar processes on their own account.

Again—though this scarcely needs pointing out—when we speak of capitalist production taking time, it is not relevant to raise the objection that, with a piece of concrete capital *once made*, say a tool, a definite product can be made more quickly than it could be without the assistance of capital; that, for instance, a tailor takes three days to sew a coat by hand, and one day to do it with a sewing-machine. For it is clear that the machine sewing forms only one part, and indeed the smaller part, of the capitalist process; the principal part falls to the making of the sewing-machine, and the total process lasts considerably longer than three days.

Thus far we have considered capitalist production as an undivided whole, and have contrasted it with production carried on entirely without capital. But here we are reminded of a fact that has to be reckoned with, viz. that in capitalist production there are stages and degrees; to speak accurately, there are innumerable degrees of "Capitalism." In the making of a consumption good the possible roundabout methods are of very varying length. We may make intermediate products from which the final good will be obtained in a month, or a year, or ten years, or a hundred years. The question now is, what influence such differences of degree have on product.

On the whole it may be said that not only are the first steps more productive, but that every lengthening of the roundabout process is accompanied by a further increase in the technical result; as the process, however, is lengthened the amount of product, as a rule, increases in a smaller proportion.

This proposition also is based on experience, and only on experience. What it says must be simply taken as a fact of the technique of production. The reader, moreover, will easily be able to check its accuracy if he follows in thought the steps which lead to the production of any consumption good. For instance, firewood can be got quite directly so long as we limit ourselves to the gathering of dry branches or breaking off of weak twigs. We take a short roundabout path in making and using a stone axe. A longer process involves digging ore out of the ground, getting the fuel and necessary tools, and smelting iron out of the ore, working up the iron into steel,

and finally turning out a finished steel axe.   Beginning
farther back, we may construct cunning machinery for mining
and raising the ore, elaborate blast furnaces for smelting it,
special machines for making and sharpening the axe.   Going
farther back still, we may put up engineering shops and
machinery for constructing each kind of appliance, and so on.
It will scarcely be doubted that every additional step increases
the productiveness of the total process; that is, results in
the obtaining of the unit, say the cubic foot of wood, at a
smaller total expenditure of labour (mediate and immediate).
But just as little will it be doubted that the first two productive methods, the use of the stone axe and then of the
steel axe, must have caused a much greater revolution in the
productiveness of woodcutting than the later improvements,
although, absolutely, these may be by no means inconsiderable.

If necessary, this may easily be proved to demonstration by a little calculation.   Assume, for example, that
a labourer working with his hands can cut in one day 2
cubic feet of wood, and working with a stone axe, which
has taken three days to make, can cut 10 cubic feet: the
three days' capitalist process is rewarded by a surplus return
of 8 cubic feet per labour day.   Now possibly the doubling of
the process—say that the more careful fashioning of the stone
axe takes six days—may also double the surplus return, and
give 16 cubic feet.   But it is scarcely likely that trebling the
roundabout process can treble the surplus return.   And it is
quite certain that extending the roundabout process a thousandfold—say by sinking of pits, from which the ore for the
axe may be got after years have elapsed—will not be able to
increase the surplus return a thousandfold.   Otherwise we
should have the all but inconceivable possibility that a worker
in one day could cut 8000 feet of wood !   From some one
point—probably a point not far off—the surplus, though still
increasing, will increase in a less ratio than the production
period.

Of course in such cases no definite figure can be named,
either for the point from which the productiveness of further
extensions of the process begins to decrease, or, speaking
generally, for the amount of surplus result connected with any
definite length of process.   These data vary according to the

technical circumstances of each branch of production, and at each stage of productive skill. Every new invention alters them. The discovery of gunpowder, for example, opened up at a flash the possibility, which did not exist the moment before, of increasing the productiveness of the chase by perhaps one half, and the productiveness of stone-quarrying by perhaps a hundredfold.[1] We may, however, with sufficient confidence repeat the proposition already formulated, that every extension of the production process (so far as it is wisely chosen, of course) leads, generally speaking, to some surplus result. It may be confidently maintained that there is not one branch of production the returns of which may not be considerably increased in this way, as against the method of production prevailing at the time; and that without any new invention, but simply by the intercalation of intermediate members long familiar to capitalist production,—whether it be by the adoption of a steam motor, or an apt transmitter, or some ingenious gearing, blast, lever, regulator, or the like. How far behind, indeed, in capitalist equipment are the most of our agricultural and industrial businesses compared with the most advanced typical businesses! And certainly these latter are no less far behind an ideally perfect equipment.[2]

The fact that the prolongation of production processes leads to surplus results, and the fact that these surplus results

---

[1] Inventions, so-called, generally mean the discovery of a new and more productive method of production. Frequently—probably in most cases—the new way is longer than the old, and in this case to utilise the invention requires the making of a great number of intermediate products, or, as it is usually expressed, a large investment of capital : *e.g.* in machinery, building of railways, and the like. But often a happy invention may lead to a better, and at the same time shorter, way of production, such as the manufacture of certain dye-stuffs from chemical instead of plant bodies. However elaborate the former may be, it is still certainly far more direct and speedy than a manufacture which has to wait on tedious processes of growth.

[2] It may be asked here, by way of objection, why man does not fully utilise the chances offered him of increasing the technical result by the technical knowledge he has at the moment. The common explanation runs—from want of capital. With the limited amount of capital at his disposal man can only utilise those chances of employment, among the infinite number of remunerative ones, which are most remunerative, and a great number of less, but still remunerative, employments must be passed over. This explanation is not quite exact, but it is at least right in the main contention. We may therefore be content with it until, in another connection, we can examine the matter with perfect accuracy.

usually decrease from a certain point onwards, have long
been noticed and acknowledged in our science; mostly, I must
say, in another form, and one borrowed from the jargon of the
Productivity Theory. It is many years since Thünen put
them in the most impartial manner, and showed that, in
the case of progressive increase of capital, the capital that
comes last does lead to an increase in the product of labour,
but in a constantly decreasing proportion.[1] On this foundation of fact he himself framed the well-known doctrine that
the rate of interest adjusts itself to the productiveness of the
last dose of capital applied in the least productive employment,
and, in the wake of this doctrine, the facts were recognised and
received in the widest circles.[2] In harmony, however, with
the fashion of the time, these facts were forced into the special
forms of presentation and terminology of the Productivity
Theory, whereby the most vexatious mistakes and confusions
slipped in along with them.[3] Before going further it seemed to
me advisable here to try to restate the facts in their naked
simplicity.

It scarcely, perhaps, requires to be proved that the capitalist production of consumption goods, although carried out in
roundabout ways and by many stages, does not, on that
account, cease to exhibit an intimately connected and united
work of production. The labour which produces the inter
mediate products—the mediate labour, as we shall call it with
Rodbertus [4]—and the labour which, out of and with the intermediate products, produces the desired good—the immediate
labour—both form a part of the production of the consumption
good. The production of timber is more than the labour of

---

[1] *Der isolirte Staat*, third edition, part ii. div. i. p. 97. See particularly
the table on p. 101.

[2] For instance by Roscher, *Grundlagen*, § 183; by Mangoldt, *Volkswirthschaftslehre*, 1868, p. 432; by Mithoff in Schönberg's *Handbuch*, second edition,
p. 663, and by many others. Jevons independently adopted quite similar views,
Theory of Political Economy, second edition, p. 277.

[3] In particular the "physical" or "technical productivity," which is founded
on these facts (that is, the circumstance that by the assistance of capital more
products can be produced than without it), was confused with a "value productivity" (that is, a pretended power of capital to produce more value than it
itself possesses). See my *Capital and Interest*, pp. 112, 131.

[4] *Das Kapital*, p. 236.

felling wood in the forest; it embraces the labour of the smith who makes the axe, of the carpenter who cuts the haft, of the miner who raises the ore, of the iron workers and steel workers who prepare it, and so on. True, our modern division of employment to outward appearance breaks up the unity of the process into a number of independent parts, but it is the theorist's business to understand economic processes in their living connection, and he dare not, of course, let himself be deceived by appearances, but must reproduce in his own mind the real unity of the work of production thus obscured. The masterly manner in which Rodbertus has done this is one of his best services to economics.

But this very consideration, essentially economic as it is, raises a doubt we must fairly meet. According to what has been said, the production period of a consumption good is, strictly speaking, to be reckoned from the moment on which the first hand was laid to the making of its first inter-mediate product, right down to the completion of the good itself. In our times, when unassisted production has almost entirely disappeared, and one generation builds on the inter-mediate products laid down by earlier generations, the produc-tion period of almost any consumption good could, in any strict calculation, trace its beginning back to early centuries.

The boy who cuts a stick with his knife is, strictly speak-ing, only continuing the work of the miner who, centuries ago, thrust the first spade into the ground to sink the shaft from which the ore was brought to make the blade. Of course the finished product of to-day owes a quite infinitesimal fraction—not worth calculation even if that were possible—to the firstlings of labour in these far-off centuries, and it would therefore give a very false view of the degree of capitalism expended in the cutting of the stick, if we were to estimate it by the absolute period of time intervening between the atom of labour first put forth and the completion of the work.

It is more important and more correct to look at the period of time which elapses *on the average* between the expenditure of the original productive powers, labour and uses of land, as successively employed in any work, and the turning out of the finished consumption goods. Production is more or less capitalistic according to the average remoteness of

the period at which the original productive powers exerted
during the process are paid. Say, for example, that the production of a commodity costs in all a hundred days of labour
—for the sake of simplification we shall leave out the co-operating uses of land—and that, of these hundred, one day was
expended ten years before the completion of the work, another
nine years, others respectively eight, seven, six, five, four, three,
two, and one year, while the remaining ninety days were
expended immediately before the completion. Then the first
day of labour is paid ten years later, the second nine years
later, the third eight years later, and so on, while the last
ninety days are paid immediately. The calculation is as
follows :—

$$\frac{10 + 9 + 8 + 7 + 6 + 5 + 4 + 3 + 2 + 1}{100} = \frac{55}{100}.$$

That is to say, on the average the hundred days of labour are
paid in about half a year. Say that the production of another
good were also to demand in all a hundred days of labour,
likewise spent in the course of a ten years' period, but spread
over it in such a way that twenty days' work was expended
ten years before, other twenty days' work nine years before,
five days' work in each year from the eighth to the first
successively, while the last twenty days were spent immediately
before the completion of the work, the average would come out
quite differently and much higher :—

$$\frac{200 + 180 + 40 + 35 + 30 + 25 + 20 + 15 + 10 + 5}{100} = \frac{560}{100},$$

or more than five and a half years. It is highly probable,
moreover, that in both cases some fraction of a day's work will
have been spent centuries before, but such a small element
will scarcely influence the average, and may in most cases be
simply neglected.[1]

[1] The first of the above schemes corresponds to the case of a production
where one single tool is employed, and where the total process extends over ten
years—for instance, the making and using of an axe of Bessemer steel. The
second scheme, again, corresponds to a production where, besides the axe, a
number of other capitalistic tools, auxiliary mechanism, and materials, are
employed, the existence of which, however, does not date from farther back than
ten years. This comparison clearly shows how, without increasing the absolute
length of the production period, the degree of capitalism may be very considerably

Where I have spoken above of extension or prolongation of the roundabout process of production, and of degrees of capitalism, I must be understood in the sense just explained. The length or the shortness of the process, its extension or its curtailment, is not to be measured by the absolute duration of the period that lies between the expenditure of the first atom of labour and the last—otherwise the cracking of nuts with a hammer which might chance to be made of iron brought from a mine opened by the Romans would perhaps be the most "capitalistic" kind of production. Nor is it to be measured by the number of independent intermediate members which the production process embraces—otherwise when, by means of the three intermediate products, twig, lime, and bird-lime, a boy catches birds on the same day as he commences making these three forms of capital, his bird-catching would be more capitalistic than the far-back labour of the miner who devotes years to the sinking of a shaft. But it is to be measured by the average period which lies between the successive expenditure in labour and uses of land and the obtaining of the final good. It is only in methods of production where the expenditure in original powers is distributed equally over the whole production period that the absolute length of the process affords at the same time the proper measure for the degree of capitalism.[1]

Let us now apply what has been said of single acts of production to the circumstances of an entire community. Every year a community comes anew into possession, and gets the disposal of a certain quantum of original productive powers, the powers represented by its labour and land. The farther away its production is from capitalist production—there is no production, of course, absolutely without capital—the greater

increased ; all that is necessary is to alter the proportion between the number of early workers and that of the finishing ones. Whether it is ten workers employed in the final stage against one worker employed ten years before, or one worker in the final stage against ten workers ten years before, in either case the total production process extends over a period of ten years. But in the former case the finishing workers would be very sparingly provided with tools, machines, etc. ; in the latter case they would be very amply provided. The latter, of course, would be far and away the more capitalistic of the two.

[1] See the interesting calculation and graphic statement of the amount of investment of capital in Jevons's *Theory of Political Economy*, second edition, p. 249.

will be the proportion of the year's productive powers that is changed into consumption goods during the same year. The more capitalistic the production is, the smaller will be the proportion of the year's productive powers consumed within the year, and the greater the proportion invested in intermediate products that will come to maturity as finished goods only in future years. And again, the higher the degree of capitalism is, the more remote will be the period at which these intermediate products mature. Thus a community producing from hand to mouth consumes in each year the fruits of the productive powers of that same year. A capitalist community consumes only to a small extent the fruits of the productive powers of the present year, and to a great extent the fruits of the productive powers of past years, while it again is making intermediate products for the service of future years. And the higher the degree of capitalism, the farther back in the past, on the average, are the years whose productive powers it consumes, and the farther on in the future are the periods for which it provides.

And now, I trust, the following proposition, which puts together the chief features of the capitalist production process, will be understood beyond possibility of mistake.

All consumption goods which man produces come into existence through a co-operation of human power with natural powers, which latter are partly economic, partly free. By means of these primary productive powers man may make the consumption goods he desires, either immediately, or through the medium of intermediate products called Capital. The latter method demands a sacrifice of time, but it has an advantage in the quantity of product, and this advantage, although perhaps in decreasing ratio, is associated with every prolongation of the roundabout way of production.

CHAPTER III

THE FUNCTION OF CAPITAL IN PRODUCTION

AFTER what has been said in the preceding chapter it should not be difficult accurately to indicate the rôle which capital plays in economic production.

Capital has, first, a symptomatic importance. Its presence is always the symptom of a profitable roundabout production. I say, deliberately, "symptom" and not "cause" or "condition" of profitable methods of production; for, as a fact, its presence is rather the result than the cause. If men to-day are fishing with boats and nets instead of picking the fish out of pools on the shore with their hands, it cannot be said that they have adopted those more fruitful methods because they possess boats and nets. Obviously they possess boats and nets because they have adopted these methods. They must have already chosen the roundabout way of production before these goods, speaking generally, come into existence.[1]

This, however, does not exhaust the importance of capital. It is, secondly,—and herein lies the chief point of its productive efficiency,—an effective intermediate cause of the consummation of this profitable roundabout process. Every piece of capital is, to a certain extent, a store of useful natural powers, the working of which helps to bring to a successful issue the roundabout process in the course of which the piece of capital has come into existence. I say "intermediate cause," not

---

[1] It would be somewhat different if we were to adopt the other conception of capital, and understand by it, not intermediate products only, but the entire national subsistence fund, which would therefore include the labourers' subsistence. In that case, but only in that case, one might say that capital was the cause of these profitable roundabout ways of production being adopted.

"cause." Capital gives no independent impulse; it only transmits an impulse given by the original productive powers, just as one billiard ball transmits motion to another. The function of capital, indeed, has been called the "prisoning of natural powers." The expression is quite appropriate, and very happy. Only it must never be forgotten that this attribute belongs to the entire capitalist process, not only to the "descending branch," generally called the use of the capital, but also to the "ascending branch," in which the capital itself is first made. Man does not first prison natural powers by means of capital; capital itself originates as the result of a previous imprisonment—by the original productive powers that are at man's own bidding—of certain compliant natural powers. Taken all in all, among the many predicates which economists have given to capital, the one that best fits this aspect of the case is that of "Tool of Production."

But, thirdly, capital is also the indirect cause of other profitable roundabout ways of production being entered on — other, that is, than those in the course of which it itself has come into existence. When a people possesses much capital not only can it successfully complete those processes in the course of which the capital presently existing has come into being, but it can also adopt other and new methods. For the stock of capital in hand (which, essentially, is nothing else than an aggregate of consumption goods in a transition state [1]) throws off every year a certain quantity of its constituents, which have just completed their transition state and become finished goods, and places them at the disposal of the current economic period for purposes of immediate consumption. In this way the greater the stock of capital, the larger is the share taken by the productive powers of the past in providing means of consumption for the present, and the less are the new productive powers of the present drawn on for the present. Thus a larger proportion of these current powers is free for the service of the future, that is, for investment in more or less far-reaching processes of production.

If a community is so poor that the consumption goods

---

[1] Schäffle very finely speaks of capital as "Consumption wealth as it were in the stalk, when it is still only swelling bud and ripening fruit" (Schönberg's *Handbuch*, second edition, vol. i. p. 208).

maturing out of capitalist intermediate products in any year, say in 1888, scarcely cover $\frac{1}{20}$ of that year's wants, then the remaining $\frac{19}{20}$ must be provided out of the labour and uses of land of 1888, and only a fractional part of the productive powers of that year remains over to initiate methods of production that will turn out consumption goods in the years following. If, on the other hand, the past has accumulated a treasure of intermediate products—raw materials, tools, machines, factories, workshops, etc.— so great that their successive maturing covers the consumption demand of the year 1888 to the extent of $\frac{5}{10}$, that of 1889 to the extent of $\frac{4}{10}$, that of 1890 to the extent of $\frac{3}{10}$, and so on, then only one half of the productive powers of 1888 will be claimed to make up the current wants, while the entire other half may be spent unhesitatingly in producing intermediate products which will come to maturity, as consumption goods, only in later years—all the later in proportion as the next year's wants are already covered by accumulations of capital in the past.

In this sense, but only in this sense, is it correct to say that man must already have capital before he can enter on roundabout ways of production ; that want of capital prevents man taking advantage of far-reaching and profitable methods of production, such as the laying of railways, building of canals, irrigation schemes, altering of river-beds, and so on. It would be quite incorrect to understand this proposition as meaning that a community must have, finished and ready to hand, that kind of concrete capital with which the methods of production in question are carried out, or even the concrete capital (raw materials, tools, etc.) out of which are made the forms of capital first needed. All that is required is, that the community possess so much capital, whatever its shape, as will cover—while it is being gradually changed into consumption goods—the demand of the present and near future for such goods sufficiently to leave the current production powers free for investment in intermediate products of the kind required. It would be essentially more correct to say that we require *consumption goods* before we can enter upon roundabout ways of production, whether these be in the form of finished stocks of goods ready for consumption, or in the transition form of intermediate products.

Lastly, we can now answer, easily and categorically, the much-disputed question, whether any independent productive power is inherent in capital; or, to put the question in its usual form, whether capital is a third and independent "factor in production" alongside of labour and nature?

The answer must be a most distinct negative. This seems to me the only conclusion any one can come to, provided he makes clear to himself the sense in which this question is put, and must be put if it is worth the trouble of putting at all. And this sense is a very emphatic one. The following analogy will make it perfectly clear. A man throws a stone at another man and kills him. Has the stone killed the man? If the question is put without laying any special emphasis it may be answered without hesitation in the affirmative. But how if the murderer, on his trial, were to defend himself by saying that it was not he but the stone that had killed the man? Taking the words in this sense should we still say that the stone had killed the man, and acquit the murderer?

Now it is with an emphasis like this that economists inquire as to the independent productivity of capital. The question comes up in the course of the inquiry concerning the elements which constitute our material goods. A similar interest to that which the chemist has in the analysis of compound bodies leads the economist to analyse the multiform transition stages of material goods, to trace them back to their source, and to resolve the thousandfold instruments and auxiliaries of production, to which, directly or indirectly, they owe their existence, into the simple fundamental powers from the co-operation of which everything proceeds. In this connection the doubt arises whether capital is an independent productive power or not. The whole spirit of the inquiry allows only one meaning to be given to the question, and the emphasis is very marked. We are not asking about dependent intermediate causes, but about ultimate independent elements. The question is not whether capital plays a part in the bringing about of a productive result—such as the stone does in the killing of the man—but whether, granted the productive result, some part of it is due to capital so entirely and peculiarly that it simply cannot be put to the credit of the two other recognised elementary factors, nature and labour. Now can this question be answered in the affirmative?

Emphatically it can not. Capital is an intermediate product of nature and labour, nothing more. Its own origin, its existence, its subsequent action, are nothing but stages in the continuous working of the true elements, nature and labour. They and they alone do everything from beginning to end in bringing consumption goods into existence. The only distinction is that sometimes they do it all at once, sometimes by several stages. In the latter case the completion of each stage is marked outwardly by the appearance of a fore-product or intermediate product, and capital has emerged. But, let me ask, is a thing any the less the work of its author that it is not produced all at once, but in instalments? If to-day, by allying my labour with natural powers, I make bricks out of clay, and to-morrow, by allying my labour with natural gifts, I obtain lime, and the day after that make mortar and so construct a wall, can it be said of any part of the wall that I and the natural powers have *not* made it? Again, before a lengthy piece of work, such as the building of a house, is quite finished, it naturally must be at one time a fourth finished, then a half finished, then three-quarters finished. What now would be said if one were to describe these inevitable stages of the work as independent requisites of house-building, and maintain that, for the building of a house, we require, besides building materials and labour, a quarter-finished house, a half-finished house, a three-quarters-finished house? In form perhaps it is less striking, but in effect it is not a whit more correct, to elevate those intermediate steps in the progress of the work, which outwardly take the shape of capital, into an independent agent of production by the side of nature and labour.

This would never have been called in question had it not been that the introduction of division of vocations and labour had split up the united work of producing consumption goods into a number of apparently independent acts of production. It was this that made economists forget to look at it as a whole, and made them, with singular modesty, bow before the dependent intermediate creations of previous human activity as if they represented an independent power. But

even as it was, it was scarcely possible for any acute theorist
to make this confusion if another circumstance had not
conspired to assist it.   That was the accepted parallelism
between factors of production and branches of income, and
the awkwardness economists feared to encounter in the
explanation and justification of interest if they had to
refuse recognition to capital as an independent factor of
production.   All natural income, it was taught, is based on
participation in the production of goods.   The various branches
of income are nothing else than the forms in which the
different contributories to production are paid.   Rent of land
is the payment for the factor of nature, wage the payment for
the factor of labour, and interest—well, interest appeared to
have no substantial foundation if it also could not be interpreted as a payment for a third independent factor of production.   It did not seem to be explained theoretically, nor—
what indeed might be more serious to the theorists in question
—to be justified practically.   Thus it was that many a learned
thinker was driven into a corner, and preferred rather to shut
an eye to clear facts than to sacrifice the independent productivity of capital, and with it the welcome basis for the
current theory of interest.

Facts certainly spoke with perfect distinctness.   It was
impossible to deny that capital is no element in the proper
sense of the word, inasmuch as it itself springs from the
co-operation of nature and labour.   Not only so, but by a
singular irony of fate this had to be expressly proved—as it
had been by Adam Smith before them- —by those very theorists
who maintained its independent productivity.   In their theory
of price, in having to show how all prices resolve themselves
finally into rent, wage, and interest, they were forced to
demonstrate in the most minute way that concrete capital is
not an element; that, for instance, copper and steel, which
serve as capital in the manufacture of watches, originate in the
co-operation of the natural mineral deposits, of the work of
miners, and of older capitals, which themselves have orig nated
in similar ways, and so on.[1]   In the face of this, to maintain
the independent productivity of what they had just demonstrated to be a dependent and intermediate product, they were

[1] *e.g.* Say, *Traité*, seventh edition, p. 344.

driven to adopt very singular expedients. The favourite ones were obscurity and brevity. Instead of making an earnest effort to bridge the yawning contradiction, they either did not suggest the doubt at all, or, if a doubt had already been raised, they dismissed it with some laconic phrase or other. A long series of writers make no scruple about expounding capital on one page as a factor of production " derived " from nature and labour, and on the next as a third independent factor of production along with nature and labour.[1] Mill has so far yielded to the pressure of facts as to admit that capital is itself the product of labour, and that its instrumentality in production is therefore in reality that of labour in an indirect shape. But with a quick turn he saves its independence. " Not the less," he continues, " does it require to be specified separately. A *previous application of labour* to produce the capital required for consumption during the work is no less essential than the *application of labour* to the work itself." [2] Therefore, because labour must be applied twice, in two different stages of production, something else besides labour must be recognised as the independent condition of production !

Some writers, of course, treat the matter more seriously. They do not evade the difficulty, but try to get a real solution of it. They cannot overlook the fact that capital first comes into existence through combination of simpler factors. Quite correctly, therefore, they do not attempt to claim for capital itself the character of an element ; but they still require an independent support for interest. This they obtain by resolving capital into its elements, and finding that, besides nature and labour, there is still a third independent element : Senior calls it Abstinence, Hermann calls it the Use of Capital. These attempts at solution, which I went into in detail and pronounced upon in my former book, *Capital and Interest*, were certainly not very happy. Hermann's, in particular, is singularly unfortunate in being obliged to explain the " use " which capital gives as more elementary than capital itself—as if the egg which the hen lays is antecedent to the hen !

---

[1] Of older writers, *e.g.* B. Fulda, *Grundsätze der Oek. pol. or Kameralwissenschaften*, second edition, 1820, p. 135 ; Schön, *Neue Untersuchung der National-Oekonomie*, 1835, p. 47. Of later writers Cossa himself, *Elementi*, eighth edition, p. 34 ; and Gide, *Principes d'Éc. Pol.* 1884, pp. 101, 145.

[2] Book i. chap. vii. § i.

Nevertheless as regards our present question these theories are very instructive. They show that several of our most clear-sighted thinkers preferred to take refuge in the most hazardous and artificial constructions rather than agree in the current doctrine that capital itself, while originating in the co-operation of nature and labour, is, all the same, an "independent" factor of production along with them!

We may confidently, then, strike capital out of the list of independent productive powers, as a portion of the English school did long ago, and as the Socialists have done more recently. I may say, however, that the manner in which they have done so is not quite appropriate. In the instrumentality of capital they see only the instrumentality of the labour expended in producing it; they explain it as "previous stored-up labour." This is not correct. Capital—to keep the same form of expression—is "stored-up labour," but it is something more; it is also stored-up valuable natural power. It is the medium through which the *two* original productive powers exert their instrumentality. To the instrumentality of gold, which is employed as capital in gilding the lightning-rod, the labour of the miner, who finds the ore and refines it, is not the only contributory: nature also has contributed her share in depositing the valuable vein or placer.

Although, then, we have traced its instrumentality in production to nature and labour, is capital itself not productive at all? Certainly it is, in more than one sense of that too ambiguous word.[1] It is, first, "productive" because it finds its destination in the production of goods; it is, further, productive because it is an effectual tool in completing the roundabout and profitable methods of production once they are entered on; finally, it is productive indirectly because it makes the adoption of new and profitable methods possible. One thing, however, it is not; it is not *independently* productive in the sense on which the most important part of the controversy turns. As the old economist Lotz expressed it, briefly and succinctly: "Of any independent labour in capital there is simply no question."[2]

[1] See *Capital and Interest*, p. 114.
[2] *Handbuch der Staatswirthschaftslehre*, Erlangen, 1821, i. p. 66, in note.

CHAPTER IV

THE THEORY OF THE FORMATION OF CAPITAL

IN our science there are three views in circulation as to the formation of capital. One finds its origin in Saving, a second in Production, and a third in both together. Of these the third enjoys the widest acceptance, and it is also the correct one. But the formula will have to be amplified to some extent, and presented in a way that is, at once, clearer and more true to life than has usually been the case.[1]

---

[1] The dispute as to the share which Saving plays in the formation of capital is almost as old as economic science. The theory which ascribed it the prominent place was the first to appear. Already suggested by the Physiocrats, it was formulated by Adam Smith in the often-quoted proposition, "Parsimony and not industry is the immediate cause of the increase of capital" (*Wealth of Nations*, book ii. chap. iii.) Supported by his authority it was for a long time almost the only one that held the field, and, although in later times it has suffered many reverses, it still finds some notable apostles: thus, among others, Mill—"Capital is the result of saving" (book i. chap. v. § 4); Roscher—"Capital is mainly the result of saving" (*Grundlagen*, § 45); Francis Walker—"It arises solely out of saving. It stands always for self-denial and abstinence" (*Political Economy*, p. 67). But from a very early period there was sharp opposition to the theory, first from Lauderdale (*Inquiry*, 1804, chap. iv.); then, after some time, from the socialist theorists, Rodbertus (*Das Kapital*, pp. 240, 267—"Just as the capital of the isolated individual originates and increases, so does the national capital,—only through labour and not through saving"); Lassalle (*Kapital und Arbeit*, p. 64); Marx (*Das Kapital*, i. second edition, p. 619). To these opinions a great many recent writers of other schools more or less incline; thus, very clearly and decidedly, Gide (*Principes*, p. 167); less decidedly, Kleinwächter (in Schönberg's *Handbuch*, second edition, p. 213), and R. Meyer (*Das Wesen des Einkommens*, 1887, p. 213); more by way of reconciliation, Wagner (*Grundlegung*, second edition, § 298); and, a little obscurely and confusedly, Cohn (*Grundlegung*, 1885, § 257). Although, however, this tendency to ascribe capital to labour is unmistakably rapidly gaining ground, that view which ascribes to saving a share in the formation of capital is still the view of the majority. But the later representatives of this view are in the habit of rightly limiting it, and

To put the matter, first of all, in its simplest conceivable terms. Suppose a recluse working absolutely without capital —say some Robinson Crusoe thrown on a lonely shore without either tools or weapons. Being without capital he must at first support life in the most primitive fashion, as, for instance, by gathering berries which grow wild. Now what must happen before he can get possession of his first capital, say a bow and arrow ?

Let us put the first theory to the test. Is saving by itself sufficient to call capital into existence ? Certainly not. With the one possession that he has—his wild fruits—our Crusoe may save and stint as much as he please ; he will accumulate a store of berries—goods for consumption—but that will never give him a single bow or arrow. As we can easily see, these must be positively produced.

Is it sufficient, then, for the origination of capital that it be produced ? Again, certainly not. Of course, once Crusoe has got the length of commencing to produce capital, the formation of capital is as good as accomplished. But before he gets that length, there is something else to be done, and that something is by no means self-evident. Productive powers are to be set free for the proposed formation of capital, and this can only be done, as we shall see, through saving.

The amount of original productive powers which our Crusoe has daily at his command is equivalent — leaving natural gifts out of account—to one day's labour, which we shall assume to be ten hours of labour. Suppose, now, that the berries within reach of his hut are so scarce that a full day's labour of ten hours is necessary to provide as much food as will just support him in bare life, obviously no formation of capital is possible. There is no use advising him to produce a bow and arrows. Producing requires time and strength, and all the time and strength our Crusoe has is fully claimed

expressly emphasising the fact that saving alone is not sufficient, and that there must also be "labour," or "devotion to productive purposes," or such like— which, indeed, may very well have been the true meaning of many of the older adherents of the Saving theory, and only not expressed by them because of its assumed obviousness. See, *e.g.*, Rau (*Volkswirthschaftslehre*, eighth edition, i. § 133), Ricca-Salerno (*Sulla Teoria del Capitale*, chap. iv. p. 118—"Il capitale deve la sua origine all' industria e al risparmio "), Cossa (*Elementi*, eighth edition, p. 39), and many others.

already to keep him in life. To produce capital, then, may be difficult enough without something else ; and what that is will appear immediately on our varying a little the assumed facts of the illustration.

Suppose there is such wealth of berries that the result of nine hours' gathering is sufficient to support bare life, while ten hours' gathering gives a return such as to guarantee a subsistence amply sufficient to maintain Crusoe in health and strength. Obviously he has now a choice between two lines of conduct. Either he may take advantage of the opportunity thus offered to complete his provision, and consume each day the fruits of an entire ten hours' day of labour—in which case it is perfectly clear that he has now no time and strength left to make a bow and arrows ; or, although the productive power at his disposal would enable him to live better, he may content himself with the barest living, which, as we said, can be provided by the nine hours' labour of gathering ; then, and then only, has he a tenth hour free in which to make weapons for future use. This amounts to saying, in other words, that, before capital can actually be formed, the productive powers necessary to its making must be *saved* by encroaching on the moment's enjoyment.

To anticipate and avoid a mistake very apt to be made, it must be said distinctly that this encroaching on the moment's enjoyment need by no means involve downright privation. With more productive labour, Crusoe's choice would not lie, as in the above illustration, between bare living and comfortable living, but, perhaps, between comfortable and ample living. It is not a question of the absolute insignificance of these claims on the moment's enjoyment, but on their relation to that amount which I may indicate in the shortest and most generally intelligible way by the word " Income "—an expression, unfortunately, not yet strictly enough defined in scientific usage.[1] The essential thing is that the current endowment of

[1] On the many divergent and contradictory readings of the conception of Income, see R. Meyer's *Das Wesen des Einkommens*, 1887, particularly pp. 1-27. I purposely avoid going into the controversy as to this conception, which Meyer's work, notwithstanding its many merits, seems to me to have by no means adequately settled. Where I use the word Income in the sequel it is to be understood, not in Meyer's sense, but in a sense very much in agreement with popular usage.

productive powers should not be entirely claimed for the immediate consumption of the current period, but that a portion of this endowment should be retained for the service of a future period.   But such a retention will undoubtedly be called a real saving of productive powers.

A saving of *productive powers*, be it noted; for productive powers, and not the goods which constitute capital, are the immediate object of saving.   This is an important point, which must be strongly emphasised because, in the current view, too little consideration is given to it.   Man saves consumption goods, his means of enjoyment; he thus *saves* productive powers, and with these finally he can *produce* capital.[1]   It is only exceptionally that capital itself is the immediate object of saving; it may happen in the case of those goods which, by nature, admit of being used either for consumption or for production, such as grain.   To the extent that a man withdraws such goods from immediate use in consumption, his saving directly lays the foundation of capital. To build on that foundation, of course, the negative element of saving must have added to it the positive element of devoting the saved goods to production, as intermediate products.

It is easy to show that every further increase of the existing stock of capital is limited by the same conditions as the first formation.   Assume that for a month our Crusoe consumes daily only so much fruit as he can gather in nine hours' labour, and devotes the tenth hour to making weapons. As result of this thirty hours' work he now owns a bow and arrows, and in them he has the possibility of making his living much more easily and amply than before.   Naturally his desires widen.   He wishes decent clothes, a house, all sorts of things that minister to comfort.   But for these he requires the suitable intermediate products—axes, nails, braces, etc. Now we ask further what kind of conditions must be fulfilled that Crusoe may obtain this new capital?

This is very easily answered.   If he makes use of the improved circumstances, which he owes to the possession of

---

[1] Adam Smith's celebrated proposition therefore—"Parsimony and not industry is the immediate cause of the increase of capital"—is, strictly speaking, to be turned just the other way about. The immediate cause of the origin of capital is production; the mediate cause is a previous saving.

the bow and arrows, simply to increase his immediate consumption—that is, if he spends the whole labour time at his disposal in the service of the moment, hunting, gathering fruits, and sleeping,—not only is it impossible for him to acquire new capital, but he will lose the old. Bows and arrows do not last for ever. In a month's time, we shall say, his arrows will be spent, and his bow worn out. If, therefore, his capital is to remain in existence, he must, obviously, employ at least one of the ten hours in renewing his weapons, and, at the most, he can employ nine only in gathering and hunting.

To put it in propositional form. To retain capital in existence, man must make over, and devote to the service of the future, at least so much of the productive powers of the *current* period as he has consumed, during the current period, of the produce of *former* productive powers.[1] Or, to put it in other words, the consumption of the current period is limited by the produce of as many productive powers—present and past taken together—as come into existence anew during the current period.

Finally, if an increase of capital is to become possible, obviously a still greater proportion of the current productive powers must be withdrawn from the consumption of the present, and transferred to the service of the future; of his ten hours of labour our Crusoe must devote *one* to renewing his weapons, and *less than nine* to gathering berries and killing game, if he is to make the new capital he desires in what remains free of his labour time. To put it generally, he must curtail the immediate consumption of the current period to such a point, that it uses up the produce of fewer (past and present) productive powers than come into existence anew in the same period; he must, in a word, save productive powers.

All this is quite clear and simple; indeed it is even a little too simple for our purpose. Robinsonades and pictures

---

[1] It is only in cases where, in the meanwhile, the technique of the particular production has improved, that the transference of a less amount of productive powers to the service of the future is sufficient. If, for instance, Crusoe learns how to make in fifteen days those weapons which formerly had taken thirty days, it is, of course, sufficient for the upkeep of the capital if he works only half an hour daily at the repair of his weapons, and nine and a half hours can now be spent in directly obtaining a more plentiful maintenance without prejudice to his economical position.

of primitive circumstances are very good when the object is to present clearly the simplest typical principles—to give a kind of skeleton of economical procedure,—and to that extent, I trust, our Robinsonade also has done good service.   But, naturally, they cannot give us an adequate picture of those peculiar and developed forms in which this skeleton clothes itself in the living actuality of a modern economic community And it is just at this point that it becomes important to fill out the abstract formula with explanation and illustration taken from life.   We shall, therefore, leave the lonely shore of our Crusoe, and come to the industrial conduct of a great nation with its millions of people.

CHAPTER V

FORMATION OF CAPITAL IN A COMMUNITY

LET us take the case of a community embracing ten millions of able-bodied persons. Leaving out of account the current uses of land, so as not to cumber the statement unnecessarily, the annual endowment of such a nation—its original productive powers—thus amounts to ten million years of labour. Its accumulated stock of capital, we shall suppose, represents the fruit of thirty million labour-years (and a corresponding amount of uses of land) invested during previous economic years in intermediate products. Now look at the constitution of this stock of capital more closely.

Every capital is, by its nature, composed of a mass of intermediate products, and the common goal of all these products is to ripen into consumption goods or means of enjoyment. They reach this goal through the continuation of that production process in the course of which they themselves have come into existence. They are all, as it were, on the way towards the goal of human consumption. But the length of the road which they have had to travel is different. This is partly because the various branches of production adopt roundabout ways of various length : mining, for instance, or railway building, takes a much more roundabout and lengthy method than wood-cutting. But it is partly, also, because those goods which constitute the community's capital at the moment are at various points on their respective roads. Many an intermediate product has just entered on a very lengthy roundabout road, as, for instance, a boring machine, whose life-work it will be to drive a gallery in a mine. Some are midway. Others, again, like clothing stuffs ready for making into coats

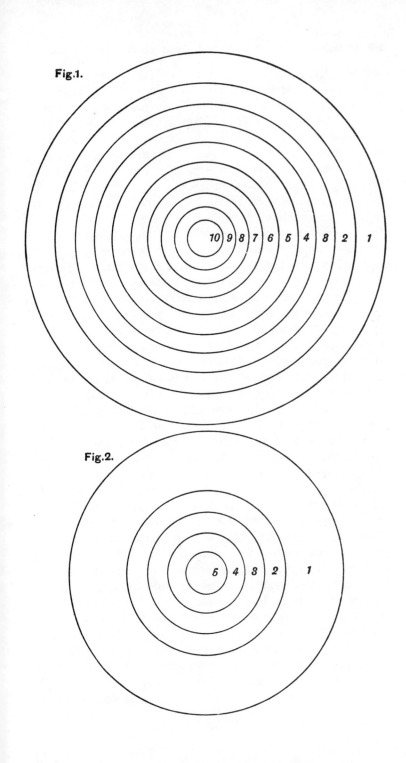

Fig.1.

Fig.2.

and mantles, are near the end of the journey their particular production process has to take. Now the inventory of capital lays a kind of cross-section through the production processes, thus unlike in length and unlike in stage of progress, and intersects them, of course, at the most different points, just as a national census lays a section through the paths of life, and encounters and registers the individual members of the nation at the most different stages of life.

Considered with reference to the varying distances at which intermediate products lie from the goal of consumption, the total mass of capital divides itself into a number of annual classes or stages of maturity, which may be very appropriately pictured by a diagram of concentric annual circles. The outmost circle (Fig. 1) embraces those goods which will be transformed into goods ready for consumption within the coming year; the second circle represents those goods which will ripen into consumption goods in the year after; the third circle, those which will be ready the year after that, and so on. In a community where production is not yet strongly capitalistic, the inner circles will rapidly contract (Fig. 2), because, in such a community, very lengthy roundabout ways of production, such as turn out their finished goods only after many years, will be rare. In rich and well-developed communities, again, there will be a considerable number of comprehensive circles, and of these the inner ones will have a content that, although relatively smaller, is not inconsiderable.

This representation of the stages of maturity by concentric circles is peculiarly appropriate on this account that it also gives a very happy expression to the quantitative relations of these stages. Exactly as the outmost of the concentric circles possesses the greatest area, while the inner circles possess a gradually decreasing one, does the first of these classes—that nearest to the completion of the process—always, by its very nature, embrace the largest quota of the total mass of capital, while a decreasingly smaller quota falls to the more remote classes. There are two reasons for this. The first is that the various branches of production generally adopt processes of different lengths—lengths varying with the technical circumstances of each branch. Many complete the entire work of production, from the preliminary processes to the turning out of the finished product, within a year; many require two, three, and five years; only a few have a production period extending over ten, twenty, and thirty years. The result is that in the highest classes—those farthest removed in time from the finished product—only a few branches of production are found; intermediate products, for instance, in the tenth circle can only be provided by those branches of production which have at least a ten years' production period. But the lower circles are filled, not only by those last-named branches of production (for the intermediate products of these very long processes must pass circle by circle towards maturity), but also by those branches of production which have shorter periods. Thus the quantity of intermediate products grows larger and larger up to the first class, and to this first class every branch of production, without exception, sends its representative.

But there is still another circumstance that works in the same direction. The ripening of intermediate products into consumption goods demands a steady addition of current productive powers. At each stage of the production process new labour is added to the intermediate products which have been passed on to it from the previous stage, and they pass on to the following stage in a more advanced state. In one stage the intermediate product wool is changed, by the addition of labour, into the intermediate product yarn; that again in a following stage, by the addition of labour, into the intermediate product cloth, and so on. This has the natural result that, within each branch of production, the amount of invested capital increases with each advancing stage of the production, or, what is the same thing, at every change into a lower circle. Consequently not only are the lower circles, as has been shown, supplied from more branches of production, but they are supplied with relatively larger amounts of capital, and this gives the lower classes a twofold numerical superiority over the higher ones.[1]

On these lines we may now put our illustration into figures. To facilitate our survey we shall assume that the

---

[1] Durable productive goods, which give off their use gradually in the course of several years, belong naturally (in various parts of their content as useful goods, or in various annual circles of their activity) to several circles simultaneously.

total capital of the community is comprised in ten yearly
circles. If thirty million labour-years are embodied in this
total capital (for simplicity's sake I again leave out invested
uses of land) we may assume the following division of the
circles. The

1st circle contains the intermediate products of 6 million labour-years.
2d	„	„	„	5	„	„
3d	„	„	„	4	„	„
4th	„	„	„	3·5	,,	„
5th	„	„	„	3	„	„
6th	„	„	„	2·5	„	„
7th	„	„	„	2	„	„
8th	,,	„	„	1·7	„	„
9th	„	„	,,	1·3	„	„
10th	,,	„	„	1	„	„

In the normal course of things the outmost circle becomes
divided off from capital each year, and is changed into consumption goods, but the succeeding circles press forward, each
circle, by the addition of new labour, advanced one stage,
both as regards nearness to maturity and amount of capital
invested. The first class, therefore, is changed into consumption goods, the second class into the first, the third into the
second, and so on. Now the following important questions
suggest themselves. What use must the community make
of the original productive powers which come anew into its
possession during the current year—that is to say, the new
ten million labour-years if, for simplicity's sake, we still leave
out uses of land—in order to conserve the capital that is in
existence ? And how must it act to increase that capital ?

These questions are easily answered. To keep the capital
at the present level the community must not spend more than
four million labour-years in present-time production.[1]

With the remaining six million labour-years the stock of

---

[1] Under this name (*Gegenwartsproduktion*) I mean to group, for the sake of
shortness, all those acts of production which agree in this, that the original productive powers which are put forth in these acts reach their goal, and turn out
consumption goods, within the same economic period. This applies to two kinds
of productive acts ; partly and principally to those of the final stages, the labour
required to transform the first circle of capital into consumption goods (*e.g.* agricultural labour, the labour of the miller, baker, shoemaker, tailor, etc.), partly
to industries where the production process is short, and can be carried through
from beginning to end within a single economic period.

capital, reduced by the separating off of the first year's circle, must be brought up in quantity and quality to its former level. This demands that the nine other yearly circles be brought each one step nearer maturity by the addition of the requisite labour, and that the tenth class, which is now non-existent, be new created. The amount of labour necessary for this may be exactly determined. The former second class, in which as yet only five million labour-years have been embodied, needs, in order to make it entirely equal in value to the former first class, an addition of 1 million labour-years.

The	3d class needs an addition of	1		"	"
"	4th	"	"	0·5	"	"
"	5th	"	"	0·5	"	"
"	6th	"	"	0·5	"	"
"	7th	"	"	0·5	"	"
"	8th	"	"	0·3	"	"
"	9th	"	"	0·4	"	"
"	10th	"	"	0·3	"	"

And the creation of a new 10th class requires the labour of 1 " "

In all 6 " "

It should be noted that it is not a matter of indifference at what point, in which particular circles, the six million labour-years are spent. If, for instance, they were to be spent in making intermediate products, but not according to the above distribution—say they were all spent in making intermediate products of the first circle, which would come to maturity in a year's time—the disadvantage would be two-fold : first, the production processes which had only got the length of intermediate products of the higher classes would be brought to a standstill ; and second, as we know, the shorter methods would be less productive. With six million labour-years invested in a one year's process, the present would hand over to the future the same number of productive powers indeed, but—what in the last resort is the important thing—these powers would, in virtue of their one year's process, be capable of producing only a smaller amount of products than the present has received for consumption from the past. The next year's production, therefore, would necessarily be reduced, and the stock of capital would not be maintained at its former level.

Again, if the present stock of capital is to be increased, it is evidently necessary that the community give up a portion of the consumption which it might have enjoyed—while still maintaining the stock at its former height;—that it withdraw a portion of the productive powers at its disposal from the service of the present; that it save and employ them for additional future production. Productive powers may be saved in various ways. (1) Other dispositions remaining unchanged, a smaller portion of the current productive powers—say three instead of four million labour-years—may be employed in immediate " present-time production." Or (2) the arrangements for saving may have been already made, and the total capital organised in such a way that the circle which is now passing over into the stage of full maturity contains a less quantity of capital, say five instead of six million labour-years. Inasmuch, then, as only five instead of six million labour-years are now required for the replacement of capital, there remains—if, as before, four out of the ten million labour-years which are the current productive endowment are spent in "present-time production"—one million over, available for the formation of new capital. Or (3) it is conceivable that, at the last moment, the disposition of the capital should be so altered that less passes into the stage of full maturity than was originally contemplated. It is a familiar fact that there are many goods which admit of being employed in a variety of ways. This often makes it possible to put back goods which have already attained full maturity, or which stand quite near to maturity, by several stages. Grain, for instance, instead of being ground for food purposes, may be stored for seed, or used in distilling; coal may heat the blast furnace instead of the domestic oven ; iron may build machinery instead of park railings; and so on. If, by thus disposing goods differently, the amount of capital which arrives at maturity becomes reduced from six to five million labour-years, there will, after four million labour-years have been expended in " present-time production," be one million labour-years free for the making of new capital.

All three methods, then,—of which, in practical life, the second is most common, and the first is least so,—agree in one essential point, that during the current year the produce of nine million labour-years only is consumed, while ten million labour-years come forward; that accordingly, in other words, one million labour-years of the current productive endowment are saved.[1]

Hitherto we have spoken of the formation of capital by a community as if in such a community there was one single economy, guided by one individual will. Of course this is not the case. It remains, therefore, for us to show how, in a community where industry is divided up and managed by many heads, the productive forces that conduce to the formation of capital are actually disposed, and to inquire whether, as we have maintained, these dispositions presuppose " saving." And since it is claimed, and not without reason, that universal truths should be proved to hold not only in the present and historical organisation, but in every social organisation, I propose in this inquiry to look both at the actual economic form, which is pre-eminently individualistic, and at that form which is at least conceivable, the socialistic. We may begin with the latter as being the easier from the standpoint of our present problem.

In a socialist state from which private capital and private undertaking were banished, and where the entire national production was organised by the state, the formation of capital, and the previous saving of productive powers necessary thereto, would be controlled officially. The method would

---

[1] If, during the current year, there should be introduced such improvements in the technique of production that the capital, which had taken six million labour-years to produce, could be fully replaced by an expenditure of five million labour-years, there would be a change in the figures of our illustration, but the principle would remain the same. It would now be possible to preserve the capital already in existence, even if five million labour-years were spent in present production, and if the produce of eleven million labour-years in all were spent in immediate consumption (see above, note to p. 104). But in any case the formation of new capital would require the renunciation of some portion of that immediate consumption which would be possible if it were only wished to preserve capital at the same level; in other words, would require that a portion of the "income," which might be consumed without diminishing the stock of capital, be not consumed but saved. Moreover, if technical improvements did not continue to be made, then, after some years—that is to say, when the capital produced according to the old methods of production was quite used up,—the old figures would come true again; capital would be kept at the same level if in any period the produce immediately consumed just corresponded to the productive powers which came forward anew in the same period.

simply be to put a considerable proportion of the national workers to very lengthy processes, whereby the making of capital, in the form of intermediate products, would be very great, and the amount of matured products in the future would be much increased.   Many workers, relatively speaking, would be put to mining, railway-building, regulation of rivers, machine-making, and the like, and few to wine-growing, silk-spinning, lace-making, beer-brewing, cloth-making, and the like.   The people would thus be compelled to save by pressure from above, inasmuch as, of the national production thus conducted by the state, in each year relatively few goods would be put at their disposal for immediate consumption—less, that is to say, than might be annually produced and consumed if the existing stock were merely to be maintained.   The productive powers left free would be invested in lengthy capitalist processes of production.

Somewhat more complicated, but still easy to grasp in principle, is the procedure in the individualistic organisation of society as we find it in the present day.   Here, in the first instance, it is the undertakers who decide how the productive powers, as they come forward annually, shall be employed, and they thus decide the direction which the national production takes.   But they do not decide it at their pleasure ; they follow impulses given by the prices of products.   Where lively demand promises a profitable price they extend their production, and curtail it in those kinds of goods where failing demand can no longer take off the supply, and the prices fall below a paying level.   Extension and contraction of supply continue till such time as production has adapted itself to the desire for the particular commodities.   In the last resort, therefore, it is not the undertakers who decide the direction of national production, but the consumers, the "public."   All depends on the effective desire they exert by means of their income.   The income of a people is, in the long-run, identical with the return of its production.   The circle that represents a year's income coincides, roughly,[1] with the circle that re-

---

[1] I have neither time nor desire to go into subtle distinctions here, although there is material enough for them.   Interesting investigations into the relation between national product and national income—although I cannot altogether agree with them—may be found in R. Meyer's book, pp. 5, 84.   See also the investigations of Lexis (which appeared while the present volume was passing

presents a year's return of its productive powers. If every individual in the community were to consume exactly his year's income in the form of consumption goods, there would arise a demand for consumption goods which, through the agency of prices, would induce the undertakers so to regulate production that, in each year, the return of a whole year's circle of productive powers would take the form of consumption goods. If ten million labour-years (and the corresponding uses of land) form the annual endowment of a people, and this people wishes to consume, and does consume, the whole of its income in the form of consumption goods, it is a necessity that the produce of the whole ten million labour-years (together with the corresponding uses of land) be changed each year into the form of consumption goods. In this case there is no productive power left to dispose of in increasing capital, and capital only remains as it was.

If, on the other hand, each individual consumes, on the average, only three-quarters of his income, and saves the rest, obviously the wish to buy, and the demand for, consumption goods will fall. Only three-fourths of the former consumption goods will find demand and sale. If the undertakers, however, were for some time to continue the old dispositions of production, and bring to market consumption goods to the amount of ten million labour-years, the over-supply would very soon press down the price, business would become unremunerative, and the pressure of loss would compel the undertakers to adapt their production to the changed circumstances of demand. They will now provide that, in one year, only the produce of seven and a half million labour-years is transformed into consumption goods (whether it be by the maturing of the first class, or by adding to "present-time production"[1]), and the two and a half millions which remain of the current year's endowment may and will be spent in the increasing of capital. I say "will be spent," for an economically advanced people does not hoard, but puts out what it saves—in the purchase of

through the press), entitled *Ueber gewisse Werthgesammtheiten und deren Beziehungen zum Geldwerth* (*Tübinger Zeitschrift*, forty-fourth year, part ii. p. 221), where also the yearly "consumption sum," "production sum," and "primary income sum" are treated as "quantitatively, approximately equal" amounts.

[1] The change of disposition will, as we have seen, be made essentially easier by the adaptability of many forms of capital to various uses.

valuable paper, in deposits in a bank or savings-bank, in loan securities, etc. In these ways the amount saved becomes part of productive credit; it increases the purchasing power of producers for productive purposes; it is thus the cause of an extra demand for means of production or intermediate products; and this, in the last resort, induces those who have the regulation of undertakings to invest the productive powers at their disposal in these intermediate products.

We see, therefore, as a fact, an intimate connection between saving and formation of capital. If no individual saves, the people, as a whole, cannot accumulate capital, because the great consumpt of consumption goods forces the producers, by the impulse of prices, so to employ the productive powers that, every year, the produce of a whole year's endowment is demanded and used up in the shape of consumption goods, and no productive powers are left free for the increasing of capital. But if individuals save, the altered demand, again through the impulse of prices, compels the undertakers to dispose of the productive powers differently; fewer powers are put, each year, at the service of the present, and thereby is increased the amount of those productive powers whose produce will be found in suspense as intermediate products; in other words, the economical capital will be increased with a view to an increased consumption in the future.

Now there is still a third possibility. Individuals may consume, on the average, more than their income; instead of saving they may waste their parent sum of wealth. According to our theory, this must lead to a diminution of the community's capital, and, as a fact, it does so. The steps of the process are as follows. By the prevailing extravagance more than a year's income of the community, and, therefore, more than the produce of one year's circle of productive powers, is demanded in the shape of consumption goods. Production, compelled by the impulse of prices, yields to the demand. For instance, the former disposition was that the first circle, with its six million labour-years, should mature during the current year, and that, of the ten million labour-years that form the current endowment, four millions should be spent in "present-time production," and the other six in replacing the capital consumed. Now we shall suppose that, through the extravagant manners of the citizens, the year's demand for consumption goods rises till it requires the produce of twelve million labour-years.   The undertakers will act in something like the following manner.   Of the current labour endowment they will invest, perhaps, not four but five million labour-years in present production, and, in correspondence with this, the amount devoted to the replacement of capital will shrink from six to five millions.   This will cover one million of the extra amount required.   At the same time, by differently disposing of such goods as allow of more than one employment, they will perhaps divert the produce of another million of labour-years from a more remote class into the first class, and thus add it to the consumption of the current year.   This will cover the second million of the extra demand.   The community now receives and consumes what it desires, the produce of twelve million labour-years in the form of consumption goods;[1] but it does so at the expense of the stock of capital, which is insufficiently replaced, and so diminished by two million labour-years.[2]

Possibly I have wasted too many words in proving a truth so obvious that no thinking man unskilled in science would ever doubt it.   Every child knows that a piece of capital, say a hammer, must be produced if it is to come into existence. And to every simple man it is obvious that no stock of capital can be made, or can increase, if men regularly consume their whole available income ; if, in other words, they do not save. It was reserved for the sharp and subtle wits of learned theorists to suggest the first doubt about it.   This, however, it would have been difficult to do if, instead of dogmatising on the formation of capital, they had attempted to give a complete and faithful representation of the process by which capital is formed.   Here lies the entire, but almost the only, difficulty of these and many other economical doctrines ; and this suggests, I might add, the reason why so many abstract

[1] Viz. six million from the original provision of the first circle, one million diverted and added to that by changed disposition, and five millions from the current labour endowment.

[2] The stock originally embraced the return of thirty million labour-years ; it now gives seven millions to the consumption of the current year, and it receives only five millions to replace them, whereby it falls from thirty to twenty-eight million labour-years.

deductions are discredited and fail of result. It is not the deductive method that deserves the distrust, but the persons who misapply it. Vulgar errors in thought, indeed, are quite exceptional among capable thinkers; and here the fault lies mostly in this, that the economists in question could not put a sufficiently clear and life-like picture before their minds of the circumstances and processes which they introduced into their deductive arguments as assumptions, or, at least, did not keep it persistently enough before them through all stages of the deduction. Hence, losing touch with life, they began to make deductions, not from truth of facts, but from words of formulas, and so fell without knowing it into the emptiest dialectic. It is because so many economists, as it seems to me, have made this mistake, that I risk being tedious rather than being suspected of sophistry.

CHAPTER VI

POSSIBLE OBJECTIONS

IT is perhaps advisable to supplement our positive statement by a brief critical consideration of the most important objections that might be urged. Two of these appear to me particularly worth noticing. The first is, that the majority of goods which constitute capital are, by nature, quite unfitted to immediate consumption. There is, therefore, no sacrifice in withdrawing them from a use which they could never serve. Indeed, it is ridiculous to speak of the "non-consumption" of steam-engines and land improvements, of roofing tiles and bars of metal, as an act of saving or abstinence.[1]

To me this seems a somewhat cheap, but still perfectly good, argument against those who formulate the theory of saving superficially or falsely. But, as against the essence of the theory, it proves nothing. If any one is stupid enough to interpret the theory of saving as meaning that finished capital. in its form as concrete capital, must be "saved," he must submit to the retort that man cannot eat iron machines.[2] But this is not at all the meaning of any thoughtful representative of the theory. What is maintained is only that, without saving, capital cannot be made or increased; that saving is as indispensable a condition of the formation of capital as is labour. And this is literally correct. The machines themselves have

---

[1] This is very strongly put by the Socialist writers, as, *e.g.*, Lassalle (*Kapital und Arbeit*, p. 69); Rodbertus (*Das Kapital*, p. 271). In a somewhat diluted form the same doctrine appears in Wagner (*Grundlegung*, second edition, p. 600), who makes a distinction between goods in which the peculiarities of capital are inherent, and those in which they are not. The former are not, at least "directly," objects of saving. Similarly Kleinwächter (Schönberg's *Handbuch*, first edition, p. 173).   [2] Lassalle.

not been saved, but built. But in order to build them, men had previously to withdraw the productive powers necessary to building them from the service of the present; they had, therefore, in the strictest sense of the term, to save them.[1]

It may serve towards the settling of this controversy to remark that the idea of sacrifice, of renunciation, and thus of moral desert, need not be associated with the conception of saving.[2] There *may* be sacrifice in saving, and it *may* be praiseworthy, but not at all necessarily. A man with a small income will, of course, feel it a sensible privation, and it will require strong self-denial in him to lay past anything; while one who has an income of £100,000, and is content to consume one half of it, has little claim to be considered a hero of asceticism because he saves the other half as capital. It is simply the *fact* of a saving that is indispensable to the formation of capital; whether there is sacrifice and moral desert in it or not is all the same to the result. And it follows from this that the theoretical truth, that "saving" is necessary to the formation of capital, cannot and must not be used to justify, either morally or socio-politically, all and every taking of

---

[1] In the second edition of Schönberg's *Handbuch* (p. 214) Kleinwächter comes a long way nearer our conception in assenting to it, as regards at least one of the chief forms of capital—tools of production. He allows that the making of such tools "always involves, to a certain extent, the renunciation of an immediate enjoyment," because the materials which are made use of in making the tools of production might have been employed in making some kind of consumption goods; and thus there is no reason for objecting to call such a renunciation of enjoyment by the name of Saving. But it is different, he says, with the materials of production. Such things as raw wool, stone, and lime, etc., could not in any way be objects of direct consumption, and so could not be saved; they must be looked on, therefore, economically as products of labour only, and not as the result of saving. In this Kleinwächter is not logical. As regards the tools of production he, quite correctly, does not consider whether the finished tools themselves might have been consumed, but whether, by the instruments from which the tools were made, any consumption good might have been made; and because this is the case he answers the question as to saving in the affirmative. But if he had kept to this line of thought as regards the materials of production, he must have seen that, by means of the same productive powers as man uses to quarry stone, to build a house, or obtain lime for mortar, he might have made himself goods for immediate consumption,—*e.g.* hunted wild animals or caught fish,—and that here, consequently, on exactly the same grounds and in exactly the same way as in the case of tools, saving does come into the question.

[2] See above, p. 102.

interest. This is another instance of that confusing of the theoretical with the socio-political problem of interest which I adverted to in another place[1] as having done so much harm. One side mixed up the theoretical doctrine that the formation of capital must be preceded by saving, with the moral judgment that interest is justified as the " reward of abstinence," and the other side, which saw, quite correctly, that interest could not be justified in such general terms, was misled, by the same confusion of the problems, into denying not only the false socio-political deduction but the true theoretical premiss.

If these two problems are kept distinct it will help us to give both parties their due. To Rodbertus and Lassalle we may grant at once that saving need not be moral heroism, and therefore is no sufficient socio-political justification of interest ; but we must stand for the recognition of the theoretical truth that the fact of saving is in any case required to the formation of capital.

A second objection lays emphasis on the fact that, for a man to be able to accumulate capital, he must *acquire more* than he uses, and draws the conclusion that it is essentially the productivity of labour—industriousness and not abstinence —to which the formation of capital is due. Thus Rodbertus says, in so many words, that if, in the beginnings of economic development, an " isolated worker has no time to make a tool because he must always live from hand to mouth," the blame lies simply in the productivity of labour being too small. If, later, this productivity increases so much that, say, eight hours' labour is sufficient to produce the day's maintenance, then " from the labour time, which up till now he had to devote entirely to make what was absolutely necessary, he has a portion over for other labour, and it is this spare labour which he is now able to devote to the making of a tool." And from this quite correct consideration Rodbertus draws the conclusion that it is *only* the increasing of the productivity of labour, and *not saving*, which makes the existence of such a primary capital possible.[2] And still more briefly and strongly does Klein-wächter give expression to the same idea when he says : " He who transfers a portion, say a half, of his revenue to the bank is merely industrious. He might, for instance, by a five hours'

---

[1] See *Capital and Interest*, p. 3.   [2] *Das Kapital*, p. 242.

day of labour earn his bare maintenance, and devote, say, every afternoon to his recreation or enjoyment; instead of which the man works ten hours a day, and regularly carries what he earns in the afternoon to the savings-bank." [1]

1 think this objection is very easily met. It is simply not correct to say that the man is " merely industrious." He is industrious and saving. If he were simply industrious he would. every day, spend the produce of the afternoon's labour, along with the produce of the forenoon's labour, in immediate enjoyment of life. That he does not do so is because he is saving as well. I freely admit that greater industriousness, causing a return far exceeding necessary require- ments, and, similarly, greater productivity of labour, very much facilitate saving, just as I admit also that, without acquisition, saving, as well as formation of capital, is absolutely impossible. But I must as emphatically claim recognition of the fact that the greatest acquisition could not lead to the formation of capital if a portion of it were not withdrawn from present use and " saved." Production and Saving form two equally indispensable conditions of the formation of capital, and it is only dialectical one-sidedness—which, unfortunately, has already played much too great a part in the doctrine of capital—that could deny the co-operation of either of them. [2]

But does not this involve me in contradiction with the proposition so earnestly contended for in last chapter, that all goods (and consequently all capital) proceed from wo elements, of which saving is not one, viz. from nature and labour ? [3] Certainly it does not. It is not my intention to do as Senior

---

[1] Kleinwächter, in Schönberg's *Handbuch*, second edition, p. 215.

[2] A very striking illustration of these words may be found in the already-mentioned utterances of Rodbertus on the subject. On p. 242, from the fact that, if the productivity of capital is too small, there can be no saving and no forma- tion of capital, he contents himself with drawing the quite correct conclusion that "necessarily some other element besides saving must intervene." Thus he ascribes to saving its proper place, as not sufficient by itself, but, all the same, as a factor of the formation of capital. It is only on p. 243 that the fact of a certain degree of productivity of labour being indispensable is dialectically changed into the statement that *only* the increase of productivity, and *not* saving, makes the formation of capital possible.

[3] A similar objection was urged by the old economist Lauderdale against the Saving theory, *Inquiry*, pp. 207, 272.

did,[1] and try to make Saving a third factor in production along with Nature and Labour. It does not stand *beside* these factors, but behind them. It does not share with them in the work of production in such a way that any part of the same is due to it solely and peculiarly ; it only effects that the productive powers, nature and labour, which in any case must do the *whole* work of production, are directed straight to this and no other goal—the production of capital and not of consumption goods. In a word, it has its place, not among the *means* of production, but among the *motives* of production— the motives which decide the *direction* of production. The proposition, then, that nature and labour are the only true productive powers, can stand perfectly well beside the wider assertion, that, if capital is to come into existence at all, there must, first, be certain intellectual dispositions through which renunciation is made of a portion of the immediate consumption that is otherwise possible ; in other words, there must be " Saving."

Saving, it is objected again, is a " non-consumption "— something purely negative ; and a pure negation can bring forth nothing.[2] To my mind there is more dialectic than truth in this argument. Is it quite correct to say that saving is something purely negative ? How comes it, then, that, although nothing is easier than a " pure not-doing," so many people feel saving an uncommonly difficult and disagreeable thing ? In truth, saving is a mental business ; and often, indeed, though

---

[1] *Political Economy*, third edition, p. 57, where three great agents or in-struments of production are distinguished — Labour, Natural Agents, and Abstinence.

[2] Marx, *Das Kapital*, second edition, i. p. 619, in note (English translation, p. 608) : "It has never occurred to the vulgar economist to make the simple reflection, that every human action may be viewed as 'abstinence' from its opposite. Eating is abstinence from fasting, walking abstinence from standing still, working abstinence from idling, idling abstinence from working, etc. These gentlemen would do well to ponder, once in a way, over Spinoza's *Determinatio est Negatio*." Gide, *Principes d'Éc. Pol.* p. 168 : "Un act purement négatif, une abstention ne saurait produire quoi que ce soit. . . . Sans doute on peut dire que si ces richesses avaient été consommées au fur, et à mesure qu'elles ont pris naissance, elles n'éxisteraient pas à cette heure, et qu'en conséquence l'épargne les a fait naître une seconde fois. Mais à ce compte, il faudrait dire qu'on produit une chose toutes les fois qu'on s'abstient d'y toucher et la non destruction devrait être classée parmi les causes de la production, ce qui serait une singulière logique."

not always, a very troublesome mental business, preceded by long deliberation and conflict between contending motives. This, of course, does not constitute an act of production, and the representatives of the above dialectical objection are, in the end, quite right in raising it as an argument against those theorists who would dignify saving by the name of a third factor in production. But, indeed, simply mental as saving may be, it is sufficient to effectually fill the rôle which we have assigned to it in the formation of capital, viz. exerting an influence on the direction of production.

For the rest, whether it be a " pure negation " or not, we can, in no case, allow dialectical considerations to interfere with establishing important scientific facts. And it is an important scientific fact, which must be reiterated all the more emphatically that it has been disputed, that the progress of capital stands in a causal relation with the extension of the immediate claims put forward by individuals and peoples. Whatever body—be it an individual or a people—extends the claims of the moment so far as to exhaust, during the current period, the entire amount of consumption goods which its income makes possible for the current period, can neither make new nor increase old capital ; and this fact finds accurate and straightforward expression in the proposition that saving is an indispensable condition of the formation of capital.[1]

Suppose now that we have succeeded, after considerable trouble, in establishing the proposition that capital comes into existence through saving and devotion to production of what is saved, we have still got but half the answer to our inquiry as to the formation of capital. We have now to face the further question : On what does it depend that people can, will, and actually do save and produce intermediate products ? Strictly speaking, this second question is the more important of the two ; it points to the impelling and working forces in the formation of capital, while all that has preceded has merely laid down the external forms of the process.

[1] I will not, *a priori*, deny that possibly one might contrive to hunt up some subtle examples where capital (particularly social capital) comes into existence without saving properly so called. But all the more strongly do I hold by my proposition that, as regards the great mass of the economic formation of capital, saving, in the way I have indicated, has its place.

The most general answer, but still, it must be confessed, insufficient for all its generality, runs thus : what people look to in economic life is the Value of goods.   Here we touch a subject which is too important and too difficult to be spoken of merely in passing.   To obtain the basis for the principal part of our work—the explanation of interest—we require to go into the theory of value.   I shall, therefore, leave the theory of the formation of capital at this stage, returning to it shortly in the last chapter, where we shall give it the logical conclusion that it still lacks.

BOOK III

VALUE

CHAPTER I

THE TWO CONCEPTIONS OF VALUE [1]

In the science of Political Economy, as in ordinary speech, two
very distinct things have usually been classed together under
the one name of Value. From the first it could scarcely escape
notice that there was a difference between them, but the full
extent of the difference was certainly underrated. Instead of
being recognised as phenomena belonging to entirely distinct
categories of thought, they were, quite falsely, represented as
members of one and the same group of phenomena, and, under
the not very felicitous names of Use Value and Exchange
Value, they were assumed to be sub-species of one universal

---

[1] My views on the subject of Value have already been published at length
in another place (*Grundzüge der Theorie des Wirthschaftlichen Güterwerths*, in
Conrad's *Jahrbücher für Nationalökonomie und Statistik*, vol. xiii. 1886, pp.
1-86 and 477-541). Since then I have seen no reason to change them. What I
have now to say on the same subject can, therefore, offer but few new features.
On the whole, what follows is an extract from my former work adapted to the
requirements of the theory of capital, and, in the composition of it, I have gone
on principles suggested by the nature of my present task. Those fundamental
ideas on which the understanding of the whole depends, and those lines of thought
with which the theory of capital is specially connected, I have taken in all their
detail from my other book ; and, as a simple change of form would have been as
troublesome as it was useless, I have taken them, for the most part, without
change. I have omitted, on the other hand, all those explications, demonstrations, and so on, which were important for the Value theory, but seemed not
altogether indispensable for the understanding of the theory of Capital. In place
of these I have added a good deal of matter in which I have taken advantage of
the newest literature on the subject, and have tried to give a still clearer formulation to several ideas, and, particularly, to develop with more exactitude special
points where the value theory comes into more intimate connection with the
theory of capital. The most important additions occur in chapter vii. of the
present book, and at the end of chapter v. and in chapter vii. of the next book.
Readers who are interested in the theory of value and price for its own sake, I
should ask to consult the statement in Conrad's *Jahrbücher*, which is much more
complete, and which I tried to make easier by numerous references.

conception of Value, and distinguished from each other as such. This distinction once made, however, the so-called Use Value was almost entirely dropped out of sight. Economists took no trouble to inquire any deeper into its nature, nor did they make any use of it in further investigations. They simply catalogued it, as it were, among the conceptions of political economy, and left it lying in a corner of their systems like a stone for which there was no use. It is only of very recent date that economical investigation has discovered in this "stone rejected of the builders" the basis and support of one of the most important conceptions of economics, and has awaked to the fact that on it depends a group of most notable laws—laws with consequences reaching far beyond the boundaries of the theory of value, and laws to which almost every branch of economic theory must go back for its root and spring.

But, first of all, it is important that we give right names to those things which tradition has handed down to us under the inadequate designations of Use Value and Exchange Value. The two groups of phenomena, to both of which popular usage has given the ambiguous name "Value," we shall distinguish as value in the Subjective and value in the Objective sense.[1]

Value in the Subjective sense is the importance which a good, or a complex of goods, possesses with regard to the wellbeing of a subject. In this sense I should say of any particular good that it was valuable to me, if I recognised that my wellbeing was so associated with it that the possession of it satisfied some want, secured me a gratification or a feeling of pleasure which I should not have had without it, or saved me from a pain which, otherwise, I should have had to endure. In this case the existence of the good means my gain, the absence of it my loss, in wellbeing: to me it is a matter of importance, for me it has value.

By Objective value, on the other hand, is meant the Power or Capacity of a good to procure some one objective result. In this sense there are as many kinds of value as there are external results with which man may be connected. There is a nutritive

---

[1] I frankly confess that I would gladly exchange these pedantic and clumsy expressions for terms more euphonious and popular, if they could be got to indicate the opposition referred to with even approximate correctness. But I have not been able to find such expressions. The words Use Value and Exchange Value are not suitable at all, because, as we shall see, there is a Subjective exchange value.

value of food, a heating value of wood and coal, a fertilising
value of manures, a blasting value of explosives, and so on.   In
any expressions of this kind all reference to the wellbeing or
illbeing of a subject is excluded from the conception of value.
If we affirm that beech has a superior heating value over pine,
we only express the purely objective and, as it were, mechanical
fact that with a definite weight of beech a greater amount of
heat can be raised than with the same weight of pine.   In the
above connections, then, instead of the word "Value" we use,
as entirely synonymous with it, the expressions "Power" or
"Capacity"—expressions which themselves suggest a purely
objective relation.   Instead of "nutritive value," "heat value,"
"explosive value," we use "nutritive power" or "nutritive
capacity," "heating power," "explosive power," and so on, as
meaning exactly the same thing.

The varieties of Objective value just mentioned by way of
illustration do not, however, belong to economical but to purely
technical relations; and, however frequently they are referred
to in economical text-books, they do not properly belong to
political economy at all.   It does not fall within the province
of our science to expound the heating value of wood, nor, in
explaining other economical phenomena, has it occasion to lay
stress on this heating value any more than it does on any other
physical or technical fact.   I have given these illustrations
purely as illustrations, with the intention of putting in clearer
relief the very intimately related nature with the above of that
branch of objective values which, of course, has the greatest
possible importance for political economy, namely, the objective
Exchange value of goods.   By this expression I mean the
objective worth of goods in exchange; or, in other words, the
possibility of obtaining in exchange for them a quantity of
other economical goods, this possibility being looked upon as
a power or a property of the former goods.   In this sense we
say that a horse is worth £50, or a house worth £1000, if, in
exchange for these, we can obtain, respectively, £50 or £1000.

Here, again, it must be noted that, as in the kindred
expressions heating value and the like, we say nothing at all
as to the influence which goods may exert on the wellbeing of
any subject whatever; we simply indicate the objective relation
that for a particular good a certain amount of other goods may

be had in exchange. In this case also the characteristic phenomenon recurs, that the word "Value" can be, quite adequately, replaced by the word "Power," and is, indeed, so replaced in popular speech. Besides the expression "value in exchange" English economists use, quite indifferently, the expression "purchasing power," and we Germans are beginning in the same way to put in general use the term *Tauschkraft.*

The economical theory of value has, then, the double task of interpreting, on the one hand, the laws of Subjective Value, and, on the other, the laws of Objective Exchange Value, as from the economic point of view by far the most important branch of objective value. The first part of this task we shall take up in the present book, the second in the following book dealing with the theory of Price. It is true that the two conceptions, "Price" and "Exchange Value," are by no means identical. Exchange Value is the capacity of a good to obtain in exchange a quantity of other goods. Price is that other quantity of goods. But the laws of these two coincide. So far as the law of price explains that a good actually obtains such and such a price, and why it obtains it, it affords at the same time the explanation that the good is *capable,* and why it is capable, of obtaining a definite price. The law of Price, in fact, contains the law of Exchange Value.[1]

[1] The foundations of the modern value theory have been laid by three writers whose work is in substantial agreement—Carl Menger, Jevons, and Walras. Of these, in clearness and completeness, Menger's statement takes the first place. Twenty years before his time, several of the most weighty and fundamental ideas had been already propounded by Gossen in his remarkable book, *Entwicklung der Gesetze des menschlichen Verkehrs und der daraus fliessenden Regeln für menschliches Handeln,* Brunswick, 1854. Like the book itself, these ideas sank into complete but undeserved oblivion, and had to be rediscovered by the economists just mentioned. That this was done almost simultaneously by three different men, belonging to three different nations, and quite independently of each other, is a very remarkable coincidence, and is, at the same time, no small guarantee for the correctness of the principles on which all three were certainly agreed, although in thoroughness their statement of them was unequal. Since then these principles have had a notable development, and received wide acceptance. Not long ago, in the preface to his *Theorie de la Monnaie* (Lausanne, 1886), Walras could give an imposing list of writers as adherents of the new theory. Since then we may add the name of E. Sax (*Grundlegung der theoretischen Staatswirthschaft,* Vienna, 1887, p. 250),—with whom, however, I cannot agree in many particulars, particularly in those where he tries to establish original ideas that are not in harmony with those of his predecessors ; and that of R. Meyer (*Das Wesen des Einkommens,* Berlin, 1887).

CHAPTER II

ALL goods without exception—indeed according to the very conception of them as "good"—possess a certain relation to human wellbeing. There are, however, two essentially distinct grades of this relation. A good belongs to the lower grade when it possesses the general *capacity* to subserve human weal. The higher grade, on the other hand, demands that a good should be more than merely a sufficient cause; it must be an indispensable *condition* of human wellbeing—a condition of such a kind that some gratification stands or falls with the having or wanting of the good. In the expressive vocabulary of everyday life we find a separate designation for these grades. The lower is called Usefulness, the higher Value. This distinction, already recognised in common speech, we must try to make as clear and well-marked as its fundamental importance for the whole theory of value deserves.

A man dwells beside a bubbling spring of water. He has filled his cup, and the spring goes on pouring out enough to fill a hundred other cups every minute. Another man is travelling in the desert. A long day's journey over glowing sand still divides him from the nearest oasis, and he has come to his last cup of water. What is the relation in each case between the cup of water and the wellbeing of its owner?

A single glance shows us that the relation is very dissimilar; but wherein lies the difference? Simply that, in the former case, we have only the lower grade of the relation we call wellbeing, that of usefulness; in the latter case we have the higher grade as well. In the first case, just as in the d, the cup of water is useful, that is, capable of satisfying int, and, moreover, in exactly the same degree; for evidently the refreshing qualities of the water—the qualities on which its capacity to quench thirst is based, such as coolness, taste, etc.—are not in the least degree weakened by the fact that other cups of water chance to possess similar properties; nor, in the second case, are these refreshing qualities in the least augmented by the accidental circumstance that there is no other water near. On the other hand, the two cases become essentially distinct when considered with reference to the second grade. Looking at the former case we must say that the possession of tne cup of water does not provide the man with one single satisfaction more, nor its loss with one satisfaction less, than he could have obtained without it. If he has that particular cup of water he can quench his thirst with it; if he has not that cup —well, he can quench his thirst quite as well with one of the hundred others which the spring puts freely at his disposal every minute of the day. If he likes, therefore, he may make that one cup the *cause* of his satisfaction by quenching his thirst with it; an *indispensable condition* of his satisfaction it cannot be; for his wellbeing it is dispensable, unimportant, indifferent.

It is quite otherwise in the second case. Here we must say that, if our traveller had not that one last cup, he could not quench his thirst; he must bear its pangs unassuaged, perhaps even succumb to them. In the cup of water then, in this case, we see not merely a sufficient cause, but the indispensable condition, the *sine qua non* of human wellbeing. Here it is of consequence, even of urgency; it possesses importance for his wellbeing.

Now it is not too much to say that the distinction here drawn is one of the most fruitful and fundamental in the whole range of our science. It does not owe its existence to the microscope nor to any hair-splitting distinctions of the logician. It has its life in the world of men, who know it and use it and take it as guide for their common attitude towards the world of goods, not only as regards the intellectual estimate they apply to these goods, but as regards their actual business transactions. About goods which are only useful the practical business man is careless and indifferent. The academic knowledge that a good may be " of use " cannot evoke any efficient interest in the good, in face of the other knowledge that the same use may be obtained without it. Such goods are practically naught as regards our wellbeing, and we treat them as such; we are not put about when we lose them, and we make no effort to gain them.   Who would fret at, or make an effort to prevent, the spilling of a cup of water at the spring, or the escape of a cubic foot of atmospheric air ?   Where, on the other hand, the sharpened glance of the economic man recognises that some satisfaction, wellbeing, gratification, is connected with a particular good, there the effective interest which we take in our own wellbeing is transferred to the good which we recognise as its condition ; we see and value our own welfare in it; we recognise its importance for us as value; and finally, we develop an anxiety, proportioned to the greatness of that importance, to acquire and hold the good.

Thus, formally defined, value is the importance which a good or complex of goods possesses with respect to the wellbeing of a subject.   Any addition to this definition, regarding the kind and reason of the importance, is, strictly speaking, not necessary, since goods can only have an effective importance for human wellbeing in one way, viz. by being the indispensable condition, the *sine qua non*, of some one utility which subserves it.   In view of the fact, however, that in other definitions of value it is very often translated as an " importance," while the importance spoken of rests, erroneously, on a simple *capability* of utility, or, not less erroneously, on the necessity of expenditure of costs, or the like,[1] we shall define it, unambiguously and exactly, as : That importance which goods or complexes of goods acquire, as the recognised condition of a utility which makes for the wellbeing of a subject, and would not be obtained without them.

All goods have usefulness, but all goods have not value. For the emergence of value there must be scarcity as well as usefulness—not absolute scarcity, but scarcity relative to the demand for the particular class of goods.   To put it more

---

[1] See Conrad's *Jahrbücher*, vol. xiii. p. 11.

exactly : goods acquire value when the whole available stock of them is not sufficient to cover the wants depending on them for satisfaction, or when the stock would not be sufficient without these particular goods.   On the other hand, those goods remain valueless which are offered in such superfluity that all the wants which they are fitted to satisfy are completely supplied, and when, beyond that, there is a surplus which can find no further employment in the satisfaction of want, and which, at the same time, is large enough to spare the goods or quantities of goods that we are valuing without imperilling the satisfaction of any one want.

After what has been said as to the nature of value, it should not be very difficult to prove these propositions.   When the supply of goods is not sufficient, and some of the wants which they are adapted to satisfy must remain unsatisfied, it is clear that the loss of even a single good involves the loss of a possible satisfaction, while the addition of a single good involves the acquisition of a satisfaction otherwise impossible ; and it is clear, consequently, that some gratification or form of wellbeing depends on the existence of that good.   Conversely, it is quite as clear that, if goods of any class are to be had in superfluity, there is no harm done if one of the goods be lost— since it can be immediately replaced from the superfluous stock ; nor any utility got if another such good be added— since it cannot be employed in any useful way.   Suppose, for instance, that a peasant requires ten gallons of water per day, and no more, for general purposes—say, for his own drinking, for that of his family and servants, for watering his cattle, for cleansing, flushing, etc.—and suppose that the only spring within reach supplies no more than eight gallons a day.   It is quite evident that he cannot spare one single gallon from his water-supply without suffering, to a more or less sensible extent, as regards the wants and aims of his economy.   Every gallon in this case is the condition of a definite sphere of usefulness. Even if the spring supplied just ten gallons this would still be true.   But if the spring supplied twenty gallons per day, it is just as obvious that the loss of one gallon would not do the slightest injury to our peasant.   He can only employ ten gallons usefully, and he must let the other ten gallons flow away unused.   If one gallon is spilled it is replaced from the overflow, and the only effect is that now the unusable surplus is reduced from ten gallons to nine.

Now as it is the insufficient, or the barely sufficient, goods that are the objects of economical care —the goods we "economise" or endeavour to acquire and keep,—while such goods as are to be had in superfluity are free to everybody, we may express the above propositions shortly in the following form: All economical goods have value; all free goods are valueless.[1] In any case it must steadily be borne in mind that it is only relations of *quantity* that decide whether any particular good is merely *capable* of use, or is also the *condition* of a utility for us.[2]

[1] Some very interesting phenomena of value may, in certain circumstances, be exhibited by free goods also. For the explanation of this see my *Grundzüge*, p. 15.

[2] Those numerous writers of whom Scharling is the latest instance (Conrad's *Jahrbücher*, vol. xvi. pp. 417 and 513, and particularly 424, 430, 551), who say that the distinguishing criterion of "economical" and "valuable" goods is difficulty of attainment, the necessity of expending labour, and the like, are giving a secondary ground of definition instead of the really decisive and primary one. It is only when and because we are suffering, or fear to suffer, loss of satisfaction from insufficient supply of goods that we decide, generally speaking, to submit to the hardships of acquiring them, to labour, and so on. Labour and hardship could not by themselves confer an economical character on goods were it not that, for the most part, another circumstance, and that the really decisive one, is also present; in other words, that those kinds of goods, which are difficult or troublesome to obtain, are, at the same time, the goods that remain scarce. That, however, it is not the difficulty but the scarcity that decides is vividly shown in those cases—not, I grant, very common—where the technical circumstances are of such a nature that the good can be got only, indeed, by conquering difficulties, but then in superfluous amount. When the peasant obtains good drinking water, *e.g.*, by bringing it along a pipe to a house, it may occasion him a permanent expenditure of labour and costs for construction, upkeep, and management of the water-supply. But if this brings the water in greater quantity than he requires, it will not occur to the peasant, in spite of the labour, that he must "economise" the water.

CHAPTER III

THE AMOUNT OF VALUE

IN asking what is the principle that regulates the amount of value, we pass to a sphere where lies the chief task of a theory of value, and where at the same time lie its greatest difficulties. These difficulties are the result of a peculiar coincidence of circumstances. From one point of view the true principle almost suggests itself. If the value of a good is its importance to human wellbeing, and if this "importance" means that some portion of our wellbeing is dependent on our having the good, it is clear that the amount of the good's value must be determined by the amount of wellbeing which depends on it. Goods will have high value if our wellbeing depends on them to any important extent, low value if it does not.

But from another point of view, there are certain facts in the economical world which seem to give the lie to this very simple and natural explanation. Everybody knows that, in practical economic life, precious stones possess a high value, while bread and iron have a moderate value, and air and water usually no value at all. Now everybody knows that without air and water we simply could not exist, and that the uses of bread and iron are extremely important, while precious stones, for the most part, only satisfy the love of ornament, and have, accordingly, a very inferior importance for human wellbeing. It would appear, then, that one who holds fast by the principle that the amount of a good's value is determined by the importance of the services which it may render to human wellbeing, must expect to find in precious stones a low value, in bread and iron a high value, and in water and light the very highest value. But facts show that exactly the opposite of this is the case.

This startling phenomenon has been a veritable rock of offence in the theory of value. The highest utility accompanied by the smallest value is a strange paradox. It is true that, in confusing Usefulness and Use Value, economists did not apprehend and describe the state of the case quite exactly. When they falsely ascribed to the iron a high " use value " and to the diamond a low " use value," the only reason for surprise was that the " exchange value " of these goods went so entirely in the opposite direction. But this was only to change the name of the opposition, not to take away any of its sharpness. There were plenty of attempts to bridge the fatal contradiction by involved explanations, but these were unsuccessful ; and so it happens that, from Adam Smith's time to our own, innumerable theorists have despaired of finding the nature and measure of value in any relation to human wellbeing, and have fallen back upon quite foreign and often wonderful lines of explanation, such as labour or labour time, costs of production, resistance of nature to man, and the like. But, unable to get rid of the feeling that the value of goods must have something to do with utility and human wellbeing, they put down the want of harmony between the utility and the value of goods as a rare and perplexing contradiction, a *contradiction économique.*

In what follows I mean to prove that the older theory had no need to abandon the most natural explanation. The measure of the utility which depends on a good is, actually and everywhere, the measure of value for that good. To prove this nothing more is necessary than a dispassionate but keen casuistical investigation into the question, What is the gain to our wellbeing that, in any given circumstances, depends on a good ? I say deliberately " casuistical " investigation ; for the entire theory of subjective value is, properly, nothing else than a system of casuistry, determining when, under what circumstances, and how far our wellbeing *is* dependent upon any particular good. It is very remarkable that the ordinary man in everyday life is constantly making casuistic distinctions of this kind, and making them with great certainty. He seldom makes a mistake, and he never makes a mistake in the principle. He may, of course, ascribe a trifling value to a diamond if he mistakes it for a glass bead. But the theoretical consideration—which is quite irrelevant here—that without water the human race could not continue in life, would never lead him to the casuistical conclusion that every gallon of water which flows from the village spring is a good of priceless value, or worth thousands of pounds. Our task, then, is to hold the mirror up to those casuistical distinctions which men make in the ordinary affairs of life, and to bring those laws, which the ordinary man instinctively handles with certainty, to clear and conscious presentation.

What human wellbeing may gain from a good, and thus the advantage which is dependent on a good, is, in most cases,[1] the satisfaction of a want. The casuistical consideration that really determines how far a person's wellbeing depends upon a particular good is found in the answer to two questions: first, *which*, among two or more wants, depends on it? and, second, what is the *urgency* of the dependent want or of its satisfaction?

For convenience we shall take the second question first, and answer it in the present chapter. It is a familiar fact that our wants vary very greatly in importance. We are accustomed to rank them according to the seriousness of the consequences which their non-satisfaction has on our wellbeing. Thus we attach the greatest weight to those wants the non-satisfaction of which would be followed by death. Next to these we place wants the non-satisfaction of which would result in some serious permanent injury to our health, honour, or happiness. Below these again come such wants as expose us to more temporary injuries, pain, or deprivations. Finally, we put in the very lowest class those wants the non-satisfaction of which costs us nothing more than a very slight unpleasantness, or the deprivation of some quite insignificant pleasure. Arranging our wants according to these characteristics we obtain a regularly graduated scale of wants. Of course as differences of bodily and mental disposition, culture, and so on, result in very marked differences of wants, this scale will come out very different for different individuals, and even for the same individual at different times. All the same, every practical man whose means are limited must have a scale

---

[1] On certain comparatively rare exceptions see Conrad's *Jahrbücher*, vol. xiii. p. 42.

more or less clearly before his mind if he would make a choice
among these wants, and even theorists have often had occasion
to sketch such a scale from the " objective " standpoint of
impartial scientific consideration.

So far everything would be simple and certain were it
not that there is an ambiguity when we speak of graduation
or ranking of wants. We may mean by these terms either
the graduation of wants as *kinds* of wants, or the graduation
of *degrees* of wants, the concrete individual feelings of want ;
and these two are essentially different, even divergent.   If
we compare kinds of wants, looked at as a whole, according
to their importance for human wellbeing, there is no doubt
whatever that to the needs of subsistence would be allotted
the first rank, to the needs of housing and clothing a rank
not much inferior, to the wants satisfied by tobacco, spirituous
liquors, music, etc., a very much less important place, while
the wants of ornament and the like would have a very insignificant rank indeed.

Now the graduation of *concrete* feelings of want is essentially different from this.   Within one and the same kind of
want the feeling of want is not always uniform, not always
equally strong.   Every feeling of hunger is not equally
intense, and every satisfaction of hunger is not equally perfect.   In the class of " needs of subsistence," for instance,
the concrete want of a man who has not eaten a morsel for
eight days is infinitely more urgent than that of another man
who has already got through two courses of his ordinary dinner,
and is meditating whether he should have a third.   In
the graduation of concrete wants we have to deal with an
entirely different state of affairs, and with a much greater
variation.   In the scale of *kinds* of wants the " needs of subsistence " came far and away before the desire for tobacco, for
liquor, for ornament, etc.   In the scale of concrete wants,
wants belonging to the most various kinds cross and intersect
each other.   It is true that, even here, the most important
concrete wants in the most important classes of wants stand
at the top of the scale ; but the less important concrete wants
of these classes are frequently overpassed by concrete wants
of much inferior classes—the bottom members of the highest
class, perhaps, overpassed by the top member of the lowest

It is very much the same as if a geographer were one ,e to arrange the Alps, Pyrenees, and Harz by their height s mountain ranges, and another time were to arrange their single summits. As ranges the Alps would, of course, come before the Pyrenees, and the Pyrenees before the Harz. But, in comparing individual heights, a great many of the Alpine summits would take rank below individual peaks of the Pyrenees, some even below hills in the insignificant Harz.

And now the question is, When goods have to be valued, by which scale shall we measure the importance of the wants they subserve—the scale of kinds or the scale of concrete wants? When the older theory came to this dividing of the ways—the very first opportunity offered it of making a mistake—it chose the wrong way. It adopted the scale of kinds. On this scale the class "Needs of Subsistence" occupies one of the most conspicuous places, while the class "Desire of Ornament" has a subordinate place. Thus the older theory decided that bread, universally, has a high "use value," and diamonds a low "use value," and, naturally, was very much astonished that the value practically put upon those two kinds of goods was exactly the reverse of this.

Now their conclusion was quite wrong. What the casuist must say to himself is: If I have a slice of bread I can indeed still this or that concrete feeling of hunger as it arises, but I can never satisfy the totality of such feelings—the actual and possible, present and future, feelings of hunger which, together, make up the kind "needs of subsistence." Obviously, then, it is quite out of place to attempt to measure the service which the piece of bread can render me by the fact that the totality of such feelings possesses much or little importance. To do so would be like the act of a man who, on being asked as to the height of the Kahlenberg, an insignificant off-shoot of the Alps near Vienna, were to ascribe to it the height of the Alpine chain! As a fact it would never occur to us in practical life to value every bit of bread in our possession as a treasure of infinite importance. We do not rejoice every time we buy a baker's roll as if we had saved a life, nor do we blame a man as spendthrift when he carelessly gives away a slice of bread or throws it to a dog. Yet this is the judgment we must pass if we would transfer the import-

ance of the kind " needs of subsistence," on the satisfaction of
which our very life depends, to the goods which actually
minister to that satisfaction.

This much is clear, then, that the value we ascribe to goods
has nothing to do with the graduation of kinds of want, but
only with the graduation of concrete wants.   In order to bring
out all that is involved in this conclusion, it may be desirable
to put more clearly certain points relating to the composition
of this graduated scale, and to put the whole argument on a
surer basis than has been done in the foregoing analysis.

Most of our wants are divisible, in the sense that they are
susceptible of piecemeal satisfaction.   When hungry I am not
compelled to choose between satisfying my hunger completely
and going entirely unsatisfied.   I may take the edge off my
appetite by a moderate meal, intending, perhaps, to dispel the
feeling of hunger altogether later on by a full meal, or, perhaps,
to make shift with the partial satisfaction I have got.   Naturally
the partial satisfaction of a concrete want has another and a
smaller importance for my wellbeing than a complete satisfaction of the same ; and, to a certain extent, this of itself would
suffice to call attention to the above-mentioned phenomenon
that, within a kind of wants, there are concrete wants (or
degrees of want) of varying importance.   But with this is
connected a further notable fact.   It is an experience, as
familiar as it is deep-rooted in human nature, that the same
enjoyment, when constantly repeated, gives us, beyond a certain
point, a constantly decreasing gratification, till, in the end, it
changes into its opposite.   Any one can prove for himself
that at a meal when the fourth or fifth course is reached, the
appetite is not nearly so keen as at the first course, and that,
if there are too many courses, a point is reached where enjoyment turns into discomfort or disgust.   The same occurs in
too long a concert, lecture, walk, play, and, generally speaking, in the case of most physical as well as intellectual
enjoyments.

If we put the essence of these well-known facts into
technical language we get the following proposition : The concrete degrees of want into which our sensations of want may
be divided, or the successive degrees of satisfaction obtained
from similar amounts of goods, are usually of very dissimilar

importance—indeed, of importance which diminishes step by step to zero.

This will explain a whole series of propositions which were simply asserted above. It explains, firstly, how, in one and the same kind of wants, there may be concrete wants, or degrees of want, of varying urgency. Indeed in the case of all divisible satisfactions as the term is defined above—that is, in the great majority of cases—this not only may be but must be so, quite normally and, so to speak, organically. It explains, again, that, even in the most important kinds of wants, there are lower and lowest grades of importance. Properly speaking, the more important kind is marked off from the less important only by the fact that, to some extent, its head rises higher than the others, while its base stands on the same level as all the others. And, finally, it explains that, not only may it occasionally happen, as I have just said, that a concrete want belonging to a kind which, on the whole, is more important, may be out-weighed by some individual concrete want of a kind, on the whole, less important, but that this happens as a perfectly normal, ordinary, and organic occurrence. There will always, for instance, be innumerable concrete subsistence wants which are weaker and less urgent than many a concrete want of quite unimportant classes; such things as the desire of ornament, the love of dancing, the craving for tobacco, etc., will often be stronger than the need of good food and warm clothing.

If we try to represent the classification of our wants by a typical scheme we must, on the principles just laid down, give it something like the following shape [1]:—

I	II	III	IV	V	VI	VII	VIII	IX	X
10									
9	9								
8	8	8							
7	7	7	7						
6	6	6	.	6					
5	5	5	.	5	5				
4	4	4	4	4	4	4			
3	3	3	.	3	3	.	3		
2	2	2	.	2	2	.	2	2	
1	1	1	1	1	1	.	1	1	1
0	0	0	0	0	0	0	0	0	0

[1] See Menger's *Grundsätze der Volkswirthschaftslehre*, p. 93.

In this scheme the Roman figures indicate the various kinds of wants, decreasing in order of importance from I to X. I indicates the most urgent kind, say the needs of subsistence ; V indicates a kind of medium importance, say that of spirituous liquors ; while X indicates the least important conceivable kind.

The Arabic figures 10 to 1, again, indicate the concrete wants and degrees of want that occur in the different kinds, their rank being shown by assigning the figure 10 to the most important conceivable want, the figure 9 to that next in importance, and so on, till the last figure 1 indicates the most insignificant want likely to occur.

This scheme now puts before us the fact that the more important the kind, the higher stands the most important concrete want contained in the kind ; but it shows at the same time that in each kind there are all grades of importance, from greatest to least. The only exceptions in the scheme occur in classes IV and VII, in which some individual members of the descending scale are wanting. These represent the (comparatively rare) kinds where, on technical grounds, a successive satisfaction by means of partial acts is either incomplete or quite impossible, and where, accordingly, the want must either be entirely satisfied or not satisfied at all. The want met by kitchen ranges, for instance, is generally met so completely by one range that we should have absolutely no use for a second. Finally, the scheme shows that in the most important kind (I) there occur concrete wants, which bear the lowest figure of importance, while, in almost all the other kinds which stand under it in importance, there are concrete wants that bear higher figures.

CHAPTER IV

THE MARGINAL UTILITY

TURNING now to the second question suggested in last chapter we ask, Of several or many wants which one is it that actually depends on a particular good ?

This question would not be put at all if the circumstances of economic life were so simple that single wants always stood over against single goods. If a good were adapted to satisfy a single concrete want, and if it were at the same time the only one of its kind, or, at least, the only one of its kind available, it would be quite clear without further consideration that the satisfaction of the single want depended on our command over the single good. But in practical life the matter is scarcely ever so simple as this ; on the contrary, it is usually complicated simultaneously from two sides. First, one and the same good is usually adapted to satisfy various concrete wants, which wants again possess various degrees of importance ; and second, several goods of one and the same kind are frequently available, thus leaving it to caprice which good will be used for the satisfaction of an important, and which for an unimportant want. To give the simplest possible example. I have been shooting for a few days on the mountains, and by some accident I miss my companions. I am far from any house or village, and the only food I have for myself and my dog is two entirely similar baker's rolls. It is clear that the satisfaction of my hunger is of infinitely more importance to me than the satisfaction of the dog's hunger and it is just as clear that it lies with me which of the two rolls I shall consume and which I shall give to the dog. And now the question arises, Which of the two wants here is dependent on the bread ?

One is tempted to answer, That want to which the bread was actually devoted. But it is evident at once that this is an erroneous conclusion. It would amount to saying that the two rolls, devoted as they are to the satisfaction of wants of different importance, must possess different values; while it does not admit of question that two similar goods, available under similar conditions, must be entirely equal in value.

Here, again, an easy casuistical consideration gives the proper solution. The problem is: Which, among several wants, is dependent on a commodity? This resolves itself very simply when it is known which want it is that would *fail of its satisfaction* if that commodity were not present: that want is evidently the dependent one. And now it is easy to show that the want which failed of its satisfaction would not be that want which the particular commodity was, accidentally and capriciously, selected to satisfy, but would always be the *least important* among all the wants in question; that is to say, among all those wants which would formerly have been provided for out of the total stock of this class of goods.

Consideration for one's own convenience, as obvious as it is imperative, induces every reasonable man who acts economically to maintain a certain fixed order in the satisfaction of his wants. No one would be so foolish as to exhaust the resources at his command in satisfying trifling wants, or wants that could be easily ignored, and thus to deprive himself of the means of satisfying necessary wants. On the contrary, every one would take care to use the resources at his command, in the first instance, to provide for his most important wants; then for wants that come after these in importance; then for those of the third rank, and so on;—always arranging in such a way that the lesser wants were only provided for when all the higher wants had been supplied, and there still remained some means of satisfaction to spare. We act according to the same obvious and reasonable principles when our stock undergoes a change by the loss of one member of that stock. Naturally this will alter the plan according to which we have been employing our resources. Not all the wants we had arranged to satisfy can now be provided for, and some abatement in the totality of satisfaction is unavoidable. But, of course, the wise man will try to lay the burden on the least sensitive spot; that is to say, if the loss chances to be in a commodity which was destined to a more important use, he will not give up the satisfaction of this more important want, and, by holding on obstinately to his old plan, provide satisfaction for the less important wants. We may be sure that he will satisfy the more important want, and will do so by withdrawing provision from that want, among all the wants hitherto marked out for provision, on the satisfaction of which *least* depends. To put it in terms of our former illustration: if our sportsman loses the roll which he has meant for himself, he will scarcely feed his dog with the one that remains, and expose himself to the danger of starving. He will suddenly change his plan, elevate the roll that remains into fulfilling its more important function only, and shift the loss to the least important function, the feeding of the dog.

The case, then, stands as follows. Wants which are more important than this "last" want will not be affected by the loss of the good, for their satisfaction is, as before, guaranteed in case of need by the replacement of substitutes. Nor will those wants be affected which are less important than this "marginal want," for they go unsatisfied whether the good is there or not. The only want affected is the last of those that otherwise would be satisfied : it will be satisfied if the good is there ; it will not be satisfied if it is not there. It is thus the dependent want we were seeking.

Here then we have reached the goal of the present inquiry, and may formulate it thus : the value of a good is measured by the importance of that concrete want, or partial want, which is *least urgent* among the wants that are met from the available stock of similar goods. What determines the value of a good, then, is not its greatest utility, not its average utility, but the least utility which it, or one like it, might be reasonably employed in providing under the concrete economical conditions. To save ourselves the repetition of this circumstantial description—which, all the same, had to be somewhat circumstantial to be quite correct—we shall follow Wieser [1]

[1] *Ueber den Ursprung und die Hauptgesetze des wirthschaftlichen Werthes,* p. 128. Jevons has the expressions "final degree of utility" and "terminal utility." With Menger, who first formulated the above law with entire clearness, but gets along without the convenience of a short technical expression,

in calling this least utility—the utility that stands on the margin of the economically permissible—the economic Marginal Utility of the good.   The law which governs amount of value, then, may be put in the following very simple formula : The value of a good is determined by the amount of its Marginal Utility.

This proposition is the key-stone of our theory of value. But it is more.   In my opinion it is the master-key to the action of practical economic men with regard to goods.   In the simplest cases, as in all the tangle and complication which our present varied economic life has created, we find men valuing the goods with which they have to deal by the marginal utility of these goods, and dealing with them according to the result of this valuation.   And to this extent the doctrine of marginal utility is not only the key-stone of the theory of value, but, as affording the explanation of all economical transactions, it is the key-stone of all economical theory.[1]   Those who have observed practical life closely will, I think, be convinced that this claim is not exaggerated.   Rightly to observe and rightly to interpret what has been observed, however, is an art not always easy ; and in what follows accordingly we shall make use of the value theory to guide us in observing and interpreting what falls within its sphere.   We begin, then, with an illustration of the greatest conceivable simplicity.

A colonial farmer, whose log-hut stands by itself in the primeval forest, far away from the busy haunts of men, has

the law runs as follows (p. 98) : " In every concrete case, accordingly, of the satisfactions of want guaranteed by the total quantity of goods, it is only those which have the *smallest* importance for the person that are dependent on his command over a definite part-quantity of the amount of goods at his disposal ; and the value of a part-quantity of the available amount of goods is, accordingly, equal to the importance which the satisfactions of want that are least urgent among all the satisfactions guaranteed by the total quantity, and obtainable with a similar part-quantity, have for that person."

[1] Even where men do not act egoistically but altruistically, they have occasion to consider the marginal utility, viz. that marginal utility which the goods given away have to the persons who get them.   One gives donations, charities, and the like, when the importance of such, measured by their marginal utility, is very much higher as regards the wellbeing of the receiver than as regards that of the giver, and almost never when the converse is the case.   I am glad to know that, in the idea expressed above, I am at one with so distinguished an economist as Walras. I can only express my entire concurrence with what he says, in the preface to his *Théorie de la Monnaie*, p. 11, as to the universal importance of the idea of marginal utility, both as regards theory and as regards the practice of economic life.

just harvested five sacks of corn.   These must serve him till the next autumn.   Being a thrifty soul he lays his plans for the employment of these sacks over the year.   One sack he absolutely requires for the sustenance of his life till the next harvest.   A second he requires to supplement this bare living to the extent of keeping himself hale and vigorous. More corn than this, in the shape of bread and farinaceous food generally, he has no desire for.   On the other hand, it would be very desirable to have some animal food, and he sets aside, therefore, a third sack to feed poultry.   A fourth sack he destines for the making of coarse spirits.   Suppose, now, that his various personal wants have been fully provided for by this apportionment of the four sacks, and that he cannot think of anything better to do with the fifth sack than feed a number of parrots, whose antics amuse him.   Naturally these various methods of employing the corn are not equal in importance. If, to express this shortly in figures, we make out a scale of ten degrees of importance, our farmer will, naturally, give the highest figure 10 to the sustenance of his life ; to the maintenance of his health he will give, say, the figure 8 ; then, going down the scale, he might give the figure 6 to the improvement of his fare by the addition of meat, the figure 4 to the enjoyment he gets from the liquor, and, finally, to the keeping of parrots, as expressing the least degree of importance, he will give the lowest possible figure 1.   And now, putting ourselves in imagination at the standpoint of the farmer, we ask, What in these circumstances will be the importance, as regards his wellbeing, of *one* sack of corn ?

This, as we know, will be most simply tested by inquiring, How much utility will he lose if a sack of corn gets lost ? Suppose we carry out this in detail.   Evidently our farmer would not be very wise if he thought of deducting the lost sack from his own consumption, and imperilled his health and life while using the corn as before to make brandy and feed parrots.   On consideration we must see that only one course is conceivable : with the four sacks that remain our farmer will provide for the four most urgent groups of wants, and give up only the satisfaction of the last and least important, the marginal utility—in this case, the keeping of parrots.   The only difference, then, that his having or not having the fifth sack of corn makes to his wellbeing is that, in the one case, he may allow himself the pleasure of keeping parrots, in the other he may not; and he will rightly value a *single* sack of his stock according to this unimportant utility.   And not only one sack, but *every* single sack; for, if the sacks are equal to one another, it will be all the same to our farmer whether he lose sack A or sack B, so long as, behind the one lost, there are still four other sacks for the satisfying of his more urgent wants.

To vary the illustration, assume that our farmer's wants remain the same, and that he has only three sacks of grain. What now is the value of one sack to him ?   The test again is quite easily applied.   If he has three sacks he can and will provide for the three most important groups of wants.   If he has only two sacks, he will be obliged to limit himself to the satisfying of the two most important groups and give up the satisfying of the third, that of animal food.   The possession of the third sack—and the third sack, be it remembered, is not a definite sack but any of the three sacks, so long as there are other two behind it—directly carries with it, therefore, the satisfaction of his third most important want; that is, the last or least of those wants covered by the three sacks which constitute his total stock   Any estimate other than that according to the marginal utility would, in this case also, obviously run counter to facts, and would be quite incorrect.

Finally, suppose that our farmer's wants remain as before, and that he only possesses one single sack of corn.   In this case it is perfectly clear that all less important methods of employing the corn are out of court, and that it will be devoted to and spent in sustaining the farmer's life—a function for which it just suffices.   And it is as clear that if this single sack fails the farmer will no longer be able to support himself in life.   His possession of the sack, therefore, means life ; his loss of it means death ; the single sack of corn has the greatest conceivable importance for the wellbeing of the farmer.   And all this is still in conformity with our principle of marginal utility.   The greatest utility—the preservation of life—is here the sole, as well as the last or marginal utility.

These estimates according to marginal utility are not merely " academic."   No one will doubt that our farmer on due occasion

—say, on an offer made him for the corn—would act practically according to the same estimates. Any one of us, placed in his position, would undoubtedly be inclined to let one of the five sacks go pretty cheap in consideration of and in correspondence with its small marginal utility. He would charge considerably more for one of the three sacks. And he would not let the irreplaceable *single* sack, with its enormous marginal utility, go for any price whatever.

Transfer, now, the field of illustration from the solitary in the primeval forest to the bustle of a highly organised economic community. Here we encounter, in an altogether dominating position, the empirical proposition that quantity of goods stands in inverse ratio to value of goods. The more goods of one kind there are in the market, the smaller, *ceteris paribus*, is the value of the single commodity, and *vice versâ*. Every one knows that economic theory has made use of this empirical proposition—the most elementary proposition in the doctrine of price—to establish the law of " Supply and Demand." But this proposition maintains its validity quite apart from exchange and price. For instance, how much more value does a collector put upon the single specimen, which represents a class in his collection, than upon one of a dozen of such specimens? It is easy to show that well-authenticated facts of experience like these follow, as a natural consequence, from our theory of marginal utility. The more individual goods there are available in any class, the more completely can the wants to which they relate be satisfied, and the less important are the wants which are last satisfied—those whose satisfaction is imperilled by the failure of one of the goods. In other words, the more individual goods there are available in any class, the smaller is the marginal utility which determines the value. If, again, there are available so many individual goods of one class that, after all the wants to which they are relative are completely satisfied, there still remains a number of goods for which no further useful employment can be found, then the marginal utility is equal to zero, and a commodity of that particular class is valueless.

Here, then, we have an entirely natural explanation of the phenomenon which originally struck us as so surprising, that comparatively " useless " things, such as pearls and diamonds, have so high a value, while infinitely more " useful " things, like bread and iron, have a far less value, and water and air no value at all. Pearls and diamonds are to be had in such small quantities that the relative want is only satisfied to a trifling extent, and the point of marginal utility which the satisfaction reaches stands relatively high.[1] Happily for us, on the other hand, bread and iron, water and light, are, as a rule, to be had in such quantities that the satisfaction of all the more important wants which depend on them is assured. Only very trifling concrete wants, or no wants at all, are dependent, for instance, on the command over a piece of bread or a glass of water. It is, of course, true that in abnormal circumstances—as, for instance, in besieged towns, or in desert journeys, where water and food are scarce, and small stores only suffice to meet the most urgent concrete wants of meat and drink—the marginal utility flies up. According to our principles the value of those goods, otherwise of so little account, must rise also, and the inference finds ample empirical confirmation in the enormous prices paid in such circumstances for the most wretched means of subsistence. Thus those very facts which, at first sight, seemed to contradict our theory that the amount of value is dependent on the amount of utility conditioned, on closer examination afford a striking confirmation of it.

---

[1] To guard against possible confusion it should be noted that the German writers on value generally speak of "satisfaction of want" under the metaphor of a descending scale : the increasing satisfaction creeps *down* the scale, and the point of saturation is zero, not 100.—W. S.

CHAPTER V

COMPLICATIONS

THE cases we have hitherto considered have been comparatively easy of interpretation; but practical economic life brings out a great many complications which the practical man treats with easy assurance, but the theorist finds considerable difficulty in explaining.[1] To understand these everything depends on the correctness of our casuistical decision as to that amount of utility which, in the given circumstances, is the marginal utility. For this purpose the following general direction may serve as master-key to all the more difficult problems of value. We must look at the economic position of the person who is estimating the value of a good from two points of view. First, we must in thought add the good to his stock, and consider what further and lesser concrete wants can *now* be satisfied. Second, we must in thought *deduct* the good from his stock, and consider again what concrete wants will *still* be satisfied. In the latter case, of course, it becomes manifest that a certain layer of wants, viz. the lowest layer, has lost its former provision; this lowest layer indicates the marginal utility that determines the valuation.[2]

---

[1] On the relation of theory and practice in the sphere of valuation see Conrad's *Jahrbücher*, vol. xvi. p. 74.

[2] Generally speaking, there are two occasions on which a man is called on to form a judgment as to value. One is on parting with a good in his possession, *e.g.* in giving it away, or exchanging, or consuming it; the other, on acquiring a good. In the two cases the form which the valuation assumes in thought is, externally, a little different. A good which a man has he values according to the injury which he would suffer by its loss; he values it, therefore, according to the last satisfaction which is assured him by having it. A good which a man has not he values, on the contrary, according to the increment of utility which its acquisition brings; *i.e.* according to the most urgent among those satisfactions which,

The first very obvious but, theoretically, not unimportant application, leads us to recognise that in valuing a good sometimes it is the importance of some one individual concrete want that is taken into consideration, sometimes it is the importance of many concrete wants that has to be summed up. That is to say, in the nature of things the layers of want that depend on the object we are valuing may turn out to be very various, in compass and extent, according to the constitution of that object. If it is a single individual of a perishable group of goods, for instance a food, the marginal utility will usually include no more than one single concrete want, or even a partial want. If the object, again, is a durable good, and thus susceptible of repeated acts of use, or if it is a number of goods considered as a whole, it is natural that an entire sum—in certain circumstances, a very great sum—of concrete wants may be included in the layer of wants that depends on it. On the possession or non-possession of a piano, for instance, depend hundreds of musical enjoyments ; on the possession of a cask of wine hundreds of pleasures of the palate ; and the importance of those pleasures naturally must be summed up in valuing these goods.[1]

To pass on now to another far-reaching complication. It follows from our earlier analysis that the marginal utility which determines the value of a good is not (or is only accidentally) identical with the utility which the good itself actually affords.[2] As a rule, the marginal utility of any good is a foreign utility, the utility of the last individual good (or of the last similar part) which may be taken to replace it. In simple cases this utility, although the utility of another good, is at the least the utility of a good of the same kind. In the illustration already made use of, the value of each individual

in the conditions of his fortunes up till the present time, he has not been able to obtain. Naturally we get the same result by either method, for the final satisfaction which is assured *by* a good is always identical with the first which would be lost *without* the good. In the text I have put the formula in such a way that it will sufficiently embrace either method.

[1] On certain far-reaching complications which may be connected with this, see Conrad's *Jahrbücher*, vol. xvi. p. 34.

[2] The latter occurs only with individual goods, or with those particular goods which may have chanced to be selected just for the most insignificant service.

sack of corn—and therefore the value, for instance, of the first sack—was determined by the utility of another, the last sack of corn, but always by the utility of *a* sack of corn. The existence of organised exchange, however, may cause considerable complications here. In making it possible to exchange goods of one kind, without loss of time, for goods of another kind, it also makes it possible to shift a loss, which occurs in one kind of goods, over to another kind. Instead of replacing the loss of an individual good by withdrawing another good of the same kind from a less important employment, and leaving there a vacancy, we may summon goods of entirely different kinds from the occupation in which they have previously been employed, and, by way of barter, procure the good required to supply the loss. What is here lost in losing a good of class A is really the utility which the goods taken from class B would otherwise have afforded; and since, of course, we should not think of taking the replacing good from the more important but from the least important employments in their spheres of utility, the loss comes upon the marginal utility of the foreign good, that transferred from class B to class A. Here, therefore, the marginal utility and the value of a good of one kind is measured by the marginal utility of a good of another kind—by the good (or portion of goods) devoted to replace it.

To illustrate this. My only overcoat has been stolen. There is no question of replacing it directly by another coat of the same kind, because I had only the one. But, all the same, I shall not willingly let the loss caused me by the theft rest where it originally fell. For the want which now makes itself felt—that of warm winter clothing—is a very urgent one; its non-satisfaction may involve the most serious consequences to my health, and even endanger my life. I shall accordingly try to shift the incidence of the loss on to other kinds of goods, and I shall do so by parting, in exchange for a new overcoat, with goods which, in other circumstances, would have been put to other uses. The goods needed for this exchange I shall, naturally, withdraw from those uses which are of least consequence to me; that is to say, I shall take the goods which are of least marginal utility to me. If I am well off I shall probably take the £3, the price of a new greatcoat, out of my cash-box, and I shall be able to buy one luxury the less with my diminished funds.   If I am not well off, but am not exactly a poor man, I shall have to fill up the deficit in the cash-box by economising on my house-keeping expenses for a couple of months.   If I am so poor that I neither have the money nor can save it out of my monthly income, I may have to sell or pawn some articles of furniture which can be most easily dispensed with.   Finally, if I am so far reduced that I can provide only for the most urgent concrete wants in all the other classes, then I cannot shift the loss to other classes of wants, and needs must get along without an overcoat.

If we put ourselves for the moment into the position of the owner of the overcoat, and ask what it is, as regards his wellbeing, that depends on the coat being stolen or not, we shall find that the dependent circumstance is, in the first case, the spending of money on some luxury; in the second, some little curtailments in house-keeping; in the third, deprivation of the utility of the goods sold or pawned; in the fourth, the actual preservation of health.   Only in the last case, therefore, is the value of the coat determined by the immediate marginal utility of its own class (which marginal utility here happens to coincide with the utility of the good itself because the class is represented by a single individual); in all the other cases it is determined by the marginal utility of foreign classes of goods and wants.

Under the present economic system, where exchange is very highly organised, a notable importance attaches to the casuistical modification we have just described.   We might almost say that it includes the majority of subjective estimates of value.   For reasons which may be easily inferred from what has been said, we scarcely ever value goods that are indispensable to us by their direct utility, but, almost always, according to the "substitutionary utility" of foreign classes of goods.   I should say, however, emphatically that, even where exchange is most highly organised, we do not always have occasion to employ this latter method of valuation; it is only under certain conditions, although of course conditions that very often occur.   That is to say, we employ the "substitutionary" method only when the marginal utility of the replacing good is less than the immediate marginal utility of the class into which it is transferred ; to put it more exactly, when the prices of goods, and, at the same time, the circumstances of provision for the various kinds of wants, are such that, if a loss occurring in one kind were borne inside the kind itself, wants relatively more important would go unsatisfied than if the purchase price of the replacing good were drawn from other kinds of wants. But through all complications it is always the *least* utility, mediately or immediately dependent on a good, that determines its true marginal utility and value.

Casuistical complications similar to those made possible by exchange may be caused by the fact that replacing goods can be quickly obtained by production. This kind of complication also has a very notable place in the theory of value, from the fact that it gives the key to the influence of cost of production on value. It requires, on that account, particularly careful treatment. But it will be more appropriate to give an independent consideration to this and to certain other casuistical complications somewhat later, and to return meantime to the simple fundamental law, the statement of which requires to be supplemented in a particular direction.

CHAPTER VI

THUS far we have traced the amount of value which goods possess to the amount of their marginal utility. We may, however, pursue the causes which determine value one step farther back, and ask on what circumstances the amount of this marginal utility itself depends. The answer is;—on the relation between Wants and their Provision. The way in which these two factors influence the amount of marginal utility has been suggested so often and so fully in the foregoing analysis, that I need not say anything further in way of explanation. I shall content myself with shortly formulating the law relating to it. It runs thus: the more comprehensive and the more intense the want, the higher the marginal utility, and *vice versâ*. That is to say, the more numerous and the more intense the wants demanding satisfaction on the one hand, and the less the quantity of goods available to satisfy them on the other hand, the more important are the layers of want that must remain unsatisfied, and the higher, therefore, the marginal utility. And conversely, the fewer and the less urgent the wants, and the more goods there are to satisfy them, the deeper down the scale goes the satisfaction, and the lower falls the marginal utility and the value. It comes nearly to the same thing, only in a less precise form, to say: Usefulness and Scarcity are the ultimate determinants of the value of goods. In so far as the degree of usefulness indicates whether, in its way, the good is capable of more or less important services to human wellbeing, so far, at the same time, does it indicate the height to which the marginal utility, in the most extreme case, *may* rise. But it is the scarcity that decides to what point the marginal utility actually does rise in the concrete case.[1]

---

[1] In his recently published essays on *Werththeorien und Werthgesetze* (Conrad's *Jahrbücher*, N. F., vol. xvi. pp. 417-437, and 513-562) Scharling will not allow that the relation of Wants and Provision is the ultimate universal determinant of the value of goods, and would substitute Difficulty of Attainment in its place (*ibid.* p. 425, and particularly p. 430 in note, and p. 551). Notwithstanding some striking things in it I frankly confess—and all the more frankly that I attach so much scientific importance to the Danish economist, and so much weight to anything he says—that I consider not only this proposition, but the whole treatise he has written in its proof, as a lamentable relapse in scientific analysis. Scharling has done everything possible to re-entangle certain things that had up till now scarcely escaped from confusion. And what makes it worse is that he has done it with skill, and with a certain semblance of truth. I consider " difficulty of attainment " one of those unlucky catch-words which can be stretched and stretched like an indiarubber band ; it leads out of one ambiguity into another, and it either explains things falsely or does not explain them at all. I mean that either one connects with it a definite, limited, and narrow meaning, and holds fast by that—in which case the explanations that one would base on this narrow conception prove to be positively false ; or one draws and stretches the rubber band, and, by making perverted and violent constructions, forces all sorts of foreign things under the elastic—in which case we avoid open contradiction, but at the cost of making the proposition expressed by the catch-word an insipid and weak phrase, which does not explain, but goes round about an explanation. And just this has been Scharling's fate. What does he mean by "difficulty of attainment"? He explains it as the amount of effort that every one must take on himself to obtain a good, or the effort which is spared him by the possession of the good (p. 430). And what does the word "effort," again, mean ? If any precise conception is to be attached to it, it can scarcely be understood as anything else than as some sort of exertion, pain, or labour. But if this is the meaning attached to it then the appeal to "saved effort," as the principle of the value of goods, is positively false. To give one example out of a thousand, take the case of a pensioner past work with an income of £60. He is told to value the overcoat which he possesses according to "saved effort." What kind of effort may that be ? Perhaps the effort which he would have to expend to produce the overcoat himself ? Certainly not ; he would never himself make the coat, but always buy it. Or the effort which he would have to put forth if he were to produce those goods which he had to give away as equivalent for the coat ? Neither can this be the case ; for, past work as he is, he would never acquire this purchase price through effort, but simply take it from his income, and for that, of course, he must curtail the satisfaction of other less important wants. What, therefore, the possession of the overcoat spares him is not an effort, but a *deprivation*, and a deprivation the amount of which, as I have indicated in the work disputed by Scharling, depends exactly on the importance of those last needs which are satisfied by the good, which lose their satisfaction in losing it, and the urgency of which itself, again, is determined by the existing relation of Wants and Provision. It is only in those rare cases mentioned by me in Conrad's *Jahrbücher* (*ibid.* p. 42) —the exceptional character of which I most distinctly maintain in spite of Scharling's remarks (p. 430, note 1)—that the amount of an effort or the pain of labour can be the immediate standard of value.—Now I admit that Scharling

This proposition, that the height of marginal utility is determined by the relations of Wants and Provision, admits of a great number of useful applications.   Just now I shall only emphasise two of these, which we shall have to make use of later on in the theory of objective exchange value.   First, since the relations of Wants and Provision among individuals are extremely various, one and the same good may possess an entirely distinct subjective value for different persons—without which, indeed, it is difficult to see how there could be any exchanging at all.   And thus, second, under otherwise similar circumstances, the same quantities of goods have a different value to rich and poor; to the rich they have a smaller, to the poor a larger value.   The rich being amply supplied with all classes of goods, their satisfaction extends, generally speaking, to the more unessential wants, and the added or deducted satisfaction dependent on any particular good is, consequently, inconsiderable; while to the poor man, who is generally able to provide for only his most urgent wants, the utility which depends on each good is much greater.   Experience also shows that poor men find it a pleasant thing to acquire goods and a painful thing to lose them, where a similar gain or loss does not affect the rich at all.   We would scarcely compare the state of mind of a poor clerk, who received his month's salary of £5 on the first day of the month and lost it on his way home, with that of the millionaire who dropped the same sum.   To the former the loss would mean most painful privation over a whole month; to the latter it would only involve the want of some idle luxury.

sometimes gives the word "effort" quite another meaning from that of a pain. To avoid repetitions, however, I will show what that leads to, a little later, under the theory of price.—Finally, the illustration, with which Scharling thinks he has signally refuted my doctrine, will not mislead any one who has rightly understood the doctrine of marginal utility.   If a boy, who hitherto had only had a single apple, were allowed for once to pull as many apples as he liked in a neighbour's garden, he would, I admit, immediately reduce the value he put upon the good called "apple."   But why?   Not, as Scharling thinks he may assume as self-evident, because "his relish and his enjoyment in consuming the fruit remain unchanged."   This enjoyment may run down a whole graduated scale from the consumption of the first and single apple to entire satiation with apples, but it is perfectly clear that the boy with the single apple sacrifices the enjoyment which stands highest in this scale, while, "with one of many apples to choose from," he sacrifices only a very trifling one.

M

CHAPTER VII

ALTERNATIVE USES

In the present and following chapters of this book we shall continue the discussion of various casuistical complications which arise in practical life in the formation of value. We must go into these for two reasons : first, in order to put on a surer foundation the perfect agreement of our theory of value with the phenomena of actual life, and, second, because the conclusions arrived at now will find important applications later when we come to the theory of capital.

It often happens that a commodity permits of being employed or used in two or even several entirely different ways. Wood, for instance, can be used for burning or for building; grain for bread, for seed, or for distilling; salt as a relish, or as an auxiliary material in the making of chemicals. Since, then, in each different employment the commodity supplies different wants, and these wants have, of course, different degrees of importance; since, further, in these different classes of wants, the relations of want and its provision are frequently dissimilar; and since, finally, the good, if it possesses a complex usefulness, does not usually possess this usefulness in the same degree at all times,—on all these grounds it is easy to see that the increment of utility which a good causes, or the marginal utility which it may afford, may vary very greatly from one employment to another. For instance, it may very well be that a pile of boards, used for building material, affords its owner a marginal utility that may be indicated by the figure 8, while the same boards, used as fuel, would only afford a marginal utility indicated by the figure 4. The question now is : In such cases which is the true economical marginal utility that determines the value of the good ?

The answer is easy enough: it is always the *highest* marginal utility. As has been already shown at length,[1] the true marginal utility of any good is identical with the least utility which it may be employed, economically, in providing. If, then, several mutually exclusive employments compete for any particular good, it is clear that, in any rational scheme of economy, the most important among them will get the preference; it alone is economically permissible; all less important uses are excluded; and, as the good cannot be used in these employments, they can have no influence on the value set upon it. To put it in terms of our concrete example. If a peasant, after using his stock of wood to provide for all the more urgent wants of building and fuel, has still two uses for wood—two employments to which he could profitably put it—indicated by the numbers 8 and 4, but has only one pile of boards remaining, it is clear that he will apply them to the more important of the two uses, and leave the less important unprovided. So long as he can get a utility indicated by 8 in building, he will not burn the wood to get a utility indicated by 4. What depends, then, on his having or not having that particular pile of boards, is the obtaining or not obtaining of the greater utility 8. We may put the rule in general terms thus: in the case of goods which allow of alternative uses or employments, and are capable of furnishing different marginal utilities in these uses, that employment which yields the highest marginal utility is the standard for the economical value of the goods. This rule will be found amply confirmed by experience. Nobody would price oak furniture at its value as fuel, or sell a fine picture for the price of old canvas, or estimate a lady's hunter by its capacity to draw a butcher's cart!

The formula, however, as now stated might easily give rise to mistakes, and it will be advisable to anticipate these before going further. It might seem as if what I have just said was contradictory of what was said a little ago. I now say that, among several alternative employments having different marginal utilities, the highest is the standard, while a few pages ago it was demonstrated that, if the immediate marginal utility of a good (say the utility of the last good of its own class) was greater than its mediate marginal utility (say the marginal

[1] See above, p. 147.

utility of goods of another class employed as substitutes), the lower marginal utility was the standard.[1] The seeming contradiction is very simply explained. In the former case we were dealing with a distinction between several ways in which a stock of goods could be employed; now we are dealing with a distinction between two or more employments for which the stock of goods is not sufficient, and, as I have already shown [2] on a former occasion, the least of those uses to which a good is put always coincides exactly with the greatest of those uses which fail of provision if there is no such good.

When, then, in the above formula I spoke of *several* alternative employments and of alternative marginal utilities, it must be understood as a method of expression which, literally speaking, is not quite correct. For, naturally, of those competing employments only *one* can, economically, be the last; only one, therefore, can be the true "marginal employment"—that in which we find the marginal utility—while all the other employments are, economically, inhibited. They make the more demand on our attention, however, as being the first or most conspicuous representatives of an entire branch of employment. As soon as we think of this latter branch at all, these representatives force themselves, in the first place, on our consideration, and it is by choosing between them that we, as it were, give a casting vote for one among entire groups of employment, such as carving and burning of wood, hacking and knacking of horses, and so on—an actual psychological procedure which appears to me best and most concisely indicated by the above formula.

Here, however, it must be emphasised that the precedence given in the course of our inquiry to those pseudo-marginal employments is only formal: in our economical decisions they enjoy no sort of material preference. Generally speaking, the fact that the employments to which a good *may* be put fall into several distinct branches has really not the slightest influence on our calculations of value. Just as we do not value goods according to *kinds* of wants,[3] so we do not distribute them according to *branches* of employment. Every concrete employment is only looked on as a possible employment according to the rank which it maintains in virtue of its importance among all competing employments of every branch.

[1] See above, p. 157.   [2] See above, p. 154 in note 2.   [3] See above, p. 142.

And thus, in obedience to the principle of economic conduct, we always follow one and the same course; we allocate our stock of goods among the concrete uses which are of most importance on our scale, and the last of these determines for us the marginal utility and the value of the good.

Now in doing so it will often happen that only one single branch of employment is taken into consideration. This will of course be, quite regularly, the case where we have only a single individual commodity to dispose of. But it will also happen where a whole series of concrete employments of one kind outweighs that of another kind in importance, and where, at the same time, this series is long enough, or the available stock of goods is small enough, to leave no provision for employments of less importance. If, for instance, in any branch of industry, there are a hundred opportunities of employing certain goods, and the importance of each opportunity is indicated by the figure 8, while the opportunities in another branch of employment are indicated only by the figure 6, and if our stock of goods consists of fifty individual commodities only, naturally all the fifty will be devoted exclusively to the first kind of employment, and their value will be fixed, according to the highest utility, at 8. But often it will happen that wants representing different branches of employment—say, for instance, timber wanted for building and for burning—demand satisfaction simultaneously; in such cases it is the ratio that chances to exist between the opportunities and the goods that decides to what branch of want the "last" employment will belong; that is to say, the employment which determines the value. Suppose that in one branch of employment there are four opportunities, indicated, according to importance, by the figures 10, 8, 6, 4; and that in another branch there are four opportunities, indicated by the figures 9, 7, 5, 3; and suppose that a man possesses in all five individual goods; there is no doubt that the five goods will be allotted to the opportunities 10, 9, 8, 7, 6, and that the last figure (which, accidentally, belongs to the first branch of employment) is the real marginal utility and determines the value of the good, while the employment that comes next in the second branch, that indicated by the figure 5, must, according to our formula, become the "pseudo-marginal utility."

CHAPTER VIII

WE are now ready to consider a concrete application of what has just been said, and one that lies at the root of a very wide-spread phenomenon. Hitherto we have mostly had before us cases where a commodity, in virtue of some technical adaptability peculiar to it, becomes susceptible of being employed in various ways. Quite apart from any such special assumption, however, the existence of an organised system of exchange gives almost every good a second kind of employment—that of being bartered for other goods. It is customary to put this against, and in opposition to, all other kinds of employment, and to associate this opposition between "Use" and "Exchange" with a division of value into "Use Value" and "Exchange Value."

Understood in a certain sense, to which in this place we shall adhere, both of these—exchange value as well as use value—are kinds of subjective value. Use value is the importance which a good obtains for the welfare of a person, on the assumption that it is used immediately in furthering his wellbeing; and, similarly, exchange value is the importance which a good obtains for the welfare of a person through its capacity to procure other goods by way of barter. The amount of use value is measured, according to rules already known to us, by the amount of the marginal utility which the good in question brings its owner when used by himself. The amount of (subjective) exchange value, on the other hand, obviously coincides with the amount of the use value of the goods got in exchange. When I employ a good by bartering it I procure for my welfare exactly what the goods I get in exchange procure for me in utility. The amount of the good's subjective exchange value, therefore, is to be measured by the marginal utility of the goods got in exchange for it.

Now nothing is more common than that the use value and the exchange value of a good to its owner are of unequal amount. To a scholar, for instance, the use value of his books would, as a rule, be considerably greater than their exchange value, while to the bookseller the contrary is likely to be the case. The question now recurs, Which of the two values in such cases is the true one ? [1]

Here we have only to deal with a special case out of a group for which we have already laid down the general rule. Employment in personal use and employment in exchange are two different ways of employing one good. If the good affords a different marginal utility in each employment, it is the higher utility that gives the standard for its economical value. If, therefore, the use value and the exchange value of a good are different in amount, the higher of them is its true value. We recognise this principle in practical life. We always employ our goods in that which corresponds to the higher and the true value. The scholar keeps his books ; the bookseller sells his. Or, if the scholar gets into reduced circumstances, he also sells his books ; but in this case, while the use value and also the objective exchange value of the books remain unaltered, their subjective exchange value to him has risen. That is to say, there are now more urgent wants of other classes clamouring in vain for satisfaction, and the possibility of satisfying these other wants through the sale of the books acquires for him an increased importance, and an importance that easily outweighs the use value of the books.

The recognition that there is a subjective exchange value, and that this is something entirely distinct from what is usually called exchange value (that is, objective exchange value), is of

---

[1] It is easy to see that we can only speak of *two* values in the same loose way as we spoke above of several "alternative marginal employments," for, naturally, a good can never have anything but one value to a person. Value is the importance which a good has for the wellbeing of a man, and this importance cannot be at the same time great and small, higher or lower. But we do now and then use this rather inaccurate way of thinking and speaking, and, therefore, I have here, as on the former occasion, adapted my formula to it.

fundamental importance in guiding us among the phenomena of
value.   It may be advisable, on that account, to devote a little
more attention to the subject.   The illustration of the scholar
is enough to convince us that the subjective importance, based
on the possibility of barter, may take a different direction from
that taken by the objective power-in-exchange and price of
goods.   For, price remaining unaltered, the subjective exchange
value of the goods may rise.   But the two exchange values
may even move simultaneously in opposite directions.   Take
the case of a poor student, whose last and sole possession—the
only thing he can call his own—is a Jubilee sovereign.   There
is no doubt that this sovereign will have a high subjective
importance for the satisfaction of his own wants ; and there
is no doubt that this importance is an *exchange* value, for
sovereigns have no use value.   Now suppose that our student
falls heir unexpectedly to a fortune of ten thousand pounds,
while, simultaneously, on account of the limited number
issued, the sovereign goes up from 20s. to 40s.   How is it
now with the " exchange value " of the sovereign ?   Here the
difference between the two conceptions becomes manifest.   The
objective exchange value, the current value of the coin, has gone
up from 20s. to 40s. ; but the importance which it has for the
satisfaction of its owner's wants, the *subjective* exchange value
of the sovereign, has, owing to the changed relations between
the student's wants and his resources, unquestionably fallen.
Yesterday our student would have lamented the loss of the
sovereign as the loss of his last defence against extremest
hunger and misery ; to-day, perhaps, he gives it away with a
light heart to a friend who collects coins.   In spite of its
increased current value it has become a mere bagatelle to him.

This fundamental and real difference between the two conceptions of exchange value is the principal reason why we cannot accept the ordinary division of Use Value and Exchange
Value as the ultimate division of the total phenomena of value.
To do so would be to separate related things, and to mix up
matters which are really so heterogeneous that it is scarcely
possible to find a common definition for them.   Obviously,
subjective exchange value is much more nearly related to subjective use value than to objective exchange value.   If we
wish to find our way with certainty among those phenomena

to which the name of "value" has been attached, it is advisable to do as we have done : place objective exchange value by itself on one side, and subjective value on the other side, and afterwards separate the latter into subjective use value and subjective exchange value.[1]

---

[1] Notwithstanding the objections of Diehl (*P. J. Proudhon.   Seine Lehre und sein Leben*, vol. i., Jena, 1888, p. 109), who approves of the "traditional distinction of Use Value and Exchange Value," I must hold by everything I have said above.

CHAPTER IX

THE VALUE OF COMPLEMENTARY GOODS

IT very often occurs that, in order to obtain an economic utility, several goods require to co-operate in such a way that, if one good falls out of its place, the utility cannot be obtained, or cannot be completely obtained. Goods whose uses thus supplement each other we may follow Menger in calling Complementary goods. Thus, for instance, paper, pen and ink, needle and thread, cart and horse, bow and arrow, right and left hand gloves, and so on, are complementary goods. This complementary character obtains generally, indeed almost universally, among productive goods.

It is easy to see that the intimate co-relation of complementary goods—the co-relation in which they afford this utility—will be reflected in the formation of their value. This leads to a number of peculiarities, all, however, occurring within the limits of the universal law of marginal utility. In stating these we must distinguish between the value which belongs to the complete group, and that which belongs to individual members of it.

The total value of the complete group adapts itself, as a rule, to the amount of the marginal utility which it is capable of affording as a group. If, for instance, three goods, A, B, and C, form a complementary group, and if the smallest utility economically obtainable by the joint employment of these three goods amounts to a value of a hundred, the three goods A, B, and C taken together will be worth a hundred.

The only exception to this rule occurs in those cases where, on the general principles with which we are now familiar, the value of a good is to be measured, not by the immediate

marginal utility of its own class, but by the marginal utility
of other classes of goods drawn on to serve as substitutes.
In the special case under consideration this will occur if every
individual member of the complete group is replaceable by
purchase, or production, or even by taking a substitute out of
some other isolated employment, and if, at the same time, the
total sum of the utility which the substituted goods would
otherwise (in isolation) have had is less than the marginal
utility they afford as combined.   If the latter, for instance,
amounts to 100, while the substitutionary value, the value of
the three members individually, is only 20, 30, and 40—that
is in all 90,—the thing that depends on the group of three is
not the obtaining of the combined utility of 100—which is,
in any case, assured by the substitutionary goods—but only
the obtaining of the smaller utility, the 90, which fails of its
provision when the members are taken away and become
substitutes in the group.   Since, however, in such cases the
complementary character has, properly speaking, no influence
on the formation of value, and the value is simply determined
according to the ordinary laws already familiar to us, we need
not give any separate consideration to this.   In what follows,
then, I shall give particular attention only to the normal case,
where the marginal utility attainable by goods in joint employment is, at the same time, the true marginal utility.

As was before remarked, this marginal utility, first of all,
determines the united value of the whole group.   But in the
manner in which this total value is divided out among the
single members of the group, considerable differences emerge,
varying with the casuistical peculiarity of the case.

First, if none of the members admits of any use other
than the joint use, and if, at the same time, no one member
which co-operates towards the joint utility can be replaced,
then one single member has the full total value of the group,
and the other members are entirely valueless.   Suppose, for
instance, I pay five shillings for a pair of gloves, five shillings
is the total value of the pair.   If I lose one of the gloves I
lose the whole utility, and, with it, the whole value of the pair ;
and the remaining glove has no value.   Of course either of the
two gloves equally admits of either valuation, and it is simply
circumstances that decide which of them is to rank as all,

and which as nothing—the glove needed to complete the pair, or the useless single glove. Cases of this kind are relatively scarce in practical life.

Second, and more common, is the case where the individual members of the group can afford another, though a less utility, outside of their joint employment. Here the value of the single member does not lie between everything and nothing, but between the amount of the marginal utility which it is capable of affording in isolation as minimum, and the amount of the joint marginal utility, after deducting the isolated marginal utility of the other members, as maximum. Suppose, for instance, that three goods, A, B, and C, in co-operation afford a marginal utility of 100; that A by itself has a marginal utility of 10, B by itself of 20, and C by itself of 30; the value of A is determined as follows. If a merchant owns this good by itself he can get from it only its isolated marginal utility of 10, and the value of the good, accordingly, is only 10. But suppose he owns the *whole* group, and is asked to sell or give away the good A out of that group, what he has to consider is that, with the good A he can get a marginal utility of 100; without it, only the smaller (isolated) utility of the goods B and C, that is $20 + 30 = 50$; and that, accordingly, on the having or losing of the good A depends a difference in value of 50. As complement of the group it is, therefore, worth $100 - (20 + 30) = 50$; as an isolated good it is worth only 10.[1] Here the difference in value is not so extreme as in the first case, but still it is very considerable.

Third, and more common still, is the case where some individual members of the group are not only employed for other purposes, but are, at the same time, replaceable by other goods of the same kind. For instance, building ground, bricks, beams, and labour are complementary goods in the building of a house. But if a few carts of bricks, intended for the building, go astray in transit, or some of the labourers engaged for

---

[1] Of course in this case also the peculiarities of the case decide which member is to be valued as the completing member of the group, and which as simply the isolated piece. If, for instance, the owner of the complete group is asked to sell the good A, he will value it as completing member, and the other goods B and C as isolated pieces. But if he is asked to sell C, he will value it as completing member at $100 - (10 + 20) = 70$, while A and B will be valued as isolated pieces.

the job refuse to work, in normal circumstances this does not in the least hinder the obtaining of the joint utility—the built house.   The labourers and materials are simply replaced by others.   The consequences as regards the formation of value are as follows :—

1. The replaceable members, even if they are needed as complements, can never obtain any higher than their " substitution value "—viz. the value conferred by the utility in those branches of employment from which the replacing goods are obtained.[1]

2. This fact considerably contracts the limits within which the value of the individual good—estimated sometimes as complementary, sometimes as isolated good—may be determined, particularly when it is a common marketable good.   The more numerous the available goods of any kind, and the more numerous the opportunities of using them, the smaller will be the difference between the importance of that use from which a replacing sample might be drawn, as maximum, and the use next to it in rank, in which a superfluous isolated good might be employed, as minimum of value.   If, for instance, besides the good A, which we shall call A_1, contained in the complementary group, there are two other similar goods A_2 and A_3, and if the possible opportunities of use (outside of employment in the complementary group) possess an importance indicated by the numbers 50, 20, 10, and so on, only the uses indicated by 50 and 20 would be filled by the goods A_2 and A_3, and if one of these two were taken to replace the good A_1 a utility of 20 would be lost.   On the other hand, if the complementary group were broken up, and the good A_1 itself obliged to seek for an isolated and inferior employment, its only chance would be the third, that indicated by 10. Thus its value would always lie between 10 (isolated) and 20 (complementary).   But if, instead of three, there are a thousand goods, and a thousand opportunities of using them, the difference between the 1000th employment (from which the good required to replace the other must in case of need be

---

[1] To put it concretely : although a load of bricks were absolutely indispensable to finish a house, the load could never obtain any higher value than that determined by the marginal utility of bricks generally ; that is, as determined by all the uses to which bricks generally are put.—W. S.

drawn) and the 1001st (in which the good must look for employment if it becomes superfluous through the breaking up of the group) will certainly fall to a quite insignificant amount.

Now, of course, it is not likely that any one individual, within the limits of his own economy, will possess a thousand goods of one kind, and a thousand different opportunities of employing them. But, all the same, the efficiency of the influences just described is in no wise annulled; it is only the scene of their operation that is changed, from individual economy to the market, and that in the following way. Individuals buy what they require, and sell their surpluses in the market. Here, then, all the stocks of goods and all the opportunities of employing them over the entire field covered by the market, come together. And now—exactly as before— everything depends on whether, in the market, commodities and opportunities of employing them are scarce or not. If the commodity is very scarce, it makes a very considerable difference in the determination of price whether we approach the particular good as buyer or as seller. For instance, suppose, as before, that there are only three similar goods, and three buyers each wishing to acquire just one such good, with the view of using it in employments that will yield 50, 20, and 10. Then, if one of these goods be withdrawn from the market to serve in a complementary employment, the two remaining goods are bought for the employments indicated by 50 and 20, and—according to laws which will be explained in next book—the purchase price must be fixed between 10 and 20, say at 15. But if now the complementary employment fails, and the third good also is thrown on the market, it must —if it is to find a sale at all—fall to the buyer who can get 10 by employing it, and the result is that the market price is in all cases fixed *below* the level of 10. Here, then, the price —and the subjective exchange value based on it—varies not inconsiderably.

If, on the other hand, there are a thousand similar goods offered, and a thousand buyers demand them, evidently it will not make the smallest difference to the market price whether there appears a thousand and first buyer, or a thousand and first seller; the good obtains a price and value independently of whether it finds a place in the single complementary employment or not.

Thus, under the assumptions now laid down, the value of the replaceable members is fixed at a certain level independently of their concrete complementary employment, and this value they have when we distribute out the total value of the group among its individual members.   The distribution, then, will be made thus : of the total value of the whole group—which is determined by the marginal utility of the joint employment —this fixed value is previously assigned to the replaceable members, and the remainder—which varies according to the amount of the marginal utility—is reckoned to the non-replaceable members as their individual value.   To use our old illustration again ; say that the joint marginal utility amounts to 100, and that the members A and B have a fixed " substitution " value of 10 and 20 respectively, 70 must be reckoned the individual value of the non-replaceable good C.; or, say that the marginal utility of the group amounts to 120, the individual value of C will be 90.[1]

Of the three cases we have discussed the last mentioned is by far the most common in practical life, and, accordingly, in the great majority of cases, the value of complementary goods is determined according to the latter formula.   The most important application of it is in the distribution of the product among the various productive powers co-operating in producing it.   Almost every product is the result of the co-operation of a group of complementary goods consisting of uses of ground, labour, fixed and floating capital.   Of the complementary members the great majority are marketable commodities, and replaceable at will ; as, for instance, the labour of wage-earners, the raw materials, fuel, tools, etc.   Only a few of them are non-replaceable, or not easily replaceable ; as, for instance, the land on which the peasant works, the mine, the railway lines, the factory walls, the activity of the undertaker himself with his peculiar and high qualifications, and so on.   It is easy to see, therefore, that here we have exactly those casuistical cir-cumstances in which the foregoing formula of distribution

---

[1] If C also were replaceable by a substitute of less value the case mentioned on p. 170 would emerge, and the marginal utility of the joint use would not determine the value of the complementary group.

obtains, and, as a fact, it is acted upon in practical life in the most accurate way. In actual business the "costs" are first deducted from the total return. If we look closer, however, we shall see that what is deducted is not all the costs—for, if so, the use of ground, or the undertaker's activity, as both valuable goods, would come under costs—but only the expenditure for the *replaceable* means of production with a given substitution value, viz. the wage of labour, raw materials, wear and tear of tools, etc. The remainder, under the name of "net return," is ascribed to the non-replaceable member or members: the peasant calculates it to his land, the mine-owner to his mine, the manufacturer to his factory, the merchant to his undertaking activity.

If the joint returns increase, it would not occur to anybody to ascribe the surplus to the replaceable members; it is always the ground or the mine that "produces more." And, similarly, if the joint returns decrease, nobody would credit the "costs" with the reduced amount; the deficiency also is conceived as exclusively due to the diminished productiveness of the ground or the mine. And this is entirely logical and correct: on goods replaceable at any moment only the fixed substitution value is actually *dependent*; the entire remainder of the joint amount of utility obtainable depends on the goods that cannot be replaced.

The theory of the value of complementary goods is the key which will solve one of the most important and difficult problems of political economy—the problem of the distribution of goods as made in the present state of society, where competition is more or less free and prices are determined by free contract. All products come into existence through the co-operation of the three complementary "factors of production," labour, land, and capital. Now our theory, in showing how much of the joint product may economically [1] be considered as

[1] Not physically. It would, in most cases, be absolutely impossible to calculate the physical share—how could one be supposed to distinguish what percentage the material and what percentage the artist had contributed physically to the making of a statue?—but it is also a matter of no importance. On the other hand it is, in most cases, quite easy to determine what share of the utility, or of the value, would have to be done without if one were not in possession of a definite individual factor, and this quota, conditioned by the possession of one factor, I call its economical share in the total product.

due to each of these, and what share of the total value may, accordingly, be assigned to each of them, lays down, at the same time, the most decisive basis for determining the amount of remuneration which each of the three factors obtains.   And thus although, as we know, capital as "factor of production" does not exactly coincide with capital as "source of income," yet this gives us at least a rough indication of the way in which the amount of the three branches of income—wage, rent, and interest—is determined.

It does not indeed do this quite directly.   That quota which the workers receive, and that other quota which the owners of the co-operating ground receive, is directly identical with wage and rent.   But the quota which falls to the co-operation of capital is not interest—as, in theories of distribution, economists have repeatedly assumed ever since the days of Say with fatal precipitation.   It is, first, the *gross* remuneration for the co-operation of capital; and, out of this, interest is got, like a kernel out of a shell, because, and to the extent that, something remains over after deducting from the gross remuneration the value of the worn-out capital. To explain how this is so is a problem in itself.   To make it quite clear by an illustration, suppose that a commodity, produced by the co-operation of all three factors, is worth £100.   The law of complementary goods will carry us thus far; it will enable us to determine that the share of labour (the labour directly employed in the production) amounts to, say, £20, that of ground to £10, that of capital to £70.   But it does not tell us what, or how much, of that £70 remains over *net*, as interest, after deduction of the wear and tear of capital.   On the contrary, the law of complementary goods in itself would rather lead us to the conclusion that nothing remains over.   For, according to it, it would be most natural to assume that the capital, to the co-operation of which the return of £70 is ascribed, and which has been consumed in obtaining that return, had already been valued at the entire £70; and, if this were the case, the return to capital would naturally be entirely absorbed by the wear and tear of the capital.   That this is not the case is, so to speak, an internal matter—a matter which plays its part *inside* the gross share of capital determined by the law of

N

complementary goods, and is the object of an independent problem, the peculiar problem of Interest.   But before we can discuss interest there is still a great deal to be explained.[1]

[1] The confusion, so common in economic literature, between the gross share assigned to the co-operation of capital (*Rohzins*) and net interest, has been fully discussed in my *Capital and Interest* (see the criticism of Lauderdale, p. 146 ; of Carey, p. 155 ; of Strasburger, p. 175 ; of Say, p. 189, etc.)   It will not be expected of me to give a complete theory of distribution in the passing, as it were.   I purposely refrain from going deeper into the subject than is necessary for my special task, the development of the Interest theory.   And for this it is sufficient to sketch only in the broadest lines the principles which limit the gross share of capital, as against the shares of labour and uses of land that co-operate with it : our special task will be to lay down what is the state of the case as regards the gross share of capital.   Moreover I hope that on this question of the shares allotted to the various factors, which I am compelled to treat in a very cursory way, the eagerly expected work of Wieser will very shortly shed a clear light.   (Wieser's *Der Natürliche Werth*, Vienna, 1889, appeared while this was passing through the press.—W. S.)

CHAPTER X

THE VALUE OF PRODUCTIVE GOODS. VALUE AND COSTS

IT has been almost a commonplace of economical teaching that the value of goods is regulated by the costs of their production. This doctrine has very seldom been questioned on grounds of theory,[1] but very often its validity has been closely limited by the enumeration of exceptions, and insertion of all sorts of saving clauses. In this contracted sphere, however, it has held almost unquestioned authority down to our own times; it has a certain amount of support in practical experience, and, what is most serious, it seems to contradict the theory of value just put forward. For "Costs of Production" are nothing else than the sum of productive goods which must be used up in the making of a good—the concrete capital consumed, the labour expended, and so on. Now to the question as to the ground and amount of value which a good has, our theory answers: it depends on the marginal utility which a good is capable of rendering; that is to say, it depends on its *future* employment. But the other theory answers: it depends on the value of the productive goods consumed in producing it; that is to say, on the conditions of its *origin*. Putting aside this contradiction for a moment, and forgetting everything we have been taught as to costs, let us inquire impartially what

---

[1] Among older writers it was disputed by Say, *Traité*, vol. ii. chap. ix. seventh edition, p. 404 : "Ce qui nous ramène à ce principe déjà établi, que les frais de production ne sont pas la cause du prix des choses, mais que cette cause est dans les besoins que les produits peuvent satisfaire." In more recent literature what M'Leod has said (*Elements of Political Economy*, 1858, p. iii.) is worth notice. But the matter was really first grasped in its entirety by Menger, Jevons, and Walras, whose books mark an epoch as regards the whole value theory, and of these again the work of Menger was the most profound.

our theory of marginal utility, logically carried out, has to say as to the value of productive goods, and as to " costs."

For the sake of clearness it is desirable, before going further, to define with more exactness the object of our present inquiry, viz. Productive Goods.   As compared with consumption goods (*Genussgüter*), which directly serve to satisfy human wants, all productive goods have this common feature— they serve to satisfy human wants only indirectly.   But they differ, again, from one another in the degree of indirectness. The flour, for instance, from which bread is baked, stands nearer the final satisfaction of want by several degrees than the field which grows the wheat.   To express these degrees— which we shall find to be of importance both theoretically and practically—we shall avail ourselves of Menger's division of goods into ranks.[1]   In the first rank we shall place consumption goods—those goods which serve immediately for the satisfaction of wants , such as bread.   In the second rank we place those goods which assist in producing the goods of first rank— the goods which co-operate in the production of bread; as the flour, the oven, and the baker's labour.   In the third rank we place those goods which serve for the production of goods of second rank ; as the wheat from which the flour is ground, the mill in which it is ground, the building materials of the oven, etc.   In the fourth rank we put the means of production of goods of third rank ; as the land which grows the corn, the implements used in cultivation, the labour of the agricul- turist, the building materials of the mill, etc.   And so on to the fifth, sixth, and seventh ranks, which embrace those goods, the useful service of which consists in producing goods of the rank immediately below them.

On the lines of our conception of value it must be self- evident that a productive good, like any other good, can only obtain value for us through our recognition that on its possession or non-possession depends our gain or loss of some one utility, of some one satisfaction of want.   And it is equally self-evident that its value will be high when the dependent satisfaction is important, and low when it is unim- portant.   The only difference is that, in the case of goods for immediate consumption, the good and the satisfaction stand

[1] *Grundsätze*, p. 8.

beside each other in a direct causal relation; while, in the case of productive goods, there is interposed, between them and the satisfaction finally dependent on them, a more or less lengthy series of intermediate members, their successive products. In this prolonged connection there is both matter and occasion for the development of new and legitimate relations, particularly between the value of means of production and that of their products. But the great law of value is neither destroyed nor disturbed by these relations. Exactly as in the analogous case of complementary goods it is only obscured, as it were, by a mass of details, to which the more ample development of the phenomena gives occasion. These details we have now to consider. To this end let us take a typical productive series.

A good for immediate consumption, which we shall call A, is made from a group of productive goods of second rank, which we shall call G_2; this from a group of goods of third rank, G_3; and this, finally, from a group of fourth rank, G_4. For simplicity's sake assume, first, that each of these productive groups passes without loss of time into the product which it creates, and that, at the same time, this particular employment is the only one of which it is capable. We have now to find out what is the relation of dependence between each member of the above series, and the wellbeing of its owner.

What depends on the final member, the good A, we already know. It is its marginal utility. Our inquiry, then, begins at the member G_2. If we had not the group G_2 we should not have its product A; that is to say, of the class of goods to which A belongs, we should have one fewer than we should otherwise have had. But, as we already know, one good less means one satisfaction less, and that the least satisfaction to which economically, one good of the stock would otherwise have been devoted. In other words, it means the loss of the marginal utility of the product A. On the group G_2, therefore, exactly as on the final product A itself, depends the marginal utility of A. Looking now at the next member we find that, if we had not the group G_3, we could not have the group G_2 which is made from it; and, as consequence, we should lose one good of the class A, or its marginal utility. On the group G_3, then, depends exactly the same utility and importance for wellbeing as on the members which come after it in the pro-

duction series. The same thing again follows in the case of
the group G_4. If it fails us, we, of course, lose one of the
group G_3, which otherwise might have been produced from it;
we lose, further, one of the group G_2, one of the class of good
A, and, finally, the marginal utility of A   Thus we arrive at
the following general proposition : On all groups of Means of
Production of remoter rank which successively pass into one
another, there depends one and the same gain to human wellbeing; that is, the marginal utility of their final product.   No
one will be surprised at this result.   It is a foregone conclusion that a series of productions, which has no relation to our
wellbeing except through its final member, can neither tend
towards any other utility, nor condition any other utility, than
that which this final member itself conditions.   In every
member of the chain successively we hold in our hand the
condition of this final utility, sometimes at a further, sometimes
at a nearer stage on the way to it.

From what has been said we may deduce the following
general principles as regards the value of means of production.
First, since on one and the same utility depend all the groups
of means of production which successively pass into one
another, the value of all these groups must be substantially
the same.   Second, the amount of this, their common value,
is regulated for all, in the last resort, by the amount of the
marginal utility of their finished product.   I emphasise " in
the last resort."   For, thirdly, the value of each group has its
immediate measure in the value of its product, the succeeding
group.   In the *first* instance, the utility and service of the
means of production consist and exhaust themselves in the
making of their product, and, naturally, the more important
and more valuable the product is for us when made, the higher
will be the estimate put on the importance of this utility, and
of that which provides it.   Substantially the third proposition
is fully covered by the second, for, in the value of the goods
of higher rank, the marginal utility of the final product is
mirrored.   From this marginal utility value is conducted to
all the groups of means of production, but the conduction is
done, as it were, by stages.   First, and immediately, the
amount of the marginal utility stamps itself on the value of
the final product.   This then forms the measure of the value of

the group of goods from which this product comes. This again measures the value of the third group; and the third group, finally, the value of the last group, the goods of fourth rank. From stage to stage the name of the determining element changes, but, under the different names, it is always the same thing that acts—the marginal utility of the final product.

Although the second and third propositions, then, agree in substance, it is necessary to formulate the third explicitly. It is important as being a convenient abbreviated formula which we use in practical life much more frequently than the principal formula. If we are estimating what amount of wellbeing a productive instrument brings us, we look, naturally, first of all to the product which we get from it, and then, beyond that, to the wellbeing which that product brings us. If we do not know this, we must, I admit, go over the entire course of the conduction of utility, member by member, till we come finally to the marginal utility of the final member, the finished product. But very often this is not necessary. From previous consideration, or from experience, we meet with some opinion, already formed, on the value of the products, and, without further consideration, we make this the ground of our opinion as to the value of the means which produced them. A wood merchant, buying timber for cask staves, will not take long to consider the value of the wood to him. He estimates how many staves he can get out of the timber, and he knows what the staves are worth in the condition of the market at the time. Further than this he need not trouble himself.

Thus far we have formulated these principles as to the value of means of production on purely theoretical grounds; to some extent, as postulates of economical logic. If, now, we ask what experience says to these postulates, we shall find that it confirms them. Indeed we can appeal for confirmation to that very " law of costs " which is apparently so hostile to our theory of marginal utility. Experience shows that the value of most goods is equal to their " costs." But " costs " are nothing else than the complex of those productive goods which have value—the labour, concrete capital, uses of wealth, and so on, which must be expended in the making of a product. The well-known identity of costs and value is only another form of expressing the identity of value between groups of goods of various ranks which pass into one another. I am quite aware, of course, that, as regards the cause of this identity, those who adopt the law of costs usually read it in the converse way. While we say that the value of means of production, and therefore the value of the costs, is regulated by the value of their products, the usual way of interpreting the law is to say that the value of products is determined by the value of their costs—that is, by the value of the means of production out of which they are made. Later on we shall have occasion to go thoroughly into this difference of opinion as to the cause of the identity. Meantime all I intend to do is simply to confirm the statement, that the asserted identity of value between groups of productive instruments which successively pass into one another—whatever be its cause,—is an actual empirical fact.

Of course this identity is not absolute, but approximate; we can only speak of a tendency towards identity of value. The divergences from absolute identity are of two kinds—partly irregular, partly normal. Both kinds arise from the fact that production costs time. In the long periods which often intervene while goods of sixth or eighth rank are passing gradually through all the transformation stages into the finished consumption good, both men and things may change. Wants may change; the relations between wants and their provision may change; and, not less important, the knowledge of these relations may change. With them, of course, changes the valuation of the goods at various stages on their way to the matured product. It is easy to understand that the fluctuations which proceed from this cause may be sometimes great, sometimes small, sometimes upwards, sometimes downwards; they are irregular fluctuations. But, besides these, we notice a divergence from complete identity which is constant and normal. It is a matter of observation that the total value of a complete group of remote rank lags somewhat behind the value of its product, and in a definite ratio; and that, indeed, the amount of this difference in value is graduated according to the time required to change the group of means of production into its product. If the value of the product, for instance, is £100, experience tells us that the total value of the labour, uses of land, fixed and floating capital spent in producing it, is something less than £100—perhaps £95 if the production process lasts a year; perhaps £97 or £98 if it lasts only half that time. This difference of value is the crease, as it were, in which Interest is caught. Its explanation is a subject by itself, with which we shall have enough to do in following chapters. It would be very far from advisable to mix it up with our present inquiry, where we are dealing with the general relation between the value of means of production and that of their products, and for the moment we shall therefore entirely disregard the existence of this particular difference of value.

Up to this point we have expounded the law which governs the value of productive goods under the simple hypothesis that each group of productive instruments permits of only one quite definite employment. But in actual life the cases in which this hypothesis corresponds with facts are very limited. It is, indeed, characteristic of productive goods that they admit of an infinitely more various use than consumption goods. The vast majority of them are adapted to several productive uses, while many of them, like iron, coal, and, above all, human labour, are adapted to thousands of different uses. In theoretical research we must, of course, take note of these actual circumstances, and see whether they do not involve some modification of our law, that the value of a group of goods of remote rank is determined by the value of its product.

Suppose, then, we vary the assumptions of our typical illustration. A man possesses a great stock of groups of productive instruments of second rank (G_2). From one such group he can, at will, make a finished commodity of the kind A, or one of the kind B, or one of the kind C. Naturally he will provide for his various wants harmoniously, and will therefore, by means of different parts of this stock, produce simultaneously finished goods of all three classes according to the measure of his requirements. In a scheme of provision that was really harmonious, the amounts produced would be so regulated that, in each kind, wants of something like the same importance would depend on the last sample of the kind, and the marginal utility of every sample would therefore be approximately equal.[1] Nevertheless there will be differences,

[1] This is demanded by the principle of "economic conduct." See Wieser, *Ursprung und Hauptgesetze des wirthschaftlichen Werthes*, p. 148.

and even considerable differences, of marginal utility, because, as we already know,[1] the gradation of the concrete wants in any kind of want is not always uniform and unbroken. One fireplace in a room, for instance, will give me a very considerable utility—which I may represent by the figure 200—while a second fireplace would not be of any further use to me. Naturally, in providing for my wants, I shall therefore, in any case, stop at fireplaces when I have one fireplace with its marginal utility of 200, even if in other branches of wants the provision goes down, on the average, as low as a marginal utility of 100 or 120. To make our typical illustration true to nature, therefore, we must assume that the marginal utility of one sample is of different amount in the three kinds A, B, and C—say 100 in A, 120 in B, 200 in C. The question now is, In these circumstances what is the value of G_2 ?

After the practice we have had in drawing distinctions of a similar kind, we can give the answer without hesitation—the value will be equal to 100. For if one of the available groups were lost the owner would naturally shift the loss to the least sensitive part; he would neither limit the production of the kind B, where he would lose a marginal utility of 120, nor of the kind C, where he would lose a marginal utility of 200. He would simply produce one less of the kind A, whereby his loss of wellbeing would be only 100. To put it generally : The value of the productive unit adjusts itself to the marginal utility and value of that product which possesses the least marginal utility among all the products for whose production the unit might, economically, have been employed. All the relations which we found to hold as regards the value of means of production and of their products under the simple hypothesis of the single employment, hold, therefore, generally between the value of means of production and their *least valuable* product.

And how does it stand with the value of the remaining classes of products, B and C ? This question brings us to the source of the " law of costs."

If, under all circumstances, the marginal utility attainable within the kind itself were to decide, the kinds of goods B and C would possess a value diverging, as well from the value of

---

[1] See above, p. 145.

the kind A, as from the value of its costs G_2.   B would have
a value of 120, C a value of 200.   But this is one of those
cases where, through substitution, a loss occurring in one kind
of goods is shifted to another kind, and consequently the
marginal utility of the latter becomes the standard for the
former.[1]   That is to say, if one of the kind C gets lost there
is no occasion to give up the marginal utility of 200, which it
would have directly afforded; we can and will immediately
procure a new C out of a productive unit G_2, and we shall
prefer to produce one less of that kind of good in which the
marginal utility, and with it the loss of utility, is least.   This,
in our illustration, is the kind A.   In virtue of the opportunity
of substitution offered by production a good of the kind C is
therefore valued, not at its own marginal utility 200, but at
100, the marginal utility of the least valuable cognate product
A.   The same holds, of course, of the value of kind B, and
would hold, generally speaking, of every kind of good which is
" cognate in production "[2] with A, and has at the same time
an immediate marginal utility greater than that of the kind A.

This leads to several important consequences.   First of all,
in this way the value of goods which have a higher individual
marginal utility is put on a level with the value of the
" marginal product "—as we shall call that product which has
the least marginal utility—and thus with the value of the
means of production, from which both in common come ; the
theoretical identity of Value and Costs, therefore, holds in this
case also.   But it is well worthy of notice that here the
agreement between value and costs is brought about in a way
essentially different from the agreement between costs and
marginal product.   In the latter case the identity was brought
about by the value of means of production adapting itself
to the value of the product; the value of the product was the
determining, that of the means of production the determined.
In the present case, on the contrary, it is the value of the
product that must adapt itself.   In the *last* resort, of course,
it adapts itself only to the value of another product, the
marginal product of the cognate production ; but, in the *first*
instance, it accommodates itself also to the value of the means
of production from which it comes, and which are mediated

---

[1] See above, p. 156.   [2] Wieser, p. 146.

by the substitutionary connection with the marginal product. Here the conduction of value describes, as it were, a broken line. First it goes from the marginal product to the means of production and fixes their value; then it goes in the opposite direction, from the means of production to the other products which may be made from them. In the end, therefore, products of higher immediate marginal utility get their value from the side of their means of production. To translate this from the abstract formula into practice. If we are considering what a good B or C (generally speaking, a product of higher immediate marginal utility) is worth for us, we must say first of all: It is worth exactly as much as the means of production from which we could replace it at any moment. Then if we examine further how much the means of production themselves are worth, we come to the marginal utility of the marginal product A. But very often, indeed, we may save ourselves this further inquiry, as we already know the value of the goods that make up the cost without having to begin at the foundation and follow it from case to case; and in all such cases we measure the value of the products in an abbreviated form, both accurate and convenient—that is to say, simply by their costs.

Here, then, we have the whole truth about the celebrated Law of Costs. As a fact people are right when they say that costs regulate value. Only they must always be conscious of the limits within which this " law " holds, and the source from which it gets its strength. It is, first, only a particular law. It holds only in so far as it is possible to obtain, at will and at the right time, substitutes through production. If there is no opportunity of substitution the value of every product has to be measured by the immediate marginal utility of its own kind, and its agreement with the value of the marginal product, and with the intermediate means of production, is disturbed. Hence the well-known empirical proposition that the law of costs holds only as regards goods " reproducible at will," or " freely produced," and that it is simply an approximate law which does not bind the value of the goods that come under it with slavish exactitude to the level of costs, but— according as production for the moment comes short of demand or runs beyond it—permits of fluctuations now on one side, now on the other

But it is still more important to emphasise, in the second place, that, even where the law of costs holds, costs are not the final but only the intermediate cause of value. In the last resort they do not *give* it to their products, but receive it from them. In the case of productive goods which have only a single employment this is perfectly clear. That Tokay is not valuable because there are Tokay vineyards, but that the Tokay vineyards are valuable because Tokay has a high value, no one will be inclined to deny, any more than that the value of a quicksilver mine depends on the value of quicksilver, the wheat field on the value of wheat, the brick kiln on that of bricks, and not the other way about. It is only this many-sided character of most cost goods—their capacity of being employed in many different uses—that gives the appearance of the contrary, and a little consideration shows this to be an appearance and nothing more. As the moon reflects the sun's rays on to the earth, so the many-sided costs reflect the value, which they receive from their marginal product, on to their other products. The principle of value is never in them, but outside them, in the marginal utility of the products. The law of costs is not an independent law of value; it only forms an incidental case inside the true universal law of marginal utility. It is simply the great counterpart to the law of Complementary Goods. As the latter disentangles and explains those relations of value which result from the temporary and causal *collocation*—the simultaneous co-operation of several goods to a common useful end; so does the Law of Costs for the value relations of those goods which act in temporary and causal *sequence*—the working of goods after one another and through one another to the same final goal. If we think of the value relations of goods that work into one another as a much-tangled net, we might say that the former law disentangles the meshes in their length and breadth, while the latter disentangles them in their depth; but both fall under the all-embracing law of Marginal Utility, and are nothing but special applications of that law to special problems.

BOOK IV

PRICE

CHAPTER I

THE FUNDAMENTAL LAW

EXCHANGES are not made simply for amusement. People who take the—not always trifling—trouble to exchange the goods which they possess for other goods, do so for a rational and material end, and, in nine hundred and ninety-nine cases out of a thousand, this end is to better their economical condition by the exchange.[1] Whether this end be attained, and in what degree it be attained, depends naturally on the current conditions of exchange, particularly on the prices which the parties get as equivalent for their goods. It is, therefore, a perfectly natural thing that the motive which gives rise to exchange in general, namely, the striving after economical advantage, should maintain a commanding influence in the fixing of the exchange prices.

In what follows I mean to inquire how prices are determined under the assumption that all who take part in the exchange act *exclusively* from the motive of pursuing their immediate economical advantage in it. The law which we shall arrive at in this way I have already,[2] for very good reasons, called the fundamental law of the formation of price. I am perfectly aware that, in practical life, this law does not exactly obtain. For, although the motive of self-advantage is almost never absent, and is almost always the most prominent motive, still, in price transactions, other motives do very often get mixed up; such motives as humanity, custom, friendship,

---

[1] Menger, *Grundsätze*, p. 153. Of course now and then exchanges may be made simply to show some person a kindness ; perhaps to conceal a present, or a charity in the guise of an exchange. But such cases form only a quite insignificant minority. [2] *Grundzüge*, part ii., in Conrad's *Jahrbücher*, vol. xiii. p. 486.

vanity, or the influence of outside institutions, such as government taxation, union regulations, boards for fixing wages, and the like, give them another direction than that they would have taken if exclusively dominated by self-advantage.   Such motives, indeed, scarcely ever get the upper hand of the other to the extent of making us conclude an exchange which would cause us positive economic loss; but they often make us decide to be content with a less amount of advantage than we should have got in steadily pursuing our interests.

I have on the same occasion [1] expressed myself with all clearness on the theoretical and practical importance of the admixture of these other influences, and I shall only now briefly sum up what I then said.   In actual life this admixture of motives causes certain modifications of the fundamental law of the formation of price, and the statement of these modifications cannot be neglected in any accurate and complete theory of it. But if all that is wanted is to grasp the characteristic features of the formation of price, it is enough to put forward the " fundamental law " above mentioned.   For just as, among the motives that determine price, that of striving after self-advantage in exchange has the lion's share, so does the lion's share in the theoretic explanation of the phenomena of price fall to the " fundamental law " here stated.   And it is sufficient for us in our present task, as we have not to pursue the theory of price as an end in itself, but only so far as is necessary to establish the theoretical connection between the elementary phenomena of subjective value and the complicated phenomena of interest.   In this law we obtain a principle which is not minutely accurate, but is amply sufficient for the further development of the theory of capital.

Before going on to state the peculiar laws of price, it may be desirable to preface them by some considerations that may, more accurately, unfold the content of the fundamental motive which forms the assumption and basis of the whole of the following inquiry.

In exchange transactions the decisions made always turn on two points; these are—(1) whether, in a given state of things, a man should exchange or not; and (2) if he decide to

---

[1] *Grundzüge*, p. 480.

exchange, what form he should try to give to the terms of the exchange. Now in making these decisions it is obvious that the man who looks to his own immediate advantage and nothing else, will act according to the following rules. First, he will exchange only if the exchange brings him an advantage. Second, he will rather exchange for a greater advantage than for a less. Third, he will rather exchange for a small advantage than not exchange at all.

It scarcely need be shown that these three rules are dictated by our fundamental motive, and constitute the practical substance of it; what does require elucidation is an expression that recurs in them all, " to exchange with advantage."

The meaning of the expression obviously is—to exchange in such a way that the exchanger gains more in wellbeing from the goods he gets than he loses in the goods he gives ; or, since the importance that goods have for life and wellbeing is expressed in their subjective value, to exchange in such a way that the goods received possess a greater subjective value than the goods parted with. If A owns a horse and is willing to exchange it for ten casks of wine, it can only be because the ten casks of wine have a greater value for him than his horse has. But, naturally, the other party to the contract thinks exactly in the same way. He, on his part, will not give up the ten casks of wine if he does not get for them a good that has a greater value for him. He will exchange his ten casks for A's horse only if the wine is worth less to him than the horse is.

From this we get an important rule. An exchange is economically possible only between persons who put a different value, even an opposite value, upon the commodity and upon the price equivalent.[1] The buyer must put a higher, the seller a lower, estimate on the commodity than he does on the equivalent. Indeed the interest which the two parties have in the exchange, and the gain they get from it, increases as the difference between their estimates increases; if the difference

---

[1] It will be observed that our author does not confine the word Price to Money price, but applies it to the equivalent good or goods obtained in exchange for what is, pre-eminently, *the* good—the object of demand from buyers, and of supply from sellers. The convenient word *Preisgut* I render by "price equivalent," or simply "equivalent."—W. S.

decreases their gain decreases ; and if the difference disappears, and their estimates coincide, no exchange is, economically, possible between them.[1]

It is easy to see that, under the regime of the division of labour, there must be innumerable chances of opposing estimates, and therefore innumerable opportunities of exchange. That is to say, as each producer makes only one or two kinds of articles, and these far in excess of his own personal requirements, he has at once a superfluity of his own products and an absence of all others. He will, therefore, ascribe to his own product a low subjective value, and to other products a relatively high subjective value. But, conversely, the other producers will ascribe a high value to all products which they have not, and a low value to their own products of which they have too many, and here we have in the fullest degree that relation of opposite valuations which is most favourable to the effecting of exchange.

Another idea that comes out in what has been said we may follow to its logical consequences. To one consulting his own advantage an exchange, as we saw, is economically possible only when he estimates the good to be acquired more highly than the good possessed. Now, obviously, this will more readily occur the less value he puts on his own commodity, and the more value he puts on the equivalent. A man who values his horse, subjectively, at £50, and values a cask of wine at £10, has, economically, a much greater possibility of exchange—or, as we shall say in future for brevity's sake, is much more " capable of exchange "—than another who values his horse at £100 and a cask of wine at £5. The former, obviously, can proceed with the exchange if six casks are offered him for his horse, while the latter must hold back unless something over twenty casks is offered him. If a third party again values his horse at £40 only, and a cask of wine at £15, obviously he would be economically capable of concluding an exchange if even three

[1] Say, *e.g.*, that A values his horse at five casks of wine, while B values it at fifteen, then, if the horse goes for ten casks, each gains an amount of value represented by five casks of wine. If A values the horse at eight and B values it at twelve, each gains only a value of two casks. Finally, if both agree in valuing the horse at twelve casks of wine, B, of course, would be glad to get the horse for ten casks, or for any price under twelve casks, but A, naturally, would not give it him at that price. See Menger, *Grundsätze der Volkswirthschaftslehre*, p. 155.

casks were offered him.   Generally speaking, then, that exchanger is the "most capable" who puts the least value on his own commodity in comparison with that offered him in exchange, or, what is the same thing, puts the highest value on the other commodity in comparison with the commodity which he offers in exchange for it.

Now that we are sufficiently acquainted with the meaning and content of our "fundamental motive," we may proceed with our proper work, and consider what are the normal effects which this fundamental motive exerts on the formation of price.   In this part of our work the method already pursued by several distinguished economists seems to me by far the most convenient: first, by typical illustrations to show how, under certain definite assumptions, price is and must be determined, and then to separate the accidental surroundings of the illustration from what is universal and typical, and formulate the latter into laws.   I shall begin with the simplest typical case, the determination of price in isolated exchange between a single pair of exchangers.

CHAPTER II

ISOLATED EXCHANGE

A PEASANT, whom we shall call A, requires a horse. His individual circumstances are such that he attaches the same value to the possession of the horse as he does to the possession of £30. A neighbour, whom we shall call B, has a horse for sale. If B's circumstances also are such that he considers the possession of the horse worth as much as, or worth more than £30, there can, as we saw, be no exchange between them. Suppose, however, that B values his horse at considerably less, say at £10. What will happen?

First, it is certain that there will be an exchange; in the assumed circumstances each of the contracting parties can make a considerable profit by the exchange. If, for instance, the horse changes hands at £20, A, who considers it worth £30, makes a profit of £10, and B, who gets £20 for an article worth only £10 to him, gets the same amount of profit. They will, therefore, in any case, according to the proposition "rather a small gain than no exchange," agree on making an exchange at a price advantageous to both of them. The question now is: How high will this price go? As to this it may be said definitely: The price must at all events be less than £30, otherwise A would have no economical advantage, and would have no motive for going on with the exchange. And it must at all events be higher than £10, or there would be no use in the exchange to B, and perhaps even loss. But the particular point between £10 and £30 at which the price will be fixed cannot be determined beforehand with certainty. Any price between the two is, economically, possible; a price of £10 : 1s. or a price of £29 : 19s. Here, then, is room for any amount of " higgling."   According as in the conduct of the transaction the buyer or the seller shows the greater dexterity, cunning, obstinacy, power of persuasion, or such-like, will the price be forced either to its lower or to its upper limit.   If both parties have equal skill in bargaining, the price will be fixed approximately midway ; that is to say, about £20.

There is no difficulty in putting this briefly in the form of a general proposition.   In isolated exchange—exchange between one buyer and one seller—the price is determined somewhere between the subjective valuation of the commodity by the buyer as upper limit, and the subjective valuation by the seller as lower limit.

CHAPTER III

FIRST: of one-sided competition of Buyers. Accommodating the conditions of our illustration to the requirements of the new typical case, let us assume that A_1 finds a competitor, whom we shall call A_2, already in the field, and that he also has the intention of purchasing the horse. The circumstances of this competitor are such that he counts the possession of the horse worth as much as £20. What will happen now? Each of the competitors wishes to buy the horse, but only one, of course, can buy him. Each of them wishes to be that one. Each, therefore, will try to persuade B to sell the horse to him, and the means of persuasion will be to bid a higher price. Thus ensues the familiar phenomenon of mutual overbidding. How long will this last? It will last till the rising bids have reached the valuation of the least capable competitor, who, in this case, is A_2. So long as the bids are under £20, A_2, acting on the motto " rather a small gain than no exchange," will try to secure the purchase by raising his offer, which attempt, naturally, A_1, acting on the same principle, will counteract by raising his offer. But A_2 cannot go beyond the limit of £20 without losing by the exchange. At this point his advantage dictates " better no exchange than a loss," and he leaves the field to his competitor.

This is not to say that the price A_1 pays must be just £20. It is possible that B, knowing A_1 to be in urgent want of a horse, will not be content with £20, and will try, by holding back and by skilful bargaining, to extort a price of £25, £28, or even £29:19s. The one thing certain is that the price cannot exceed £30 (the valuation of A_1 who concludes the purchase) and cannot be under £20 (the valuation of A_2, the excluded competitor).

Assume now that, in addition to A_1 and A_2, three other buyers, A_3, A_4, A_5, compete for the horse, and that their circumstances are such that they count the possession of the horse equivalent to £22, £25, and £28 respectively.   It is easy to show, in the same way, that, in the ensuing competition, A_3 will bid to the limit of £22, A_4 to £25, and A_5 to £28 ; that the most capable competitor, A_1, will always be the successful one ; and that the price will be fixed between £30 as higher limit, and £28—the valuation of the most capable of the excluded competitors—as lower limit.

The results of this investigation may therefore be expressed in the following general proposition :—

In one-sided competition of buyers—where there is one seller and more than one buyer—the most capable competitor will be the purchaser; that is, the one who puts the highest value on the commodity he wishes to buy in comparison with the good he wishes to sell; and the price will lie somewhere between the valuation of the purchaser as higher limit, and the valuation of the most capable among the unsuccessful competitors as lower limit—always understood that the price can in no case be lower than the subsidiary lower limit of the seller's own valuation.   Comparing this proposition with the result arrived at under the former typical case, we see that competition of buyers has the effect of narrowing the sphere within which price is determined, and narrowing it in the upward direction.   Between A and B the limits within which price was determined were £10 and £30 ; by the added competition the lower limit was moved up to £28.

Second: of one-sided competition of Sellers.   This forms the exact converse of the foregoing.   Entirely analogous tendencies lead to entirely analogous results—only in an opposite direction.   The statement of this need not detain us long.

Suppose that our friend A is the only buyer, and that five dealers, whom we shall call B_1, B_2, B_3, B_4, and B_5, are competing to sell him a horse.   We assume that all the horses are equally good, but B_1 values his horse at £10, B_2 values his at £12, B_3 at £15, B_4 at £20, and B_5 at £25.   Each of the five rivals tries to utilise the present as the sole opportunity of sale, and endeavours to secure a preference over his competitors by underselling, as in the former case by overbidding. But as no one will care to offer his commodity for less than what it is worth to himself, B_5 will cease offering at £25, B_4 at £20, B_3 at £15; then B_1 and B_2 will compete for a while till, finally, at £12 B_2 finds himself "economically excluded,"[1] and B_1 alone keeps the field. The price at which he remains a seller must necessarily be higher than £10—otherwise there would be no use in the exchange, and therefore no motive for it—but neither must it be higher than £12, otherwise B_2 will continue his competition.

In general terms, then, we have the following proposition. In one-sided competition of sellers—where there is one buyer and more than one seller—the most capable competitor will be the actual seller; that is, the one who puts the lowest value on the good he wishes to sell in comparison with the commodity he wishes to buy; and the price will lie somewhere between the valuation of the seller as lower limit, and the valuation of the most capable among the unsuccessful competitors as higher limit.[2] Compared, therefore, with the case of isolated exchange, where, according to the first formula, the price had to lie between £10 and £30, the sphere within which price is determined will be narrowed by the competitions of sellers, and narrowed in the downward direction.

---

[1] Menger, p. 183.

[2] Always without prejudice to the second or subsidiary upper limit formed by the valuation of the buyer, which the price can in no case go beyond. Where there is anything like full competition of sellers, however, this is seldom of practical importance.

THE case of two-sided competition is the most common in economic life, as it is the most important in the development of the Law of Price. It demands, therefore, our most careful attention.

The typical situation which the present case assumes may be represented by the following scheme. It shows us ten buyers and eight sellers, each of them wishing to buy or sell a horse, and it tells us at the same time the degree of the subjective valuation put upon the horse by each of the exchangers. It will be seen that the figures which represent these valuations are very different, and this exactly corresponds with facts. Indeed, the individual relations of want and provision for want, which regulate subjective value, are so very various that it would be difficult to find two persons who had an entirely similar opinion about the value of any one thing.

BUYERS.				SELLERS.			
A_1 values a horse at	.	.	£30	B_1 values a horse at	.	.	£10
(and will buy at any price under)				(and will sell at any price over)			
A_2	,,	,,	£28	B_2	,,	,,	£11
A_3	,,	,,	£26	B_3	,,	,,	£15
A_4	,,	,,	£24	B_4	,,	,,	£17
A_5	,,	,,	£22	B_5	,,	,,	£20
A_6	,,	,,	£21	B_6	,,	,,	£21:10s.
A_7	,,	,,	£20	B_7	,,	,,	£25
A_8	,,	,,	£18	B_8	,,	,,	£26
A_9	,,	,,	£17				
A_{10}	,,	,,	£15				

To complete the scheme, it must be added that all the competitors appear simultaneously in the one market; that all the horses offered for sale are of equal quality ; and, finally, that the buyers and sellers make no mistake about the actual state of the market, such as would prevent them from really pursuing their own egoistic interests.[1]   We ask now, What will happen in this situation ?

The circumstances of A_1 are such that he considers a horse to be worth £30 to him ; it would therefore be to his advantage to buy even at £29 ; and it is quite certain that any of the eight sellers would be glad to sell him a horse at a price so advantageous to them.   But, evidently, A_1 would be a very poor business man if he rashly bought at such a high price.   For his self-interest demands from the exchange not merely a profit, but the greatest possible profit.   Instead, then, of buying at the highest price—which, all the same, he might do in the worst possible case—he will prefer to begin by offering a price as low as his least capable rivals, and will only raise his offer when, and in the degree that, it is necessary to save himself from being shut out of the market.

In the same way B_1, who, economically, could quite well sell at a price of £11, and at that price could very easily find buyers, will carefully hold back from offering his horse at the lowest figure which he would accept, and will not reduce his price below what he must take if he is to keep his place in the competition.   It may be assumed, then, that the transaction will begin with the buyers holding back and offering low prices, and with the sellers holding back and asking high prices.[2]

---

[1] If, *e.g.*, a buyer erroneously imagines the number of horses brought to market to be much less than it really is, it may very well happen that he hastily consents to pay a higher price than he would have found necessary if he had given better attention to his own interests.   The influence of errors like this on the formation of price must not, of course, be overlooked in a theory of price, but where we are merely trying to bring out the simplest fundamental law it is not necessary to go into such details.   See *Grundzüge*, as before, part ii. p. 486.

[2] The more experienced both parties are, and the more familiar with the condition of the market, the shorter will be the time spent in "trying the market" by preliminary offers.   In an old and well-organised market competitors will save themselves the trouble of making offers that are not meant to be taken, and will make their first offers at least somewhere near that zone within which the market price will finally be fixed.   The extreme limit of this curtailment is given in the "fixed prices" of sellers.   In this case, trying the market is entirely dispensed with, and sellers undertake at one throw, as it were, to hit the very zone into which the condition of the market will force the price.   They must try

Suppose the buyers begin with an offer of £13. It is at once clear that—putting aside the case of gross error as to the condition of the market—the buying cannot be concluded at this price. For at £13 all the ten buyers would be willing to buy, since all of them put a greater value on the horse than £13 ; but, at that price, only two horses, those of B_1 and B_2, could (economically) be offered for sale. Now evidently B_1 and B_2 would be very poor sellers if they did not make use of the active competition of buyers to raise their price, and the others would be as poor buyers if they let the best chances of purchasing be snatched away by two of their members without attempting to obtain the preference by bidding a price somewhat higher, but still advantageous to themselves. Exactly, then, as in the case discussed in last chapter, the surplus buyers will be weeded out by means of mutual overbidding. How long will this weeding process go on ?

At any price under £15 all ten buyers can compete. From that point the least capable competitors must, one after another, withdraw from the competition. At £15 A_{10} is knocked out, at £17 A_9, at £18 A_8, at £20 A_7. But as the bids rise on the one side, the number of those sellers who, economically, become capable of selling increases on the other side. At any price above £15 B_3 may seriously think about selling, above £17 B_4, and above £20 B_5. Thus the marked disproportion, which existed at first between the horses demanded and the horses actually offered for sale, is gradually reduced. At £13 there was an effective demand for ten horses, and only two could, economically, be offered ; while, at any price over £20, only six horses are demanded and five offered, the majority of buyers over sellers being thus reduced to one. So long, however, as the rival buyers are in the majority, and this fact is accurately known in the market, there can be no final settlement. For, on the one hand, the sellers have always the chance, and the temptation, to take advantage of the excess of buyers and stand out for higher prices ; and, on the other hand,

to hit this zone quite exactly ; for if they put the price lower they lose their profit, while if they put it higher the buyers in the market get supplied by other competitors, and the sellers are left with their commodities. Fixed prices, however, are less common in the open market than in shops, where selling is never conducted under the full pressure of competition, and where, consequently, any mistake in the price asked is not so hazardous.

the mutually opposed interests of the rival buyers compel them
to bid still higher against each other. Obviously, A_6 would
scarcely consult his own interests if he were calmly to look on
while his five rivals went off with the five cheapest horses, and
left him no chance of an exchange, and, therefore, no chance of
a profit.[1] But, at the same time, no one of these rivals would
allow A_6 to purchase one of the five horses most "strongly"
offered for sale. For, if so, the man who withdrew in favour
of A_6 might indeed purchase a horse, but only under less
favourable conditions—the conditions, that is, offered by the
most conservative sellers B_6, B_7, and B_8, and at a price which,
at least, exceeds the subjective valuation of £21 : 10s. that
B_6 puts on his horse. Thus if the buyers know their own
interests, the whole body of them will feel impelled to continue
their bidding against each above the level of £20.

Finally, the situation becomes essentially different when
the rising bids have reached the limit of £21. At that price
A_6 is compelled to cease bidding, and there are now only
five sellers against five buyers. These buyers can all be satisfied simultaneously, and there is no occasion for further competition among themselves : on the contrary, as against the
sellers, their common interest is to close at the lowest possible
price. The bidding of buyers against each other, which
hitherto has prevented the final settlement, now comes to an
end, and the bargains *may* be concluded at the price of £21.
But they need not be concluded at that price. The sellers
may possibly be stiff and refuse £21, in hope of a still higher
offer. What will happen in this case ? First of all, the
buyers, rather than have a fruitless errand and go away without
making any exchange, will bid higher. But their limit is now
very near at hand. If the sellers stand out for a price above
£22, A_5 must give up all idea of purchase, and there will be
five sellers against four buyers. One of the sellers, then, will
have to fall out, and as no one would care to be that seller
there will—from motives quite analogous to those which before
prompted the surplus buyers to overbid each other—ensue a

---

[1] If the horses of B_1 to B_5 are sold, the most capable seller remaining is B_6,
who values his horse at £21 : 10s.—that is, higher than A_6. As we know, then,
an exchange between A_6 and B_6 is economically impossible, and the same is true
a fortiori of the less capable sellers B_7 and B_8.

mutual underselling among the surplus sellers, till such time as the fifth seller meets a buyer: this will be the case somewhere under the limit of £22.[1]

Indeed, in the present case, the limit must go still lower. So long as a price over £21 : 10s. was possible, there would be a sixth possible seller in the person of B_6; this would give the sellers a majority of one over the five buyers, and compel them to offer under each other, if they are not to be shut out from the exchange. In this competition the weakest must first go to the wall, and this fate will overtake B_6 the moment that his rivals are content to take a price below the level of £21 : 10s. —at which figure the number of competitors on either side will be equalised, and the level of price found at which the competition may cease. Thus assuming, as we do in this illustration, that each competitor knows what is the condition of the market, and intelligently follows his own interests, the limits within which the price must necessarily be determined are narrowed to £21 and £21 : 10s.; those being the only limits within which there occurs the relation favourable to the final settlement—that all who are able to take a share in the business find it their advantage to do so, while all who do not find it their advantage, the unsuccessful competitors, have no power to prevent the others from coming to terms.[2]

Let us try now to apply the results of these lengthy analyses to our theory of price.

We notice, first, that what decides success in two-sided competition is, as in the case of one-sided competition, the degree of "capability" for exchange. On either side

---

[1] It need scarcely be said that the gradual bidding up of buyers, and the gradual under-offering of sellers, do not usually take place in two separate and succeeding stages, but generally occur simultaneously.

[2] In the nature of things the result shown in our abstract scheme will be the more exactly realised in practice, the better known the total condition of the market is to all interested; that is to say, the more organic the market, and the more publicly the negotiations are conducted. Where, on the other hand, as is usually the case, transactions are conducted in groups that are, indeed, in communication, but are yet somewhat separated from each other either in space or time, the relations of competition that would prevail over an entire market will, naturally, not be quite active in the single groups, and this has for result that the prices formed in the single groups are frequently only more or less approximate to the ideal market price represented in our scheme, without necessarily exactly coinciding with it.

it is the most capable competitors who come to terms, namely, those buyers who put the highest value on the commodity (A_1 to A_5), and those sellers who put the lowest value (B_1 to B_5), while all less capable competitors are excluded. And, indeed, if we look more closely, we shall find that the series of successful competitors includes all competing pairs, arranged by capability, between whom there exists the relation necessary for exchange, viz. that the buyer considers the commodity worth more than the seller does. In our illustration A_5 considers B_5's horse worth more than B_5 himself does, and, accordingly, they can exchange with each other.[1] A_6, on the other hand, values the horse of B_6 at £21 only, while B_6 values it at £21 : 10s., and therefore they cannot come to terms—and still less can those competitors who are less capable.

Very closely related to the grounds on which are decided the successful competitors in the struggle of competition are, secondly, the grounds on which is decided the market price that results from this struggle. This price—to recur to our illustration—cannot, in any case, be higher than the valuation of A_5, nor less than that of B_5; otherwise the fifth buyer in the one case and the fifth seller in the other would not have come to terms. But, again, the price cannot in any case be higher than the valuation of B_6, nor less than that of A_6; otherwise in the former case a sixth buyer would begin competing with the other five buyers, and in the latter case a sixth seller competing with the other five sellers; the equilibrium would thus be destroyed, and the overbidding and under-offering would inevitably be continued till such time as the price was forced within the limits already indicated.

To put these results in general form :—In two-sided competition the market price is determined within a latitude of which the upper limit is constituted by the valuation of the last buyer who actually exchanges (the last buyer) and that of the most capable seller excluded (the first excluded seller), and the lower limit by the valuation of the least capable seller who actually effects a sale (the last seller) and that of the most capable buyer excluded (the first excluded buyer). The meaning of this

---

[1] Or with one of the more capable competitors, but in no case with a weaker one. See more exactly on this point in my *Grundzüge*, p. 499.

double limitation is that, in every case, it is the narrower limit that decides.[1]   If, finally, we substitute the short and significant name of "Marginal Pairs" for the detailed description of the four parties whose competition determines the price, we get this very simple formula : The market price is limited and determined by the subjective valuations of the two Marginal Pairs.

This suggests a number of reflections.

The first thing that strikes us is the analogy between the formation of price and the formation of subjective value.   We saw that the subjective value of any good, unaffected by the more important uses to which single members of the same stock might be put, was a "marginal value"—a value determined by the good's marginal utility, or that utility which stands on the very limit of the economically permissible.   Now we see that every market price is a "marginal price"—a price determined by the economical relations of those competing pairs which, also, stand on the very limit of exchangeability It is easy to see that the analogy here is no chance coincidence, but one that results from closely-related and internal causes. In the case of subjective valuation, the motive of economical advantage demanded that the available stock of goods should be employed in satisfying the wants that stood highest on each man's scale, the last of the wants thus supplied indicating the "marginal utility."   In the case of the formation of price, the motive of the competitors' economical advantage demands that the pairs which are most capable on the scale of competitors should come to terms, and one of these again is the last, the "marginal pair."   In the former case, the provision for all satisfactions more important than the marginal utility was assured without the particular good whose value was the subject of discussion, and the only utility dependent on this latter good was the last, the marginal utility.   In the latter case, all the contracting pairs more capable than the marginal pairs may come to terms at prices higher or lower, and here again it is only the fate of the last, the marginal pair, that

---

[1] In our illustration it is the valuation of the excluded parties A_6 and B_6.   If, however, the valuation of A_6, instead of being £21, had been £19, and that of B_6, instead of £21 : 10s., had been £23, the limits would have been determined by the valuation of the last pair who actually came to terms : the price would have been fixed between £20 and £22.

depends on the price just reaching a definite height, neither greater nor less. And, finally, as in the former case the importance of the last dependent want, in virtue of its dependent relation, gave the good its value, so, in the latter case, the economical circumstances of the last dependent pair— here also in virtue of their dependent relation—confer on the commodity its price.

But this analogy does not exhaust the connections between price and subjective value. Of still greater consequence is the fact that price, from beginning to end, is the product of subjective valuations. Look back over what we have said. It is the relation of the subjective valuation of commodity and price-equivalent which decides the persons who may consider it worth their while to compete, either as buyers or sellers; that is to say, decides which parties are " capable of exchange." It is the same relation which decides on the degree of each competitor's capability of exchange. With perfect exactness it decides for each man the figure at which his advantage calls him to join in the competition, and it decides, at the same time, the limit at which he is beaten and obliged to withdraw from it. As further result, it decides the parties who, among the most capable competitors, actually come to terms; it decides to which pair falls the rôle of being marginal pair; and, finally, it decides on the price at which the bargains are concluded in the market. Thus, as a fact, in the whole course of the formation of price —so far as it is conducted on purely egoistic principles—there is not a single phase nor feature which is not traceable, wholly and entirely, to the position of subjective valuations as its cause. And this is at bottom perfectly natural. For, as we know, these subjective valuations point out whether any importance, great or little, attaches to a good as regards our economic wellbeing, and how great the importance is; and, consequently, these valuations, wherever we acquire or part with goods solely with regard to our economic wellbeing, mark out the natural, indeed the only possible compass of our transactions. We are, therefore, fully justified in defining price as the resultant of subjective valuations put upon commodity and price-equivalent within a market.[1]

[1] Sax, who, in his theory of value and price, stands wholly and entirely on the foundation laid by Menger, repeatedly and with emphasis characterises market

Of course it is a resultant of a peculiar kind. The amount of price is not the resultant of the sum, or of the average of all the valuations that come to the surface : in the formation of price these take very different shares. One class of them has no effect on price at all; viz. those valuations made by all the unsuccessful competitors except the most capable pair. It is all the same whether there are no such valuations, or whether there are scores of them in the market : they make not the slightest difference on the resultant price. In our illustration, whether there are unsuccessful buyers A_7 to A_{10} or not, whether the category of the unsuccessful is composed of them alone, or of a hundred others besides,—so long as they cannot bid more than £20, it is easy to show that the resultant price will always run between £21 and £21 : 10s. The excluded competitors may increase the congestion of the market, but they are not factors in that condition of the market which determines the formation of price.[1]

A second group plays a very peculiar part in this resultant, viz. that consisting of the valuations of all the contracting parties who actually come to terms, exclusive of the last. What they do is simply to bind and neutralise each other. Recur again to our typical illustration. If we inquire what, for instance, the presence of A_1 contributes to the formation of price, we find that he takes up one member of the opposing series, namely, B_1, with the result that now the formation of price proceeds exactly as if neither A_1 nor B_1 were in the market. Similarly it is not difficult to see that the efficiency of A_2, A_3, and A_4 simply consists in cancelling the efficiency of B_2, B_3, and B_4 : if they are in the competition the resultant

price as an "average of individual values" (*Theoretische Grundlegung der Staats-wirthschaft*, p. 276 and *passim*). This expression, if given without commentary, is exceedingly unfortunate, indeed directly misleading. As may be seen from what follows above (and more exactly from what I wrote in my *Grundzüge*, pp. 505 and, particularly, 522), the characteristic thing, on the contrary, as regards the resultant price, is that it is *not* an "average" in the usual sense of the word.

[1] At least under the assumption distinctly made in our inquiry, that the competitors who appear in the market have a correct knowledge of the condition of the market. If we depart from this assumption, the appearance of more than a hundred demanders might give rise to the erroneous opinion that there may be among them a great many persons of higher "capability," and this might mislead the few capable competitors who are present into rashly making higher offers.

price falls between £21 and £21 : 10s.; if they were all absent A₅ and B₅ would still make their exchange at a price between £21 and £21 : 10s. And it is worth emphasising that the *degree* of the subjective valuations made in this group is quite indifferent to the result. A₁, for instance, whose valuation, in our scheme, is put down at £30, would cancel B₁ not less thoroughly if his valuation amounted to only £25 or £22 ; and, conversely, suppose that his estimate were £200 or £2000, of this enormous amount absolutely nothing would affect the resultant price except the sum, in any case, absorbed in neutralising B₁.

If, however, the valuations of this group have no direct influence on the formation of price, it cannot be said that they are quite without effect. When the valuations of A₁ to A₄ cancel those of B₁ to B₄ they have a twofold result. First, they prevent any stronger seller than B₅ getting into the marginal pair which immediately determines the price. And second, they prevent the strongest sellers from cancelling the next strongest buyers—as they might do if not cancelled already—and they thus prevent any weaker member of the buying series than A₅ from getting into the marginal pair.[1] The part played by all those exchanging pairs who are stronger or more capable than the last may therefore be accurately characterised in the following words : Their valuations contribute nothing directly to the formation of the resultant price, but they do indirectly, in so far as they neutralise each other, and thus reserve the rôle of marginal pair for another couple.

Finally, the real decision of price lies exclusively with a

---

[1] To show this, suppose we leave A₁ to A₄ out of our illustration. The position of the parties, then, is as follows :—

A₅	.	.	.	. £22	B₁	.	.	.	. £10
A₆	.	.	.	. £21	B₂	.	.	.	. £11
A₇	.	.	.	. £20	B₃	.	.	.	. £15
A₈	.	.	.	. £18	B₄	.	.	.	. £17
A₉	.	.	.	. £17	B₅	.	.	.	. £20
A₁₀	.	.	.	. £15	B₆	.	.	.	. £21 :10s.
					B₇	.	.	.	. £25
					B₈	.	.	.	. £26

Here we see that the last pair within which the economical conditions of exchange are present consists of A₈ and B₄. The buyers, therefore, are now represented in the decisive marginal pair by a weaker member, the sellers by a stronger one. Accordingly the limit of price, which in the last case stood between £21 and £21 : 10s., moves down to between £17 and £18.

third group, and that a small one—the valuations of the two marginal pairs.   All weaker competitors being, absolutely, without influence, and all stronger ones cancelling each other, they and they alone are the directly effective components, and the market price is their resultant.

At first sight it may appear strange that so few persons, and those so little conspicuous, should decide the fate of the whole market, but on closer examination this will be found quite natural.   If all are to exchange at one market price, the price must be such as to suit all exchanging parties; and since, naturally, the price which suits the least capable contracting party suits, in a higher degree, all the more capable, it follows, quite naturally, that the relations of the last pair whom the price must suit, or, as the case may be, the first pair whom it cannot suit, afford the standard for the height of price.[1]

---

[1] Students of economic literature will not fail to notice an interesting relation in which the above theory stands to certain doctrines that have for long obtained full recognition.   When Thünen—and with him the whole body of economic doctrine—said that the rate of interest was determined by the productivity of the "portion of capital last applied," and the rate of wage by the return of the "last worker employed in the undertaking"; or when, much earlier, the question as to which, among several costs, regulates market price was decided in favour of the "highest costs of production that were still necessary to provide for the market," *i.e.* in favour of the "last seller,"—we recognise in all these, without difficulty, adaptations to special cases of the same principle on which we have built the doctrine of marginal utility and the theory of the formation of price. The only thing is that at that time economists were not yet conscious of the universal importance of these peculiar lines of thought.   They meant simply to state a couple of special rules of limited range, while in reality they had hit upon the dominating *Leitmotiv*, which underlies the entire mechanism of industry carried on under the guidance of self-interest, and which, therefore, runs through the entire formation of value and price.

CHAPTER V

THE LAW OF SUPPLY AND DEMAND

THE zone within the limits of which the struggle of competition forces the formation of price is, as we have seen, characterised as lying between the subjective valuations of the marginal pairs, and on this characteristic feature we have formulated our law of price. But this zone has a second characteristic feature: it is that in which exactly as many commodities are offered for sale as are wanted to purchase;[1] or, to use the common expressions, in which supply and demand are quantitatively in equilibrium. In our scheme, at a price which did not rise to £21 more horses were demanded than were offered; at a price which rose above £21 : 10s. more horses were offered than were demanded; while in the zone indicated by our law of marginal pairs—that between £21 and £21 : 10s.—the position requisite to end the competition was reached, and at that price exactly as many horses were asked as were offered.

Now, if it should be thought preferable, the formulation of the law of price may be based on this second characteristic feature, and it will then take the following shape: The market price is found in that zone in which supply and demand quantitatively balance each other. This formula is as correct as the other. It indicates the same zone in another way. But it is less expressive (1) in so far as it only points to the level of the determining zone in a roundabout way,

---

[1] I need scarcely say in so many words that it is not the number of persons wishing to buy and sell on which the formation of price depends, but the mass of commodities desired and offered, and that in the typical scheme it is only for simplicity's sake that I have assumed each person to desire and offer for sale only one commodity, whereby number of persons and mass of commodities go *pari passu.*

while, by our formula, the limits of this zone are directly and positively indicated ; (2) as it has to contend to some extent with the difficulty of having to use the expressions Supply and Demand,—for the protean ambiguity of these terms is sure to bring innumerable errors and misconceptions in their train, just as it has brought the terms themselves into thoroughly bad repute with many.[1]   Still, these drawbacks may very well be overcome by critical attention ; and there is no objection, in my opinion, to treat the theory of price under the good old catchwords Supply and Demand, if care is only taken to avoid the errors and misunderstandings which so plentifully surround them, and to inform the old forms and formulas with new and clear knowledge.[2]

In one special case this second formulation of our law of price is even the more exact of the two.   In the vast majority of cases, the zone within which supply and demand just balance each other exactly coincides with the zone whose limits are marked out by the valuations of the marginal pairs.   But there is one quite definite coincidence of circumstances in which it may happen that the equilibrium between supply and demand does not make its appearance within the whole of the last-mentioned zone, but only within a distinctly narrower part of that zone ; and, in such cases, the price is always fixed within these narrower limits.   The very peculiar coincidence of circumstances which produces this result occurs very rarely indeed in economic life, but, among the cases where it does occur, there is one that is very important for the theoretical explanation of interest, and for that reason, in spite of its somewhat " exotic " character, I must devote a few words to it.

The casuistical conditions of this case are the following. First, there must be considerable latitude between the valuations of the marginal pairs.   This condition is most thoroughly fulfilled where all the competing exchangers come to terms (there being, therefore, no excluded competitors), and when, at the same time, the buyers, as a body, value the commodity

---

[1] See my *Grundzüge*, p. 525.

[2] On the relation of the above theory of price to the old doctrine of Supply and Demand, as well as on the truth and error contained in that doctrine, I have already written at length in my *Grundzüge*, pp. 524-534 ; here it is sufficient to refer to that work.

considerably higher than the sellers do. If there are, for instance, ten buyers who each value the commodity at £10, and ten sellers who each value it, subjectively, at £1, obviously all the ten pairs can come to terms, and the zone which lies between the valuations of the last buyer and the last seller represents the wide latitude between £1 and £10. Secondly, that this latitude should be narrowed down, the further circumstance must be present, that the desire of the buyers is directed to an unlimited number of goods, while, at the same time, the total amount of means of purchase must be strictly limited, and the buyers must be determined to spend the whole of this sum in purchase of the commodities in question—in the purchase of fewer goods if the price be high. in the purchase of a proportionately larger number of goods if the price be low. To put it in terms of our illustration. Say that each of the ten buyers is resolved to spend the sum of £100 in buying cotton goods; that is to say, at any price under £10 he will buy as many pieces as he can obtain for £100. And suppose that against this total competing demand of £1000 there is a supply of 200 goods, which their owners are inclined to let go at any price above £1. It is easy to see that the price must be fixed at £5 the piece. For if the price were to be less, say £4, the 200 pieces offered would be purchased for £800, and £200 of the available means of purchase would remain unemployed Here the owners, acting on the motto "rather a small gain than no exchange," will continue bidding up against each other, and so raise the price to £5, at which figure the whole capital of £1000 finds employment. If, on the other hand, the price were to be put still higher, say £8, only 125 pieces of cotton goods could be bought with the £1000 available, and 75 would remain unsold. Now, obviously, no seller (considering that the price remains profitable to him till it is brought down as low as £1) would willingly forego taking part in the exchange, and thus the sellers, in fear of being shut out, would offer below each other, and the price would be pressed down to the equilibrium point of £5. Inside the wider zone, then, of £1 to £10—that determined by the valuations of the marginal pairs —the necessity for equilibrium between supply and demand determines the price with much more exactitude, and fixes it at £5, that being the point at which, if the competitors follow their own interests without let or hindrance, the market price must be fixed.

As we have already said, the extremely peculiar coincidence of circumstances necessary to this result occurs very seldom, but, as it happens, the cases where it does occur are very notable. One of these is the formation of the price of Money—which, however, does not concern us here.[1] A second is the formation of price in the Labour market, and this is the case which we shall have to take up later on, on account of its close connection with the origin and height of Interest. It should, however, be carefully noted that, even in these two cases, the conditions under which this special form of the law of price appears are seldom met with in economic life in entire isolation. Thus the practical importance of such cases is still further diminished, and, if the recognition of them cannot well be ignored in the course of any theoretical exposition, still, as regards the infinite majority of cases, the first formulation of the law of price—that which determines the height of price by the subjective valuations of the marginal pairs—may be relied on with perfect confidence. This formulation is always correct, and, for the infinite majority of cases, is sufficiently exact. Moreover, without losing its practical usefulness in the majority of cases, it permits of being still further simplified. Before going on to this, however, some other explanations are necessary.

---

[1] Without being a blind adherent of the "Quantity theory," I believe that, along with other important circumstances, the quantity of money, the amount of the supply of money, exerts a powerful influence on its purchasing power. But the supply of money has exactly the peculiarity described in the text, that, rather than let money lie entirely unused, holders will be content with a comparatively unremunerative employment, and that, at the same time, the entire given quantity of money strives to realise itself in the purchase of an unlimited quantity of commodities—the more the better.

CHAPTER VI

THE INDIVIDUAL DETERMINANTS OF PRICE

In the chapter before last we saw that price is determined at a level fixed by the valuations of the marginal pairs. We have still to ask, What are the circumstances which determine whether this level itself is high or low ?

The first few steps in the answer are very easy. It is clear at a glance that the two things which must have the decisive influence on the position of the marginal pairs are the *number* and the *intensity* of the desires or valuations on both sides. In this way. The level of the valuation of the marginal pairs will tend to be high when, on the side of the buyers, there are very high valuations, and, relatively, a great many of them, and when, on the side of the sellers, the low valuations are relatively few. For, in this case, the few low valuations of the sellers will be cancelled by a portion of the more numerous high valuations of the buyers, and since, after this is done, there are still buyers with a high valuation, while at the same time the only remaining sellers also have a high valuation, the marginal pairs on both sides are composed of persons with high valuations. On quite analogous grounds the level of the valuation of the marginal pairs will tend to be low when, on the side of the buyers, there are (relatively) few high valuations, and on the side of the sellers there are (relatively) many low valuations.

If we single out the individual factors from the combined action of which, as we have shown, the valuation level of the marginal pairs results, we get the following individual determinants of price : [1]—

[1] I should like to say that I here bring forward the theory of the determinants of price only in the briefest of epitomes, because the details of it have no imme-

1. The number of desires directed towards the commodity (Extent of Demand).
2. The figures which the buyers put upon their valuations (Intensity of Demand).

The latter, however, is not a simple matter. The figures in which valuations are expressed are in no wise simple expressions of the absolute amount of subjective value which the commodity has for the valuer. They only express a relation obtained by comparing two different valuations—that of the commodity and that of the equivalent price. When we said in our scheme that A values a horse at £30, that is not to say or prove anything of the absolute importance of a horse to A's wellbeing; all that it expresses is the relation in which the value of the horse to A stands to the value of the money to A. It simply says that A values the horse thirty times more highly than he values one pound sterling. If, therefore, we wish—and this is the task in which we are at present engaged —to lay down the *elementary* factors in the formation of price, we must put down, instead of the combined amounts which make up the figures of our valuation, the elements out of which they are combined. These elements are two—first, the absolute amount of subjective value which the commodity has for the valuer; and second, the absolute amount of the subjective value which the unit of the equivalent price has for the valuer. And, indeed, they obviously work towards combination in this sense, that the figures are high in direct ratio to the absolute value of the commodity, and in inverse ratio to that of the equivalent, and *vice versâ*.

Thus, in our scheme of the determinants of price, instead of the valuation figures, we have to lay down as the determinants of these figures—

(a) The subjective valuation of the *commodity* by the buyers (which itself, again, according to the law of marginal utility already laid down, depends on the relation of wants and provision for want); and

(b) The subjective valuation of the *equivalent price* by the buyers. Since, under present conditions, it is money

diate interest for the theory of capital. Any one interested in the theory of price as such, I would refer to the full statement in Conrad's *Jahrbücher*, vol. xiii. pp. 508-524.

that mostly serves as equivalent, and since, as we saw in a former chapter, the unit of money has a smaller subjective value for the rich than for the poor, it is, in the last instance, the standard of comfort of the buyers which has the preponderating influence on the formation of this determinant.[1]

Continuing our enumeration we have—

3. The number in which goods are offered for sale (Extent of Supply).

4. The figures which the sellers put upon their valuations (Intensity of Supply).

As in the former case, this latter determinant may be split up into two simpler factors—

(*a*) The subjective valuations of the commodity by the sellers.

(*b*) The subjective valuations of the equivalent price by the sellers.

These two find their own further determination according to the law of marginal utility. But frequently this leads to a very noteworthy peculiarity. In the present condition of industry most sales are made by men who are producers and merchants by profession, and who hold an amount of their commodities entirely beyond any needs of their own. Consequently, for them the subjective use-value[2] of their own wares is, for the most part, very nearly nil; and the figure which they put on their valuation (in which the subjective use-value is the standard element) also sinks almost to zero. Finally comes the result that, in such sales, the limiting effect which, according to our theoretical formula, would be exerted by the valuation of the last seller, practically does not come into play, and price is actually limited and determined by the valuations of the buyers alone. In other words : when goods are once produced, and the owner can do nothing with them for his own personal wants, they must, all the same, seek a market. To find this market the seller must, in the usual way, put his

---

[1] The older theory was misled by this into substituting, for the determinant "subjective valuation of the equivalent price," the "ability to pay" of the buyers, which is not exactly false, but is very one-sided. See the more exact statement in Conrad's *Jahrbücher*, pp. 520, 527.

[2] This, and not subjective exchange value, is the important thing for the formation of price. See the *Grundzüge*, p. 516.

goods at a price low enough to find buyers for the whole stock he offers for sale. In the case of a stock of 1000 pieces, for instance, he will find his market at a price which is somewhat less than the valuation of the thousandth buyer, and somewhat higher than the valuation of the thousand and first. If, now, the relations of production and sale are normal, the whole stock offered will, almost invariably, be taken off by the demand at a price which is far above the minimum use-value of the commodity to the sellers, and which, beyond the full amount of costs, brings them a business profit. If the circumstances, however, are unfavourable, it may well happen that the seller must seek for his market at considerably lower levels of demand, and be content to take prices which show a loss when compared with costs of production. But, as a rule, even those forced prices are still above the subjective use-value of the commodity to the seller, and the function of this subjective use-value, as lower limit of price, does not come into operation. It is only if the price should sink almost to zero that it would be checked in its descent by this latter limit, the valuation of the seller, finally coming into play. But it can scarcely ever come to this : in almost all cases the competition of buyers is sufficient of itself to stop the downward movement at a higher point on the scale. Thus, in regard to the prices actually established within a large and organised market, the law of price undergoes a great simplification. Of the four valuations which, as "valuations of the two marginal pairs," limit the zone within which price is determined, the valuations of the seller, for the reasons mentioned above, fall out altogether. But, if the buyers are very numerous, the interval between the figures which two successive buyers put on their valuation is so small, that the zone limited by the figure of the last buyer and that of the first unsuccessful competitor, is narrowed almost to a point. And so far as this is the case it may be asserted, with sufficient exactness, of the economic exchange which goes on in large markets, that the market price is determined by the Valuation of the Last Buyer.[1]

[1] This may be a suitable place to finish the analysis of Scharling's argument, which I began on p. 160. Scharling explains (Conrad's *Jahrbücher*, vol. xvi. p. 542) that in all essential respects he can agree with my theory of price ; only, he says, it does not go far enough. My "determinants," and even the deter-

minants of these determinants, do not go to the very root of the explanation ;
there is still something wanting; and this something, this *Schlussstein* or "element
which, in the last resort, determines the conditions for an exchange," Scharling
thinks that he has found in the "exertion (*Anstrengung*) which is spared the man
who wishes . . . to obtain possession of a good by the fact that the good is
transferred to him, in the case in question, by the other party in the exchange"
(p. 551).   If Scharling here were to mean by *Anstrengung* the toil of production
which must otherwise be expended, directly or indirectly, for the acquisition of the
good, his proposition would be positively false (see above, p. 160 in note), and
this, indeed, Scharling himself seems to see and, indirectly at least, to admit
(pp. 531, 554).   But he goes on to give this expression a wider meaning.   Under
it he now embraces, among other things, the exertion which it costs to induce an
owner to part with his commodity (p. 554), or "to meet competitors" (p. 556), or
"to meet other suitors by overbidding" (p. 558), or "to overcome the indisposition
of the owner to part with the good" (p. 558), and so on.   "The right of the owner
to possess the good," explains Scharling in the most significant passage of this
kind, "is the last hindrance which stands in the way of the buyer's acquisition of
the same, and this is now the thing to remove.   The exertion which is required for
this determines the value, the conditions for the exchange" (p. 558).   Now, what
kind of "exertion" is this ?   Scharling himself speaks of it more than once with
all desirable plainness (*e.g.* p. 555, line 15 ; p. 558, lines 5, 16, etc.)   It consists
simply in the offering of a sufficiently high or higher price, in a bidding up or
bidding higher.   And now I ask : First, is there any justification, material or
linguistic, for calling the offering of a price an "exertion," and, specially, for
calling the offering of a price of £20 twice as great an exertion as offering a price
of £10 ?   Second, is the "exertion" which consists in offering the purchase price,
e.g. at an auction, *spared* the purchaser, or must he not rather take the exertion
on himself if he is to obtain the good ?   And, third and principally, is it explaining the formation of price, or going round about the explanation in a manifest
circle, to account for the height of price by the amount of the exertion which the
meeting of competition and the inducing of the owner cost, and then explain
this exertion again as the offering of a sufficiently high or higher price ?   Is this
not rather to say directly ;—the price is high when and because much must be
paid to get the good, and it is low in another case when and because but little
need be paid ?   Who will be inclined to accept this as "*der Weisheit letzten
Schluss*," as the long-sought-for coping-stone of the theory of price ?—And
now one more remark in case of misunderstanding.   I am very far from denying that "difficulty of attainment" or "amount of toil of production" may, and
very often actually does, afford one single important *secondary* determinant for
the relation of want and provision for want, thereby for the height of marginal
utility, and so, finally, for the amount of value.   But this determinant only
works in the way, and within the limits, which I have indicated in my theory
(see in particular the statement of the "exceptional case," where the amount of
a pain or strain averted determines the value of a good, *Grundzüge*, p. 42, and
especially the statement of the influence of costs of production on value and
price, p. 61 ; then pp. 521, 532, 534).   On the other hand, the more extensive
claim that Scharling puts forward with so much emphasis (vol. xvi. pp. 551, 552),
that difficulty of attainment by itself alone is the last universal determinant and
measure of value, I can only most emphatically reject.

CHAPTER VII

THE LAW OF COSTS

IN the sphere of price, as in the theory of subjective value, we find a law firmly rooted in economic literature and accredited by common experience. It tells us that the market price of goods reproducible at will tends to equalise itself, in the long-run, with Costs of Production. The following perfectly valid line of argument is usually adduced in proof of this. The market price of goods reproducible at will cannot, in the long-run, be maintained either much above or much below their cost. If at any time the price of an article rises appreciably above the cost, its production will be particularly profitable to the undertakers. This will not only induce the latter to extend their already flourishing businesses, but will encourage new undertakers to enter the same remunerative branch of industry. Thus the amount of product brought to market will be increased, and finally—according to the law of supply and demand—a fall in price will ensue. If, conversely, at any time the market price falls below costs, continued production will show a loss; many undertakers will reduce their output; the supply of the commodities will be reduced; and this, finally, in virtue of the law of supply and demand, must lead to a raising of the market price.

Round this law of costs has gathered a great mass of theoretical detail,[1] which may, for our purposes, be left entirely on

---

[1] Thus the question as to costs of production or costs of reproduction; whether, in the case of a variety of costs, it is the highest, the lowest, or an average cost that is to be taken as standard; what elements are to be reckoned among costs, and so on.

one side.   Our whole interest is centred in the question as to
the position which the law, so well accredited by experience,
takes in the systematic theory of price.   Does it run counter
to our law of marginal pairs or not ?

Our answer is that it does not.   It is as little of a contradiction as we before found to exist between the proposition
that the marginal utility determines the height of subjective
value, and the other proposition that the costs determine it.
The line of thought which, in both cases, leads to the solution
of the apparent contradiction is the same, feature for feature ;
except that, in the present case, in virtue of the intervention
of exchange,—in virtue, that is, of the translation of the
phenomena out of individual economy into social economy,—
there appear richer developments at every station on the line
of thought.

In what follows I shall try, as briefly and clearly as
possible, to describe the concatenation between Value, Price,
and Costs ; and I think I am not exaggerating when I say that,
to understand clearly this connection, is to understand clearly
the better part of Political Economy.

The formation of value and price takes its start from the
subjective valuations put upon finished products by their consumers.   These valuations determine the demand for those
products.   As supply, over against this demand, stand, in the
first instance, the stocks of finished commodities held by producers.   The point of intersection of the two-sided valuations,
the valuation of the marginal pairs, determines, as we know,
the price, and, of course, determines the price of each kind of
product separately.   Thus, for instance, the price of iron rails
is determined by the relation of supply and demand for rails ;
the price of nails, by the relation of supply and demand for
nails ; and, similarly, the price of every other product made
out of the productive good iron—such as spades, ploughshares,
hammers, sheet-iron, boilers, machines, etc.—is determined by
the relation between the supply and demand which obtains for
these special kinds of products.   To make this perfectly clear,
let us assume that the relations between requirements and
stocks of the various iron products—and, accordingly, their
prices to begin with—are very various ; that the price of a
quantum of commodity which can be made out of one and the

same unit of productive material[1]—for instance, from a cwt. of iron—varies from 2s. for the cheapest to 20s. for the dearest class of products.   These prices are the result of the position of the market at the moment, and we have first assumed that the stocks of products (the supply) are a given quantity.   But they are only for the moment a given quantity.   As time goes on, they are always getting supplemented from production, and this makes them a variable quantity.   Let us follow the circumstances of this production.   For the manufacture of iron fabrics producers, of course, require iron.[2]   Under the system of division of labour they must buy this in the iron market.   The manufacturers represent this demand for iron.   As regards the *extent* of the demand, it is clear that every producer will buy as much iron as he requires to produce that amount of the commodity which he may expect to sell among his customers.   But how will it be as regards the *intensity* of the demand ?   Obviously no producer will give more for the cwt. of iron than he can get for it[3] from his own customers in the shape of price ; but, up to this point, even in the worst case, he can and will compete rather than let his production come to a standstill for want of raw material.   The manufacturer, therefore, who can profitably employ the cwt. of iron if he gets 20s. from his customers will be a buyer in the iron market up to the price of 20s. as maximum ; he who can profitably employ the cwt. of iron at 16s. will, naturally, not buy at a price over 16s., and so on. In this way the market price which each producer of iron wares gets for his particular wares (or the share of the market price which falls to iron according to the law of complementary goods) furnishes him with the concrete valuation which he has in his mind when joining in the demand for iron.

[1] To simplify the matter, we shall omit for the moment the co-operation of any other complementary means of production.

[2] Again, for simplicity's sake, I leave out the other requisites of production.

[3] It must be remembered that here we are making abstraction of the co-operation of other complementary means of production, as Labour, Tools, Coal, etc. If otherwise, of course, according to the principles laid down above (p. 170) on the value of complementary goods, we should have to put a portion of the value of the product to the account of the other co-operating goods, and assign only a quota of the product's value to the iron.   But, in that case, exactly the same relations, as are shown in the text to exist between the value of iron and the full value of the product, would hold between the value of the iron and that quota of the product's value.

Q

The supply, which stands over against this demand, consists of the stocks of iron held by the mine-owners and ironmasters. These stocks will pass, in methods familiar to us, into the possession of the most capable buyers, and at a price which, approximately, corresponds to the valuation of the last buyer.[1] Suppose the stocks of iron are sufficient to meet the demand of all those buyers who value iron from 20s. down to 6s. per cwt., the valuation of the last buyer, and thus the market price of the iron, will stand at 6s.

And now we have to consider the causal connection which has ended in this price. It runs, in the clearest possible way, in an unbroken chain from value and price of products to value and price of *costs*—from iron wares to raw iron, and not conversely. The links in the chain are these. The valuation which consumers subjectively put upon iron products forms the first link. This helps, next, to determine the figures of the valuation—the money price at which consumers can take part in the demand for iron products. These prices, then, determine, in methods with which we are now familiar, the resultant price of iron products in the market for such products. This resultant price, again, indicates to the *producers* the (exchange) valuation which they in turn may attach to the productive material iron, and thus the figure at which they may enter the market as buyers of iron. From their figures, finally, results the market price of iron.

But still another and very important connection may be gathered from all this. It is that here we have simply the great law of marginal utility fulfilling itself. According to that law the available stock of goods is, successively, conducted into the most remunerative employments—put to the most advantageous uses,—and the last use to which the goods are put determines their value. In any individual economy the most remunerative uses are seen to be those which express the most urgent subjective wants, and the value which emerges, as result of these individual relations, is purely personal subjective value. In the more extended sphere of a market, on the other hand, everything is referred, no longer directly to subjective wants, but to those wants as mediated by money— money being, as it were, the neutral common denomination for

[1] See above, p. 221.

wants and feelings of various subjects which are not immediately commensurable. Here emerge, as the most remunerative employments, not those which express the wants absolutely most urgent, but those which are represented by the highest money valuation; that is, the *best paying* employments;[1] and the value which results is objective exchange value. Thus it is, first of all, with iron products. In their respective markets they pass to the best paying buyers, and the price which expresses the valuation of the last buyer determines their market value and price. But so it is also, in the second place, in a slightly roundabout way, with the "cost good," iron, itself. In the iron market it goes to the best paying producers, and the valuation of the last of these determines its price. But here the producers are simply mediators. In their conducting of the iron to the best paying consumers, the stock of iron really passes successively to the most remunerative forms of consumption, and the last of *these* forms provided for determines—through the valuation named by the last producer who enters the market as buyer—the market price of the cost good, iron. It is not this cost good, then, that dictates its fixed price to the products that proceed from it; on the contrary, it receives its own price by the medium of the price of its products, in conformity with the great law of marginal utility, according to which the available stock is forced into the most remunerative employments, and receives its price from the money valuations of the last of these.

But connected with this is a series of subsequent phenomena, which, obviously, have given rise to the opinion that costs exert a causal influence on the price of products. So long as the price of various products made from iron varies between 20s. and 2s., while the price of the unit of iron stands at 6s., it is an evidence that the economical principle which should guide the stocks of iron into the most remunerative employments is not fully carried out. Iron is being used in employments where the products fetch only 2s. or 3s., where, accordingly, the use is less than the "last" economically permissible; and, on the other hand, there are still numerous

---

[1] That these two, unfortunately, are not usually the same I have shown at length in Conrad's *Jahrbücher*, pp. 510-513, when discussing the causes and effects of this fact.

employments unprovided for, where the products would obtain
a greater value than 6s.   If, for instance, the market price of
an iron product stands at 20s., it is a proof that only those
consumers of that product who value it at 20s. and upwards
are actually purchasing, while other consumers, whose valuations range from 18s. down to 6s., are not supplied in the
market.   Similarly with products whose market price stands
at 16s.; there will be an unsatisfied layer of demand, with a
use for the product corresponding to the prices 14s. down to
6s., and so on.   Now this must be corrected—and the enterprise
of undertakers will usually not be long in supplying the needed
correction.   The production of those iron wares, the price of
which still stands above 6s., will, under the inducement of the
premium offered by the difference between price and cost, be
increased till all those employments where the utility is greater
than the amount of 6s. are supplied.   Of course this increase
of supply has the effect of always reducing the level in which
the "last" buyer is found, and thus the market price sinks,
till such time as the money valuation of the last buyer,
and with it the market price, comes to the normal level of 6s.
Conversely, where iron has been put to employments whose
products fetch less than 6s., the loss that ensues will prevent
more iron being thus employed.   This will be brought about by
a temporary suspension or limitation of the production of those
iron wares, the market price of which is under 6s.   This limitation of supply will soon have the effect of raising the price to
6s., and now, as the state of the case demands, the commodity,
iron, will only be attainable by those buyers who can use it to
make products that will fetch at least 6s.   Thus, from above
and from below, all iron products come together at the price of
6s., the amount of their costs; but, quite evidently, the cause
of this is not that the cost good, iron, can force its own
arbitrary fixed price on its products, but that all the products
involved, including the cost good, iron, conform to the law of
marginal utility, find their way successively into the most
remunerative employments, and together receive their price as
regulated by the last of these.[1]

---

[1] It is possible that the amount of costs may itself be shifted—raised, for
instance—by the process of correction just described. It may happen, that is to
say, that in order to satisfy the demand, hitherto unsatisfied, which is desirous

Empirical proofs of this may be had in abundance. It is a very well known fact that active building of railways raises the price of rails, and, through this, the price of iron ; that the present strong demand for copper wire in electric lighting puts up the price of copper. In these cases it is evident that the upward movement of price takes its start from the final products, and is transferred from these to the cost goods. But the objection will probably suggest itself to many readers, that there are also cases where the movement of price is from costs to products. The stocks of iron, for instance, of which we have been speaking in our illustration, are not a fixed amount, but are smaller or greater according to the circumstances of iron production. Now if there is an extension of this production, and the supply of iron increases, its price will certainly fall, and that from causes peculiar to the iron ; and this fall in prices will drag down the price of iron wares. Does the causal connection here not run from costs to price of products ?

To answer this objection we have only to carry the concatenation, of which we have hitherto examined only a few links, back to its beginning. It is quite correct to say that stocks of iron are not a fixed amount, but the varying result of a production which is capable of being extended or limited at will. For the production of iron two things are necessary,— mines, and (to put it shortly) direct and indirect labour The mines are a given quantity, and cannot be devoted to the production of anything but iron. On the other hand, the quantity of labour available as a whole for economical employment, is an amount given and limited by the current state of population, but this is not the case with that particular labour which is employed in the production of iron. Labour is a productive power capable of being employed in any number of ways, and all the branches of production carried on in the community compete for it. Who or what, now, is it that decides what exact proportion of the original productive powers

of buying iron products at a higher price than 6s., so much iron is taken out of the iron market that the stock is no longer sufficient for the demand that is willing to pay just 6s. This latter, then, will, of course, be shut out by the stronger competitors, and the market price settles at a higher figure than 6s.— another proof that costs are not the fixed point to which the price of products adapts itself, but *vice versâ*.

at the disposal of industry, namely labour and uses of land, is
employed in the production of iron, and who and what is it that
decides on the value and price of the unit of those productive
powers ?

Here, then, for the last time, is repeated, in the elements
of all economy, the movement which we saw in the case of
final products and intermediate products. The original productive powers of the nation force themselves into the most
remunerative employments one after another, and receive their
value and price from the last of these. As little as, perhaps
even less than, any other good have they any *a priori* fixed
value : they receive it only from the opportunities of employment. Whether the day's work is worth 2s. or 6s. depends
on the worth of the product which can be turned out in the
day's work, and, indeed, on the " last " product—the one worst
paid—for the production of which there is still enough labour
of the necessary quality left, after all the better paid employments have been supplied.

Production may be compared to a giant pump. Every
branch of want has its separate pipe sunk down to the great
reservoir of the original productive powers, and competes with
all the other branches of want in trying to draw its supply
by suction from that reservoir. Every branch has a different
power of suction, the power increasing with the number and
the remunerativeness (that is to say, in the case of organised
exchange, the money value) of the employments it embraces.
In the nature of the suction pipes, too, there is a difference.
Many are quite simple : others have independent intermediate
lengths, that convey the pressure that comes from the want,
as it were, by stages ; and, in correspondence with that, the
productive powers which supply the want are raised by stages.

The simile extends still further. Such wants as demand
personal services for their satisfaction, attract labour quite
directly, according to the payment which they can and will
give for them. Such wants, again, as demand material goods
for their satisfaction, get these supplied, first, by payment of a
market price which is remunerative in itself, and then the
remunerative price of the products must attract the productive
powers to their manufacture. Sometimes this is done through
one or two, sometimes through twenty or thirty, members. In

our illustration, human demand asked and paid for iron wares :
the market price of iron wares attracted people to the purchase
of iron : the price of iron, finally, attracted the original productive powers to the production of iron. In the case of
other consumption goods, the number of intermediate members,
or, to keep to the terms of our comparison, the number of
intermediate lengths in the suction pipe, may be double or
twenty times as great. But the principle of the movement,
and what chiefly interests us, the result, is always the
same. Whether there are many or few intermediate members may hasten or hinder the result, but it cannot weaken or
strengthen it ; in the end every want, according to the power
expressed by its money valuation, draws to itself, mediately or
immediately, the productive powers required for its supply
To supply the wants of the rich innumerable productive powers
are always active, even if, simultaneously, at other points of
the economy, there is want both of men and goods. The
reason of this is that the high figures, which the rich are able
to offer for the satisfaction of their wants, never fail to exert
and continue their attractive force through all the stages of
production, right down to the reservoir of the original productive
powers.

Thus all human wants exert, as it were, a suction power
indicated by the figures of their valuation. Now, that layer of
wants which is willing and able to pay, say, 20s. and upwards,
for the day's work devoted (mediately or immediately) to its
satisfaction, is soon entirely provided for. After it those layers,
in succession, draw supply to themselves which can and will
pay the day's labour with 18s., 16s., 14s., and 12s., even down
to 10s., 8s., 6s., and 4s. If, at the limit of 4s., the entire stock
of original powers is required and is taken, this decides two
things :—All wants which will not, or cannot, pay the day's
labour devoted to their service at 4s., remain unsupplied ; and
the market price of the day's labour will stand at the figure of
the last buyer, namely, 4s. But if, as we may rather assume,
the available quantity of labour is greater than this, the wants
of still lower levels may be supplied. The last needs—mediate
or immediate—which are supplied may be those that pay the
day's labour at 2s. only ; and, in conformity, the market price
of labour also will be fixed at this lower figure of 2s. And,

indeed, this market price will be a general one : the uppermost layer will not be paid 20s., and the lowest layer 2s. for the same work or the same commodity : the market price will be the same for all buyers.

And now we come in sight of the answer to the doubt suggested by our former illustration. Suppose that the price of the day's labour is 2s., and the price of a cwt. of iron, which takes three days to produce, is 6s. Suppose now that, all of a sudden, new and productive mines are opened, or some great improvement in process discovered, which makes it possible to produce the cwt. of iron in two days' labour. What is the consequence ? So long as the iron and its products maintain the old price of 6s., only those wants in the department of iron wares are supplied which are able and willing to pay 6s. for two days' work ; that is, to pay the day's labour at the rate of 3s., while all round, in all other departments of want and branches of production, that layer of want is supplied which pays only 2s. for the day's labour. On economic principles— which are willingly carried out by undertakers of industry, who are always ready to seize the chance of a profit when offered them—those opportunities of employment which pay the day's work at more than 2s., and have hitherto been unsupplied, will now be supplied: more original productive powers will, accordingly, be invested in the production of iron ; and the supply of iron and iron products will be increased till such time as, here as elsewhere, that level of wants which is willing to pay the day's labour at 2s. is satisfied, and therefore the cwt. of iron, which costs two days' labour, fetches 4s. Parallel with this, of course, the price of iron and iron products [1] goes down to the level of 4s. And all this is not in opposition to, but in real fulfilment of our law of Marginal Utility, of which the law of costs, rightly understood, is only a special expression suitable to a special group of phenomena.

---

[1] It must not be forgotten that we are simplifying the matter by leaving out of account the co-operation of other complementary goods in the production of iron products. If we were to take these into consideration, and assume, for instance, that, to change the iron into the iron product, the expenditure of other two days of immediate or mediate labour was necessary, then 8s., as the price of iron product, would correspond to 4s. as the price of iron, and of this, according to the law of complementary goods, 4s. would be reckoned to the productive good, iron, as its share.

If—what is practically inconceivable—production were carried on in ideal circumstances, unfettered by limitations of place and time, with no friction, with the most perfect knowledge of the position of human wants requiring satisfaction, and without any disturbing changes of wants, stocks, or technique, then the original productive powers would, with ideal and mathematical exactitude, be invested in the most remunerative employments, and the law of costs, so far as we can speak of such a law, would hold in ideal completeness. The complementary groups of goods from which, in the long-run, the finished good proceeds, would maintain exactly the same value and price at all stages of the process; the commodity would be exactly equal to its costs ; these costs to their costs, and so on, back to the last original productive powers from which ultimately all goods come.   But this ideal symmetry is traversed by two disturbing causes.

The first of these I may call by the general name of Friction.   Almost invariably there is some hindrance, great or small, permanent or temporary, to the due investment of the original productive powers in the employments and forms of consumption which are the most remunerative at the time. In consequence the provision for wants, and likewise the prices, are somewhat unsymmetrical.   Sometimes it is that individual branches of want are, relatively, more amply supplied than others; so that, for instance, in woollens, those wants are supplied which pay the day's labour indirectly at 1s. 8d. only, while it may be that, in copper goods, no wants are satisfied which cannot pay 3s. for a similar day's labour.   But sometimes it may be that groups of productive materials, successively transformed till they are changed at last into the finished commodity, are not equally valued at all stages of the process.   If we compare the means of production to a stream, we might say that the stream is not, as it should be, of equal breadth at all stages of its course: from some disturbing cause or other there may be dams at certain particular points, and leakages at others; and these cause an unsymmetrical divergence of price compared with the prices obtained at stages before and after, or, as it is usually conceived and expressed, a divergence of the price of a product (or intermediate product) from its costs.   Thus it is, in our illustration of the iron, when production is suddenly cheapened from

6s. to 4s.   As a consequence the production of iron is at first
increased, and presses down the price of raw material, while
the products of iron may still for some time maintain a price
greater than their costs.   But gradually the increase of supply
presses forward to the later stages of production,—passes from
the production of raw materials to the manufacture of final
products,—and by reducing the price here also to 4s. restores
the disturbed symmetry between price and costs.

In practical life such frictional disturbances are innumerable.   At no moment and in no branch of production are
they entirely absent.   And thus it is that the Law of Costs
is recognised as a law that is only approximately valid; a
law riddled through and through with exceptions.   These innumerable exceptions, small and great, are the inexhaustible
source of the undertakers' profits, but also of the undertakers'
losses.

The second disturbing cause is the Lapse of Time—the
weeks, months, years which must stretch between the inception
of the original productive powers, and the presentation of their
finished and final product.   The difference of time, in exerting
a far-reaching influence on our valuation of goods, makes a
normal difference between the value of the productive groups
standing at different points of the production process through
which they must all pass; and is, therefore, a difference to be
kept quite distinct from the unsymmetrical divergences caused
by frictional disturbances.   It is this second disturbing cause
which gives rise to Interest.   Our further task will be to
intercalate the theory of interest in its place within the value
and price theory already outlined.

BOOK V

PRESENT AND FUTURE

CHAPTER I

PRESENT AND FUTURE IN ECONOMIC LIFE

PRESENT goods are, as a rule, worth more than future goods of like kind and number. This proposition is the kernel and centre of the interest theory which I have to present. All the lines of explanation, by which I hope to elucidate the phenomena of interest, run through this fact; and round it, both essentially and superficially, is grouped the whole of the theoretical work we have to do. The first part of our explanation will try to prove the truth of the proposition; the second will then show that, out of the fact, spring, naturally and necessarily, all the manifold forms which the phenomena of interest take. In the present book we have to take up the first part, and I shall try to go into it with that minuteness which is due to the cardinal importance of such a proposition. To this end we shall, first of all, make a general survey of the relations between present and future in human economy—a subject, obviously, of the highest importance, but one which, strangely enough, has up till now attracted but scanty scientific attention.[1]

[1] A history of the theory of this subject—which I have no intention of writing here—would probably start with Adam Smith's emphatic opposition of "present enjoyment" to "future profit" (ii. 1). In more recent times there are some good observations on the subject in Senior (*Political Economy*, third edition, p. 58) under the headings of "Abstinence" and "Capital"; in Rae (*New Principles of Political Economy*, quoted in Mill's *Principles*, book i. chap. xi.); and in Menger (*Grundsätze der Volkswirthschaftslehre*, p. 127). The first, so far as I know, to treat it as a subject by itself, was Jevons (*Theory of Political Economy*, 1871, second edition, 1879). Jevons's work is exceedingly interesting and suggestive, but, on the whole, it is rather imperfect—as could scarcely be otherwise in a first attempt, and on a field of speculation hitherto all but untouched. It shows a good deal of incorrectness, a good many contradictions, and, in particular, many obvious gaps. Jevons may be said rather to have

In the present we live and move, but our future is not a
matter of indifference to us, and our desires are, with reason,
directed towards a wellbeing not limited by the present. It is
only as the logical carrying out of this general principle that
we set before us, in our economical arrangements, the larger
object of providing for our future as well as for our present
wellbeing. As a fact, the future has a great place in our
economical provision ; a greater, indeed, than people usually
think. It is, of course, a commonplace, but, all the same, it
is a truth seldom seen in all its bearings, that our economical
conduct has exceedingly little reference to the present, but is,
almost entirely, taken up with the future.

shown, by a bold stroke of genius, that here was a new circle of ideas waiting
to be taken up, than shown what was to be done with them. Closely following
Jevons, without going beyond their master, are, quite recently, Launhardt
(*Mathematische Begründung der Volkswirthschaftslehre*, 1885) and Emil Sax
(*Grundlegung der theoretischen Staatswirthschaft*, 1887, pp. 178, 313). A little
before these G. Gross (*Die Zeit in der Volkswirthschaft*, in the *Zeitschrift für die
ges. Staatswissenschaft*, 1883, p. 126) had made a well-meant suggestion,—which,
however, was by that time carried out by Jevons and then by myself,—that the
element of time in economical theory was worthy of a fuller consideration.
Finally, as concerns my own work, I owe it to myself to say that I arrived at
my views on this subject in complete independence, and altogether uninfluenced
by Jevons—and, naturally, still less by later writers. I first became acquainted
with Jevons's writings in 1883,—shortly before the printing of my *Capital and
Interest*,—when completing the historical material already collected in that work
by a review of the latest English literature on the subject. The principles of
my own theory of capital, on the other hand, were laid down by me as early
as 1876. In that year I first suggested them in a youthful work never published.
In later writings I gave many plain, if still cautious, hints of my leading ideas
(*e.g.* in *Rechte und Verhältnisse*, p. 68 in note on the phenomenon of *Abnützung*,
pp. 76 and particularly 109, 115 in note, on the computation of the future use,
and p. 152 ; in *Capital and Interest*, pp. 257, 276, 343, 424, and particularly
on p. 428 where I formulated the programme of my positive theory in saying
that the explanation of interest was to be deduced from the influence of Time
on human valuations of goods). The cautious tone which I still deliberately
adopted in giving these hints was due to my desire not to compromise my new
ideas by any premature or incomplete formulation of them. I meant that they
should not go before the public till I was in a position to produce them as a
finished whole, all harmoniously fitted in to a system of carefully planned
economic doctrine. That is why I preferred to work for ten years at laying
the foundation of the present theory by completing the theory of goods (1881), the
criticism of the theories of capital (1884), and the theory of value (1886), rather
than snatch, as I might easily have done, at the glory of priority by publishing
original but still immature ideas a decade earlier. Moreover my theory, if it
touches that of Jevons at several points, by no means agrees with it in essence ;
and in the most important points, such as the explanation of interest, it is in
distinct opposition to his.

Let us clearly understand what this latter statement means. It means that our anxiety in the present is to have at our disposal, in the future, means for the satisfaction of wants that will not emerge till the future. In other words, it means that pleasures or pains, which we will only experience in the future, determine us now to provide goods or services, which, again, will only assert their use in the future. But how is it possible that feelings which are not yet felt, and therefore feelings which, essentially, do not exist, can be motives to will and deed?

Now, as a suggestive writer has said, we do not indeed possess the gift of feeling future sensations, but we possess the other gift of anticipating them in imagination.[1] Either it is

---

[1] When Jevons calls that intellectual phenomenon which impels us to provide for future wants and to value future goods, a "present anticipated feeling" (*Political Economy*, second edition, p. 37), the expression is very apt to be misleading. We must distinguish between two fundamentally distinct things, which Jevons seems to me not to have sufficiently kept apart. It is one thing to represent to ourselves, or imagine, a future pleasure or future pain, and to estimate its presumable intensity on the ground of this imagination. It is quite another thing to experience, in this imagination itself, a pleasure, an actual present pleasure of anticipation. To give an example. I think of taking a pleasure trip to Italy. From personal experiences, or from travellers' tales heard or read, I represent to myself the pleasures of the journey, and I put the intensity of these pleasures so high, that it seems to me worth the sacrifice of £50 to realise them. But, beyond this, in picturing to myself the future pleasure of the journey, a real present pleasure of anticipation is kindled. Thinking on the journey affords me an actual pleasure, but, in any case, it is an entirely different pleasure and, in all probability, its intensity is ever so much less than the pleasure of the journey itself. If I value the latter at £50, the pleasure of anticipation is, perhaps, not worth more than 10s.—of which it may be sufficient proof that I am willing to lay out so much money, and no more, in buying a book of travels that lifts me into the pleasant world of thought. The concrete figures here are of no moment. No constant or normal quantitative relation can be established between an anticipated pleasure and a pleasure of anticipation : the relation will vary in the wildest way according to persons, motives, and circumstances. With dreamy imaginative men, for instance, who are apt to be strongly excited by their own imaginings, the pleasures of anticipation may be relatively strong ; with hard-headed unimpassioned men, on the other hand, they will be disproportionately weak. For our purpose it is sufficient to establish two things : first, that the intensity of the represented future pleasure and that of the actually felt pleasure of anticipation, are two different quantities ; and second, in the vast majority of cases, the intensity of the pleasure of anticipation is less than the anticipated pleasure, not by a few per cent, but infinitely.

The question now is : When we value future goods, and when in conformity with that valuation we are making these economical determinations on which we provide for future wants, with which of these two intensities have we to do ? On

that we have already in the past, once or many times, experienced the same want as we expect in the future, and retain a picture

this, at any rate, there can be no doubt : we shall all agree that it is the intensity of the future pleasure (or of the averted future pain) valued on the representation or imagination of it. A good which I have every reason to expect will bring me an intensity of satisfaction indicated by 100, I shall value at 100 and not at 1, even if, in anticipating the same, I experience only an actual pleasure of anticipation of the intensity 1. And, in the same way, in choosing whether I shall provide for any definite future want, in general, or to which of several I should give the preference, I shall try to decide, as impartially as possible, according to my reasonable valuation of the future pleasure, and *not* according to the degree of my momentary feeling of pleasure. (That we not seldom have our clear judgment clouded by the latter, and that it thus obtains an indirect influence on our determinations, is a phenomenon which belongs to quite another sphere.) If, after what has been said, there should still be any doubt on the subject—which I do not anticipate—it may be removed by pointing to the well-known fact, that enthusiastic dreamers, in whom the anticipation of future events excite very lively present emotions, are not at all the sort of people who are given to provide economically for their future needs in the most efficient way. On the contrary, it is the cold calculating men who do so ; men whose sober intellectual judgment of future situations is little or not at all affected by accompanying excitement.

Now Jevons has fundamentally confused these things. He makes out that our economical transactions have for their motive present feelings, which, according to the distance of time, remain a few per cent behind the intensity of future pleasures and pains—standing to the latter, perhaps, in the ratio of 95 to 100. But nothing is more certain than that, while we represent to ourselves feelings of that intensity and anticipate them, we do not experience them as present feelings. Sax, again, who, in this respect, has obviously followed Jevons without proving the facts of the case for himself, has made the same blunder in a ruder way. He speaks of a *Vorempfindung* of future wants—to be distinguished from a simple prescience (*Grundlegung*, p. 178), and out of these "previous feelings" he even construes actual "present wants" and "feelings of want," which should be only a little weaker, according to the distance of time, than the corresponding immediate want of the present itself (p. 314). Surely Sax has scarcely considered what tortures we must constantly endure if all the future pleasures and pains, against which we protect ourselves by forethought, are really to be experienced by us in anticipation, and only a few per cent less vividly than in reality !—Let me add the following remark. I am quite aware that the psychologists attach two distinct conceptions to the words "feeling" and "sensation" (*Gefühl* and *Empfindung*). The speech of economics, however, has not yet carried out this distinction and it is usual to speak either of sensations or feelings of want, pain, and so on. I retain these common expressions because, by giving them up, I should probably lose more, among economic readers, in plainness, than I could gain in exactness.

NOTE BY TRANSLATOR.—I may suggest here that, so far as concerns Jevons, the above criticism scarcely applies. It is based on a literal reading of two unfortunate expressions, "present anticipated feeling" and "vague though powerful feeling of the future." The whole passage, however, shows that Jevons did not mean the *present* feeling, but the represented future feeling—what he himself calls the "actual amount of feeling anticipated." The criticism, however, probably finds its mark in those German writers who have too faithfully followed the letter of Jevons.—W. S.

of it in our memory ; or, at least, we have already experienced
wants or feelings that bear a certain resemblance to the feelings
we are expecting, and can, from such analogous reminiscences,
construct for ourselves an imaginative picture which is more
or less true.   On such pictures of memory and imagination we base our economical calculations and our economical
decisions.   Certainly, as many a one will be apt to object, it
is an unsafe and deceptive foundation, but, all the same, it is
almost the only one that we have.   It is the rarest possible
thing for us to base a valuation of goods, or an economical
decision, on a pain that we are feeling at the very moment.
It is, indeed, one of the characteristics of a civilised community
that it anticipates want by providing for it, and does not
allow the pain of emptiness, which the unsatisfied want would
involve, to get to its full height.   We do not begin to prepare
our meals when hunger has reached its highest point of
torment: we do not wait till the flood has overwhelmed house
and home before we think of putting up the dam: we do not
delay building the fire-engine till the flames have broken over
us.   At the moment when we decide on an economical action,
the wants which cause us to make the decision are, almost
always, in the future, and so, however near that future may
be, they are acting on us, not as actual feelings, but as simple
anticipations.   How many a man has never, even in the past,
fully felt the want which makes him value the goods he daily
uses !   How many rich people know only from hearsay what
real hunger is !

Hence it is obvious that, however deceitful and unsafe this
gift of anticipation may be, and however far astray it may lead
us in individual cases, we still have every cause to be heartily
thankful that we have it.   Otherwise, neither actually feeling
the future wants, nor yet forewarned of them by anticipation,
we could not, of course, provide for them in advance; once
want had made itself felt, any measures we could take would
be miserably inadequate to provide for it; and, poorer than the
poorest savages, we should drag out a hazardous hand-to-mouth
existence.

But economical action means something more than thinking
generally about the wants which are to be provided for.   As,
indeed, all economising arises from the quantitative insufficiency

R

of the means of satisfaction as compared with the wants requiring satisfaction, so it demands a constant selection, a constant choosing between those wants which can and should be provided for, and those others which cannot be provided for. The selection naturally proceeds on a comparison of the importance and urgency—or, as we may say, the intensity—of the feelings of pleasure and pain which are associated with individual wants and their satisfaction. Now, if it is seldom that, in the moment of an economical decision, we actually feel that *one* want to which it refers, it is much more seldom that, on the moment of our choice, we experience, as actual feelings, *all* those sensations of pleasure and pain between which we have to choose. Our comparisons must, almost invariably, be, partially and very often completely, made on imaginative anticipations which we make of future feelings. And this leads us to a fact which I should like to emphasise: The future feelings we imagine are commensurable. They are commensurable with present actually-felt sensations, and they are commensurable with one another, and that too without reference to whether they belong to the same or to different levels of time. It is as easy for me to choose between a pleasure which seems desirable at the moment and another pleasure which I can obtain in eight days, as between two different pleasures which are both obtainable in eight days, or, again, as between two pleasures of which the one is obtainable in eight days, the other in eight months, or eight years.

The fact that we borrow from future sensations the motive for our present actions, is one side of our connection with the future. Another side is that, by our present actions, we prepare goods or material services [1] for the benefit of the future. If we analyse the totality of goods which constitutes our wealth we shall find that by far the greater part has the character of what, for want of a better name, we may call " future goods " (*Zukunftsgüter*). All productive goods, without exception, are destined altogether to the service of the future. Durable consumption goods give off only a fraction of their material services in the present, and all the remainder in the future. If a dwelling-house, for instance, remains occupied for a hundred years, and affords shelter and comfort all that time,

---

[1] On the conception of Material Services see *Capital and Interest*, p. 223.

only an infinitesimal fraction of these services is rendered to-day; a still very small fraction is rendered in the present year; the great bulk of the service is spread over remote future periods. Even in the case of those perishable goods, such as meat and drink, wood and candles, which we keep ready for immediate consumption in our domestic economy, only one portion of their use is, strictly speaking, devoted to the service of the moment ; the greater part is carried over into the future, although it may be the immediate future.   As, among our motives, future feelings are the dominant ones, so, among the goods we possess and use, "future goods" occupy the larger place.

And there is yet another important analogy.   As future feelings, whether they belong to the near or to the far future, are commensurable, alike with one another and with present feelings, so are future goods commensurable, alike with one another and with present goods.   We can compare the value of a camellia which fades in an hour, with that of a ticket for a next week's concert, or with that of a bunch of next year's roses ; or we can give one of these goods for the other. It makes no difference to the matter whether the "future good," which we compare or barter, is at hand and ready for delivery now, or whether it is represented in bodily shape by nothing more than the means of production out of which it will come, or whether, at the moment, it is neither itself ready nor is capable of being palpably represented—is, that is to say, a "future good," in the narrowest and strictest sense of that word. Thus we give present money in exchange, not only for the present consumption good Bread, but also for the present productive good Meal, in which the future good, bread, lies concealed.   But just as easily can we buy from a farmer, for money down, his next year's harvest.   In "reserved seats" we buy the future services of actors and singers.   In buying Consols we give our present money for a series of future payments.   Future goods and services are to us—I have cause to emphasise this—entirely familiar objects of economic dealing, just as future feelings are entirely familiar economic motives. Both have their ultimate ground in the continuity of our personal life.   What we shall experience in a week or a year hence affects *us* not less than what we experience to-day, and has, therefore, equal claims to be considered in our economic arrangements. Both arrangements have for their end *our* wellbeing.

Whether this theoretically similar claim of future and present is always fully recognised in practical life, is another question which will require much consideration.

Provision for the future makes no inconsiderable demands on our intellectual strength; makes some demands, even, on our moral strength; and these demands are not equally met by men at all stages of civilisation. The present always gets its rights. It forces itself upon us through our senses. To cry for food when hungry occurs even to a baby. But the future we must anticipate and picture. Indeed, to have any effect in the future, we must form a double series of anticipations. We must be able to form a mental picture of what will be the state of our wants, needs, feelings, at any particular point of time. And we must be able to form another set of anticipations as to the fate of those measures which we take at the moment with a view to the future. Our knowledge of causal processes must enable us beforehand to form an adequate picture of the forms which goods will take, of the quantity of them, and of the time when they will come to maturity as result of those productive or commercial activities which we are now commencing. To make this double work of anticipating a comparatively remote future clear and true to fact, is not possible to the infant, and not much more than possible to the child and the savage. Civilisation of course teaches us this difficult art gradually. But, even among the most advanced peoples, the art is still very far from being perfect, and the practical economic provision for the future is correspondingly inadequate. But, be the degree of anticipation and provision for the future what it may, wherever it exists in the most general way—and that is even among the most barbarous tribes —future goods and future services are as much actual objects of economical dealing as present goods. We strive to get them; we produce them; we value them; we buy and sell them.

I say, we value them; and this is a point that must be looked more closely into. On what principles do we estimate the value of future goods? The answer is: On the same principles as we estimate the value of goods in general: that is, according to the marginal utility which they will bring us in the circumstances, of Want and Provision for want.   But here, naturally, we have not to deal with the relations of want and provision that obtain at the moment, but with the want and provision of that future period when the goods in question will be at our disposal.   To the inhabitants of a besieged town, threatened with starvation, grain that was promised for delivery a year after the raising of the siege would certainly not be valued and paid according to the standard of the moment's need; while, on the contrary, a brewer who, in January, concludes a purchase for a hundred cubic feet of ice to be delivered in July of the coming summer, will, just as certainly, not measure the value of the ice according to the over-supply that obtains at the moment when the bargain is concluded, but according to the scarcity which is likely to come with the summer.[1]

Very frequently, however, there enters into the valuation of future goods an element which causes us to value them a little —or even a great deal—under their future marginal utility, but which—as I shall show presently—has no connection with the phenomenon of interest.   This is the element of Uncertainty.   To us nothing future is absolutely certain.   However closely we may have bound present and future together in economical connection, and however much reason we may have to expect the future to bring certain goods into existence, or put them at our disposal, still the actual fulfilment of our expectations is never, in the strict sense of the word, certain: it is always more or less probable.   Of course, the probability is often so great that, practically, it amounts to certainty: as, for instance, the expectation that payment will follow an acceptance by the Rothschilds.   In such cases we do neglect the infinitely small amount that is wanting of full certainty, and deduct nothing from the valuation we put upon the acceptance on the ground of uncertainty.   But, frequently, the probability falls considerably short of full certainty.   The farmer, for instance, may have done everything in his power to obtain a harvest by ploughing, manuring, sowing, and so on: but the harvest may be destroyed, wholly or in part, by hail, frost, flooding, or insect ravages.   Sometimes, indeed, the probability sinks to the level of a very faint possibility, as, for example, when a

[1] Menger, *Grundsätze*, p. 124.

man holds one of a hundred tickets in a lottery where there is only a single prize.

Cases like these cause a certain amount of hesitation to economic men. Are they to value uncertain future sums of goods exactly as if they were certain? Impossible! For then every lottery ticket that carried the chance of winning £100 would be valued at £100, and every claim, even the most doubtful, at its full nominal amount; — a course which, obviously, would land the men who tried to do business on these lines in the bankruptcy court in the shortest possible time. Or are the uncertain future sums of goods not to have any value put upon them? is no importance whatever to be attached to them with respect to our wellbeing? As impossible, and as ruinous! For then no man would give the smallest price for a chance in a lottery, or even for nine hundred and ninety-nine chances out of a thousand; no one would dare to make the slightest sacrifice to sow when harvest was uncertain. From this dilemma there is only one escape: we must ascribe to uncertain future sums of goods an importance as regards our wellbeing, but, at the same time, we must take account of the uncertainty of their acquisition according to the degree of that uncertainty. But, practically, this cannot be done otherwise than by transferring the gradation from where the gradation exists, but cannot be expressed—that is, from the degree of probability,—to where the gradation is not, but where alone it can be expressed—that is, the degree of the expected utility: thus equalising a greater, but less probable utility, to a less, but more probable utility, and this again to a still less but absolutely certain utility. In a word, we reduce all possibilities of utility to certainty, and restore the balance by deducting from this utility or value the amount we must add to the probability of the expected utility to raise it to certainty. Thus we reckon a claim on the Rothschilds at its full nominal value (disregarding for the moment the discount, as belonging to an entirely different sphere of phenomena), while one lottery ticket of a thousand, where the chance is a prize of £100, we value perhaps at 2s., one of a hundred at 20s., and one of ten, perhaps, at £10.

Strictly looked at, this kind of valuation—except where the certainty of the anticipated future utility is practically assured—is always incorrect.[1]   For, to recur to our illustration, the ticket will either draw the prize or it will draw a blank.   In the former case it will have been, as the events show, worth a hundred pounds; in the latter, worth nothing at all.   In no case will it have been worth 2s., or 20s., or £10.   But, however false this method of valuation is in the individual case, it comes at least approximately right, according to the law of averages, over a great many cases; and, in the absence of any better method of valuation—which is denied us by the dulness of our imaginative forethought—it is well justified as a practical make-shift.[2]

I repeat that the element of uncertainty, which is the cause of a lesser value being put upon particular classes of future goods, has no causal connection with the phenomenon of interest.   The lesser valuation which is its effect is a special one, and extends to one class of future goods only,[3] and there it bears the character of a deduction as premium for risk.

With the exception of this peculiarity, the valuation of present and future goods is made on identical principles.   But, to conclude from this that the *amount* of value of present and future goods must be identical, would be too hasty.   On the contrary, since present goods are available at a different time from future ones, and therefore come under different actual circumstances, and are intended for the service of a different set of wants, it is to be argued, from all we know about value, that the value of such goods must, as a rule, be different. And so it is in fact.   We arrive thus at a proposition which is a fundamental one in our inquiry : As a rule present goods

[1] This proposition has lately been disputed by Mataja (*Das Recht des Schadenersatzes vom Standpunkte der Nationalökonomie*, Leipsic, 1888, p. 149, note 1) on the ground that, in the selling of such goods, one might actually obtain their average return as price, and therefore, quite correctly, value them according to this.   But Mataja forgets that the market price is not the cause, but is itself the result of the fact that the individuals, who appear as buyers and sellers of such goods, value them *in the first instance*—that is, in the individual case, objectively falsely—according to the average return.

[2] See my former tract on *Rechte und Verhältnisse*, p. 85, where I brought out the same idea in a somewhat different connection : also Mataja, *ibid.* p. 139.

[3] It embraces also goods which, materially, are present, but are intended for future consumption ; for instance, productive goods, the technical transformation of which into consumption goods is accompanied by a danger of not succeeding.

have a higher subjective value than future goods of like kind and number. And since the resultant of subjective valuations determines objective exchange value, present goods, as a rule, have a higher exchange value and price than future goods of like kind and number.

This phenomenon is the result of the co-operation of a number of causes;—causes which, individually, are of very different natures, but which, as it happens, work in the same direction. These causes we shall consider in order.

CHAPTER II

THE first great cause of difference in value between present and future goods consists in the different circumstances of want and provision (*Bedarf und Deckung*) in present and future. Present goods, as we know, receive their value from the circumstances of want and provision in the present: future goods from the same circumstances in those future periods of time when they will come into our disposal. If a person is badly in want of certain goods, or of goods in general, while he has reason to hope that, at a future period, he will be better off, he will always value a given quantity of immediately available goods at a higher figure than the same quantity of future goods. In economic life this occurs very frequently, and may be considered as typical in the two following cases. First, in all cases of immediate distress and necessity. A peasant who has had a bad harvest, or sustained loss by fire, an artisan who has had heavy expenses through illness or death in his family, a labourer who is starving; all these agree in valuing the present shilling, which lifts them out of direst need, ever so much more than the future shilling,— the proof being the usurious conditions to which such people often submit in order to raise money at the moment.[1] Second, in the case of persons who have reason to look forward to economical circumstances of increasing comfort. Thus all kinds of beginners who have no means, such as young artists, lawyers, officials, budding doctors, men going into business, are only too ready, in return for a sum of present goods

---

[1] The proverb *bis dat qui cito dat* has therefore a quite sound economical basis.

which assists them to start in the vocation they have chosen, and acts as foundation of their economical existence, to promise a considerably larger sum on the condition that they do not require to pay it until they are in receipt of a decent income.[1]

Of course the contrary also occurs not unfrequently in economical life. There are persons who are comparatively well off at the moment, and who are likely to be worse off in the future. To this category belongs, among others, that very considerable number of people whose income is obtained, mostly or altogether, by personal exertions, and will, presumably, fall away at a later period of life when they become unfit for work. A merchant's clerk, for instance, who is in his fiftieth year, and has an income of £100, cannot expect to have anything better ten years later than, perhaps, a small retiring allowance of £30, or an annuity which he may secure by purchase at an assurance office. It is evident that to such people the marginal utility that depends on a shilling spent now is smaller than that depending on a shilling available in the more badly secured future. It would seem that, in such cases, a present shilling should be less valued than a future one. And so it would be if present goods were necessarily spent in the present, but that is not the case. Most goods, and among them, particularly, money, which represents all kinds of goods indifferently, are durable, and can, therefore, be reserved for the service of the future. The case, then, between present and future goods stands thus. The only possible uses of future goods are, naturally, future, while present goods have the same possibility of future use, and have besides—according to choice—either the present uses, or those future ones which may turn up in the time that intervenes between the present moment and the future point of time with which the comparison is being made.

Here then are two possibilities. Either it is the case that all those uses of the present and near future, which are generally taken into consideration as regards the good in

---

[1] For this reason the well-known postponement of university fees in the case of poor students in Germany (*Stundung*) is found to be a relief not much inferior to the total exemption of the same class in Austria (*Befreiung*). Or we may think of the conditions of the contract which the *impresario* makes with the singers he educates and brings out.

question, are less important than the future uses; and in this case the present good will be reserved for these future uses, will derive its value from them,[1] and will be just equal in value to a future good similarly available. Or it is the case that one of the earlier uses is more important; and then the present good gets its value from this use, and has, therefore, the advantage over the future good, which can only obtain its value from a less important future employment. But, usually, one never knows that some unforeseen occurrence in the near future may not give rise to some more urgent want. At any rate such a thing is possible, and it gives a chance of profitable employment to a good already on hand, such as, naturally, a good that will only come into our possession in the future has not got:—a chance which, as we have seen, is calculated in the amount of the value, and assessed, according to practical although incorrect methods, as an increment graduated according to its probability. To put it in figures. With £100 which will come into my hands at the end of five years, I can only aim at a marginal utility determined by the situation of things in the year 1896; we shall put this utility down at 1000 ideal units. With £100 at my disposal now, I can, *at the least*, realise the same marginal utility of 1000 units, but if an urgent want, arising in the meantime, gives me an opportunity of obtaining a marginal utility of 1200, I may, possibly, realise it. Say, now, that the probability of such an opportunity occurring equals one-tenth, I shall estimate the value of the present £100 at 1000 units certain, and, beyond that, at one-tenth of the possible surplus of 200: that is, in all, at 1020 units.[2] Present goods are, therefore, in the worst case, equal in value to future goods, and, as a rule, they have the advantage over them in being employed as a reserve. The only exception occurs in those comparatively rare cases where it is difficult or impracticable to keep the present goods till the time of worse provision comes. This happens, for instance, in the case of goods subject to rapid deterioration or decay,

[1] According to the law laid down above on p. 162, for the case of alternative employments with different marginal utilities.

[2] I need scarcely say that, in practical life, we seldom or never make out our valuations with such minute exactitude as in the above illustration. But it does give a faithful picture of the *kind* of considerations of which we avail ourselves in such cases.

such as ice, fruit, and the like.   Any fruit merchant in harvest time will put a considerably higher value on a bushel of grapes to be delivered in April than on a bushel of grapes in his store at the time.   Or say that a rich man is anticipating a long period of arrest, during which his living will be conformed to the hard fare of prison regime, how willingly would he give the price of a hundred present luxurious meals if he could ensure ten such meals during his captivity !

We may, then, draw up the balance-sheet which shows the influence of the different circumstances of Want and its Provision in present and future as follows.   A great many persons who are not so well provided for in the present as they expect to be in the future, set a considerably higher value on present goods than on future.   A great many persons who are better provided for in the present than they expect to be in the future, but who have the chance of preserving present goods for the service of the future, and, moreover, of using them as a reserve fund for anything that may turn up in the meantime, value present goods either at the same figure as future, or a little higher.   It is only in a fractional minority of cases, where communication between present and future is hindered or threatened by peculiar circumstances, that present goods have, for their owners, a lower subjective use value than future.   This being the state of things, even if there was nothing else co-operating with this difference of want and provision in present and future, the resultant of the subjective valuations, which determines the objective exchange value, would obviously be such that present goods must maintain a proportionate advantage, a proportionate agio over future. But, besides this, there are other co-operating circumstances which work, even more distinctly, in the same direction.

CHAPTER III

UNDERESTIMATE OF THE FUTURE

IT is one of the most pregnant facts of experience that we attach a less importance to future pleasures and pains simply because they are future, and in the measure that they are future. Thus it is that, to goods which are destined to meet the wants of the future, we ascribe a value which is really less than the true intensity of their future marginal utility. We systematically underestimate future wants, and the goods which are to satisfy them.

Of the fact itself there can be no doubt; but, of course, in particular nations, at various stages of life, in different individuals, the phenomenon makes its appearance in very varying degree. We find it most frankly expressed in children and savages. With them the slightest enjoyment, if only it can be seized at the moment, outweighs the greatest and most lasting advantage. How many an Indian tribe, with careless greed, has sold the land of its fathers, the source of its maintenance, to the pale faces for a couple of casks of " firewater "! Unfortunately very much the same may be seen in our own highly civilised countries. The working man who drinks on Sunday the week's wage he gets on Saturday, and starves along with wife and child the next six days, is not far removed from the Indian. But, to a smaller extent, and in more refined form, the same phenomenon is, I venture to assert, not quite unknown to any of us, however prudent, or cultured, or highly principled. Which of us has not been surprised to find that, under the pressure of momentary appetite, he was not able to refuse some favourite dish or cigar which the doctor had forbidden — knowing perfectly that he was doing an injury to his health, which, calm consideration would tell him, was much more considerable than the pleasure of that trifling indulgence ? Or, which of us has not, to avoid a little momentary embarrassment or annoyance, plunged headlong into a much greater ? Who is there that has never postponed some troublesome but unavoidable call, or business, or work which had to be done within a certain time, till the day was past when it could be done with little trouble, and has had to do it in more difficult circumstances, in haste and hurry, with over-exertion and ill-humour, to the displeasure of those who were injured or wounded by the delay ? Any one who knows himself, and keeps his eyes open to what is going on around him, will find this fact of the underestimate of future pleasures and pains exhibited under a thousand forms in the midst of our civilised society.

Of the fact, then, there is no doubt. Why it should be so is more difficult to say. The entire psychological relations, indeed, through which future feelings in general act on our judgments and our actions, are still very obscure, and it will be understood that the same obscurity covers the reasons why future feelings act with greater weakness on our judgments and actions than present feelings. Without meaning to fore-stall the pronouncement of the psychologists, who seem to me more competent to decide on both questions than the economists, I venture to think that this phenomenon rests, not on one ground, but on the joint action of no less than three different grounds.

The first ground seems to me to be the incompleteness of the imaginations we form to ourselves of our future wants. Whether it be that our power of representation and abstraction is not strong enough, or whether it be that we will not take the necessary trouble, the consideration we give our future and, particularly, our far-away future wants, is more or less im-perfect. Naturally, then, all those wants which we have not considered remain without influence on the valuation of such goods as are destined to serve those future wants, and, conse-quently, the marginal utility of such goods is put too low.

While this first ground is very much a peculiar defect in estimate, the second seems to me to rest on a defect in will. I believe it frequently occurs that a man, called on to make choice between a present and a future pleasure or pain, decides for the present pleasure although he knows perfectly, and is even conscious while choosing, that his future loss will outweigh his present gain, and that, taking his welfare as a whole, the choice is unprofitable. How well many a "good fellow" knows the painful embarrassments and privations he is bringing on himself, by running through his salary on the day he gets it, and yet has not the strength to resist the temptation of the moment! Or, how often does a man, "from weakness," let himself be hurried into taking some step, or making some promise, which he knows at the moment he will rue before twenty-four hours are over! The cause of such defects in conduct, I say, appears to me, in distinction from the former case, to rest, not on want of knowledge, but on defect of will. I should not be surprised, however, if the psychologists were to explain this case also as only a variation of the former: it may be that the weaker feeling of the moment prevails over the stronger feeling of the future only because the latter, while present in consciousness in a general way, is not lively enough and strong enough to take possession of the mind. For our purpose, however, it is a matter of no consequence.

Finally, as third ground, I am inclined to name the consideration of the shortness and uncertainty of life. In the case of future goods, their *objective* acquisition may be practically certain,[1] and yet it is possible that we may not live to acquire them. This makes their utility a matter of uncertainty for us, and causes us—in perfect analogy with the case of objectively uncertain goods—to make a deduction from their value corresponding to the degree of uncertainty.[2] A utility of 100, as to which there is 50% of probability that we shall not live to see it, we certainly do not value so highly as a present utility of 100; probably we value it as we do a present utility of 50; and I am convinced that any of us who was promised, to-day, a cheque for £10,000 on his hundredth birthday, would be glad to exchange this large, but somewhat uncertain gift, for a very small sum in present money! To determine correctly the practical influence of this factor, however, we must make a

[1] See above, p. 245.
[2] If there is objective uncertainty as well as subjective there will, naturally, be two deductions. Of these the one made on account of objective uncertainty, as a particular phenomenon of certain kinds of goods, has nothing to do with interest; we have only to deal with the deduction on account of subjective uncertainty.

somewhat more accurate calculation, both of the extent to which it prevails, and the way in which it works.

As regards this I think we shall be able to establish what follows. The factor in question is directly active only in a minority of cases: in most cases its action is indirect. It works in the most direct and powerful way in those not very numerous cases where men have the thought of death forced on them by peculiar circumstances; for example, among very old men, people suffering from fatal diseases, those placed in dangerous situations or engaged in very perilous callings, such as people in times of plague or soldiers before an engagement, and so on. The disregard of a future so uncertain not seldom finds drastic expression in the mad extravagance which seizes people in such circumstances; a fact in the history of civilisation which has often been noted—by Adam Smith among others. On the other hand, the thought of the uncertainty of life seems to me to exert no direct influence at all in that vast majority of cases where we are dealing with men in normal circumstances, and dealing, at the same time, with the valuation of goods belonging to a time not very far in the future; say, goods that would come into their possession in a couple of days, or months, or even years. I am convinced that a healthy middle-aged man, to whom a payment of £100 next year was due for certain, would not value it a single penny less on the ground that he might not live to see next year. It is only where very long periods of time are concerned that this factor, among normally situated men, obtains fully and directly. Payments which fall due in a hundred, fifty, or even twenty years, lose in value from the consideration of the uncertainty of life as regards *all* payees: payments which fall due in ten years lose in value as regards a great many.

And here finally we have the point from which this third motive may rise to universal *indirect* efficiency—although, at the same time, a very much weakened efficiency. If certain differences of valuation have once become established as regards long intervals of time, they must, through the agency of exchange transactions, to some degree affect shorter intervals. For the mechanism which determines objective value abhors any sudden leap in value. It is not possible, for example, that a payment of £100 which will be made on 1st January 1900 certain,

should be worth only £80 till 31st December 1889, and
should jump up to the full value of £100 at twelve o'clock
that night, because the due date is now only ten years off.
Equalising tendencies, and transactions which I can best compare with stock exchange arbitrage, spread the differences of
value, which obtain as regards long periods, uniformly over the
entire intermediate period —Putting all these peculiar circumstances together, I should be inclined to consider the practical
efficiency of this factor not altogether trifling. Still I should
not place it very high, especially as it is weakened, to a not
inconsiderable extent, by the consideration of closely related
heirs.   In any case, the two motives first mentioned have considerably more to do with the undervaluation of the future
utility than the third.[1]   All three causes of our underestimate
of future utility—errors of valuation through faulty representation of coming needs, defects of will, and consideration of
the uncertainty of life—manifest themselves in extremely
different degrees in different individuals, and even in the same
individual at different times, according to differences of temperament and mood.   For the same interval of time they may
cause one to make an undervaluation of 100%, another of
50%, a third of 1% or 2%: while they may send fanatics
in the matter of foresight and precaution to the opposite
extreme of overvaluing future utility.   I should like to call
special attention, further, to the fact, that the undervaluation
which results from these causes is not at all graduated harmoniously, in the subjective valuation of the individuals,
according to the length of the time that intervenes.   I mean,
it is not graduated in this way, for example, that the man who
discounts a utility which he expects to get in one year by
5%, must discount a utility due in two years by 10%, or one
due in three months by $1\frac{1}{4}$%.   On the contrary, the original
subjective undervaluations are, in the highest degree, unequal
and irregular.   In particular, so far as the undervaluation is
caused by defects of will, there may be a strong difference
between an enjoyment which offers itself at the very moment,
and one which does not; while, on the other hand, there may be

---

[1] An effect analogous to that of the uncertainty of life might be exerted by
the uncertainty of the duration of our capacity of enjoyment; but in any case
the limits of the efficiency of this motive are much more closely drawn.·

a very small difference, or no difference at all, between an enjoyment which is pretty far away, and one which is farther away. Uniformity is practically introduced into the various undervaluations, as we shall see later, only through the mediation of exchange business. At any rate—and this is sufficient for us here—all three causes have one common result; that, under their influence, we estimate the utility of future goods at a lower figure than expresses their true value: we look at the marginal utility of future goods diminished, as it were, in perspective.[1]

Now it is easy to show that this phenomenon must substantially contribute to strengthen the efficiency of the first factor in the undervaluation of future goods, the difference in the provision of goods for present and future. All persons who are worse off in the present than they expect to be in the future, —persons to whom, therefore, the true marginal utility of a future good is already less than the marginal utility of a similar present good,—are led by this second factor to put the future marginal utility still lower than it really is, and this increases the difference in value to the further prejudice of future goods. If, for example, the marginal utility of a definite present good is 100, and the true marginal utility of a similar good in a better-provided future is 80, the future good will be rated, perhaps, at 70 only, thanks to this second factor, and thus the difference of valuation rises from 20 to 30. In the same way those persons who may be supposed to be in approximately similar circumstances in present and future, and would, other things being equal, value present and future goods at approximately the same figure, will fall under the category of those who value present goods more highly than future. This second factor, then, increases both the number and the

---

[1] Jevons, like his follower Sax, as we saw in the note to p. 239, fell into a misunderstanding as to the entire nature of the phenomenon mentioned in the text, in confusing the representations and valuations which we make as regards future feelings with actually present feelings. We need not wonder, then, at not finding in these writers any sound thorough-going explanation of the phenomena, or even an attempt at such. They accept the supposed "weakened anticipated feelings" of future needs simply as fact, as a "well-known psychological fact," and they pass over much of its detail—which really very much requires explanation — without comment as "self-evident" (see, *e.g.*, Sax as before, p. 178).

intensity of the differences in valuation to the prejudice of future goods, and, naturally, in the market where present goods are exchanged against future, this must make the resultant exchange value more unfavourable to the latter.   The agio on present goods moves upwards.[1]

---

[1] Indirectly this effect will be strengthened by the fact that, through the under-valuation of the future utility, men will refrain from providing for the future so amply as they would otherwise have done. In other words, this underestimate acts to the prejudice of saving and accumulation of wealth, and still further reduces the number of persons who have to throw an accumulated surplus of present goods on the market.

CHAPTER IV

THE TECHNICAL SUPERIORITY OF PRESENT GOODS

THERE is still a third reason why present goods are, as a rule, worth more than future. The fact on which it is based has long been known in a general way, but its essential nature has been thoroughly misunderstood. Hidden in a perfect wilderness of mistakes, economists ever since Say and Lauderdale have been in the habit of going to it, under the name "productivity of capital," for their explanation and justification of Interest.[1] This name, which has already been the cause of so many errors, and which, besides, does not altogether correspond with what it is intended to convey, I shall lay on one side, and shall confine myself to the facts of the case pure and simple. These facts are as follows:—that, as a rule, present goods are, on technical grounds, preferable instruments for the satisfaction of human want, and assure us, therefore, a higher marginal utility than future goods.

It is an elementary fact of experience that methods of production which take time are more productive. That is to say, given the same quantity of productive instruments, the lengthier the productive method employed the greater the quantity of products that can be obtained. In previous chapters we went very thoroughly into this, showed the reasons of it, and illustrated and confirmed it by many examples.[2] I venture to think we may now assume it as proved. If, then, we take an amount of productive instruments available at a certain point of time as given, we have to represent the product, which may be turned out by increasingly lengthy processes, under the picture of a series increasing in a

[1] See *Capital and Interest*, p. 111. [2] See above, pp. 18, 84.

certain ratio, regular or irregular.   Suppose that, in the year 1888, we have command of a definite quantity of productive instruments, say, thirty days of labour, we may, in terms of the above proposition, assume something like the following.   The month's labour, employed in methods that give a return immediately, and are, therefore, very unremunerative, will yield only 100 units of product: employed in a one year's process, it yields 200 units,[1] but, of course, yields them only for the year 1889 : employed in a two years' process it yields 280 units—for the year 1890—and so on in increasing progression ; say, 350 units for 1891, 400 for 1892, 440 for 1893, 470 for 1894, and 500 for 1895.

Compare with this what we may get from a similar quantity of productive instruments, namely, a month's labour, under the condition that we do not get possession of the labour till a year later.   A month's labour which falls due in the year 1889 evidently yields nothing for the economic year 1888.   If any result is to be got from it in the year 1889 it can only be by employing it in the most unremunerative (because immediate) production, and that result will be, as above, 100 units.   In 1890 it is possible to have a return of 200 units by employing it in a one year's method of production ; in 1891 to have 280 units by employing it in a two years' process, and so on.   In exactly the same way, with a month's labour falling due two years later, in 1890, nothing can be had to satisfy the wants of the economic years 1888 and 1889, while 100 units may be got for 1890 by an unremunerative immediate . process, 200 for 1891, 280 for 1892, and so on.   If we group together in one table the result obtainable for the satisfaction of our wants from a similar amount of present, next year's, and succeeding years' productive instruments, we get the following scheme :—

---

[1] Naturally, in the case of lengthier processes, the labour first expended requires that the production should be continued by the addition of new labour.   By the figures given in the text is always meant that share in the product which, of the total product, falls to the productive unit—in this case the thirty days' labour. If, *e.g.*, in the case of a one year's process, other eleven months of labour follow the one first expended, this would involve, in terms of our illustration, that a total product of 2400 units was obtained in the twelve months taken together, and thus, to the one month, would be ascribed a product of 200 units.

A MONTH'S LABOUR OF THE YEAR

		1888.	1889.	1890.	1891.	
Yields for the economic period.	1888	100	—	—	—	Units of Product.
	1889	200	100	—	—	
	1890	280	200	100	—	
	1891	350	280	200	100	
	1892	400	350	280	200	
	1893	440	400	350	280	
	1894	470	440	400	350	
	1895	500	470	440	400	

Putting these figures into words, the table shows that, whatever economic period we may fix upon, our economic interests for that period are more advanced by a month's labour of 1888 than by a month's labour of 1889, by one of 1889 than by one of 1890, and so on. To meet the wants of 1888, for example, a month's labour expended in the year 1889 or 1890 gives us nothing, while a month's labour expended in 1888 places at our command at least 100 units of product. To meet the wants of 1893 a month of 1890 gives us 350 units, a month of 1889 400 units, a month of 1888 440 units. Whatever period of time we take as our standpoint of comparison, the earlier (present) amount of productive instruments is seen to be superior, technically, to the equally great later (future) amount.[1]

---

[1] On the same analogy, as a present month of labour is technically superior to a future, so is a past month to a present. According to our scheme a month of the period 1883, *e.g.*, would give for 1888, in a 5 years' process, 440 units, while a month of the year 1888 would give only 100 units. But, naturally, the past years would realise their technical superiority, as against the present, only under the condition that they also were actually invested in correspondingly lengthy and roundabout processes. But this is seldom the case as regards long past years. And, therefore, one need not be frightened at the consequences which, of course, the above theory involves; that, for instance, a month's labour of the fifteenth century is, perhaps, a hundred times, and a month's labour of the year of our Lord, perhaps, a thousand times more fruitful than a month's labour of the present year; that, accordingly, to a certain extent, the productive powers of the past were gigantic beside those of to-day, and to-day's productive powers gigantic compared to those of future centuries—a view which would seem to give us but a dreary outlook to a continuous degeneracy of our productive powers. Certainly, if any one in the year 1 had expended a month of labour with a view to the marginal utility of the year 1888,

But is it superior also in the height of its marginal utility and value ? Certainly it is. For if, in every conceivable department of wants for the supply of which we may or shall employ it, it puts more means of satisfaction at our disposal, it must have a greater importance for our wellbeing. Of course I am aware that the greater amount need not always have the greater value ;—a bushel of corn in a year of famine may be worth more than two bushels after a rich harvest ; a silver shilling before the discovery of America was worth more than five shillings are now. But for one and the same person, at one and the same point of time, the greater amount has always the greater value ; whatever may be the absolute value of the bushel or the shilling, this much is certain, that, for me, two shillings or two bushels which I have to-day are worth more than one shilling or one bushel which I have to-day. And in our comparison of the value of a present and a future amount of productive instruments the case is exactly similar. Possibly the 470 units of product which may be made from a month's labour in 1889 for the year 1895, are worth less than the 350 units which may be got from the same for the year 1892, and the latter, notwithstanding their numbers, may be the most valuable product which can be made out of a month of 1889 in general. In any case the 400 units which a man can gain by a month's labour of the year 1888 for the year 1892 are still more valuable, and therefore the superiority of the earlier (present)

and had arranged for the systematic continuation of the work during all the 1888 years intervening, in that case, thanks to the natural powers impressed into the service in the course of such a roundabout journey, the product of that long past month would be mountains high beside the product of a month of the present year. But, as things are, trees do not grow up till they meet the sky. The productive powers are too necessary for the wants of the living, to let us employ them in advance for the behoof of future centuries or future thousands of years. And thus the year of those future wants to which we look forward and work, and by which we get the measure of the productiveness of the powers, moves forward very much parallel with the year when the productive powers are exerted. It is quite certain that our productive powers of 1888 do for the wants, say, of the year 1898, as much as and more than the productive powers of the year 1 A.D. did for the wants of the year 11 A.D. And thus the productive powers of giants do not degenerate into those of pigmies, as a sophistical dialectic might easily delude us into believing : in all ages, the productive powers, according to the advance of technique, do as much or, rather, increasingly more for the wants of their own circle of provision.

amount of productive instruments—here and everywhere, however the illustration may be varied—remains confirmed.

The truth of the proposition, that the technical superiority of present to future means of production must also be associated with a superiority in value, may be made absolutely convincing by mathematical evidence if the tabular comparison, which we have drawn out to show the technical productiveness of different years of productive instruments, be extended to the marginal utility and value of the same. And since we have to deal here with a proposition which will form the chief pillar in my interest theory, I prefer to err on the side of making it too plain rather than risk not making it plain enough, and I shall spare no pains to prove it in the most complete way. In other respects, too, the trouble it costs us will not be altogether lost: as we proceed we shall get an occasional glimpse into certain relations which are seldom or never taken thought of, and yet, none the less, have some importance towards giving us a complete and thorough grasp of the whole.

The marginal utility and value of means of production depend, as we know,[1] on the anticipated marginal utility and value of their product. But the means of production of which we have been speaking, the month's labour, may be invested in a production that yields an immediate return, or in a one, two, three, or ten years' period of production, and, according as it is so invested, we may obtain the very different product of 100, 200, 280, 350 units, and so on. Which of these products is to be our standard? The foregoing chapters have already given us the answer. In the case of goods which may be employed in different ways yielding different marginal utilities, it is the highest marginal utility that is the standard. Therefore, in our present case, it is that product which produces the greatest amount of value.[2] But this need not

---

[1] See above, p. 179.

[2] See above, p. 163. To prevent a mistake which is very apt to arise through the similarity of the words, I again emphasise here that the proposition in the text is not in contradiction with the fundamental proposition on p. 186, that, for productive goods, the value of the least valuable of their products, the value of the "marginal product," is the standard. The marginal product, that is to say, is the last of several products which may all be made from the available means of production ; but, in the case we are now considering,

coincide with the largest product, the product which contains the greatest number of units; on the contrary, it seldom or never coincides with that. We should obtain the greatest number of units by an infinitely long production process, or a process lasting a hundred or two hundred years. But goods which first come into possession in the lifetime of our grandchildren or great-grandchildren, have, in our valuation of to-day, little or no value.

In determining which, of various possible products, has the highest value for us, we are guided by the two considerations of which we have just spoken. First, we are guided by the anticipated position of our provision at the various periods of time. If, for instance, a man is ill provided for in the present, or not provided for at all, the unit of product in the present may, on that very account, have so high a marginal utility and value, that the sum of value of 100 present units of product is greater to him than that of 500 units which he might have at his command in 1895. To another man, again, whose present is as well provided for, or nearly as well provided for, as his future, the advantage in numbers may give an advantage in value to the 500 units. The second consideration by which we are guided is, that our present valuation of a future good or product does not depend on its true marginal utility, but on our *subjective* estimation of the marginal utility. But, in forming this subjective estimate, there takes place, as we have already seen, a kind of perspective diminution; a diminution which is in direct ratio with the futurity of the time to which the good in question belongs. The amount of which we are in search, therefore, the greatest sum of value, will evidently belong to that one, among the various possible products, the number of whose items, multiplied by the value of the unit of product (as that value shows itself with regard to the relation of want and provision for want in the particular economic period, and with regard to the diminution which future goods undergo from perspective), gives the greatest amount of value.

We shall put our illustration in figures chosen at random. I wish to emphasise that the figures *can* be chosen quite at

it is not a matter of employing a month's labour in one *and* more years' production, but in one *or* more years' production. And of these *alternative* employments, naturally, the most important has the preference.

random and varied by the reader at will, for our proposition
maintains its validity in every conceivable position of subjective
valuations. Moreover I intentionally take figures varying
very greatly and irregularly, it being obvious enough, without
any special demonstration, that, if the value of the unit of
goods were not to vary for the different periods, or not to vary
much, the present means of production, as giving a greater
quantity of products, would inevitably give us also a greater
sum of value. Assume, then, quite at random, that, for a
certain individual, the true marginal utility and value of the
unit of product—taking into account his special circumstances
of provision, which we shall suppose are, on the whole, gradually improving—are as follows: in 1888, 5 units, of value
(pounds, shillings, or units of any ideal standard); in 1889, 4;
in 1890, 3·3; in 1891, 2·5; in 1892, 2·2; in 1893, 2·1; in
1894, 2; and in 1895, 1·5. This true marginal utility, then,
by reason of perspective, experiences, for the later periods,
an irregularly progressive reduction of this kind: for 1888
it is, subjectively estimated, 5 (without reduction); for 1889,
instead of 4, it is 3·8; for 1890, instead of 3·3, it is only 3;
for 1891, 2·2; for 1892, 2; for 1893, 1·8; for 1894, 1·5;
and for 1895, 1. If, now, on the basis of these figures, we
calculate the sums of value represented by the different possible
products of a month's labour falling due in the various years,
from 1888 to 1891, we get the following tables:—

A MONTH'S LABOUR AVAILABLE IN *1888* YIELDS

For the Economic Period.	Units of Product.	True Marginal Utility of Unit.	Marginal Utility reduced in Perspective.	Amount of Value of Entire Product.
1888	100	5	5	500
1889	200	4	3·8	760
1890	280	3·3	3	840
1891	350	2·5	2·2	770
1892	400	2·2	2	800
1893	440	2·1	1·8	792
1894	470	2	1·5	705
1895	500	1·5	1	500

A MONTH'S LABOUR AVAILABLE IN *1889* YIELDS

For Economic Period.	Units.	True Marginal Utility.	Reduced Marginal Utility.	Value.
1888	—	5	5	—
1889	100	4	3·8	380
1890	200	3·3	3	600
1891	280	2·5	2·2	616
1892	350	2·2	2	700
1893	400	2·1	1·8	720
1894	440	2	1·5	660
1895	470	1·5	1	470

A MONTH'S LABOUR AVAILABLE IN *1890* YIELDS

For Economic Period.	Units.	True Marginal Utility.	Reduced Marginal Utility.	Value.
1888	—	5	5	—
1889	—	4	3·8	—
1890	100	3·3	3	300
1891	200	2·5	2·2	440
1892	280	2·2	2	560
1893	350	2·1	1·8	630
1894	400	2	1·5	600
1895	440	1·5	1	440

A MONTH'S LABOUR AVAILABLE IN *1891* YIELDS

For Economic Period.	Units.	True Marginal Utility.	Reduced Marginal Utility.	Value.
1888	—	5	5	—
1889	—	4	3·8	—
1890	—	3·3	3	—
1891	100	2·5	2·2	220
1892	200	2·2	2	400
1893	280	2·1	1·8	504
1894	350	2	1·5	525
1895	400	1·5	1	400

The conclusion we draw from these tables is the follow-ing. The highest value of product obtainable by the month's labour available in 1888—that which determines its own valuation—is 840 : the highest value obtainable by a month's labour available in 1889 is only 720 : while the highest value obtainable by a month's labour available in 1890 and 1891 is 630 and 525 respectively. As a fact, therefore, the present month's labour is superior to all future ones, not only in technical productiveness, but also in marginal utility and value.

I repeat emphatically that this result is not an accidental one, such as might have made its appearance in consequence of the particular figures used in our hypothesis. On the single assumption that longer methods of production lead generally to a greater product, it is a necessary result; a result which must have occurred, in an exactly similar way, whatever might have been the figures of quantity of product and value of unit in the different years.

I must, further, lay particular weight on the fact, that this result does not make its appearance simply because, in our hypothesis, we have introduced, as already active, those other two circumstances which are fitted to account for a surplus value of present as against future goods—namely, a difference in the circumstances of provision at the various periods of time, and a diminution of the future utility by way of perspec-tive. The superiority in value of present means of production, which is based on their technical superiority, is not one borrowed from these circumstances; it would emerge of its own strength even if these were not active at all. I have introduced the two circumstances into the hypothesis only to make it a little more true to life, or, rather, to keep it from being quite absurd. Take, for instance, the influence of the reduction due to perspective entirely out of the illustration, and we get the following figures :—

A MONTH'S LABOUR OF THE YEAR

		1888.	1889.	1890.	1891.	
Yields for the economic period	1888	500	—	—	—	Units of Value.
	1889	800	400	—	—	
	1890	924	660	330	—	
	1891	875	700	500	250	
	1892	880	770	616	440	
	1893	924	840	735	588	
	1894	940	880	800	700	
	1895	750	705	660	600	

We see that now the absolute figures of the sums of value are increased throughout, and also that the economic centre of gravity is transferred to another year;[1] but the thing which concerns us is that the result remains unchanged;—the month's labour of 1888 shows the highest figure of value, and all the others a decreasingly smaller one.

But if we were also to abstract the difference in the circumstances of provision in different periods of time, the situation would receive the stamp of extreme improbability, even of self-contradiction. If the value of the unit of product were to be the same in all periods of time, however remote, the most abundant product would, naturally, at the same time be the most valuable. But since the most abundant product is obtained by the most lengthy and roundabout methods of production,—perhaps extending over decades of years,—the economic centre of gravity, for all present means of production, would, on this assumption, be found at extremely remote periods of time [2]—which is entirely contrary to all experience. And, besides, if such a state of things were to emerge at any particular point of time, it would immediately bring its own correction. For if every employment of

---

[1] *e.g.* the economic centre of gravity for the month's labour of 1888 in the former case lay in the product attainable for the year 1890 ; it now lies in that attainable for 1894.

[2] But here, all the same, the month's labour of 1888 remains superior to that of 1889. For, as regards any one remote period, say, the year 1988, the former, as employed in a process longer by one year, could produce a somewhat greater product than the latter.

goods for future periods is, not only technically, but economically, more remunerative than the employment of them for the
present or near future, of course men would withdraw their
stocks of goods, to a great extent, from the service of the
present, and direct them to the more remunerative service of
the future. But this would immediately cause an ebb-tide in
the provision for the present, and a flood in the provision for
the future, for the future would then have the double advantage of having a greater amount of productive instruments
directed to its service, and those instruments employed in
more fruitful methods of production. Thus the difference in
the circumstances of provision, which might have disappeared
for the moment, would recur of its own accord.

But it is just at this point that we get the best proof that
the superiority in question is independent of differences in the
circumstances of provision : so far from being obliged to borrow
its strength and activity from any such difference, it is, on
the contrary, able, if need be, to call forth this very difference.—
Thus we get, as result of our digression, the assured conviction
of two things ;—first, that the productive superiority of present goods assures them, not only a surplus in product, but
a surplus in value, and, second, that, in this superiority,
we have to deal with a third cause of the surplus value, and
one which is independent of any of the two already mentioned.[1]

We have now to ask : To what extent is this third cause
active ? Of this our former analyses give a poor and inadequate picture. What has been said is only sufficient to
explain how present Means of Production are worth more than
future means of production. But, from the same cause, as we
have now to show, present consumption goods also obtain a

---

[1] Those who prefer somewhat more venturous generalisations might, perhaps,
be inclined to put the first and the third cause together under one common
category, that of the "technical superiority" of present goods. For the preference given to present goods in virtue of the different relations of provision
also rests peculiarly on a technical circumstance ; namely, that they allow of a
greater choice of employments, both as regards present and future wants, while
future goods, naturally, are adapted to serve future wants only. At all events,
this technical superiority is so essentially distinct from the other, of the greater
technical *productivity*, that the two elements would require again to be kept
separate from each other. It appears to me, therefore, in the interests of clearness that they should be kept entirely distinct from the first.

preference over future consumption goods, so that, in this third cause, we have a quite universally valid reason for present goods having a greater value than future.

The connection is as follows. Command over a sum of present consumption goods provides us with the means of subsistence during the current economic period. This leaves the means of production, which we may have at our disposal during this period (Labour, Uses of Land, Capital), free for the technically more productive service of the future, and gives us the more abundant product attainable by them in longer methods of production. On the other hand, command over a sum of future consumption goods leaves, of course, the present unprovided for, and, consequently, leaves us under the necessity of directing the means of production that are at our command in the present, wholly or partially, to the service of the present. But this involves curtailment of the production process, and, as consequence, a diminished product. The difference of the two products is the advantage connected with the possession of present consumption goods.

To illustrate this by an example as simple as it is well-worn. Imagine, with Roscher,[1] a tribe of fisher-folk without capital, subsisting on fish left in pools on the shore by the ebb-tide and caught with the bare hand. Here a labourer may catch and eat three fish a day. If he had a boat and net he could catch thirty fish a day, instead of three. But he cannot have these tools, for their making would cost him a month's time and labour, and, in the meantime, he would have nothing to live upon. To save himself from starvation he must continue his wretched and costly fishing by hand. But now some one cleverer than the rest borrows ninety fish, promising, against the loan, to give back a hundred and eighty fish after one month. With the borrowed fish he supports himself during a month, makes a boat and net, and, during the next month, catches nine hundred fish instead of ninety. From this take, not only can he make the stipulated payment of a hundred and eighty fish, but he retains a considerable net gain to himself, and thereby affords a striking proof that the ninety (present) fish he borrowed were worth to him, not only much more than the ninety, but even more than the hundred and eighty (future) fish he paid for them.

[1] *Grundlagen*, § 189.

Now, of course, the differences in value are not always so great as in this example. They are greatest among people who live from hand to mouth. For them to get command over present consumption goods means the transition to capitalist production. Less striking, but always present, is the difference where people already possess a certain stock of goods. If, for example, their stock of goods is sufficient for three years, they may realise their means of production in an average three years' production process. If, now, by some means or other, they obtain another year's supply of present means of subsistence, they may extend their average production period from three to four years, and obtain thereby an increment of product which, absolutely, is always important, but, relatively, will be much less than in the first case.

We can see that here, again, the matter of fact, on which I base my conclusions, is an old and well-known one : even in the time of Adam Smith and Turgot, it was notorious that the possession of present consumption goods confers certain advantages. But as the older theory of capital was, generally speaking, a nest of warped conceptions and incorrect explanations, this fact also was put down in a form as singular as it was inappropriate. Consumption goods—goods for immediate consumption—were looked on as productive goods or means of production ; as such they were counted capital ; and then all the advantages inherent in them were explained by the productivity of capital. Indeed, a writer of the standing of Jevons, simply through dwelling on the great importance which attaches to the command over present goods, was misled into ascribing to consumption goods the high position of being the only capital ! In face of such misinterpretations our business now is to get at the truth of facts. And the facts are very simple. Consumption goods are not means of production : they are, therefore, not capital ; and the advantages which they confer do not proceed from any productive power they possess. Everything turns on the simple fact that, according to the quite familiar laws of value, present goods, in virtue of the above stated casuistical connection of circumstances, are, normally, the means of obtaining a higher marginal utility, and receive thereby a higher value, than future goods.

CHAPTER V

CO-OPERATION OF THE THREE FACTORS

To put together the results at which we have arrived thus far. We have seen that there are three factors, each of which, independently of the other, is adequate to account for a difference in value between present and future goods in favour of the former. These three factors are: The difference in the circumstances of provision between present and future; the underestimate, due to perspective, of future advantages and future goods; and, finally, the greater fruitfulness of lengthy methods of production. The question now is :—how do these factors, working simultaneously, affect each other?

About the two first factors we know already : their effects are cumulative. In the case of a man badly provided for in the present, if the marginal utility of a present good were 100, and its true marginal utility in a future period only 80, the present good would be valued, relatively to the future, in the ratio of 100 to 80, if no other influence intervened. But if there is, besides, a perspective diminution of the true future marginal utility, say by one-eighth, the marginal utility would be put at 70 instead of 80, and the superiority of the present good to the future would be in the ratio of 100 to 70.

It is essentially different with the co-operation of the third factor. True, it also tends to strengthen the action of the other factors, but it does so alternatively, not cumulatively; that is to say, that factor which confers the greater advantage on present goods always stands out from the other as the active agent. Say, for example, that the first factor (the circumstances of provision), together with the second factor (that of perspective), taken cumulatively, would give present goods

T

an advantage of 30%, while the factor of productivity would give an advantage of 25%, we should not get a total advantage of 55%, but of 30%, the advantage being based on the stronger factors.

The matter stands thus. The superiority of present goods, as making roundabout and more fruitful ways of production possible, cannot be increased by the perspective undervaluation of future goods, because the utility got from lengthy processes is itself a future utility, to which the perspective undervaluation applies as much as it applies to the future goods with which the present goods are compared. Say that, by employing a month's labour now, in 1888, in a one year's process, I can make, for 1889, a product of 200 units, and, by employing a month's labour of 1889, I can make for that same year—on account of the short and unproductive method—a product of 100 units only, it will be a reason for my valuing the present month of labour at double the next year's month. If, now, there comes in a ten per cent undervaluation of next year's utility, I shall, of course, value the next year's 100 units at 90 present units only; but, for exactly the same reason, I shall value the 200 units at 180 present units only; and the ratio of valuation, two to one, remains exactly as if the perspective undervaluation had never come into play at all.

As little can the third factor be strengthened by the first factor, namely, the consideration of a greater present want. For, evidently, employing a good to a great future productive utility, and employing it to satisfy an immediate pressing want, are mutually exclusive employments; and it is clear that a good, which can only be employed in the one way or the other, cannot obtain a cumulative advantage from the two together.

But these two factors do work into each other's hands in the following way. Present goods may be used to meet present wants, or they may be invested in production for the future. These are the two possible employments to which each individual may put his present goods. According to principles with which we are familiar, the stock of goods will be guided into these employments in such a way, that the most important chances of using the goods are utilised first, the next important second, and so on down the scale. Here, however, it is to be noted that the employments in producing for the future, as standing over against the employments in the satisfaction of immediate wants, must submit to the perspective diminution with which we are familiar.   Say, for instance, that a man's particular circumstances are such that he estimates a utility, falling due in the following year, at 10% less than an equally great present utility; then a future utility of 110 becomes equal to a present utility of 100, and, on that account, when there comes to be a choice between employments, the future utility of 110 may be postponed to a present utility of 102. The last employment, then, which, on these principles, is still supplied from the stock of goods, indicates, as we know, the marginal utility, and, at the same time, the value of the unit of goods.

Now the following cases may occur.   First, the individual may be badly off in the present.   In that case the pressing wants of the moment will, by themselves, absorb the small stock of present goods, and, on the ground of this bad provision in the present, these goods will obtain a high value and a preference over future goods.   The needy man prefers present goods because he *must* consume them in the present.   The opportunities of employing the goods for productive purposes in the future remain in this case—since the poverty-stricken present, naturally, cannot afford any goods for purposes beyond itself— out of court as economically impossible, and, of course, without any influence on the value, or preferable value, of present goods.

Or, second, the individual may be equally well provided as regards both present and future, but may have less forethought. This case leads to a similar result.   Before, it was urgent want that prevented portions of the stock of goods from being withdrawn from the service and enjoyment of the present, and invested in future production: now, it is want of thought for the future : and this want of thought confers, at the same time, on the present enjoyment, and on the present goods which minister to it, a preference over future.   The spendthrift, greedy of pleasure, values present goods more highly than future, because he *wishes* to enjoy them in the present.—If bad provision goes along with small foresight, the two effects, as we have seen, are cumulative.

Or, third, the individual is well provided, and takes due thought for the future.   In this case, of course, the two former sanctions of the preference do not come into play at all, or scarcely at all. In this case, beyond the satisfying of the immediate wants, the other course is economically open,—of investing a portion of his present goods in production for the future: thereby their economic centre of gravity, their marginal utility, and the formation of their value, are shifted to a sphere in which present goods enjoy a preference in value under the third sanction, that of their greater productiveness. A moderately rich and prudent man who has £10,000, must not, and will not consume his £10,000 in the present, but will, in any case, save for the service of the future. But if any one were to make him the proposal, to exchange his £10,000 of present money for £10,000 of future money, he would be fully justified in declining the transaction; as, with £10,000 (now) he can provide more effectually and richly for the future than with £10,000 at a future period.

But, finally, there is still a fourth case conceivable: an individual may be so badly off in the present, or have so little thought for the future, that, on those two accounts, he values present goods more highly than future. At the same time, however, he is tempted by business which promises him so good a return in the future that he stints himself still further in his present provision, and engages in the business. Here, after the analogy of the case worked out on p. 165, the available sums of goods are directed, successively, into the most important employments of the two spheres taken together, and the competition of these future employments has for result that the satisfaction of present wants is broken off at a higher point or level than it would otherwise be. This must, in the end, raise the value of present goods, and indirectly increase their superiority over future.[1]

Thus the various sanctions come alternatively into play.

---

[1] Suppose, *e.g.*, that a man has 6 units of goods, say 6 five-pound notes, at his disposal. There are present groups of wants, which these notes could supply, and their importance is indicated by the figures 10, 9, 8, 7, 6, 5. Now there appear opportunities of employing these in business transactions which will not yield any result for a year, but are so profitable that, even after deducting the necessary dis-agio on account of the year's delay, they are equal to a present utility of 7. The following will evidently be the disposition of the notes. Four of them will go to the present wants which bear the utility 10, 9, 8, 7, the remaining two to the future employments which, likewise, show the (reduced)

Where the first two are active the third is suspended : but where the first two are not active, or not sufficiently active, there comes in the action of the third.   One can easily understand how very directly this circumstance is calculated to give the phenomenon of the higher valuations of present goods an almost universal validity.   The needy and the careless value present goods more highly because they urgently require them in the present, or only think about the present: the well-off and the saving value them because they can accomplish more with them in the future : and thus, in the long-run, every one, whatever his economical position, and whatever his economical temperament, has some ground for valuing present goods more highly than future.   And, further, it is easy to understand how much the universal emergence of subjective differences in valuation must favour the extension of this phenomenon to the sphere of objective exchange value and price.   If the third factor were to act cumulatively with the two first there would, indeed, be many who would value present goods at an extravagant rate, but it is not certain that there would not be as many, perhaps an overwhelming majority, who would have no preference for present goods, and it is doubtful how, in this case, the resultant of exchange value would turn out.   But as the third factor is alternative in its action, it levels up, as it were, the depressions instead of exaggerating individual heights ; thus it brings about a general raising of subjective valuations; and this is necessarily connected with a raising of the average line, the resultant exchange value.[1]

figure 7.   The marginal utility which attaches to the present five-pound note is, therefore, 7, while, without the competition of the profitable future employments, it would have been only 5.

[1] The statement of how the productivity of capital works into and together with the other two grounds of the higher valuation of present goods, I consider one of the most difficult points in the theory of interest, and, at the same time, the one which must decide the fate of that theory.   It is just at this point that we discover the chief weakness in Jevons's otherwise suggestive work.   None of the groups of phenomena concerned escaped his keen observation ; what did escape him was the way in which they work into one another.   Consequently his work remains an eclectic piece of patchwork instead of being welded into an organic theory.   He gathers together quite correctly all the primary phenomena required for the explanation.   But he does not find the common channel through which they all work together to the one common end, and so he explains it differently from each different point of view, with a result that is eclectic and self-contradictory.   After a most promising beginning he quite loses sight of the element of the different valua-

Here we come to our last duty in this book : to show how
the ratio that obtains between present and future goods in
subjective valuations is transferred to their objective exchange
value.

In the case of the single individual, extremely various subjective valuations will be formed, according as the one or the other
of the above-mentioned factors is stronger or weaker.   These
encounter each other on the market where present goods are
exchanged against future.   There are many such markets and
they take many different forms.   In the next book we shall
more exactly examine their constitution.   In the meantime
we must be content to examine the method in which prices are
formed in its most general and typical outlines.   Indeed the
formation of price here takes the same course as it does elsewhere.   The divergence of the subjective valuations which
encounter each other on the market makes possible, economically,
the exchange of property between the two parties.[1]   Those
who, on any subjective grounds, put a relatively high value
on present goods, appear as buyers of present against future
commodities ; those who put a relatively low value,[2] as sellers :
and the market price will be settled between the subjective
valuations of the last competitors who actually exchange, and
the first competitors who are shut out, or, as we have put it,

tions put upon present and future wants, and for the rest gives a double explanation,
full of contradictions, and scarcely rising much above the level of the old classical
economy,—part of it taken from the Abstinence, part from the Productivity theory.
(See my *Capital and Interest*, p. 400.)   The not very independent treatment which
the subject has received from Sax is in one respect better, while in another it is
even more incomplete than that of Jevons.   It shows an advance to find the
element of the undervaluation of future wants generally interwoven into
the explanation of interest.   (See also on this point Launhardt, *Mathematische
Begründung der Volkswirthschaftslehre*, Leipsic, 1885, § 2, and again my *Capital
and Interest*, pp. 344, 427.)   But, on the other hand, it is a sensible omission that the
difference between the values of present and future goods is traced exclusively to
this factor, and that the much more important factor that co-operates with it,
that of the greater productiveness, does not get even the scanty consideration
it gets from Jevons.   (Sax, *Grundlegung*, p. 314.)

[1] See above, p. 195.

[2] For reasons with which we are now familiar almost all the competitors,
whether buyers or sellers, will value present goods, *absolutely*, above future.   But
the valuation will be higher on the part of the buyers, as a class, than on the
part of the sellers.

between the valuations of the two marginal pairs.   We may
represent the position of the market by the following scheme :—

Intending Buyers.	Present goods in units.	Next year's goods in units.	Intending Sellers.	Present goods in units.	Next year's goods in units.
A_1 values 100	=	300	B_1 values 100	=	99
A_2	„	200	B_2	„	100
A_3	„	150	B_3	„	101
A_4	„	120	B_4	„	102
A_5	„	110	B_5	„	103
A_6	„	108	B_6	„	105
A_7	„	107	B_7	„	106
A_8	„	106	B_8	„	107
A_9	„	104	B_9	„	108
A_{10}	„	102	B_{10}	„	110

In the circumstances of the market which this scheme
represents, A_7 and B_7 form the upper marginal pair, A_8 and B_8
the lower.   The market price for 100 present units of goods
will be fixed between 106 and 107, say at $106\frac{1}{2}$ next year's
units, and this determines an agio of $6\frac{1}{2}\%$ in favour of
present goods.

Once a market price of this kind for present goods has
been established, it exerts a reflex levelling influence on the
subjective valuations which were originally so strongly divergent.
Even those who, from personal circumstances, would value
future goods only a little under, or perhaps at equal terms
with, present goods, now value present goods according to the
higher exchange value which the position of the market lends
to them.   This is the reason, and the only reason, why, in
practical life, scarcely any one would be willing to exchange
present goods against an exactly equal sum of future ones.
There are plenty of people whose circumstances of want and
provision for want are of such a kind, that the subjective *use*
value of present and future goods to them stands almost equal.
But the general position of the market is, almost invariably,
so strongly in favour of present goods, that it assures them a
preference in *exchange* value, of which, naturally, every one
takes advantage.

Developed market exchange, however, brings with it a
levelling effect from another side; that is to say, it brings the

amount of agio in favour of present goods, as against future goods which fall due at variously remote points of time, into one normal ratio with the length of the elapsing time. It might easily be the case that the causes which tend to the undervaluation of future goods might chance to be quite disproportionately effective on goods belonging to different periods of time. Indeed, in the very nature of several of those causes (for instance, the consideration of the shortness of human life) they would scarcely obtain at all as against goods of the near future, while, as against goods of remote periods, they would obtain strongly and irregularly. In itself, therefore, it might be quite possible that, while 100 present units of goods, as against 100 units of next year's goods, obtained, in the market, an agio of 5 units only, as against goods of the next year they might obtain an agio of more than twice that, say 20, and, as against the third year's goods, perhaps an agio of 40. But such disproportionate prices for goods of different periods of remoteness could not long hold. By a kind of time arbitrage they would very soon be brought into an equal ratio. If, for instance, the various market prices mentioned above were found quoted at one given moment, speculators would immediately appear on the scene, who would sell present goods against two years' goods, cover the purchase by buying present against next year's goods, and arrange for paying the latter a year later by a second purchase of present against next year's goods. The business would work out thus. In 1888 the speculator buys 1000 present units for 1050 units of the year 1889, and sells them at the same time for 1200 of the year 1890. In 1889 he has to deliver 1050 units, and he gets them by buying, again with a agio of 5%, the then present (1889) goods for the then next year's (1890) goods. For the 1050 units he requires to deliver he must thus give $1102\frac{1}{2}$ units of 1890. But, from the first transaction, he then receives 1200 of these very (1890) units. He has thus, on the whole business, a utility of about 100 units. Such arbitrage transactions must evidently bring the prices obtainable for goods of various future years to a level. The speculative demand for the much undervalued two years' goods must raise their price; the supply of next year's goods must depress *their* price; till such time as the agio is brought directly into proportion with the length of the time.

When this happens—say, for example, that the agio has become equalised at 5% *per year*, it may hold on at that rate undisturbed. For then it is equally remunerative to exchange present goods against next year's goods for three years successively, or to exchange present goods directly against three years' goods, and the arbitrage we have just sketched has no further occasion to interfere in the formation of price.

Thus we may accept the following as positive result of the present book.

The relation between want and provision for want in present and future, the undervaluation of future pleasures and pains, and the technical advantage residing in present goods, have the effect that, to the overwhelming majority of men, the subjective use value of present goods is higher than that of similar future goods. From this relation of subjective valuations there follows, in the market generally, a higher objective exchange value and market price for present goods, and this, reflecting back on present goods, gives them a higher subjective (exchange) value even among those whose personal circumstances happen to be such that the goods would not naturally have any preference in subjective use value. Finally, the levelling tendencies of the market bring the reduced value of future goods into a regular proportion to their remoteness in time. In the economic community, then, we find universally that future goods have a less value, both subjective and objective, corre-sponding to the degree of their remoteness in time.

BOOK VI

THE SOURCE OF INTEREST

CHAPTER I

IN the previous book I tried to show, and account for, the natural difference that exists between the value of present and the value of future goods. I have now to show that this difference of value is the source and origin of all Interest on Capital. But as the exchange of present commodities for future commodities takes various forms, the phenomenal forms of interest are as various, and our inquiry must necessarily deal with them all. In the following chapters, therefore, I intend to take up, in succession, all the principal forms of interest, and I shall endeavour to show that, notwithstanding all differences in shape and appearance, the active cause in them all is one and the same, namely, the difference in value between present and future goods.

By far the simplest case of this difference in value is presented in the Loan. A loan is nothing else than a real and true exchange of present goods for future goods; indeed, it is the simplest conceivable phenomenal form, and, to some extent, the ideal and type of such an exchange. The "lender," A, gives to the "borrower," B, a sum of present goods— say, present pounds sterling. B gets full and free possession of the goods to deal with as he likes, and, as equivalent, he gives into A's full and free possession a sum of entirely similar, but future, goods—say, next year's pounds sterling.

Here, then, is a mutual transfer of property in two sums of goods, of which one is given as recompense or payment for the other. Between them there is perfect homogeneity, but for the fact that the one belongs to the present, the other to the future. I cannot imagine how an exchange in general, and an exchange between present and future goods in particular, could be expressed more simply and clearly. Now, in the last chapter, we proved that the resultant of the subjective valuations which determines the market price of present and future goods is, as a rule, in favour of present goods. The borrower, therefore, will, as a rule, purchase the money which he receives now by a larger sum of money which he gives later. He must thus pay an "agio" or premium (*Aufgeld*), and this agio is interest. Interest, then, comes, in the most direct way, from the difference in value between present and future goods.

This is the extremely simple explanation of a transaction which, for hundreds of years, was made the subject of interpretations very involved, very far-fetched, and very untrue. Since the days of Molinæus and Salmasius,[1] the Loan has been conceived of as a transaction analogous to the Hire; as a transfer of the temporary use of fungible goods. This method of interpretation seems simple and natural enough. It has, too, the advantage and support of being in harmony with popular ideas and popular speech. We do not say, "I sell you, or exchange you £100," but, "I lend you £100." The transaction is a loan, and interest a *usura*, a use of money. But, before a scientific basis could be given to this popular conception, a whole series of subtilties had to be invented, and to obtain these out of the circumstances of actual life taxed all the resources of sophistry.

First it had to be shown that, in transferring a thing, it is possible to transfer more than the whole of it; namely, that in giving the borrower possession of the loaned thing, it is possible to transfer to him the right to all and every use that can be made of the thing, even to the consumption that annihilates it, and, besides that, the right to a separate kind of remnant use, for which a separate claim, the claim of interest, can be made. Then the further subtilty had to be invented, that, in perishable goods—goods which perish in the act of use—there is, all the same, a continuous use, ever rising anew from its own ashes; a use which lasts even when the good "used" has long ceased to exist! It had to be discovered that a cwt. of coal can be burned to cinders on 1st January

[1] See my *Capital and Interest*, p. 29.

1888, and yet be "used" uninterruptedly throughout the whole year, and, perhaps, for five, or ten, or a hundred years to come; and, what is best of all, that this lasting use can always be bought for a particular price, although and after the coal itself, and the right to consume it to the last atom, has been given away for another and a different price!

In my former book, *Capital and Interest*, I subjected this singular theory to a searching critical examination. I showed how, under peculiar historical conditions, it came into the world as the birth of circumstances, in which, to save interest and justify it against the unquestionably unjust attacks of the canonists, a decent foundation had to be found for it at any price, or, if not found, invented. I showed that this theory had its troubled source in a fiction. It was a fiction adopted, in its time, by the old jurists, in full consciousness that it was simply a fiction set up for certain practical legal purposes; but afterwards, by a strange misunderstanding, this fiction was adopted as a sufficient scientific fact. I tried, further, to show that this theory is, in itself, full of mistakes, internal contradictions, and impossibilities, and how, finally, when carried to its logical conclusion, it leads inevitably to further contradictions and impossibilities. In opposition to it, and in place of it, I now offer my own positive theory, then unpublished, and confidently leave it to the reader to judge on which side lies illusion and error, and on which truth.[1]

I would gladly refrain from any further commentary here, were it not that, quite recently, we have had a new literary pronouncement in favour of the Use theory which I opposed, and directed against the Exchange theory which I advocated; and were it not that this revived pronouncement emanates from no less authority than Karl Knies.

In 1885 Knies published a second edition of his book *Das Geld*. In it he replies to the criticism I made on some passages of his first edition, and, at the same time, expressly repeats certain positive objections he had made to the conception of the loan as an Exchange. On both counts I feel bound to answer.

It is unfortunate that Knies's reply touches only one of the many points on which I attacked his Use theory. I had,

---

[1] See *Capital and Interest*, pp. 214-259.

among other objections, put forward this;—that his method
of proving the actual existence of a durable use in perishable
goods rested on a dialectical confusion; and I had endeavoured
to strengthen my contention by an exact analysis of the very
words of his argument.[1]   To this Knies answers that I have,
notwithstanding, mistaken his meaning, and he repeats his
positive statement in such "altered expression, and with such
additions" as may put his real meaning beyond question.   As
now put, Knies's demonstration is very much amplified (in the
first edition it occupies pp. 72 and 73; in the second edition,
pp. 106 to 114), but, substantially, I cannot consider it any
more satisfactory.   On the contrary, it seems to me to bring
out more clearly that the existence of this durable use, which
I disputed, is not proved, but only assumed.

In one of the weightiest of the new passages (p. 109),
Knies has no hesitation in explaining, in so many words, that
in the Loan, although "not the same individual grains of corn
and pieces of money are returned, but (only) an equally large
and equally valuable amount of grains of corn and pieces of
money," still, "to economical consideration, the *same* goods are
given back."   Here he sanctions the fiction of identity between
fungible goods, *in optima forma*, within the sphere of economical
theory and economical discussion.   All that follows he bases
on the foundation thus obtained.   He finds the essence of
hire and lease in the fact that here "the hirer, leaseholder,
etc., gets the land, house, or the like, transferred to him to
use for his own purposes for such and such a continuous

---

[1] See *Capital and Interest*, p. 239.   It goes without saying that I could
mean nothing else than an involuntary dialectical confusion in the writer's
mind, and nothing was further from my intention than to charge a scholar, so
much esteemed by myself and by all the world, with wilfully misleading his
readers.   I should have thought that the very sincere expressions, in that and
other writings, of the respect in which I have always held the person of that
past master of our science, and particularly the express recognition of his
"thorough and conscientious efforts" with which I introduced this very
criticism (p. 239), might have sufficiently protected me against any such mis-
conception.   I was therefore more than astonished to learn that Professor
Knies had taken my words as conveying an offensive imputation of wilful
misleading of his readers.   Although I scarcely think that any one of my readers
will have understood me in this sense, I do not hesitate to explain here,
emphatically and publicly, not only that I had not the slightest intention of any
offensive imputation, but that I am exceedingly sorry if my inconsiderate choice
of words should unwittingly have made such an interpretation possible.

period, at the expiry of which he has to give back the good in question." In the Loan, perishable goods are likewise transferred "to be employed by the borrower for such and such a continuous but limited period of time." Consequently Hire and Loan are, essentially, analogous transactions—which was the point to be proved.

To this I would simply answer, that the second premiss is not truth but poetry. The sober, prosaic truth is that, in the Loan, perishable goods are not transferred to the borrower "for a continuous but limited period of time"; they are transferred definitely and for ever; they are never given back. What is given back is, in fact, other goods. What now becomes of the inferred analogy?

I am not blind to the use of analogies, and even to the demonstrative force which analogies may have under certain circumstances. I have myself often used them in the course of this book to drive home an argument. But an analogy is a weapon which requires careful handling. Comparisons, as every one knows, are always imperfect; if the compared things have one side in common, they have always another in which they differ. The "legal person," for instance, may very well be compared with the physical person in questions relating to property, while, in questions relating to the family, it would scarcely be safe. If, then, we draw some conclusion from the similarity of two things, our conclusion must keep within the sphere in which the similarity actually exists; from similar circumstances in one sphere we cannot draw a conclusion that the circumstances are similar in another sphere to which the similarity does not extend. No one, for instance, would consider an argument like this legitimate:—the legal person is as much a person as the physical person; a physical person can marry; therefore, a legal person also can marry!

Yet it seems to me that it is into this vicious and false use of analogies, that Knies and the other theorists of his school have fallen. I grant at once that, in a certain point of view, the individual goods replaced may be looked upon as if they actually were the same individual goods which were given away in the loan: they have identically the same effect on the economical position of the lender who receives them. Now, so far as the ground of this identification extends, so far

also is one justified in drawing conclusions from it—but no
further. The analogical conclusions of the Use theorists,
however, are entirely beyond this justifiable sphere. What
has the theoretical question whether, in perishable goods, a
continuous use is possible or not, to do with the fact that it
is all the same, as regards the interests of the lender, whether
he gets the individual goods X or the individual goods Y ?
Nothing at all—any more than the question of the marriage-
ableness of a legal person has anything in common with the
fact that, in matters relating to rights of property, an institution or a corporation may without hesitation be conceived of
as an independent "person"! Indeed, if the reader will
excuse a ridiculous but, as I think, a convincing example, one
might as well use the identity of fungible goods to prove that
oysters may keep fresh for ten years; they have only to be
lent out for ten years, and the lender receives "them" back
still fresh oysters! The application is so evident that I need
scarcely put it in words. The identity of the oysters lent
with the oysters returned is no true identity, but only an
identity assumed *ad hoc.* So far as concerns the practical
interests of the lender the identity may pass, but, as a scientific
question of fact, like the physical question whether oysters
can remain fresh for ten years, there is no identity at all.
And just such a scientific question of fact is the question
whether, in perishable goods, there is a continuous one year's
or ten years' use. It is a question that must find its answer
in considering the nature of the perishable good and the
nature of the use; properly speaking, not the shadow of an
argument can be got from the fact that it is of no moment,
as regards the practical interests of a person, whether he
receives the particular good X or the particular good Y !

Now Knies does make the attempt—and this is a second
and indeed the weightiest of the new passages in this edition—
really to point out a durable use in perishable goods, and
to give some indication wherein that use consists. He names,
by way of illustration, "the maintenance of life, and of
labour power, the averting of a loss, the attainment of a
business return or profit" (p. 112), as useful effects of this
sort, which the borrower "may obtain and make for himself
from the consumption (of the loaned goods) during the entire

period of time before the similar quantum of perishable goods is given back." But by illustrations like this Knies again shows that he is on the wrong track. The enjoyment of effects indirectly obtained from the consumption of goods is not in the least a utility which we get in addition to the consumption; it is just the utility we get *from* the consumption. Accordingly it can never be the ground of a special equivalent which we should have to pay over in addition to the equivalent of the perishable good itself. What would be said of a person who proposed to sell a cwt. of corn on the following terms:—" For the quarter of corn itself, that is, for all the useful services which may be got from the corn by its —sudden or gradual—consumption, I want thirty shillings. But for the lasting indirect use of the corn—the use which consists in the subsequent enjoyment of useful effects, such as life prolonged, labour power maintained, and so on—I want another shilling." Now, if,—as probably no one will deny,— in *selling* grain, it is not possible to conceive of the subsequent enjoyment as the ground of a special equivalent; if the subsequent enjoyment is obviously included in the purchase price of the good transferred into the buyer's possession; it is inconceivable that, all at once, in the case of the *loan* (where, too, the quarter of corn passes into the full possession of the borrower, and justifies him in drawing all the uses he can from it), every indirect use is to be separately paid for. And why, again, should this indirect use be paid for only during one, five, ten years, or for so long as the loan runs? Is the utility of sustained life not enjoyed so long as life lasts? Is the utility of preserved labour power not one which lasts so long as we can work?

In *Capital and Interest* I had so thoroughly and, in my own opinion at least, so clearly laid down the facts about the lasting "indirect use," and shown the impossibility of its being the ground of loan interest,[1] that I really did not expect to see the thing emerge once more as stay and support of the Use theory. Least of all did I expect it from a writer who knew what I had said on the subject, and that without a single word of explanation being vouchsafed in answer to the objections I had raised meantime. I cannot but express my

[1] P. 229, and pp. 235-239.

regret—not indeed for personal reasons, but in the interest of our science—that Knies has taken so little notice of, and given such meagre answers to the theoretical considerations which I brought against the Use theory. He replies on one single point, and that a point which, however important it may be in itself, has only the importance of an incident in the struggle that is to decide the victory or defeat of the Use theory; while, to the multitude of really cogent considerations directed against that theory as a whole—considerations which, quite apart from the issue of this incidental question, show it to be internally contradictory [1] and theoretically inadmissible,[2]—he has, unfortunately, found no word of rejoinder. Once submitted for discussion these considerations must be met, and certainly no one was more called on to speak in the defence of his own Use theory than was Knies.[3]

Hitherto the discussion has been limited to attack and defence of the Loan theory of other economists. I have now to reply to an attack made on my own theory. The distinguished writer we have just been discussing has now repeated the objection he urged some years ago against my conception of the loan as a true exchange; it is, he says, in contradiction of the hitherto established conception of what an exchange is. "For an exchange—as we are not taking into account senseless and frivolous actions—takes place only

---

[1] *Capital and Interest*, pp. 228, 247.

[2] *Ibid.* p. 264.

[3] The criticism which Knies directs against me in the note to page 106 of his second edition is limited unfortunately to a few passing remarks on points which are, for the most part, of secondary importance. Moreover, several errors of fact have slipped into these, and two of them I cannot let pass unchallenged. First, I cannot admit that I have done what Knies ascribes to me, and explained that the replaceableness of goods—that is to say, the fact that one sample of a class can be adequately replaced and represented by another—is simply a legal fiction. I only said that the *actual identity* of replaceable goods was a legal fiction (*Capital and Interest*, p. 253); and these are two very different statements. And, further, in my book I do *not* regard it as certain that, if a person speaks of uses in respect to perishable goods, he ought to point out, and wishes to point out, exactly the same kind of process of use as is to be observed in non-perishable goods. On the contrary, my entire criticism of Say and Schäffle (p. 232), of Hermann and even of Knies himself (p. 233), rests on the idea that it was a matter for the opposed theory to point out the existence of a something otherwise constituted than the usual material services, and that it had not succeeded in this attempt.

when goods different in some way or other are bartered.   But fungible goods, such as grain of similar kind and quality, are, economically, recognised as entirely similar goods."[1]

I must say that this statement seems to me to beg the whole question.   Instead of *inquiring* what the connotation of the conception of exchange is, and arguing from that whether the loan can be called a true exchange or not, Knies starts with a *preconceived* conception of exchange, and that an arbitrarily and unnaturally limited conception.   As a fact, Knies's limitation of the conception of exchange to the barter of goods of different kinds is one we do not find in the nature of exchange, nor does it correspond with the "hitherto established" use of the conception.   In the nature of exchange what is involved is that two goods are given, the one for the other—nothing more; as to "established usage," it is very easy to show that transactions in which entirely similar fungible goods are bartered for one another are considered by all the world true exchanges, and are called so.   In proof of this I might point out that two people, simply from whim or fancy, will "exchange" two fungible goods, the one for the other, *e.g.* two new copies of the same book.   Knies guards himself, indeed, against this argument by saying that "we are not taking into account frivolous and senseless actions," but this is making too light of the matter.   For, certainly, it cannot be denied that such capricious actions may happen, and occasionally do happen, and it cannot very well be denied that such transactions, when they do happen, are neither Hire nor Loan, nor anything else than true Exchange.

But there is no need to appeal to rare cases like these. There is one group of instances where men, quite deliberately and on entirely rational economic grounds, do barter similar fungible goods; that is where goods, otherwise perfectly similar, are available under different modalities—to use a philosophic term—as, for instance, in different places.   Take the case of a farmer A, who owns a plantation of trees two hours' journey away from his farm, while there is a plantation belonging to his neighbour B immediately beside him.   In both plantations, the wood, cut or ready for cutting, is of

---

[1] *Der Kredit*, part i., Berlin, 1876, p. 10: shortly repeated without new arguments in the second edition of the book *Das Geld*, p. 106, note 1.

exactly the same quality. Now, evidently, it is more convenient and more profitable for A to have ten loads of wood near his house than ten loads ten miles away from it. It will, therefore, be considered quite reasonable, and quite intelligible, to propose that B should make over to A ten loads from the near plantation, in return for which A will give B ten loads— or perhaps twelve loads, including a premium—of the similar wood from his far-away plantation. And if this is agreed to, everybody would pronounce it a real and true exchange.

Or can we imagine anybody, from the fiction of identity between fungible goods, drawing an analogical conclusion like the following about the nature of the transaction :—" A makes over to B ten loads of wood at a spot ten miles away from his house, and receives from B ten loads of wood here at his house. It is all the same to A whether he receives back the same ten loads or ten other loads. 'From an economic point of view,' therefore, it is essentially the same ten loads which he receives back, only at a different place. The essential nature of the transaction is, accordingly, not an exchange—since no exchange takes place between similar goods—but a transfer of the same goods to a different point in space,—that is to say, a freight transaction. And if, for the advantage which lies in this transfer from one place to another, A pays B a premium of two loads, the payment is essentially, from an economic point of view, an expense of carriage." I very much doubt whether anybody would follow him in this conclusion from analogy, although it is, feature for feature, the same as the one above. We should rather have expected that Knies would have been ready to own that the exchange of two amounts of wood, alike in every respect except that they are available in different places, was a real and true exchange.[1]

And now I ask : If it falls within the limits of the conception of exchange when goods present in one place are bartered for goods entirely similar but present in another place, with what right can we exclude from the conception the case where goods present at one time are bartered for

---

[1] I may note that it would be easy to multiply examples in which the same state of things occurs. Grain merchants, *e.g.*, may find it to their advantage to exchange stocks held in different stores ; bankers, to exchange sums of money disposable at different places, etc.

goods entirely similar, but present at another time ? When
so much has been made of analogies in the whole course of
this controversy, why exclude the one analogy which is,
most evidently, the appropriate one ?   If the difference of the
place at which goods are available is a sound economic reason
for exchanging fungible goods that are in other respects
entirely similar, and if the advantage and convenience of the
present *place* may justify the claim and allowance of a premium,
just as much may the difference of the *time* at which similar
goods are available be a sound reason for their exchange, and
a guarantee that there will be a premium on the—more
valuable—present goods.   This premium, and nothing else, is
Interest.

A great tree does not fall at one blow.   And I cannot
expect that a loan theory, which has dominated human intel-
lects for centuries, should fall at the first attack.   But I
venture to hope that I have at least awaked a general feeling
that it is necessary to submit the principles of that theory to
critical revision.   There is one task which the next economist
who proposes to maintain the Hermann-Knies loan theory will
not, I imagine, venture to omit ; namely, once and for all, to
point out positively the existence of that " enduring use " of
perishable goods, distinct from their consumption, for which
interest is supposed to be paid, and to say, clearly and distinctly, wherein that use peculiarly consists.   Up till now its
defenders have acted in a somewhat curious way ; they have
pointed out, by more or less questionable analogies, that, in
the loan, a temporary use is *transferred*, and concluded from
this that there must be such a use ; the consequence being
that—with the exception of this last unfortunate attempt of
Knies's—the nature of the use, its contents and so on, were
left entirely in the background.   I consider that our science
has a right to demand the opposite and the natural method of
demonstration.   Let it first be shown that there is such a use,
and wherein it consists ; if that can be done, we shall willingly
believe that it is transferred in the loan.   If that cannot be
done—and I doubt very much if it can—then I shall have
the greater confidence in pointing to my solution of the
question.   To the latter, at any rate, I have no fear that
the stigma of sophistry and unnaturalness can be attached.

Passing from this polemical digression—which I considered only due, as well to the importance of the subject under dispute, as to the scientific standing of my esteemed opponent, —let us return to the main subject.   According to our conception interest is a complementary part of the price payable for a sum of present goods in future goods. It is a part-equivalent of the "principal" lent.   In itself there would be nothing to prevent this part-equivalent being paid along with the bulk of the price; in other words, interest and "principal" might be put together in one single payment at the end of the whole loan transaction.   Reasons of practical convenience have, however, made it the general rule that, in loans made for any considerable length of time, the premium should be paid separately, and in rates graduated according to time,—monthly, half-yearly, yearly, etc.   With the essential nature of interest this method of payment has nothing to do; it may, indeed, be expressly provided otherwise by the loan contract.   But quite possibly it is the case that this custom, which, practically, has prevailed from time immemorial, of separating the payment of interest from the payment of principal, has assisted—perhaps, even, directly caused—the popular opinion that the principal sum paid back is, by itself, the equivalent of the sum originally given, and that interest is a thing by itself, an equivalent for another and separate *something*.

Now and then a loan may be granted without interest; but the reason of this is seldom·or never that the market price of present goods, as against future goods, is so favourable to the latter, that, in the general loan market, they can purchase an equal amount of present goods without premium.   Almost invariably these are cases where the lender dispenses with the payment of premium on some special personal ground, such as friendship, charity, humanity, class obligation, and so on.   It has been usual to conceive of the loan without interest as a gift of the temporary "use" of the thing lent.[1]   Our theory, of course, demands another conception.   We put this kind of loan simply among cases where a man, from some personal motive, parts with his commodity under the market price. We say it is the same thing as where a manufacturer gives

---

[1] "A loan without interest is a gift of the use of so much capital," Roscher, *Grundlagen,* § 189.

personal friends at the cost price, say, of 4s. the article which he can sell anywhere at the general market price of 5s.

Lastly, it very seldom occurs, and then never as regards present and future goods in general, but only as regards one particular kind of goods, that the relations of supply and demand are such, that future goods obtain a higher price than present goods of the same kind, and that a premium in present goods must be paid for future goods. It will only happen in cases where, presumably, the relations of supply and demand in the future will be essentially more unfavourable than in the present, and where, at the same time, for personal or technical reasons, it is not possible to preserve the present ample stocks till that future point of time when they are assured of a higher value.[1] Suppose the case of a brewer whose ice-cellars are too small for his requirements. If in January he puts in as much ice as the cellars will hold, and has still two hundred carts of ice over, he may be very willing to exchange these for one hundred carts of ice deliverable in August.[2] But the possibility of such a case seems to me rather to afford a not insignificant proof of my loan theory. For, I should like to ask, how would the Use theorists explain this? As a transfer of use like the loan; only that the use has a *negative* value, and that the borrower, instead of paying a premium, demands a premium? Or, perhaps, as a storage transaction, the difference between the quantity given and that received being considered a fee for safe deposit?

I think both interpretations are so clearly artificial and fictitious that very few people would seriously entertain them. Probably the Use theorists would be quite willing to admit this as a case of real exchange; but, so far as they did so, they would be untrue to their own contention, according to which exchange is only possible between goods of different kinds, and not between fungible goods of the same kind. Our theory, on the other hand, explains everything naturally, and by one formula. Without forcing an interpretation, it can recognise that, here, the position is exactly the same as in the loan. There is a mutual transfer of property

---

[1] See above, p. 251.

[2] Similar cases may perhaps occur after very abundant harvests, where the producers have not enough storage accommodation to secure the surplus.

in two sums of goods, which are entirely similar in every other respect but that of being disposable at different points of time. And to this entirely similar state of matters it gives an entirely similar explanation: that, in both categories, there is an exchange between present and future goods, the prices of which are the resultant of the subjective valuations put upon these two classes of goods within the market.

CHAPTER II

WE come now to the principal form assumed by the interest
problem. Among the phenomena of interest it is the one
which has, practically, been of most importance. Usually,
indeed, it passes for the spring and source from which all the
others are derived. And it has chiefly been the attempt to
explain this form of interest that has led to the terribly
involved war of opinions which gave only too ample material
for my *Capital and Interest.*

A word or two will indicate generally the peculiar kind of
activity which the undertakers exert, and from which they
draw their profit. They buy goods of remoter rank, such as
raw materials, tools, machines, the use of land, and, above all,
labour, and, by the various processes of production, transform
them into goods of first rank, finished products ready for consumption. In doing so they obtain—independently of compensation for their own personal co-operation in the work of
production as leaders of industry, head-workers, etc.—a gain
approximately proportioned to the amount of capital invested
in their business. This gain is called by some "Natural Interest
on Capital" or "Profit," and, by others, "Surplus Value."
How is this gain to be explained?

I must introduce the explanation by establishing one
important fact. Goods of remoter rank, although, materially,
present commodities, are, economically *future* commodities.
As present commodities they are incapable of satisfying
human want; they require first to be changed into consumption goods; and since this process, naturally, takes time, they

can only render their services to the wants of a future period,
—at the earliest, that period distant by the time which the
productive process necessarily takes to change them into
consumption goods. A group of productive instruments, such
as Seed, Manure, Agricultural Implements, Labour, etc., which
cannot be transformed into the finished product Grain under
a year's process, can only serve for the satisfaction of next
year's subsistence wants. In this respect, then, goods of
remoter rank available in the present (present productive
goods) are similar to future consumption goods ; their utility
is a future utility ; they are "future commodities."

It is evident that this fact cannot be without some far-
reaching influence on the value which such goods obtain. As
we know, we value goods of remoter rank, in general, according to the marginal utility and value of their finished and final
products. The group of productive instruments from which we
get one hundred bushels of corn, has exactly the same importance for the satisfaction of our wants as the hundred bushels
of corn into which it is transformed. But these hundred
bushels, the value of which is the standard for the value of
the productive group, are still, for the time, a hundred *future*
bushels, and, as we saw in previous chapters, future goods are
worth less than present goods. A hundred future bushels are,
therefore, worth, we may say, only as much as ninety-five
present ones. From this it follows that Means of Production
also, *if estimated against present goods*, are found of less value
than the amount of finished and final products which can be
made out of them. Our group of productive instruments
which, in a year's time, will furnish us one hundred quarters
of grain, is equal in value to one hundred quarters of *next*
year's grain ; but, like that grain, is equal to, say, only ninety-
five quarters of *this* year's grain. Or, if we translate the
whole matter into terms of money economy, and assume that,
next year, the quarter of corn will be worth twenty shillings,
then our group of productive materials, wherewith we hold in
our hands the condition of our obtaining a money return of
£100 next year, is equal in value to £100 next year, but to no
more than £95 now. If, then, we buy or exchange these means
of production *now*, the purchase price, naturally, is measured
in present money, and we buy them for a smaller number

of pounds sterling than they will bring their owner in the future.

This, and nothing else, is the foundation of the so-called "cheap" buying of productive instruments, and especially of labour, which the Socialists rightly explain as the source of profit on capital, but wrongly interpret, in round terms, as the result of a robbery or exploitation of the working classes by the propertied classes. The buying is not so cheap as it seems. The appearance of cheapness comes, for the most part, from this; that the price is measured by a different standard from the commodity; measured, as it were, by one of these cheap measuring tapes which stretch with wear and indicate a foot by 11 inches. The means of production, and their result,—the finished product towards which the buyer is looking in purchasing them,—are future commodities, and the price is measured and paid in (more valuable) present goods. That, in this case, the greater number of less valuable future goods is purchased by a smaller number of more valuable present goods, is not "cheap buying," any more than it would be cheap to acquire one hundred florins of fifty florin standard for ninety pieces of forty-five florin standard. The circumstances of possession are only to a very limited extent responsible for the fact, that the future commodity which the labourers have to sell (their labour), is less valuable than the present goods which the capitalists have to offer (wages). For the most part, it is elementary facts of human nature and the technique of production that are to blame; facts which we have gone into in detail in the foregoing book. The social importance of the phenomenon of interest, however, will take up our attention later on; in the meantime I have only to explain what Interest is, and why it is.

Knowing now that the undertaker buys the future commodity, "Means of Production," for a smaller number of pieces of present goods than the number of pieces which will compose their future product, we ask, How does he come by his profit? The answer is very simple. From his "cheap" purchase, indeed, he does not get any result; for, estimated by its present value, the commodity is dear.[1]

---

[1] Of course it may happen in individual cases, that, outside of the reasons for apparently cheap buying discussed in the text, there may be other reasons for

The profit comes first into existence in his hand. It is during the progress of production that the future commodity ripens gradually into the present commodity, and grows at the same time to the full value of the present commodity. Time elapses; what was next year becomes this year; and on the great changing stage of life everything—man himself, his wants and wishes, and with them the standard by which he measures his goods—shifts one scene forward. The wants which, last year, were future wants, and little thought of as such, attain their full strength and their full right of present wants; and a similar advance attends the goods which supply these wants. A year ago they were goods of the future, and had to be content with the lower value that attached to them as such; to-day they are present goods, ripe for consumption, and enjoy the full value of such goods. A year ago it was to their prejudice that they were measured in the, then, " present " goods. To-day that standard has sunk into the past, and if the men of to-day measure them again in " present " goods, they stand equal with them in the first and chiefest rank, and suffer nothing by the comparison. In short, as time passes it cancels the causes by reason of which the then future commodity suffered a shrinkage of value, and brings it up to the full value of the present good. The increment of value is the profit of capital.

This is not to say, of course, that, to make present goods out of future goods, it is sufficient that time should elapse and the future become the present. The goods themselves must not remain stationary. On their part they must bridge over the gap which divides them from the present, and this they do through the production which changes them from goods of remote rank into finished and final products. If there is no production process, if the capital is left dead, the means of

<hr>

really abnormal cheap buying; as, *e.g.*, skilful utilising of favourable conjunctures, usurious oppression of the seller, and, in particular, of the labourer. The emergence of such factors in this case results in a still further limitation of the purchase price, and in the obtaining of an extra profit. This extra profit is to be distinguished from normal profit on capital in every respect: in its nature—for it is not a true profit on capital but strictly a profit of the undertaker; in its theoretical explanation—for it owes its origin to other and quite special causes: and, finally, in the social and political judgment we must form of it. I need scarcely say in so many words that what is said in the text has only to do with profit on capital pure and simple.

production always remain undervalued future goods.   In the year 1888, a group of means of production which can be changed into a finished product in a year's process,—that is to say, by 1889,—is one year away from satisfying the wants of the present.   If this group is left unused till 1889, its product, of course, cannot now be obtained till 1890 at the earliest, and it remains, as before, one year away from satisfying the wants of the present ; its value has no opportunity to expand, and suffers the common fate of " dead capital " ; it bears no surplus value, and no interest.

This is the truth about Undertakers' Profit, and I trust it will be found simple enough.   The Socialists are fond of calling this profit " surplus value."   The name is more applicable than they have any idea of.   It is, literally, a profit from the increment of value of the future commodity transmuted, in the hand of the undertakers, into a finished present good.

CHAPTER III

THE principle laid down in last chapter is simple, but in practical life it is, as usual, obscured by a multitude of casuistical details and developments.   These do not, indeed, prevent its operation, but they conceal it under various phenomenal forms such as make recognition of it not always easy.   Some of these developments we must take up, and we shall begin with one of the simplest.

The contraction of value from which, in our estimation, future goods suffer, is, as we know, by no means uniform for all future goods.   It is graduated according to the time which intervenes between the present and the date at which the goods are ready for use.   £100, for instance, which will be available in a year's time, will be valued at, perhaps, something like £95 in present money; £100 available in a couple of years, at £90; £100 available three years hence at £85, and so on.[1]   To this graduated *contraction* of value corresponds a steady graduated *increase* in value of those goods which are in process of ripening into present goods.   A group of instruments which, at the end of a three years' production process, promises a product of the value of £100, and, in virtue of that promise, is valued at £85 at the beginning of the process, does not remain stationary at the value of £85 till the moment when the production is completed, and then make one bound up to its full present value of £100.   Its value increases gradually as the time passes which divides the group from maturity, and the production process nears its completion.   This circumstance

---

[1] Not quite exactly: for easier understanding the figures in the text are calculated roughly, and without consideration of compound interest.

is of great practical importance. Under the division of labour, scarcely any kind of production is carried through from beginning to end in the hands of one person. The separate stages of production become branches of production, visibly independent, and conducted by separate undertakers. As the value thus increases by stages, a corresponding gain accrues, as profit on capital, not only to the last undertaker,— the one in whose hand the good becomes an actual present commodity,—but to each of the undertakers, even to one who has brought the product only a single step nearer maturity.

A very common complication arises from the fact that productive goods contribute various portions of their useful content to the making of various final products, which products arrive at maturity at various points of time. This is the case with all durable productive goods. A plough, for instance, which lasts twenty years, will contribute a twentieth part of its life-work and use to the ingathering of twenty different harvests. Corresponding with this twofold property—that of being means of production, and at the same time durable goods—such goods, both in the formation and in the increase of their value, manifest a peculiar combination of phenomena ; they unite the phenomena already known to us as characteristic of *productive* goods with certain other special phenomena which accompany all *durable* goods—even those that are not devoted to productive purposes. We have, however, to deal particularly with this latter class of phenomena in a later chapter, and accordingly we must postpone the full explanation of this complication until then.

Another complication arises from the fact, that almost all productive instruments admit of various kinds of employment, and that these employments turn out their finished products at different points of time.[1] The same fuel, for instance, may be employed in cooking a meal, or in keeping up a smithy fire where the tools are made for boring a coal seam. In the

[1] The analysis which follows is devoted to the circumnavigation of one of those hidden rocks which, I suspect, might rise suddenly in the way of those readers who venture on their own account to go further into the circle of ideas here opened up. The digression which it necessitates forms one of the numerous sacrifices of time which I imagine myself compelled to make with a view to the safety of my theory, at the cost of brevity and ease of comprehension.

first case, only a few hours elapse till the finished product is turned out; in the latter it may be years, perhaps decades of years. This is true in particular of that most important productive good, "unskilled labour." Various portions of it are always being employed simultaneously for productive purposes that come to maturity in the most varying periods of time. Some labourers must always get finishing work, which pays its wages almost on the moment: others must be employed in the intermediate stages; others, again, at the very beginning of the total work of production. Yet none of them has it written on his forehead whether his work is spent for the present, or for the coming year. or for the remote future.

At first sight it might appear that this complication must sensibly prejudice what we have laid down as to the formation and the increase of value. Here is a good which will be used, perhaps as a present good, perhaps as a future good. Suppose that it is valued as a future good, and therefore suffers a proportionate diminution of value, it seems as if this diminution were unjustifiable if, after all, the good is used as a present good. But, again, suppose it is valued, without deduction, as a present good, and is, after all, employed as a future good, there is no room for increase of value. But obviously, again, it is least of all possible to estimate different portions of the same commodity at different values,—one portion as a present good without deduction, another as a future good with deduction. Of ten loads of fuel of exactly the same kind and quality, one load is worth just as much as the other, as well to the householder as in the timber market.

The apparent difficulty, however, entirely disappears if we apply the universal law of value carefully to the special circumstances of the case. The value of a good is determined by its marginal utility. This marginal utility is the least important use or employment that is provided for out of the available stock of goods. Suppose the stock contains five hundred pieces of a kind which we shall call A. These goods possess the three-fold capability of serving (1) immediately as consumption goods, (2) as means of production in a five years' process, or (3) as means of production—in another branch of employment—in a ten years' process. If they are used for immediate consumption the capabilities are as follows:—one hundred pieces can be used with a useful result which we shall represent by the figure 6, another hundred with a result which we shall call 5, and a third hundred with a result which we shall call 4. But if the goods are employed in a five years' production process, there will be a product—call it X—of which the first hundred can be remunerative at 9, the second at 8, and the third at 7 per piece.[1] But these products will not be available before five years. In to-day's estimate, therefore, their value, like the value of all future goods, suffers a reduction: the amount of this reduction depends upon the amount of the agio which emerges in favour of present goods as resultant of the many intersecting subjective valuations in the market. If this agio, for instance, amount to 5%, the value of the products available in five years, as compared with present goods, suffers a reduction of a little over a fifth part.[2] In the valuation of to-day, therefore, the prospect of obtaining in five years, from one of the pieces employed as a means of production, a product which will then have the value of 9, is equal to a use realisable at the moment of 7·05. In the same way the prospect of obtaining products of the value of 8 and 7 in five years is equal to present uses valued at 6·26 and 5·48 respectively. Similarly if the goods are employed in a ten years' production process. If this gives the prospect of obtaining a product—call it Y—of which the first hundred can be remunerative at 16, the second hundred at 12, and the third hundred at 8, these products, as not available before ten years, suffer a reduction in to-day's estimate of something like two-fifths, and are equal, respectively, to 9·82, 7·35, and 4·91.

If we group together the present valuation of all these possibilities, we get the following table.

---

[1] In order to remain true to actual cases, so far as possible within the narrow limits of the illustration, I purposely assume that the value of product decreases as production in the same branch increases—the more units the less the value of each unit. The fact that even the most remunerative branch of production ceases to be remunerative when it is over-stocked, is the very thing that makes it possible for means of production to seek different employments simultaneously.

[2] To be accurate it is 21·65%, or as 100 : 78·35.

POSSIBILITIES OF EMPLOYING 100 PIECES

	In immediate consumption.	In a five years' process.	In a ten years' process.
Amount of utility per piece.	6	7·05	9·82
	5	6·26	7·37
	4	5·48	4·91

The stock of five hundred pieces admits of only five of the above possibilities being utilised. Naturally those five will be taken which, in the valuation of to-day—the only standard for to-day's decision—are the most remunerative. They are indicated in the above table by black figures, and we find them to be as follows :—

100 pieces used in immediate consumption; 200 pieces employed in a five years' process, in making the goods X ; 200 pieces employed in a ten years' process, in making the goods Y.

The least remunerative of the employments indicates the marginal utility, and with it the value of the single good A. That least remunerative use bears the value 6, and, as it happens, belongs to the present. A good of the class A, then, will be valued at 6.

How does this stand now as regards the increment of value and the interest on capital? In the case of the hundred pieces which are employed in the service of the present, and fetch a utility measured by 6, there is no room for an increment of value. But as they afford their marginal utility immediately, they do not require to bear any interest. The pieces invested in the five years' process are worth 6, and in five years turn out a product which will be worth 8.[1] Here there is room for an increase,—at the usual rate of 5% for five years,—in the ratio of, say, four to five; that is, from 6 to 7·5.

---

[1] If 200 pieces of the good are produced naturally all the pieces obtain one equal value, and not only the second hundred but the first hundred gets its value according to the lower rate of 8, at which the second hundred can be made remunerative.

Indeed, the room for increase, and the gain in value, is much greater. Beyond the normal interest, which is secured when the product obtains the value of 7·5, there is a further profit of 0·5 per piece as premium for finding and utilising the most favourable opportunities of employment in the present conjuncture; in other words, as undertaker's profit. But usually this premium will not long continue. According to principles with which we are familiar, its existence attracts competition, and competition depresses price. How far will it depress it?—Not lower than 7·5, for 7·5, obtainable in five years, is equal, in present valuation, to 6 of present money, which is just the value of the productive good itself. Anything less than this price of 7·5, consequently, would not be thought a sufficient equivalent for the sacrifice of a good valued at 6, and, in this unremunerative branch, production would be suspended until the limitation of supply again raised the price of the product to 7·5 of future money, as equal to 6 of present money. This being a state of things favourable to permanence, although the productive (and, therefore, future) good has received its value of 6 from a marginal utility which belongs to the sphere of the present, and so suffers no deduction on account of its future nature, there remains quite sufficient room for a rise to the higher value of the future product.

It is the same with the value and increase of value of those pieces invested in the ten years' process. At the moment, valued at the common marginal utility, they are worth 6. Their product, which becomes attainable in ten years, will then be worth 12. This leaves room for the normal increase of 5% per annum, from 6 to 10; and, therefore, over ten years, makes possible an increment of about two-thirds of the original value. Beyond this again it leaves room—at least in the first instance—for the obtaining of an undertaker's profit. Should this profit disappear later on in consequence of competition, the future value of the product remains, all the same, at 10, and thus leaves room permanently for the normal increase of value, in which consists the customary interest.

Thus we see that, although all the pieces of class A were valued at the one figure, this one value guarantees to each of the possible uses exactly that room for increase of value which the remoteness of its finished and final result demands. To the immediate use, where the utility of the good is at once realised, it guarantees nothing; to the five years' process it allows an expansion of about one-fourth; to the ten years' process an expansion of about two-thirds more than the original value. Perhaps there is even a greater expansion, in which case there remains a premium to the undertaker, but, in any case, it guarantees the expansion just named.

And this nice harmony is easily explained from what has just been said. In estimating the *present* value of the many-sided good, its possible *future* employments had already been reduced to present value, whereby they experienced a discount in exact ratio to their futurity. But only those future employments are found economically permissible, whose present (reduced) value is, at least, equal to the fixed value of the good, and whose effective future importance, therefore, is at least greater by the amount of the discount made *pro rata temporis*. Therefore each of these future uses has assured it in advance a corresponding scope for recovery of its value. The lapse of time replaces the value which was taken from the estimate by way of discount, and this, in the near-hand uses which require to bear little interest, is small, and is correspondingly great in the remote uses which must bear much interest.[1]

What has here been represented on a small scale by one slight instance, obtains over the whole field of industrial employment. It is not a few hundreds, but millions of productive units —days of labour, tons of coal, bars of iron, and so on—that are invested; they are invested, not in two, or three, but in hundreds and thousands of separate employments; and each of these employments has a different period of production. All those means of production enjoy one homogeneous market price. That price is formed by the available stock being

---

[1] By varying the figures the reader may very easily convince himself that exactly the same result emerges if the marginal utility, which determines the value, lies within the sphere, not of the immediately remunerative, but of the productive employments. The only difference is that, in this case, the chances of a temporary "conjuncture profit" between the individual branches of employment, are somewhat altered. That production which itself yields just the marginal utility bears no conjuncture profit, while such a profit is now possible temporarily in the present employments, and in the other branches of production.

distributed out among the most remunerative employments, and according to the degree of advantage which they bring.[1] The most remunerative branches, in virtue of having the strongest purchasing power, are supplied first and with the greatest certainty; then the next remunerative branches; and so on down the scale till the stock gives out. Some last portion of the stock, then, is taken for some last branch of employment, and the modest advantage that accrues determines the modest measure of what those last buyers can pay for the productive unit. But as the market price for all portions of the commodity is a homogeneous one, the value of the employment last supplied determines the total market price of the means of production. But how, then, has the advantage and value of the individual kinds of employment been determined?—By applying the same discount to employments for future advantage as has been described in our illustration; only that, in rough, practical life, the discounting is made in a rough way that takes a great deal for granted. In practical life men generally find already in existence the things of which we have tried to explain the elements, and are glad to accept them, without much reflection, as accomplished facts. In the same way do they take interest for granted as an every-day fact, and without more ado, in all calculations relating to future employment, they add or deduct it. If an undertaker is considering whether or not he should lay out one hundred pounds on a productive instrument which will yield a result in two years' time, he simply calculates whether the future return will leave, at least, one hundred pounds over and above the two years' interest, and after deduction of the same. If he has thus deducted, in advance, from the future result an amount of interest proportioned to time and capital, it is a very natural thing that the future proceeds, when actually realised, should contain and yield that very amount of interest.

The foregoing cases do not by any means exhaust the series of casuistical complications which obscure the working of our principle in the infinite variety of practical life. Happily it is not necessary to exhaust them. Many are not

[1] See above, p. 230.

of sufficient importance to justify us going into the tedious abstract demonstrations that would be needed to explain them, and, for the rest, I venture to hope that, in what has been already said, the careful reader will find enough to guide him among complications not expressly discussed, without further assistance from me.

There still remains for us, however, another important and by no means easy task. It is, in a word, to follow the abstract into the actual, and give it form and colour. Hitherto, by an argument which I hope is incontrovertible, but which I know to be highly abstract and general, I have tried to prove that it must be as I have maintained: I have now to show how it actually is so in the world of industry. So far I have deduced everything from the general proposition that productive goods are, by nature, " future commodities." I have shown that, as logical result, the general reasons which explain how future commodities have a less value, must also apply to productive goods, and thus explain how there is room for expansion into the full value of present goods, and for the appearance of a surplus value. I shall now attempt to show positively that all this is as I have said, and why it is. To this end I shall give a description of the markets, where, in economic life, means of production or productive instruments are exchanged against present goods, and shall try to show that, in these markets, the same motives, to which we ascribe in general the power of calling forth a difference of value between present and future goods, do really emerge, and emerge indeed in such combinations, and with such strength, that, as the result of the formation of price, there must always appear a *disagio* to the prejudice of the means of production. In doing so I hope not only to bring forward an adequate proof of the correctness of my general deductions, but also to obtain a number of new and important lights on the subject generally.

CHAPTER IV

THE PROFIT OF CAPITALIST UNDERTAKING. THE LABOUR MARKET

THE exchange of Means of Production against final and finished present goods—practically against Money—is made in three kinds of market: the Labour market, the market for Uses of Land, and the market for Intermediate Products, such as raw materials, tools, machines, factories, etc. Inasmuch as labour and uses of land are the original means of production from the co-operation of which all finished products come into existence, the formation of their price is peculiarly the one which decides the existence of profit on capital. In the markets for intermediate products we have only the continuance of a process which has received its own peculiar impulse in the other two markets. And, of these two markets, again, the labour market is by far the more important. I shall, then, first take up the circumstances of this market, and shall endeavour to show and explain how the market price of the productive good "Labour" must always be less than the value and price of the finished product of labour.

Let us assume that, in the methods of production current in economical society at the moment, the making of a product ready for consumption requires a period of time extending in all over two years. The technical productiveness of this method, we shall assume, is such that it takes a week's labour to turn out a product which will have the value of 20s. The same product may be turned out by shorter methods, but the result will be disproportionately unfavourable. If a three months' process is adopted, the technical result falls to one-half; if the worker has no capital, and his process is, accordingly, one that yields its return immediately, the productiveness falls to one-quarter;—that is, respectively, to 10s. and 5s. The price which can be paid for the commodity "labour" in these circumstances is the question now under discussion un the labour market between the labourer and the employers of labour. The price is fixed, in methods with which we are familiar, as resultant of the subjective valuations of both parties. How is it now with these valuations?

In the circumstances of modern industry, the wage workers scarcely ever possess sufficient means to utilise their own labour in methods of production extending over years.[1] They have, therefore, to face the alternative of selling their labour, or of employing it on their own account in such short and unproductive processes as the scanty means at their disposal permit. Naturally they will make that choice which is most advantageous to them. Those workers who are well enough off to embark, on their own account, on a production process lasting at least three months, and yielding a return of 10s. per week, will be willing to sell their labour at any price over 10s.;[2] at any price under 10s. they will rather work on their own account. On the other hand, those workers who are entirely without means, and who, working on their own account in a hand-to-mouth process, could only have a return of 5s., will be willing to sell their labour at any price above 5s. As, unfortunately, the labourers who are entirely without capital, form to-day the great majority, we may assume for our illustration that the "Supply" of labour will be represented by a long row of workers who are ready, in the worst case, to sell the week's labour for 5s., and a shorter row who will do the same for 10s. present money.[3]

How is it now with the Demand for labour that confronts this supply?

[1] Whether it take the form of completing the two years' production process from beginning to end by their own labour, or that of introducing their own labour at a later stage,—*e.g.* in the fourth half-year of the total production process,—and buying the fruits of the preparatory labour,—raw materials, tools, etc.,—from the others who have performed that previous labour.

[2] The pleasure of an independent position may indeed very often create a preference for labour on one's own account, even although the labourer might obtain a somewhat greater income by taking a wage. Influences of this kind, however, can alter only the figures, not the principle.

[3] Of course the possibility open to the labourer in question of realising

The demand comes from the Capitalist-Undertakers. The valuation they put upon the labour they wish to buy is so far more definite, inasmuch as the commodity labour, capable of so many employments, is looked at by them in connection with one definite employment; namely, the one carried on by themselves. To them, accordingly, the week's labour, which they wish to buy for the capitalist process, is worth just so much as the product which it will turn out in this capitalist process. On our assumption, this will be 20s. available in two years. But the question for the undertaker still remains: what are 20s., available in two years, worth in relation to the present shillings in which he must pay the week's labour.

Once for all, let us make this entirely clear. If the capitalists were to realise their entire resources as present goods,—that is, to consume their wealth in present enjoyment,—the want of the present would evidently be provided for in superfluity, while the want of the future would have no provision whatever. They must, therefore, find it positively advantageous to change a part of their resources into future goods of some kind or other. In other words: if we look only at the relations of want and provision for want in present and future, present goods, as such, are worth even less than future to the owner of a stock of wealth which is greater than his present wants. It is true, of course, that there is a very simple way of changing present goods into future: they can be stored away either *in natura*, or in the neutral form of future money. This possibility naturally saves them from the prejudice to their value, which would, in itself, result from the overabundant provision for the present, but, on the other hand, it does not give them any positive advantage in value, or, at any rate, a very trifling one.[1]

his labour in other branches of activity, can do little or nothing to alter the position of circumstances assumed in the text. For if the other branches are such as likewise demand a somewhat long production period the matter stands just the same with the labourer of this branch ; and the few branches which a man with no capital, or almost no capital, can take up with any result,— such as in particular the performance of personal services, domestic service, and the like,—can, from their nature, afford a remunerative refuge only to a limited number of workers, while any strong pressure would immediately result in overstocking and a corresponding curtailment of the advantage.

[1] See above, p. 250.

Nor can the underestimate of future wants form a reasonable basis for any such advantage. It will seldom be strong enough to outweigh the counteracting consideration of the overabundant provision for the present, and to prevent the capitalists from preferring to employ part of their wealth in the service of the future. Persons, moreover, in whom this want of foresight might, exceptionally, be found, are not, or at least would not long remain, capitalists. An estimate like theirs, dictated by momentary desire and carelessness of the future, would soon bear its consequences, and bring their fortunes into spendthrift consumption.

Of the three considerations, therefore, which, as we have seen, generally serve as foundation for the preference of present over future goods, the first two do not apply as regards the great majority of capitalists. It is our third consideration, the well-known technical superiority of present goods, or, as it is usually called, the "productivity of capital," which is decisive with them. The way in which it takes effect is essentially different in simple circumstances from what it is in the full development of our modern economic life.

In simple circumstances, where the undertaker is himself a worker, and has no capital to speak of, present goods immediately obtain a higher use value. An undertaker, for instance, has just enough wealth to defray the subsistence of one working person for four years,—or to advance that amount. The choice is now open to him, either to work by himself in a four years' process, or to assume a helper and work alongside of him in a two years' process. In a two years' process the week's labour yields, as we have assumed, 20s. : in a four years' process— since longer methods are, technically, more productive—it will yield, say, 24s. The balance now stands as follows. If our capitalist pays his helper, for the week's work, the full 20s. in present money, he has to pay him £104 for the two years' work ; from its product he recovers just this sum of £104 ; and finally, he can pay himself only 20s. a week, that is, in all, £104. His total net income, for the two years, thus amounts to £104. On the other hand, if, instead of spending £104 in paying a labourer, he spends it on his own maintenance during a third and fourth year of production, he may, from the 104 weeks of his own labour time at the higher

rate of 24s. per week, recover £124 : 16s. ; so that his two
years' net income is increased by £20 : 16s.   In these circumstances it is obviously more advantageous for the capitalist to
have no helper.   To obtain any advantage from a helper it
must be possible to pay him at such a price, that the capitalist
gains more by the buying of another person's labour than what
he loses in the realisation of his own labour by the shortening
of the production period : in other words, that 20s. a week
present money paid in wages should bring him more than 24s.
a week, future money, in products.   This will only be the case
if he can pay a weekly wage that is under 16s. 8d.[1]

Were the circumstances of capitalist production generally
so simple as this, the value to the undertakers of 20s. in future
products would, speaking generally, be equal to the value of
16s. 8d. present money,—the actual figures varying a little,
but not the tendency.   And if the buyers value the commodity
labour at not more than 16s. 8d., while the sellers value it at,
perhaps, 5s. or 10s., it is clear that the resultant of these
valuations, the price of labour, will, in no case, exceed the
amount of 16s. 8d., and must *a fortiori* come under 20s., the
full sum of the future product—which was the point to be
proved.

But the circumstances of present-day industry are not so
simple.   The great majority of our undertakers are not themselves workers, and their capitals, moreover, are generally so
great as to be far above what any one man could use for his
subsistence during the very longest practicable process.   The
possibility, which capital gives its owner, of employing his *own*
labour in longer production processes does not, therefore, as a
rule, under present conditions, give any higher use value to
present goods.   Our illustration of simple circumstances has
very great importance in other lines of proof,—of which later,—
but it does not suffice to explain the profit of capital in the
circumstances of capitalist industry.   These very complicated
circumstances, however, develop a phenomenon which works,
in another form, to the same end ; this phenomenon is Credit.
The capitalist cannot use his present goods to make his own
labour more fruitful, but others are willing to take them in
exchange for future goods to make their labour more profitable,

[1] 16s. 8d. : 20s. = £104 : £124 : 16s.

and are very willing to pay an agio in future goods. And, evidently, the capitalist need not barter his present money at par with the workers for their future product, when he can obtain on the loan market, for a certain sum of present goods, a greater sum of future goods.

One is tempted to apply this fact to the explanation of profit, as if it were owing to the chances offered on the market for loans that the capitalist's present goods had, in all cases, a higher subjective exchange value than future goods. But this is not my idea of explanation. We have no right either to represent loan interest as a *fait accompli*, and explain natural profit on capital from it, or, conversely, to represent the latter as a *fait accompli*, and explain loan interest thereby. The fact is that the Loan market and the Labour market are two markets on which one and the same commodity is mutually offered and demanded, viz. Present Goods. On both markets the demand is for means of subsistence, with the view of making labour more profitable by longer processes of production; only the circumstances of demand are different. For the present goods which he receives the wage worker gives, wholly and entirely, the indefinite future product which his labour may create : the borrower in productive credit—consumptive credit is much less important, but manifests its effects, in the long-run, in exactly the same direction—gives, in exchange for present goods, a *definite* quantity of future products, and, if the actual product differs from this quantity, may gain or lose by it. Thus wage workers and borrowers form two branches of the same demand; they mutually support its effect; and jointly help to form the resultant price. Only in outside appearance are they two distinct markets ; in reality they overlap each other ; and the market price of present goods is their joint result.

To get to the root of the matter therefore, before considering isolated and partial markets, we must take a comprehensive survey of that total market for advances of subsistence which, in every economic community, is built upon numerous communicating partial markets.

CHAPTER V

At the outset we must enunciate a proposition, as simple as
it is fundamental, but one on the proper understanding of
which everything depends : In any economical community the
supply of subsistence, available for advances of subsistence, is
—with one trifling exception—represented by the total sum
of its wealth (exclusive of land).   The function of this wealth
(*Vermögen*) is to maintain the community from the time that
their original productive powers are put in motion till these
powers obtain their final and mature fruits—in other words, to
maintain the community during the average social period of
production.   The greater the total stock of wealth in the community the longer may be this social period of production.

Here we really have three propositions, but they are so intimately connected that they may be conveniently grouped into
one, and explained and proved by one and the same argument.

If we look at the uses to which a country's accumulated
wealth is destined and put—leaving land out of account—we
get something like the following picture.   Some few owners
of wealth, whether from necessity or from prodigality, themselves consume it.   Others who produce on a moderate scale
for their own account spend their wealth in furnishing themselves with the necessary maintenance during their production
period.   But all other wealth—and that is by far the greater
amount—is, in some form or other, brought to the great
market for Advances of Subsistence as Supply.   The owner
either puts it into some undertaking carried on by himself, or
he lends it to other people.   If he puts it into his own

business it is, directly or indirectly, employed in giving advances of subsistence to labourers. I say directly or indirectly, for the division of labour, splitting up, as it does, the one united work of production into a series of apparently independent stages, causes an important distinction in form, although it does not affect the essence of the matter. If the different stages of one and the same production process were united in the hand of one and the same undertaker, he would not *buy* any previous product: all previous and intermediate products needed would be made, from the beginning, by the workers in his employment. Here, therefore, his entire "business capital" would evidently be directly devoted to advancing subsistence to labourers. As it is, under the division of labour, he gets his previous products made by other undertakers, and buys them from these other undertakers. This amounts to saying that, by this purchase, he takes upon himself the burden of the advances hitherto borne by the other undertakers, and thus puts them again in a position to take upon themselves the burden of advancing subsistence for the following period of production. These previous and intermediate products, then, thus purchased, he gets worked up by labourers who are directly in his pay. In this way, therefore, by his wage payments he advances subsistence directly to one set of workers, and indirectly by his "outlays" to a number of other sets (employed in the preceding stages).[1]

---

[1] It will perhaps be objected that the purchase amounts which the undertakers of the previous stages receive contain, not only a simple replacement of the advances of subsistence paid by them to workers, but frequently also replacement of the uses of land consumed, and, in any case, some profit on capital. The fact is correct, but it makes no difference in the conclusions which I think are to be drawn from what I have said above. The necessity of paying in advance for uses of land, the return of which will not be obtained till after long methods of production have been completed, has the same effect on the price relation between finished present goods and original productive powers, as the necessity of paying for labour in advance has. The market for uses of land is only a third part-market in addition to the market for credit and the market for labour, where, in similar ways, present goods are sold against future goods (see above, p. 313), and, consequently, as regards its effects on price, the demand of this market for present goods mutually assists, and is assisted by, the demand of the other part-markets. This, however, will be made clearer as we go on. Finally, I must here leave out of consideration the profit of the undertaker, if I would not beg the question. Its existence is the *result* of a certain market condition in the subsistence market, and therefore cannot be assumed. It is not because the

If, again, the owner lend his wealth to others, it may be either for consumption or for production. If the former, the sum lent is a direct advance of subsistence to the borrower: if the latter, it passes, as already described, from the borrowing employer to the labourers, as advance of subsistence. Thus the entire accumulated wealth of society—with the very trifling exception of that portion which the owners themselves consume[1]—is really brought into the market as supply of advances of subsistence.

But the objection may be raised: How can the entire stock of wealth be offered as advances of subsistence when that stock consists only partially, and, indeed, to a very small extent, of actual means of subsistence, such as food, clothing, dwelling-houses, etc., while the great bulk of wealth is represented by goods that are not adapted for immediate consumption, such as tools, machines, raw materials, factory buildings, and the like?

The seeming inconsistency is, however, easily explained; it is simply that men never need their subsistence for the entire production period all at once. If, in any community, ten millions of men invest their original productive powers, Labour and Uses of Land, in an average production period of two years, it is quite unnecessary—indeed undesirable—that at any one moment the means of subsisting the ten millions for the whole two years should be accumulated in finished form. It is sufficient if there is enough in finished form for, say, one month, and if, in the meantime, the means of subsistence for the following month are ripening into finished goods.

profits of the undertaker absorb a part of the available means of subsistence that the supply of means of subsistence is so weak as to give them an agio as against productive goods. It is because the supply of means of subsistence, even without consideration of profit, is insufficient, that these means of subsistence receive an agio, and the undertakers who advance them receive a profit. Moreover it is easily seen that, by eliminating profit from the argument with which I started in the text, I do not make it any easier to reach the final result, that of giving a reason for the agio on means of subsistence, but make it more difficult. That is to say, if, as I assume, the *whole* stock of means of subsistence is disposable for the granting of advances to labourers, it will be more difficult in any case for this more ample supply to be exceeded by the demand, than if a portion of the supply appears to be already hypothecated to profit.

[1] The much more important matter of the consumption of the income from capital does not belong to the present question : as was shown in last note it is only a result of the supply of wealth being insufficient as against the demand.

In other words, all that is needed is that previous labour should have provided so many goods—partly ready for consumption, partly in the intermediate form of products ripening successively into consumption goods—as will cover the subsistence needs of two years, and thereby make it possible for the workers to invest their current labour in methods of production that will turn out the finished product in two years.

Here we come to the second part of our threefold proposition. The entire wealth of the economical community serves as subsistence fund, or advances fund, and, from this, society draws its subsistence during the period of production customary in the community. All goods which appear to-day as the stock or parent wealth of society, so far as they are not already consumption goods, will, in the more or less near future, after a certain addition of finishing labour, ripen into consumption goods, and will consequently cover, for a more or less lengthy time to come, the people's demand for consumption. Of course this must not be understood as if there were some sharp line of division separating the period which is covered by the wealth already on hand from that later period which is not yet covered, and for which, consequently, provision must be made through the current productive powers. What I mean is that the stock of wealth projects itself into the future, as provision for the consumption of the future, as it were by stages, and not all at once.

It does so in two respects: in respect of the number of classes of goods for which provision is made, and in respect of the degree of maturity at which the work of production stands in the present. As regards the first; it is to be noted that, for technical reasons, in many classes of goods (*e.g.* in various foods) provision is limited to the near future, perhaps to a couple of months, while, simultaneously, in other classes of goods, provision may be made for a couple of years. In others, again, where permanence is aimed at, or goods must be got ready long in advance (*e.g.* in dwelling-houses, mining products, machinery, and the like), the means of provision must be prepared perhaps twenty or fifty or even a hundred years before. Thus, then, it is in the nature of things that goods required in the immediate future must now be ready or almost ready; for goods needed later, it is enough if, at the moment, they have gone through, perhaps, half of the production process; while, for goods required still later, it may be enough if their production should have just begun.   If a commodity, for instance, requires five years to make, then, in the year 1888, the goods of this class destined to be used in the year 1889 must be ready, perhaps to the extent of four-fifths; those to be used in 1890 to the extent of three-fifths; those to be used in 1891 to the extent of two-fifths; while, as regards goods destined for the service of the year 1892, it is enough if, at the moment, they have gone through the first fifth of their total production process.

Thus it comes that the stock of wealth existing at the moment makes provision for the future in a doubly decreasing ratio: in proportion as the time of consumption is remote there are fewer classes, and the goods in these classes are less advanced or mature.   To get an adequate representation of the circumstances of provision, then, we should have to suppose that the stock of wealth existing on 1st January 1888 [1] contains $\frac{9}{10}$ of the goods required during 1888 and those goods are, on the average, $\frac{9}{10}$ finished, so that, on the whole, the labour required for the needs of 1888 is already finished and incorporated in the existing wealth to the extent of $\frac{81}{100}$: that, further, it contains $\frac{8}{10}$ of the goods required during the year 1889 $\frac{7}{10}$ finished, thus incorporating $\frac{56}{100}$ of the labour required for 1889: that it contains $\frac{6}{10}$ of the goods wanted for 1890 $\frac{4}{10}$ finished, thus incorporating $\frac{24}{100}$ of the labour required for 1890, and so on for 1891, 1892, 1893, incorporating respectively $\frac{12}{100}$, $\frac{6}{100}$, and $\frac{4}{100}$ of the total labour required for the service of these years.   Adding up these amounts we come to the result which I wished to elucidate by this illustration; viz., that the entire existing stock of wealth provides in advance for something like two years' [2] demand of the population, with this peculiarity that the stock of wealth, instead of covering the exigencies of two continuous years, covers successively a decreasing portion of the exigencies of a greater number of calendar years.

Now the way in which this provision is made by the existing wealth, and the extent to which it is made, exercise

---

[1] The figures are, of course, only chosen for illustration.

[2] $0\cdot81 + 0\cdot56 + 0\cdot24 + 0\cdot12 + 0\cdot06 + 0\cdot04 +$

a very suggestive and important influence on the employment of the original productive powers, labour and uses of land, coming into operation in the current year. For simplicity's sake we shall consider the former only in detail. If the stock of wealth in existence in 1888 covers the want of the current year to the extent of $\frac{8}{10}$, it is clear that from the labour of this year the other $\frac{2}{10}$ will first be covered. But it is as certain that the remainder of the current labour will not be devoted to the service of the year 1888, and that for two reasons: (1) that any return in the year 1888 could only be obtained by an unremunerative hand-to-mouth method of production, and (2) that the few products thus obtained would come upon a market already stocked and find poor sale and poor prices. The other $\frac{8}{10}$ of the labour of the year will, therefore, be directed to the service of later years. And here, again, the following is clear: the fewer the wants of 1889 covered by the existing stock of wealth, the greater will be the amount of the current year's labour directed to the service of the year 1889—if there is not to be a gap in the provision from year to year—and the smaller will be the amount of labour directed to the service of the years that come after it. Conversely if the wants of 1889 are already (relatively speaking) amply covered by the stock of wealth, only a small fraction of the current labour will go to the service of 1889, and a proportionally greater amount can be reserved for remoter periods.[1] The current labour thus adapts itself naturally to the existing stock of wealth. The one begins where the other ends. If it were to begin sooner, and so duplicate the provision already existent, it would come under the double disadvantage, already mentioned, of overstocked markets and less productive methods of production; and if it were to begin later, there would be a gap in the provision which would immediately cause scarcity prices, and thus call out speedy assistance from the productive powers.

[1] It would be erroneous to assume that, after the demand of the current year is covered, the current labour must be directed to the demand of the next annual period till such time as this is *fully* covered; that, *e.g.*, if $\frac{1}{10}$ of the demand of 1889 is covered by existing wealth, the labour of 1888 must, or even might, immediately prepare the remaining $\frac{9}{10}$. But in 1888 the maturing of finished products is carried forward only one stage, and is itself fully terminated only in the year 1889 by an addition of the labour of 1889.

Thus it is—and here we come to the last part of our threefold proposition—that, in reasonable economic speculation, the current productive powers will and must, on the average, be directed to remote productive purposes (or, in other words, invested in longer production periods), in proportion to the length of time for which the existing stock of wealth is able to provide. If the accumulated wealth is so small that it only provides subsistence for one year, it is perfectly clear that it is impossible to invest the current productive powers in processes that average three years, since, in the interval that must elapse between the consumption of the old wealth and the production of the new, the people would starve. And it is equally clear that it would be, in the highest degree, foolish and uneconomic to make the production period shorter than the existing wealth allows. The average period of production in a community is in exact correspondence with the amount of its stock of wealth, and is entirely conditioned by it.

The principle is clear, but one not unimportant question of figures still remains to be considered : What is the numerical ratio between the amount of a nation's wealth and the average production period which that wealth limits ?

At the first glance one would be inclined to answer ;— the average production period may be just so many months or years as there is months' or years' provision in the accumulated wealth. If, for instance, the year's wants of a nation are five hundred millions, and the nation's wealth contains goods to the value of a thousand millions, we should be inclined to say that the average production period would be two years.

This answer, however, would be incorrect : or, to put it more exactly, it would only be correct under conditions which do not actually occur in practical life. It would only be correct, that is to say, if the work of production was not carried on by stages. If production were so arranged that all the workers co-operating generally in the manufacture of a finished product were employed simultaneously in the same stage—I mean if all the workers were to begin with the first and preliminary processes simultaneously; were then to pass on simultaneously, as it were in line, to the second, third, fourth stage, till, in the end, they simultaneously turned out the total product finished and completed,—then, of course, the community's wealth must contain, in the form of finished goods, enough to supply the wants of just as many years as there are years in the production period. Suppose, for instance, that the manufacture of clothing were so arranged that all the workers employed in it prepared the wool in the first year, built machinery in the second, spun yarn in the third, wove it in the fourth, and made up the cloth in the fifth, the stock of wealth would require to contain finished provision for the entire demand of all the workers during five years. For, under a division of labour of this kind, during all the five years there would be no addition of finished goods to the original finished stock.

It is quite different if production is arranged in stages, as it actually is in modern industry. Of the workers occupied in the production of clothing—to continue our illustration —various groups are employed simultaneously at various stages of it. In each year a fifth part of them, perhaps, will produce wool, another fifth make machinery, another spin, another weave, and another do the making up.[1] The result is that, during the five years that elapse between the growing of the wool and the making of the coat, additions are successively made to the fruits of labour which constituted the stock of wealth at the beginning of the period: that is to say, other fruits of labour, the results of labour expended at later periods, are arriving at the stage of finished goods. Say, for instance, that on 1st January 1888 a group of labourers begin the manufacture of woollen clothing. Nothing of the fruits of *this* labour will be ready before 1st January 1893. On the other hand, besides the wholly or partially finished products contained in the inventory of 1st January 1888, the following goods will arrive at maturity before 1st January 1893;—viz. the fruits of one year's labour of those workers who are busy with the final stage in 1888; of two years' labour of those busy with the second last stage in 1888 and with the last

---

[1] It is all the same as regards the effect whether the same persons perform the labour of all stages of production successively, or whether—as is the case under the division of labour—certain persons remain constantly occupied in one and the same stage.

stage in 1889; of three years' labour of those who in 1888 reach the third last and in 1890 the last stage of production; and, finally, the fruits of four years' labour of those who, in 1888, are occupied with the second stage, and will reach the final stage in 1891.   Now since these goods, thus successively maturing, would provide for a very considerable portion of the subsistence needed for the five years 1888-92, it is evidently not necessary that the community, before entering on a five years' production period, should have a stock of wealth equal to the entire five years' needs.   Or, if there is such a stock, a longer process than five years can be entered on.

If we look at the same thing from another side, and one perhaps better suited to illustration, it is clear that, where workers are employed in stages, subsistence need be provided five years in advance only for those who work on the lowest or earliest stage of the production.   The workers on the second stage, the fruit of whose labour matures after four years, require subsistence advanced them only for four years.   The workers on the third and fourth stage require subsistence only for three and two years respectively.   The workers on the last stage, those whose products will be finished in a year, require advances only for a year.   Striking the average, we may say that, to allow the entire body of labourers to embark on a five years' production process, all that is required is subsistence for $\frac{5+4+3+2+1}{5} = 3$ years, or a little more than *half* the period of production.

What is true of a five years' process is true for all periods. If we take the trouble of calculating a number of concrete examples,[1] we very easily come to an exact statement of the law relating to it as follows.   The stock of wealth must be sufficient for half the production period, plus half the usual stage period.   If, for example, the work of production is carried on only by yearly stages—that is to say, if finished products are turned out by the process in question only at intervals of one year—then, in a five years' production period such as we have been discussing, the stock of wealth must last for half the production period (*i.e.* for $2\frac{1}{2}$ years), and, beyond that, for half what we have called the "stage period" (*i.e.* for half a year); in all, three years.   If again the stages of

---

[1] Not to cumber the text I have done this in Appendix.

production are monthly, so that every month there is an output of finished products, the stock of wealth need only be such as will last $2\frac{1}{2}$ years $+\frac{1}{2}$ month.   To put it in general terms we may say: If the production period embraces x stage periods the stock of wealth must always be sufficient for $\frac{x+1}{2}$ stage periods.

Obviously, the greater x is, the smaller is the difference between this exact formula and the rough expression of "half the production period"; while x again increases with the length of the production period and the subdivision of the stages.   In a two years' process where goods are turned out once a year, the production period embraces two stages: the value of the exact expression is, therefore, $\frac{2+1}{2} = 1\frac{1}{2}$ years —that is, fully 50% higher than the rough expression.   If, again, the process takes five years, and the goods come forward by monthly stages, $x = 60$, and the exact expression has the value $\frac{61}{2} = 30\frac{1}{2}$ months, which shows very little difference from "half the production period" of $2\frac{1}{2}$ years.   And if the production period be ten years, and the output be a weekly one, x will equal 520, and the exact expression will have the value of $260\frac{1}{2}$ weeks, which practically coincides with the rough expression of "half the production period."   Now since, in any organised industrial community, the average process is pretty long, and the subdivision into stages very minute—for not a day passes but finished products are turned out of some workshop or other—it may be assumed without much error that a community may, on the average, engage in production processes which are twice as long as the period for which the accumulated stock of wealth would provide subsistence.[1]

---

[1] Of course many productions are, for technical reasons, very little divided up into stages; agriculture, *e.g.*, yielding its harvests only from year to year. All the same the above formula will be found to give an approximately correct presentation of the case, and we may be the better pleased with it that I do not intend to draw a single deduction in which anything depends on definite figures.   What I have to do with is rather the mere negative recognition, that the period of time, for which the accumulated subsistence fund must contain provision, need not be so great as the average economical production period.

CHAPTER VI

THE PROFIT OF CAPITALIST UNDERTAKING. THE GENERAL
SUBSISTENCE MARKET—(*continued*)

IT may be thought that in the disquisition of last chapter we have wandered entirely from our subject, the subsistence market. This, however, is not the case. We are here, indeed, at the very centre of the question, for we are speaking directly of those things which form and regulate the supply and demand on the subsistence market. Who are the people that require to get subsistence advanced them? The answer is: Every one who wishes to produce in capitalist methods.[1] How much is required?—An amount proportioned to the length of the production process. And in what form is it required?— By instalments. Again, who are the people that have subsistence to give?—All owners of wealth who do not consume but "save" it. How much can they give?—As much as their stock of wealth contains. And in what form can they give it?—Similarly, in instalments—in the proportion that the unfinished goods contained in their inventory successively mature. This is the true nature of what occurs in our market for means of production and in our market for credit—over which, I admit, the division of labour and the use of money throw a veil very difficult to penetrate.

Now at what price will finished present goods be exchanged

---

[1] I repeat again that it is quite true that, during the period of the national production process, the idle capitalists and rentiers also must be maintained by advances of wealth, and, indeed, as a rule maintained at a pretty fair rate. Their claims on subsistence, however, are not causes but effects of the condition of the market creating an agio on present goods. If there is no agio, and so no interest, then no one could live in idleness as a rentier; he would either have to work or positively consume his parent wealth. See above, p. 320 in note.

for future goods on the subsistence market ? This is the question in which our whole interest peculiarly centres. To answer it we must describe, with more care than hitherto, both the extent and, in particular, the intensity of supply and demand. To begin with Supply.[1]

The extent of the supply of subsistence we have already gone into with sufficient exactness. It is represented by the total stock of wealth accumulated in a community, exclusive of land, and after deduction of those amounts which are consumed partly by owners who are getting poorer, partly by owners producing independently and spending either on themselves or by way of advances.

As to the intensity of supply, it may be assumed from what was said on p. 315 as regards modern economic circumstances, that, to the capitalists, the subjective use value of present goods is not greater than that of future goods. In the most unfavourable case, then, they would be willing to give almost 20s. present money for 20s. obtainable in two years, or, what is the same thing, for one week of labour which would bring them in 20s. in two years.[2]

Over and against this supply of present goods stands, as Demand :—

1. An enormous number of wage-earners who cannot employ their labour remuneratively by working on their own account, and are accordingly, as a body, inclined and ready to sell the future product of their labour for a considerably less amount of present goods. Recurring to the figures of our illustration on p. 313 we may assume that, for the future product of 20s. value—the product turned out complete as the result of a week's work, and valued after two years at 20s.—one class of the labourers will, in the most unfavourable circumstances, accept a price or wage of 10s., while another class will accept as low a sum as 5s. in present money.

---

[1] It is scarcely necessary to note that we have now changed the names of the parties who enter the market. So long as we were considering the special relations of the labour market, we thought of labour as the commodity offered, and of the means of subsistence as the equivalent price. Now, conversely, the means of subsistence appear as the commodity looking for a market, or as Supply.

[2] Never, of course, quite 20s. ; otherwise they would have no advantage from the exchange, and consequently no motive to conclude it; but, perhaps, 19s. 6d. or 19s. 9d.—a difference so insignificant that it may be entirely neglected in our inquiry.

2. A number of independent producers, themselves working, who by an advance of present goods are put in a position to prolong their process, and thus increase the productiveness of their personal labour, say, from 20s. to 24s. per week. Since these persons, obviously, get an advantage from this advance so long as it enables them to obtain *anything* over 20s. a week, they will be prepared, where necessary, to give up a portion of the surplus product of 4s. a week, as agio on the present goods to which they owe this surplus product. I purposely here mention only those undertakers who demand productive credit for the assistance of their own labour, and not those who demand it for the employment of workers auxiliary to themselves. The demand of these latter forms only a passing stage : they take some part of the supply, provided by the owners of wealth, out of the market, but only to offer it again, on a different part-market, to the auxiliary workers.

3. A small number of persons who, on account of urgent personal wants, seek credit for purposes of consumption, and are also ready to pay an agio for present goods.[1]

Here then we see that, in these groups constituting the demand, the circumstances are such that those who demand are willing and are able to pay for the present goods they require, where necessary, by a larger sum of future goods ; that is to say, by an agio. This being the state of the case, then, that all who own the supply value present and future goods *alike*, and all who form the demand value present goods *higher* than future, the determination of the price simply depends on which side has the numerical preponderance. If more present goods are offered than are desired by the united demand there can be no interest. The resultant market price, as we know, must always be lower than the subjective valuation of those would-be sellers who do not effect a sale. Now if the demand

---

[1] I might name, as a fourth group of demand, those landowners who live, not on the return of their labour but on their rents, and who, like the labourers, get the price of a future commodity sold by them—in this case the productive good, use of land—advanced them in the form of subsistence. I intentionally, however, make no mention here of this group of demand since there need not be in every economy landowners living on their rents, and since, in any case, the emergence of interest which we have to prove in the text is quite independent of the simultaneous existence of rent from land.

is, numerically, too weak, and if, in consequence, all the present goods offered cannot find a sale, and if all capitalists—even those who cannot find a sale for their present goods—value 20s. present money at something like 20s. future money, the market price of twenty present shillings cannot be higher than twenty future shillings, and there is no agio on present goods.   If, on the contrary, more present goods are wanted than are offered, all the suitors cannot be supplied.   In methods with which we are familiar the weeding-out process of competition now ensues; those who are able to offer the highest agio for present goods succeed in effecting an exchange; while the others, be they few or many, are shut out, even although they may have been ready to offer some (smaller) agio.   But since the market price must always be higher than that bid by the excluded buyers, and since this latter contains an agio, it is clear that, in the circumstances, the market price also must contain an agio—great or small—for present goods.

Now it can be shown—and with this we come to the goal of our long inquiry—that the supply of present goods *must* be numerically less than the demand.   The supply, even in the richest nation, is limited by the amount of the people's wealth at the moment.   The demand, on the other hand, is practically infinite: it continues at least so long as the return to production goes on increasing with the extension of the production process, and that is a limit which, even in the richest nation, lies far beyond the amount of wealth possessed at the moment.

Where a people, as in the case of Roscher's poor fisher-folk, live from hand to mouth, it goes without saying that they will be eager to acquire the first hardly saved stocks which allow them to make boats and nets, and their exchanges will be made with an agio against future goods.   But among comfortably-off and wealthy people the position is different, not in kind, but in degree.   If the stock of wealth be sufficient to maintain the population during an average one year's production period, every one will wish to engage in a two years' process with its greater productiveness, and, the stock of wealth not being sufficient to advance subsistence to everybody for two years, there will be, as before, bidding against each other; the circle of suitors will be weeded out; and the agio on present goods will appear. Nor does it make any difference if the community's wealth is sufficient for an average of five or ten years' production period. Since the provision for human wants would be still more abundant if, instead of five or ten years, six or eleven years were the average periods, men will always wish to embark on these more fruitful methods, will compete to obtain the subsistence that is not sufficient for all, and will thereby inevitably call forth an agio for present goods.

Interest and Agio *must* appear. Assume for a moment that they do not. Present goods and future goods are exchanged on the great subsistence market at par, and the labourers, for the week's work, get the whole value of their future product paid down to them in present goods. Say that the average production period, assuming the nation to be enormously wealthy, is ten years: that the week's work consequently yields 40s. and that the labourer receives the whole of this as wage. What will happen? The undertaker who employs people to work with him in a ten years' process makes no profit outside of his own personal labour. For the 40s., which the labour of his people yields him at the end of the production period, has already been wholly expended as wage. But how if he extends the production period still further? If the week's labour has returned 40s. in the ten years' process, experience tells us it will return more in a twelve years' process, say 44s. In still longer processes, say, fifteen years, it may return perhaps 48s. Now as the undertaker, by hypothesis, can buy present goods at par on the subsistence market, it would be foolish of him not to extend the production period for himself and his employés to fifteen years. If he does so, he pays his workers out of the borrowed advances 40s., the price on the labour market: in fifteen years he recovers 48s. from the product: from that sum he pays back the advanced 40s. at par, and has remaining the respectable profit of 8s. out of each week of labour. And with this we have the "surplus value," the profit on capital.

To prevent its appearance the labourer's wage would have to be raised from 40s. to 48s. But this is not possible. For the well-known levelling tendencies of competition do not allow wages to rise permanently in any isolated branch—so long as it does not presuppose peculiar personal qualities—inasmuch as there will at once be a rush from less paying branches into any particularly paying branch. But neither is a general rise of wages to 48s. possible, because the existent stock of wealth is only sufficient for an average ten years' period. The extension of the process to fifteen years, consequently, can occur only in isolated cases; the bulk of productive employments must continue the ten years' process which yields only 40s. per week, and cannot, therefore, permit of any higher wage than 40s.

On the other hand, it is obvious that something else will make its appearance. However sharp undertaker A may be in borrowing money free of interest, and securing a nice surplus value of 8s. per week of labour, undertakers B, C, D and E will not be far behind. The desire to prolong the production period, and, with that, the demand for increased advances of subsistence, will become general: it will not be possible to supply this increased demand from the limited funds of subsistence: and, finally, the weeding out of competition will begin among the classes who constitute the demand. Here, then, we have the agio again appearing in the universal market price of present goods, from which, by hypothesis, we had for the moment banished it.

And this result, as regards the normal and really economic provision of society, is no less healthy than it is necessary. The possibility of obtaining means of subsistence free of agio would be certain to tempt undertakers into immoderate extension of the production period. If this were to occur only partially and in a few branches of production, naturally the limited stocks of subsistence would leave so much less for the other branches of production; these latter would have to curtail their processes unnaturally; and there would ensue a deficiency in the social provision which would outweigh the increased return got from the favoured branches through the immoderate extension of their processes.[1] But if the excessive

---

[1] The deficiency is greater, because it is well confirmed by experience that the surplus return constantly tends to decrease as the production period is extended. (See above, p. 84.) The difference between the return which can be obtained in a five years', and that which can be obtained in a ten years'

extension were to be introduced all over, the community's stock of subsistence would come to an end sooner than the fruits of processes thus unduly extended could mature; there would be deficiency in provision, want, and distress; famine prices would recall the misdirected natural powers, and put them, with difficulty, to supply provision for the moment. All this could not happen without serious disturbance, expense, and loss.

Now the constant presence of the agio on present goods is like a self-acting drag on the tendency to extend the production period; without checking it all at once it makes it more difficult, and more difficult in proportion to the projected length of the process. Extensions which would be harmful as regards social provision are thus made economically impossible. Moderate extensions over the average process, however, are not absolutely prevented, but are limited to those branches where, from peculiar economic or technical circumstances, the productiveness that goes with the extension of the period is so great that they can bear the progressive burden of the agio. Branches, again, where longer processes are somewhat, but only a little, more productive, are tempted to escape the burden of agio by recurring to periods under the average. Thus, finally, under the influence of the agio, the total fund of subsistence is divided out automatically among the individual branches of production, in such amounts that each branch adopts that length of process which—in the given condition of the fund—is most favourable to the total provision.[1]

production period, is greater than the difference between the returns of a ten and a fifteen years' period. If now, in a community where the stock of wealth is such as to allow of an average ten years' period, one branch is forced to limit its own period to five years because another branch has extended its period to fifteen years, the greater difference is lost to the community, and the lesser one is won. The total result of such a procedure is, therefore, uneconomic.

[1] The fact that the agio stands at a certain height may now and then lead to the appearance of there being a deficiency in remunerative opportunities of employment, and a "glut of capital." The truth is that there is always a surplus of remunerative opportunities of employment, and a deficiency of capital; only that the high agio, which is the result of the deficiency of capital, excludes a mass of remunerative opportunities as not remunerative *enough* economically. It is exactly the same as when, in a year of bad crops, sufficient buyers cannot at the moment be found in some one market for the strongly appreciated grain, on account of the price being so high. It cannot be truly said that there is a surplus of grain and a deficiency of demand; on the contrary,

At this point I think we may congratulate ourselves on having finished one of the most important demonstrations in the scope of our present task. It fully confirms those inferences which we had drawn from the nature of the productive instrument Labour as a future commodity, and it gives us the key to the explanation of the much-disputed " Surplus Value " of the undertakers. It shows that, in the great combined subsistence market of society, present goods must have an agio, as legitimate consequence of the constant fact that present goods are more useful, and are more desired, than future goods, and that they are never present and offered in unlimited abundance. This agio, thus organically necessary, is given directly on the loan market in the shape of interest, while, on the labour market, it is given in the form of a price for labour which remains under the amount of the future product of labour, and which, on that account, leaves room for the accretion of a surplus value.

The same principles as regulate the price of the productive instrument, Labour, regulate the price of the original productive instrument " Nature," or those services rendered by the earth which possess an economical character—generally called, from their chief representative, Uses of Land (*Bodennutzungen*). If a piece of land—after deducting the share of the complementary productive goods which co-operate—will produce in one year 100 bushels of corn, or will rear in five years 100 cwts. of beef, no one would be willing to pay the par value of 100 present bushels of corn or 100 present cwts. of beef for the use of the land, when these last-named amounts, employed in lengthening the production process, or directly exchanged against future goods on the loan market, or spent in buying labour, could obtain *more* than the 100 future bushels or cwts. Thus Uses of Land, when exchanged against present goods, cannot escape a deduction in price any more than can the productive good Labour.

And, finally, on exactly similar grounds the very same is true of the price of Intermediate Products. Concrete capital

there is so great a deficiency of grain that, after the weeding out which has resulted from the war of competition, only a very small part of the demand finds. economically, admittance to the scanty stocks.

generally—raw materials, tools, and so on—is bought and sold at a price which remains under the amount of the future product resulting from it. It would be a very easy matter to prove this point by point, as we did with the price of labour, but the case of intermediate products is so closely allied that it seems to me quite unnecessary.

Speaking generally, the importance of the demonstration we have just completed does not consist in its proving that productive instruments are bought at a price which remains under the price of their future product, for this is an old and familiar fact taught not only by daily experience but by the theory of the most diverging schools. The really important result of our investigations is, that this well-known fact has been shown to be the necessary outcome of the same causes as give present goods the superiority in value over future goods.

A few chapters back I assented to one feature of the Socialist interest theory—that which explains surplus value from the low price at which productive powers are purchased. I may now add wherein the theory is wrong. It is wrong, first, in explaining interest by the cheap purchase of *labour* only. Interest is got as much by the cheap purchase of uses of land. Quantitatively, of course, the profit from buying labour bulks much more largely in importance. The profit from the "cheap" purchase of intermediate products need not be mentioned here; it is explained on the same principles as the profit from the purchase of the original productive powers.

Second, as I have already said on p. 301, the purchase is not so cheap as it seems to be, because the object of purchase is measured in (undervalued) future goods, while the price is measured in (full-valued) present goods.

And, finally, the fact that the price of labour is relatively low, is not the naked result of an exploitation in which want forces the labourers to acquiesce. To some extent, although, probably, to a less extent, the same would be the case without any compulsion, if wealth were divided almost equally among all. To prove this let us recur for a moment to the consideration of those primitive circumstances which I hurried over as not immediately appropriate to modern economy.[1] Suppose a society where all are owners of wealth, and all independent

[1] See above, pp. 316, 317.

z

producers. Their labour, embodied in, say, a two years' process, is moderatively productive. Suppose that, in this society—which is not a poor one—a certain producer possesses means enough to make it possible for him, either to maintain himself for six years, or to maintain himself and one worker for three years. The product of a year's labour, we shall suppose, is as follows :—in a two years' production period £52 (at 20s. per week), in a three years' process £60, in a six years', £65.[1] If this man employs his wealth in lengthening the period of his production without employing an assistant, he obtains by his six years' labour $6 \times 65 = £390$. If he employs an assistant, and works along with him in a three years' process, he reaps from his own labour in six years $6 \times 60 = £360$, while the same amount is produced by the labour of his employé. How much can he pay this employé in wages ?

Obviously it is quite impossible to give him the full £360 (that is £60 per year) in wage, for this would be to inflict positive injury on himself. Working by himself he would have obtained in six years £390 ; by employing another he gets only £360. To avoid loss he must, therefore, keep back of the product of the employé at least £30, and thus he will be able to pay him at most £330, or £55 per year. If he does so, the whole advantage of the business is, obviously, still on the side of the labourer. The undertaker gains nothing, but the labourer gains, inasmuch as he now earns £55 instead of the £52, which is all he could have earned as an independent undertaker with a two years' process. In these circumstances the idea of exploitation is out of the question : so is the idea of a forced agreement : and still the wage, although stretched in favour of the labourer to the extremest limit of the economically possible, remains under the full amount of his future product. Surely this is a clear enough proof that there is some other reason for the " cheap " buying of labour than compulsion and exploitation !

[1] I assume that the figures of the return in a six years' period are a little, but not very much higher than those in a three years', in harmony with the experience, so often alluded to, that gradual extension of the production period tends to always decreasing surplus returns.

CHAPTER VII

INTEREST FROM DURABLE GOODS

MATERIAL goods are of use to mankind through the action of
the natural powers that reside in them, or, as I have expressed
it in another place, through the rendering of their material
services.   On the nature and importance of these material
services I have said enough in my former work,[1] and I shall
repeat only a few considerations which seem necessary to
connect what was then said with the subject now before us.

Many goods are so constituted technically as to be capable
of rendering one single service, and in that service to exhaust
the whole of their useful content.   These are what we call
Perishable goods.   In them the good and the service coincide.
Many other goods, again, are able to render several successive
services.   We call these Durable goods: tools, dwellings,
clothes, land are instances of such.   Here the single service
forms a smaller economical unit clearly distinguished from
the good itself, and is capable of obtaining a certain economical
independence.   To afford a single and limited act of satisfaction, a single service may be detached from the useful
content of the good.   Various services of the same good
may be independently and differently disposed of.   Single
services, or groups of services, may be independently transferred, gifted, or sold to different people, as we see every day
in the familiar legal contracts of Lease and Hire.   Such
services may obtain an independent price, and, as this of
course presupposes, an independent value.[2]   It is the value of
these material services that now claims our attention.

[1] *Capital and Interest*, p. 219.   Also *Rechte und Verhältnisse*, p. 57.
[2] Are Material Services themselves "Goods"?—Many writers will have it so,

This value cannot be subject to any other laws than those which regulate the value of goods in general. A service obtains value exactly as a good does—that is, by the satisfac-

as Hermann (*Staatswirthschaftliche Untersuchungen*, second edition, p. 109), or Menger (*Grundsätze*, p. 132). Other recent writers, like Sax (*Grundlegung*, p. 209) and R. Meyer (*Das Wesen des Einkommens*, pp. 155, 168), emphatically exclude the services themselves from the conception of Goods. (Sax speaks primarily of personal services, but what is true of them must logically be true of material services.) To my mind the matter appears to stand as follows. First of all, the whole question is not one of scientific knowledge, but simply one of terminology. And provided that the nature and the place of material services in economics were really and properly recognised, in the end it would not much matter whether the name Good was attached to them or not. Those authors who refuse to recognise material services as goods appear to me, however, to have some notions that are not really and properly correct. Thus Meyer (pp. 156, 157, note 4) denies to material services the character of economic *means*, and explains them rather as "satisfactions of want." Now the material service, as I understand it, is a real mean towards the satisfaction of want, not that satisfaction of want itself. It stands as independent intermediary between the good from which it comes, and the satisfaction of want which it is intended to cause but does not by any means always cause. If, *e.g.*, I hire an oven for the baking of bread—that is to say, buy its use or its material service—what kind of thing is it I really have bought? Have I directly bought the satisfaction of want, the allaying of hunger?—Certainly not. Or the oven itself?—No. Or, perhaps, the bread that is to be made by the oven?—Again, no. But what I have bought is just one material service, or group of services, of the good called Oven; these services are means to the production of bread, and thus, beyond that, to the satisfaction of one of the needs of subsistence. The material services are, therefore, true and—according to the sense indicated in the text—independent economical instruments and objects.—If now, with the view of settling the terminological question, we inquire as to the position of the material services among the other economical instruments, we seem to arrive at the following. There can be no doubt as to the inventory of the causes of wellbeing,—the causes which we summon to the satisfaction of our wants. Our wellbeing is furthered, on the one side, by *persons* who are useful to us (such as teachers, guardians, clergymen, artists, workers, domestics, etc.), and, on the other side, by useful *things*. And the use of both comes to us through the exertion of their useful powers,—that is, through useful services. In the sphere of material instruments of wellbeing we treat both the things and their services as economical objects : in the sphere of personal instruments of wellbeing, since the abolition of slavery, we do not treat the useful persons themselves, but only their services, as economical objects. Thus the scheme of our economical means of satisfaction would receive something like the following shape :

Economical Means of Satisfaction

(Useful Persons)	Material Goods
Personal Services	Material Services

And now it is a question of appropriate terminology to which of these categories the name "Good" should be attached. Personally I believe that the science has great need of one short expression which would embrace all kinds of means of

tion of some want being dependent upon it—and the amount of its value is measured by the importance of the dependent want—that is, by the amount of the marginal utility which may be obtained from a service of such kind and such extent.

Thus there is, naturally, an intimate relation between the value possessed by the material good itself, and the value possessed by its services. The nature of this relation scarcely requires explanation ;—a material good obviously has the same value as the sum of all its services. If a good is capable of rendering ten services, and if the satisfaction of a certain want depends on each of these services, it is obvious that what depends on the possession of the good is the receiving of these satisfactions, and, indeed, of all the ten satisfactions from which the services get their value.

Naturally the case of perishable goods is the simplest. Here the value of the single service coincides purely and simply with the value of the good itself. The value of the service rendered me by a cartridge is identical with the value of the cartridge. The case of durable goods is more complicated. We have always to think of the value of a durable good as a compound amount; as made up of the importance of more or less numerous wants to which it ministers by its successive services ; or—to put it another way—as made up of the individual values of the services on which those satisfactions depend. If a farmer is calculating the use value of a threshing-machine with a view to buying it, he will take into account the time the machine will last and the work it is capable of doing, and will calculate from that how many services it will render, and how much each service will be worth to him.[1]

satisfaction. Now, since the word "good" is quite suitable for this purpose, and has already long been used for this purpose, I see no reason why it should now be deposed. Of course there is quite as strong a need to keep the material services in their turn separate from the material goods which bear these services. But this can be done, both simply and sufficiently, by instituting the distinction, inside the universal conception of the "Good," between "Material Goods" and "Material Services."—Things like Rights, Relations, Properties, would, for good reasons, find no room even in the widened conception.

[1] The perception of the above is made very difficult by the usual method of valuation according to "Costs" which, naturally, is always directed to the unit of goods as a whole (see my *Rechte und Verhältnisse*, p. 64, note 1). The reader, however, who has followed our conception of what the nature of the law of costs

In this, however, there may be another complication. If the services of the durable good be exhausted in a short space of time, the individual services, provided they are of the same quality—which, for simplicity's sake, we assume—are, as a rule, equal in value, and the value of the material good itself is obtained by multiplying the value of one service by the number of services of which the good is capable. But in the case of many durable goods, such as ships, machinery, furniture, land, the services rendered extend over long periods, and the result is that the later services cannot be rendered, or at least cannot be rendered in a normal economic way, before a long time has expired.

As consequence, the value of the more distant material services suffers the same fate as the value of future goods. A material service, which, technically, is exactly the same as a service of this year, but which cannot be rendered before next year, is worth a little less than this year's service; another similar service, but obtainable only after two years, is, again, a little less valuable, and so on; the value of the remote services decreasing with the remoteness of the period at which they can be rendered. Say that this year's service is worth 100, then next year's service—assuming a difference of 5% per annum—is worth in to-day's valuation only 95·23; the third year's service is worth only 90·70; the fourth year's service, 86·38; the fifth, sixth, seventh year's services, respectively, worth 82·27, 78·35, 74·62 of present money. The value of the durable good in this case is not found by multiplying the value of the current service by the total number of services, but is represented by a sum of services decreasing in value. If the current year's use of a machine is worth 100, and the machine is capable of doing work of equal quality for five years

is, and has, consequently, recognised that, even where goods seem to get their value from their costs, the utility of the goods always stands in the background as the true source of value, and that, in any case, the "costs" must always be in harmony with the—independently established—marginal utility of the goods, will not be misled by any appearance to the contrary. Even in the consideration, for instance, of whether a durable good in general is worth its cost, and whether, consequently, we should produce or buy it, we must form an opinion to ourselves as to its utility, and I should be puzzled to know how this opinion is to be formed if not on the basis of the value which the material services of the good—singly and taken together—have for us.—On the whole question treated in the text see also my *Rechte und Verhältnisse*, pp. 61-68.

more, the machine is not worth $6 \times 100 = 600$, but $100 + 95\cdot23$ $+ 90\cdot70 + 86\cdot38 + 82\cdot27 + 78\cdot35 = 532\cdot93$ [1] Now what happens during the working life of this machine ?—In the first year of its use the owner realises the "current" service with its value of 100. Naturally this service, thus consumed or rendered, comes off the value of the machine (which we may call the "bearer of the use"), and the good suffers a loss of value. But this loss of value cannot be quite so great as the value of the service rendered and deducted. It is partly compensated by the increased value of the services that still remain embodied in the machine. That particular service which, at the beginning of the year of use, figured as "next year's," and had a value of only $95\cdot23$ in present money, figures by the end of the year as "this year's use"; it has advanced one year nearer maturity and grown into the full present value of 100. Similarly the former third year's service has now become next year's, and its value has grown from $90\cdot70$ to $95\cdot23$: the fourth, fifth, and sixth year's services have passed into the rank and value of third, fourth, and fifth year's services. Behind each of these latter services there remains another service ready to take its place, and entirely supply it. It is only the last, the sixth year's service, that is not replaced by any succeeding one. And thus we find that the loss of value which the durable good

---

[1] These figures are based on the assumption that the whole year's utility is obtained all at once, and, indeed, obtained in anticipation at the beginning of the year ; *e.g.* by hiring the good at a year's interest of 100 payable on each 1st January. If, on the other hand, the year's use can only be had at the end of the year, a valuation undertaken at the beginning of the year will show figures not inconsiderably lower. That is to say, on 1st January 1888, the present year's use which will be obtained only by 31st December,—that is, practically, a whole year later,—will not be valued at the full 100, but at $95\cdot23$ only ; and again the "next year's use," that obtainable 31st December 1889,—that is, practically, two years later,—will be valued at $90\cdot70$, and so on. Now this shows, for the whole good, a sum of value of $95\cdot23 + 90\cdot70 + 86\cdot38 + 82\cdot27 + 78\cdot35 + 74\cdot62 = 507\cdot55$. If, finally, the utility were always obtainable in the middle of the year, or, what comes to the same thing, were to be spread equally over the whole year, the figures would be—for a valuation taken on the 1st January—$97\cdot56 + 92\cdot85 + 88\cdot38 + 84\cdot12 + 80\cdot07 + 76\cdot21 = 519\cdot19$.—That the figures should alter according as the date of the valuation stands nearer or farther from the date of obtaining the utility, is an entirely natural thing, and one quite familiar in financial life. The value of paper—which is just a "durable good" with annual uses—always stands a little higher shortly before the interest or dividend terms than some time before. I may note that the above figures are taken as before from Spitzer's *Tables*, and are based on an interest rate of 5%.

suffers during the year's use turns out exactly equal to the
initial value of the *most remote* service inherent in the good.
This value, of course, is less than the value of the present
service, the service known as the " current return ": and
thus it happens again that, to the owner of the durable good,
something of the current return always remains over as net
profit or net interest, after deducting the loss of value which
the good suffers during its year of use (that loss of value
familiarly known as "wear and tear"). This "something"
amounts exactly to the customary percentage of the total value
(the "capital value") of the parent good, the bearer of the
utility—a coincidence which it is the easiest thing in the world
to explain. For this "something" is got from the increasing
value of the total services of the goods as these services come
nearer to the present. Now, naturally, each service increases
in value as it comes nearer the time of its realisation in the
same ratio as it was underestimated formerly by reason of its
remoteness : that is to say, it increases in value by the usual
market percentage on its individual value. But since, as we
saw, the sum of the individual values of all the services inherent
in a good constitutes the value of that good, the increment of
value of all the services added together must be exactly equal
to the usual market percentage on the total value of the good.

To put all this into figures. At the beginning of the first
year of its use the good, as bearer of six annual services, was
worth in present value $100 + 95 \cdot 23 + 90 \cdot 70 + 86 \cdot 38 + 82 \cdot 27
+ 78 \cdot 35$; that is, $532 \cdot 93$. At the end of the first year, as
now capable of five annual services of the present value of
$100 + 95 \cdot 23 + 90 \cdot 70 + 86 \cdot 38 + 82 \cdot 27$, it is worth $454 \cdot 58$.
The loss in value is, therefore, $78 \cdot 35$, which is exactly the
same as the former most remote service was. But since the
sum received from the current year's service—the value of
the service sold and now deducted—amounted to 100, there
remains a net gain of $21 \cdot 65$, which is exactly 5% of $432 \cdot 93$,
the sum which the good became worth immediately on deduc-
tion of the first service realised, as one might say, to account.[1]

---

[1] On the part return of 100, which was separated off from the good on the
first day of the year, the good naturally will no longer yield any interest. If, on
the other hand, the year's utility is only obtainable at the end of the year, it
must naturally pay interest on the full initial value of the bearer of the utility,
as will be brought out somewhat more fully later on.

Similarly, in the second year's use, the owner again realises the service now become present and worth 100. This comes off the value of the parent good. But the succeeding service, which before had become worth 95·23, now arrives at the full value of 100: that succeeding it, becomes worth 95·23, and so on. Only the last service, that originally worth 82·27, finds nothing to replace it. At the end of the second year's use, then, the good, as capable of four remaining annual services of the individual values of 100 + 95·23 + 90·70 + 86·38, is worth 372·31. As against the value of 454·58 which it had at the beginning of the year, it has suffered a loss of value of 82·27 which is equal to the value of what was the last service; and as against the receipt of 100, it returns 17·53 net, the interest on the somewhat reduced capital[1] that remains. And thus it goes on from year to year, the gross return always remaining the same (because by hypothesis the amounts of service remain unchanged in technical quality), the quota for wear and tear always increasing (because the marginal service, that which determines the loss of value, stands nearer to the present, and so to the full present value), and the net interest always decreasing (in correspondence with the decrease of the capital, owing to wear and tear, on which interest has to be paid), till finally the good has entirely given up its useful content and is, as we say, consumed.

Put in general terms, then, we get the following very simple explanation of the phenomenon of interest on durable goods. The owner of a durable good can always realise the full (higher) value of the then present utility, and this represents the " gross return " of the good, its " gross interest." He loses, on the other hand, on account of the steady advance of the more remote services towards the present, only the smaller value of the last service then inherent in the good. This smaller value determines the amount of the " wear and tear," and thus there is always a difference between gross interest and the amount of wear and tear, which difference forms his net profit or net interest. The cause, then, to which net interest owes its existence, is nothing else than an

---

[1] Of 354·58, because again the 100 taken off at the beginning of the year—which may independently obtain interest—need no longer obtain interest *through* the good.

increase of value of the future services—services which were previously of less value, but during the period of the good's use have pressed forward into or towards the present.[1]

Thus our theory traces back the profit which durable goods yield their owner to the selfsame causes as explain interest on loans and undertakers' profit on production. I think I am justified in claiming this as the peculiar merit of the theory, and, at the same time, as a strong proof of its correctness. For it was just this interest on durable goods (*Nutzungsgüter*) that formed the stone of stumbling to all earlier interest theories, and stood, as it were, a standing contradiction of them. Supposing that the other kinds of interest could be explained by the productivity of capital, obviously this was no explanation of the interest yielded by a durable consumption good which produced nothing, such as a dwelling-house, household furniture, a hired piano, the books of a lending library. Or, if undertakers' profit was traced, with more or less appearance of justification, to an exploitation of the labourers, the question remained : What labourers are exploited by the owner of a house ? Suppose he has paid away the whole £2000, the worth of his house, in wages to the labourers who built it, so that in the origin of the house there is not a particle of profit from exploitation : still, the house, year after year, yields him £100 of interest on capital. Where shall we find the worker from whom the £100 could have been taken either by fraud or force ?

The " Use theory " appears, at first sight at least, better

[1] If the year's service can be obtained only at the year's end, the figures of the valuation, and with them the figures of the interest, will be altered, but the principle of the process, and, in particular, the reduction of value by the amount of the then last service, remains unchanged. I shall put together in the following tables the course of the value movement for one such case. The initial value of a good which will last six years, and has an annual utility, obtainable at the end of the year, of 100, is, as stated above (p. 343 in note), equal to 95·23 + 90·70 + 86·38 + 82·27 + 78·35 + 74·62 = 507·55.

Year.	Value on 1st Jan.	Value on 31st Dec	Gross Int.	Wear and Tear.	Net Int.
1888	507·55	432·93	100	74·62	25·38
1889	432·93	354·58	100	78·35	21·65
1890	354·58	272·31	100	82·27	17·73
1891	272·31	185·93	100	86·38	13·62
1892	185·93	95·23	100	90·70	9·30
1893	95·23	——	100	95·23	4·77

able to account for this form of interest, since it borrows its
special foundation directly from the phenomenon of the durable
use of non-perishable goods.[1]   But neither does it get beyond
the mere semblance of an explanation.   It gets entangled in
subtleties of a " wider " and a " narrower " use, of a " gross "
and a " net " utility,—terms, by the way, which may be quite
proper as convenient expressions to indicate certain phenomena, but represent anything but clear and definite conceptions
—and leaves entirely unexplained the nature of the relations
existing between the value of the net and the value of the
gross use, between the value of the parent good and the
amount of its wear and tear.   Whether net interest is high
because the value of the capital is high, or whether capital
value is high because net interest is high ; whether the amount
of gross interest is cause or effect of the value of the other
two amounts—on these questions we should seek in vain,
in the writings of Hermann, Knies, or Schäffle, for anything
approaching to clearness of inquiry and for anything like
a real explanation.   To all these questions our theory gives
one concise answer.   The value of material services (Gross
Use) forms the first link in the causal chain.   The value of
the " bearer of the use," the parent good, is the sum of the
individual values of its material services.   Wear and tear is a
result of the diminution of the services which still reside in
the good, and is, on account of the progression in time of the
later services, neither equal to the value of the material service
detached during the year of use, nor yet corresponding to the
degree of physical wear and tear [2] (which, if the good last six

---

[1] See *Capital and Interest*, p. 194, and particularly p. 233.

[2] A very noteworthy fact, which theory up till now has left entirely without
notice and entirely without explanation.   I have already called attention
to it in my book *Rechte und Verhältnisse*, p. 68, note 6.   As to the actual
fact that the successive diminution of *value*, which a good suffers in the course of
its wear and tear, does not go parallel with the degree of its physical wear and
tear, but is slower at the beginning and quicker as time goes on, there can be no
doubt.   It may be seen in its purest form, because there it is not confused through
subjective inexactnesses or caprice, in the rating of valuable paper which brings in
a fixed annual amount for a limited number of years.   A bond, *e.g.*, which assures
its owner the right of drawing ten years' coupons of £1000, and possesses (on
a calculation of 5% compound interest) an initial course value of £7722 (Spitzer's
Tables, p. 274), does not lose £772·2 for each of the ten years which make up
its lifetime, although in each of these years it loses exactly one-tenth of its
content.   In the first year it loses £614, in the second £645, in the third £677,

years, would amount yearly to one-sixth of the whole useful content), but is equal only to the value of that service which is the last, the most remote, at the time of calculation. And it is this same progression in time which causes the increase in value of the later services and from which comes a net gain, the interest on capital.

The same considerations that have elucidated the cause of interest from durable goods throw a strong light on another phenomenon, equally familiar and equally misunderstood,—that of Capitalisation. It is a well-known circumstance that, to such goods as yield us a more or less permanent return, we ascribe a certain "capital value" in consideration of this return. We estimate them as equal to a money capital which, at the ruling rate of interest in the particular country, would yield a similar amount of return for the same period. Thus a house which returns £500 a year, we value at £10,000 if the usual rate of interest is 5%, or at £12,500 if the rate is 4%; or we value a machine which, for six years, throws off annually a gross amount of £100 and certain net decreasing amounts, at something over £500.

Why do we attach just this value to them? The common explanation is: Because these goods yield a certain net return we must hold them equal in value to a sum of money which yields just the same net return. This, however, is incorrect, or rather it is not an explanation at all but a reasoning in a circle. The existence of a net return is not the primary fact which can be given as *cause* of the parent good having a definite value, but, conversely, a definite value must already be put on the good if this net return as such is to appear. If, in our example, the machine, which in six years returns in all £600, had been valued at £600, its whole return evidently would have been absorbed by the "wear and

and so on successively £710, £747, £783, £823, £864, £907, and, finally, in the tenth year, £952, the sum it was still worth at the beginning of this latter year. But in all other kinds of durable goods the same course of wear and tear may be observed with sufficient accuracy, although, for obvious reasons, we seldom make so exact and mathematical a calculation. Later on I shall have another occasion to mention cases of this kind. Now in all the literature known to me I have found no attempt to give an explanation of this fact,—which is certainly notable enough to deserve explanation. Indeed, such an explanation is simply not to be got from the machinery of previous theories, particularly the "Use theory," while it offers itself unsolicited on the lines of my theory.

tear," and there would have been nothing left over as net return.   It is simply because it was valued at less, at something only a little over £500, that there remains a net interest after deducting the quota for wear and tear.   And it is exactly the same, as I shall show farther on in another connection, as regards the return and capital value of houses, lands, etc.

The only correct conception, and the only conception which really gives an explanation of the phenomenon, is the one now stated.   The true primary fact is the lower value of future goods and future services : next we have the parent good, as capable of containing future services, estimated at a less amount than the total value which the services successively given off will represent as they are given off: and finally, as consequence, comes the fact that the capitalised sum is less than the sum of the amounts realised by the services in the course of time, and that there is a net surplus from the current return.   That, on the one hand, the value of the bearer of the use, and, on the other, its net return, are represented by such figures that the former may be held equivalent to a money capital yielding, at the current rate of interest, exactly the same net return, is a coincidence which I have already explained.[1]   And, in virtue of this coincidence, it is, finally, as intelligible as it is justifiable that, in practical economic life which finds and adopts, as facts ready to its hand, the things which we try to explain, the net return of goods should be taken as foundation for acts of valuation.   It is an abbreviated method which, practically, is quite appropriate, although it turns the relation of cause and effect exactly the other way.[2]

[1] See above, p. 343.

[2] In Menger's most valuable contribution *Zur Theorie des Kapitales* (Conrad's *Jahrbücher*, vol. xvii. p. 47), which appeared while this was passing through the press, the author likewise has urged against the Use theory that, in its conception of capitalisation, it has not solved its problems, but only gone round about them.

CHAPTER VIII

INTEREST FROM DURABLE GOODS—(*continued*)

To proceed. The phenomenon of interest just explained is characteristic of *all* durable goods, consumption and production goods alike. But, in the case of production goods, there comes in one circumstance the influence of which has to be investigated. In goods which are to serve as instruments of production, not only are the future services remote from the present, but both the present and the future services are remote from that economical goal which is first to be reached through production. The final destination from which, according to principles with which we are now familiar, they derive their value, is the product obtainable from them[1] in the future. But from the attainment of this goal the current service—even that service in the very act of realisation—is distant by the whole production period which must intervene between its incorporation in the process and the turning out of the finished product. If this period, for instance, amounts to two years, the current service is two years away from attaining its goal, and at the same time from attaining its full present value : the next year's service is three years away, the next again four years, and so on ; while, in the case of durable consumption goods, every service attains its full present value in the year, or in the moment it is rendered. Now this has a twofold result : first, the services of productive goods undergo a greater reduction as compared with their full final value, and, second, the growth of their value lasts longer on that account. After they are produced and set to work, they bear interest during the whole

[1] After deducting the share of the co-operating complementary factors.

period of the production process on which they enter ; only, in practice, this interest is ascribed, not to the durable good that forms an integral part of the " outlay "—from which, indeed, it is now separated—but to the " business " or " circulating" capital into which it is transferred at the moment of its separation.

To illustrate this. A durable consumption good which lasts six years, and yields at the end of each year a use [1] of 100, is worth, as we have seen, $95.23 + 90.70 + 86.38 + 82.27 + 78.35 + 74.62 = 507.55$.[2] A durable productive good, on the other hand, which lasts six years, and whose year's use affords a final utility of 100 *after* a further production period of two years, has the following value. Its " current " year's use, which is first obtained by the end of the year, and then brings in the amount of 100 after two years more (that is, after three years in all), is only worth in present valuation 86.38. Its next year's use, which will bring 100 in four years, is to-day worth 82.27. Similarly the third year's use has a present value of 78.35, the fourth year's, a value of 74.62, the fifth, a value of 71.06, and, finally, the sixth has a value of 67.68. The whole productive good, accordingly, has a value of 460.36.

At the end of the first year's use the first service is detached ; this, meanwhile, has come nearer to its final goal by a year, and accordingly advances in value from 86.38 to 90.70 ; the other services follow suit in the usual way. Thus the good, as still bearer of five prospective services of the individual values of $86.38 + 82.27 + 78.35 + 74.62 + 71.06$, is now worth in all 392.68. It has therefore lost 67.68 in the course of the year's use, and, as against the return of 90.70 represented by the service detached, has borne 23.02 of interest—exactly 5% on the initial value of 460.36. So

---

[1] Here I must assume that the utility is not obtained in advance, but at the expiry of the particular period, because, in the case of durable productive goods employed in a personal undertaking—with which the comparison is to be made—there is, in the nature of things, no anticipative use. The utility, *e.g.*, which an agricultural implement affords in farming, cannot possibly be obtained on 1st January, for the whole year in advance : obviously it can be realised only at the end of the year, in the harvest.

[2] P. 343, note 1. At a different interest rate, of course, the figures would be different.

far everything runs as before. But the service which was
separated off, with the value of 90·70, neither remains in its
former shape nor retains its former value. It is detached
from the fixed capital, and has passed over into the circulating
capital, where it remains incorporated in some or other of
the intermediate products, say, in the yarn spun by the
machines. In this new shape it is the object of the further
production process, and is by it brought step by step nearer
to full maturity, and so to its future value of 100. This
it attains in the following—the second—year of use.

At the end of the second year's use again, the service,
which is now the current one, is detached from the parent
good with a value of 90·70 : the parent good, now valued at
321·62, has lost 71·06, and, as against the return of 90·70,
has borne 19·64 as interest. But during this same year, the
service detached in the previous year and incorporated in the
circulating capital, has risen from 90·70 to 95·23 in value,
and bears another 4·53 of interest. And, again, in the same
way at the end of the third year of use, a service of the then
value of 90·70 is detached, by which the parent good loses
74·62 in value, and interest gains 16·08. But since
simultaneously the service detached two years before, and
incorporated in the circulating capital, increases from 95·23
to its full value of 100, and that detached one year before,
from 90·70 to 95·23, there is a further gain in interest of
4·77 + 4·53 ; that is, of 9·30.

In this way the peculiar combination of circumstances in
durable productive goods gives occasion to a twofold interest
relation. The services already detached bear interest after
the manner, and as integral part, of the circulating capital ;
that is, their claim or title to interest is based on their transformation into finished and final product. The services still
contained in the good bear interest after the manner of
durable consumption goods ; that is, their claim is based
simply on their approximation to the present. But, of these
two elements of the interest return, only the second is formally
ascribed to the parent good from which it springs : for it the
calculation is concluded at the moment in which the individual
service is detached, and with the value which it then has.
What further happens with it is ascribed to the circulating

capital into wnich it passes at the moment of its separation.[1]
And thus we come to the final result: All interest borne by
durable productive goods is borne by them simply in their
character of *durable* goods, while their second property, that
of being productive, only comes into play in the interest borne
by the services already detached and transferred to circulating capital. In this lies the complete explanation of a
developed interest phenomenon, which I before suggested but
had to delay going fully into until now.[2]

There is still, however, another highly important explanation we may gather in passing.

In goods capable of only a moderate number of services
the contraction of value, even in the case of the last services,
is but small. The result of this is, on the one hand, that the
value of the parent good is only a little behind the gradually
developing value of its collective services—in our first example
the value of the machine lasting six years was not quite 600,
but still it was over 500; and, on the other hand, that the
amount of wear and tear, even in the first year,[3] is relatively
high, and almost equal to the entire value of the current
service—in our illustration the value of the current service
was 100, the value of the last service, that which decides the
wear and tear, about 78.

In goods, again, capable of a very long series of services,
both the value of the parent good and the amount of wear
and tear fall proportionately. A good capable of rendering
services of the annual value of 100 for 100 years, is very far
from being valued at $100 \times 100 = 10,000$. At most (where
the usual under-valuation of future goods is at the rate of

---

[1] This is most clearly shown when the intermediate product made by the
assistance of the durable good—*e.g.* the cotton yarn spun by a machine—is
immediately sold to another undertaker by whom the process is completed, and
the yarn made into thread or cloth. All increment of value which the intermediate product, the yarn, thus obtains, is now naturally put to the account of
this particular intermediate product (or the money capital for which it is sold)
and not to that of the parent durable good.

[2] See above, p. 305.

[3] In the later years the "wear and tear" increases progressively, because the
last service, which is not replaceable by any one coming after it, gets always
nearer to the present, and becomes, therefore, always higher in value. See above,
particularly the table on p. 346, note 1.

5%) it is worth 2000; and the loss of value in the course of the first year's use—although a service worth 100 has been consumed and detached from the use-content of the good— is, not 100 but 76, that and no more being the present value (at a discount rate of 5% per annum) of a sum of 100 falling due in 100 years![1]

Finally, if a good is capable of rendering not only a great many, but, practically, an infinite number of services, the phenomenon just mentioned is seen in full development: the present value of the parent good is infinitely less than the successively increasing value of its services. A piece of land, for instance, which bears £100 each year for an infinite series of years, is worth, not 100 times infinity, not £100,000, not even £10,000, but only some £2000, and its loss of value sinks to zero: the piece of land whose annual current service is worth £100, yields the *whole* £100 net. The law remains just as before; but the very remote services of the second, third, tenth century, have so exceedingly small a value in the present that they can add almost nothing to the present value of the land, and the last service, the one which should decide the amount of depreciation, as infinitely far away, has no present value at all.

This is the ultimate reason why rent of land appears as a net income, and here first is the solution of the problem of rent traced to its real issue. The old rent theory gave only a preliminary and partial answer, and, strangely enough, had not the slightest suspicion that its tentative solutions had never come near the heart of the problem. All preceding attempts, from Ricardo downwards, exhausted themselves in more or less successfully pointing out that the annual uses of land have an economic value, or yield an economic return, and why they do so. But the yield of such services is in itself, first of all, a gross return. That the owner gets a net return, a net income, has nothing to do with fruitfulness, situation, kind of ground, or any such thing, but simply with the lower value put upon future goods, and the determination of the present value of the land in conformity with that. Suppose that a quarry, after deduction of all other recognised costs, produced for a hundred years a—what we

---

[1] Spitzer's *Tables*, p. 121.

may call—net annual return of £100 ; and suppose that future services were *not* less valued than present; the value of the quarry would be the full amount, 100 × 100. The quarry-owner would draw an annual income of £100, but not a shilling of that would be "rent" in the present sense of that term, that is to say, a net income. The whole of it would be a protracted consumption of the parent wealth of £10,000. And the case of all other lands is different from that of the quarry, not in kind, but only in degree. If a field is considered capable of producing crop for 1000 years—or 2000 years if one should prefer it, for literal infinity in human affairs is out of court—and if the future crops are to be valued as highly as the present ones, the valuation put upon such a field will reach an exorbitant height, viz. £100,000 or £200,000, and the yearly rent of £100 will present the character of a breaking-off of the parent stem of wealth —a very gradual destruction of the stem, but still a destruction, not a net income. Landowners would be lords of a giant stem or stock of wealth, but they would have no net income.

The theoretical explanation of rent from land, then, coincides ultimately with the explanation of interest obtained from durable concrete capital, and land rent is nothing but a special case of interest obtained from durable goods. That the two explanations do not entirely coincide, and that, on the contrary, the current rent theories are substantially so very different from the interest theories, is only traceable to the fact that, in the course of the explanation of rent, an intercalation had to be made which did not require to be made in the case of interest on durable capital ; and that, at the same time, from a faulty conception of the rent problem, economists exhausted the whole content of the rent theories in making this special intercalation. In the case of all products of labour, and, consequently, in all goods that constitute capital, it needs no explanation that they and their material services have economic value : were it not so they would not be produced. In the case of the services of land, on the other hand, this is not self-evident. And, therefore, the economist must first exert himself to show why and under what circumstances the use of land receives a value and a

price.   With a correct value theory, a few strokes of a pen
will supply this proof;—by means of the doctrines of marginal
utility and of complementary goods.   Wanting the guidance
of such a theory, and entangled in the fetters of the labour
value theory, economists gave it a shape which was unnecessarily circumstantial and clumsy, and was, at the same
time, not very satisfactory in principle.   Of Ricardo's rent
theory, which in essence has remained the ruling one up till
the present day—the theories of his opponents Carey and
Rodbertus being quite exploded—it must be said that it
contains an abundance of truth put in a formula essentially
false.   It is a brilliant piece of casuistry, which is out of
connection with the central fire of correct principles; it
lights up a bit of the road, but leaves the rest in obscurity
and error.   Hence the peculiar fate of the Ricardian theory.
It does not quite satisfy anybody.   Even its friends are fain to
discover a number of weak points in it, and its most universal
propositions are, for the most part, its weakest.   But there
remains in it an indestructible core of truth, which lives on
under the most varied metamorphoses, and, even to-day, constitutes the better part of its substance.[1]

But how far does the Ricardian, or any other rent theory,
take us, even if it were correct in every point where it is
disputable ?   It takes us no further than we get in the question
of interest, when it has been shown that a threshing-machine,
after deducting all other costs, yields an annual *gross* interest,
and why it does so.   Where Ricardo ends his rent theory,
there in truth ends the intercalation, which, because of its
obviousness, did not require to be made in the case of movable capital.   But it is just then that the chief question of
the problem suggests itself: why there is a net interest
within that gross interest which is yielded by the year's
use or service of the threshing-machine or the field, after
deduction of all other costs.   And to this question—which
the rent theory up till now has entirely omitted to put—
no answer can be given, either as regards the field or the

---

[1] On the relation of Ricardo's rent theory to the modern value theory, see
Dr. James Bonar's suggestive remarks in an article entitled "The Austrian
economists and their view of value" in the *Quarterly Journal of Economics*,
October 1888.

machine, but to point to the under-valuation of future goods and future services.[1]

[1] Manifestly the fact that Rent of Land and Rent of Capital have one common final cause is not a sufficient reason for abolishing every distinction between them.   Between land and capital there are so many important differences, both theoretical and practical, that, notwithstanding the common feature just described, we are justified in adhering to the decision made in a former chapter to keep land out of the conception of capital.—Quite lately Carl Menger, in Conrad's *Jahrbücher*, vol. xvii. p. 48, has ably put forward the necessity of a comprehensive "universal theory of the return to wealth." I trust that, in the contents of the present chapter, he will see an earnest attempt to develop such a theory.

CHAPTER IX

WE have traced all kinds and methods of acquiring interest to one identical source—the increasing value of future goods as they ripen into present goods. Thus it is with the profit of the undertakers, who transform labour—the future good which they purchase—into products for consumption. Thus it is with landlords, property-owners, and owners of durable goods generally, who allow the later services of the goods they possess to gradually mature, and pluck them when they have ripened into full value. Thus, finally, it is with the loan. Even here it is not the case, as one might easily think at first sight, that the enrichment of the capitalist comes from the creditor receiving more articles than he gives—for at first, indeed, the articles concerned are less in value—but from the fact that the loaned objects, at first lower in value, gradually increase in value, and on the moment of fruition enter into their complete higher present value.

What, then, are the capitalists as regards the community? —In a word, they are merchants who have present goods to sell. They are the fortunate possessors of a stock of goods which they do not require for the personal needs of the moment. They exchange this stock, therefore, into future goods of some form or another, and allow these to ripen in their hands again into present goods possessing full value. Many capitalists make this exchange once for all. One who builds a house with his capital, or buys a piece of land, or acquires a bond, or gives a loan at interest for fifty years, exchanges his present goods, wholly or in part, for goods or services which belong to a remote period of time, and consequently creates, as it were at a blow, the opportunity or condition of a permanent increment of value, and an income called interest which will last over this long period. One, again, who discounts a three months' bill, or enters on a one year's production, must frequently repeat the exchange. In three months or in one year the future goods thus acquired become full-valued present goods. With these present goods the business begins over again; new bills are bought, new raw material, new labour; these in their turn ripen into present goods, and so on again and again.

In the circumstances, then, it is very easily explained why capital bears an "everlasting" interest. We may dismiss any idea of an inexhaustible "productive power" in capital, assuring it eternal fruitfulness,—any idea of an eternal "Use" given off, year out year in, to the end of time by a good perhaps long perished.[1] It is because the stock of present goods is always too low that the conjuncture for their exchange against future goods is always favourable. And it is because time always stretches forward that the prudently purchased future commodity steadily becomes a present commodity, grows accordingly into the full value of the present, and permits its owner again and again to utilise the always favourable conjuncture.

I do not see that there is anything objectionable in this. For natural reasons, present goods are certainly more valuable

---

[1] The incorrectness of a theory is shown in its not being able to give a satisfactory solution for all given cases. I have already had frequent occasion to point to cases which could not be satisfactorily explained by means of the—to my mind—incorrect "Use theory" (see above, pp. 297, 347). Here I have to add another instance;—the buying of a perpetual interest, *e.g.* Consols, where the original debt can neither be called up nor paid back. In these annual payments the Use theory would see the price for a "use of capital" perpetually transferred. But what has happened with the capital stock? It has of course been transferred. But it is not simply lent, for it will never be paid back. Nor, in the view of the Use theorists, can it be transferred against payment, for the annual interest is the price of the "use," and there is nothing paid beyond that. Nor, finally, is it transferred without payment,—presented as a gift: the rentiers, the representatives of those who made the loan, have no intention of making any such present, and the government which received the loan certainly does not feel that it has received a gift.—Now what the Use theory could not explain, or explained only in a most artificial way, is explained perfectly simply by our theory: it is just an exchange of present goods (the original capital) against a series of future sums of goods (the annual interest payments).

commodities than future goods. If the owner of the more valuable commodity exchange it for a greater quantity of the less valuable, there is nothing more objectionable in this than that the owner of wheat should exchange a peck of wheat for more than a peck of oats or barley, or that a holder of gold should exchange a pound of gold for more than a pound of iron or copper. For the owner not to realise the higher value of his commodity would be an act of unselfishness and charity which could not possibly be translated into a general duty, and as a fact would not be so translated in regard to any other commodity.

In the essence of interest, then, there is nothing which should make it appear in itself unreasonable or unjust. But the essence of an institution is one thing, and the circumstances which may accidentally accompany it in its practical working out are another. That the community has a power of choosing representatives is good; but if at every election there are broken heads, and pot-house agitation and brute force instead of patriotic deliberation decide the majority, it is not good. And, like every other human institution, interest is exposed to the danger of exaggeration, degeneration, abuse; and, perhaps, to a greater extent than most institutions.

It is undeniable that, in this exchange of present commodities against future, the circumstances are of such a nature as to threaten the poor with exploitation of monopolists. Present goods are absolutely needed by everybody if people are to live. He who has not got them must try to obtain them at any price. To produce them on his own account is proscribed the poor man by circumstances; the only kind of production he could take up would be one yielding an immediate return, and this is not only unremunerative but almost impracticable under modern economic conditions. He must, then, buy his present goods from those who have them, either in the form of a loan, or, more usually, by selling his labour. But in this bargain he is doubly handicapped; first, by the position of compulsion under which he finds himself, and, second, by the numerical relation existing between buyers and sellers of present goods. The capitalists who have present goods for sale are relatively few; the proletarians who must buy them are innumerable. In the market for present goods, then, a majority of buyers, who find themselves compelled to buy, stands opposite a minority of sellers, and this is a relation which obviously is profoundly favourable to the sellers and unfavourable to the buyers.

Now, of course, the circumstances unfavourable to buyers may be corrected by active competition among sellers. The fewer the sellers, the greater are the amounts of present goods they have to dispose of. To find purchasers for them all, competition must bring down the price from extreme heights to a moderate level that leaves no room for exploitation of poor men.[1] Fortunately, in actual life this is the rule, not the exception. But, every now and then, something will suspend the capitalists' competition, and then those unfortunates, whom fate has thrown on a local market ruled by monopoly, are delivered over to the discretion of the adversary. Hence direct usury, of which the poor borrower is only too often the victim ; and hence the low wages forcibly exploited from the workers—sometimes the workers of individual factories, sometimes of individual branches of production, sometimes—though happily not often, and only under peculiarly unfavourable circumstances—of whole nations.

It is not my business to put excesses like these, where there actually is exploitation, under the aegis of that favourable opinion I pronounced above as to the essence of interest. But, on the other hand, I must say with all emphasis, that what we might stigmatise as " usury " does not consist in the obtaining of a gain out of the loan, or out of the buying of labour, but in the immoderate extent of that gain. If exchanges are to take place between present and future commodities, the existence of some gain is an entirely normal phenomenon ; is, indeed, an economic necessity. Some gain or profit on capital there would be if there were no compulsion on the poor, and no monopolising of property ; and some gain there must be. It is only the height of this gain where, in particular cases, it reaches an excess, that is open to criticism, and, of course, the very unequal conditions of wealth in our modern communities bring us unpleasantly near the danger of exploitation and of usurious rates of interest.

As little, again, will the unbiassed spectator deny that, in

[1] See below on the Rate of Interest.

the circumstances accompanying the receipt of interest, it is frequently the case that one's sense of fairness is offended by the contrast between gain and desert. Where capital has once been obtained by personal exertion and ability no one would grudge its owner the further profit he makes, without exertion, by exchanging his hard-won present goods into future goods. But often it is just the greatest fortune that falls into the lap of its owner without any personal desert on his part, simply by the happy chance of a legal enactment giving him the preference, and in this case also the lucrative exchange, of present goods for future goods which steadily ripen into more valuable present goods, is made without exertion and without personal deserving. In all other branches of exchange clever speculation is needed, timely seizing of opportunities, favourable conjunctures, if a gain is to be made by the exchange. But the merchant of present goods finds the conjuncture always favourable. He need only put out his hand to dispose of his goods, with a profit, to any one among the thousands of eager buyers, while, by his side, the poor labourer drags out a painful existence of heavy toil, at a sacrifice of personal strength and personal happiness.

But what is the conclusion from all this? Surely that, owing to accessory circumstances, interest *may* be associated with a usurious exploitation and with bad social conditions ; not that, in its innermost essence, it is rotten. And the logical conclusion is that the axe should be laid to the decayed branches, and not to the sound stem,—just as it would be foolish to take away the right of self-representation instead of simply putting down the riots at election time. But what if these abuses are so inseparably connected with interest that they cannot be eradicated, or cannot be quite eradicated? Even then it is by no means certain that the institution should be abolished. Arrangements absolutely free from drawback are never allotted to us in human affairs. Instead of the absolute good, which is beyond reach, we must choose what, on the whole, is the relative best, where the balance, between attainable advantage and the drawbacks that must be taken into the bargain, is the most favourable possible for us. Living in a great city has certainly many disadvantages ; so has living in a small city ; and so has living in the country.

But we must live somewhere, and so we make our choice of the place where, after wise consideration of all the circumstances, the unavoidable evils seem to be most outweighed by the advantages. And in the same way, before we abolish interest as such, we must first draw out a balance-sheet to show whether human wellbeing is better promoted in a society which permits gain from capital and recognises it, or in one which permits only income from labour.

In making this calculation it will not be overlooked that the institution of interest has its manifold uses; particularly as the prospect of interest induces saving and accumulation of capital, and thus, by making possible the adoption of more fruitful methods of production, becomes the cause of a more abundant provision for the whole people. In this connection the much-used and much-abused expression, "Reward of Abstinence," is in its proper place. The existence of interest cannot be theoretically *explained* by it: one cannot hope in using it to say anything about the essential nature of interest : every one knows how much interest is simply pocketed without any "abstinence" that deserves reward.[1] But, just as interest sometimes has its injurious accompaniments, so in its train it brings others, fortunately, that are beneficent and useful ; and to these it is due that interest, which has its origin in quite different causes, acts, among other things, as a wage and as an inducement to save. I know very well that private saving is not the only possible way to the accumulation of capital, and that, even in the Socialist state, capital may be accumulated and added to.[2] But the fact remains that private accumulation of capital is a proved fact, while socialist accumulation is not ;—and there are, besides, some very serious *a priori* doubts whether it can be.

Still it is neither my purpose nor my duty to inquire what organisation of society on the whole is best,—the present

---

[1] I gladly embrace this opportunity to repair an omission in my *Capital and Interest*. At the time when I published that work I unfortunately had not made the acquaintance of Loria's *La Rendita Fondiaria* (Mailand, 1880). It contains (pp. 610-624) an unusually spirited and subtle variation of the Abstinence theory, of which I can only say that, if the Abstinence theory were tenable—which, of course, I do not believe it to be—Loria's setting of it would be the first to gain recognition.

[2] See above, p. 114.

or the Socialist. I have only here to answer what comes up for answer in an inquiry as to the nature and origin of interest. And the answer here runs: There is no inherent blot in the essential nature of interest. Those, then, who demand its abolition may base their demand on certain considerations of expediency, but not, as the Socialists do at present, on the assertion that this kind of income is essentially unjustifiable.

Is the abolition of interest, then, possible? It may, I think, not be unprofitable to many of my readers to follow the fate of interest in the Socialist state.

CHAPTER X

INTEREST UNDER SOCIALISM

LET us imagine the Socialist state perfectly realised; all private property in land and capital abolished; all instruments of production vested in the hands of the community; all citizens working as labourers in the service of the commonweal; and the national product distributed to all according to work done. How is it now with the action of those causes which produced interest under the individualist economy?

First of all, it must be made clear that the causes are still there. There is always a natural difference of value between present and future goods; and since under Socialism time does not stand still, future goods gradually become present ones, and bring a surplus value with them. The difference of value between present goods and future, I say, is always there. For its peculiar causes continue to exist;—the difference between the circumstances of provision in present and future, the partial underestimate of the future which is characteristic of man the uncertainty and shortness of life. In the Socialist state no one will be allowed to be an undertaker on his own account, and, of course, the consideration of the greater technical productiveness of present goods employed as productive instruments ceases to be a motive for individuals: all the more strongly does this motive obtain as regards the great economic commonwealth which now conducts and guides the total national production.

Thus, even for the Socialist state, it is absolutely inconceivable that economic subjects, whether as individuals or as the powerful economic commonweal, should, in their economic judgment and their economic practice, treat present and future goods as on the same footing. How, for instance, could it be all the same to the Socialist worker whether he received his hard-earned wage by instalments of £1 a week, or in £52 at the end of a year, or in the shape, perhaps, of £52 five or ten or fifty years later? Or how is it conceivable that, under Socialism, a young oak sapling which will be an oak tree, with the value of an oak tree, in two hundred years, can be made equal in value to an oak full-grown now? The central authority directing the national production must base its entire arrangements and dispositions on a calculation of present and future goods having different values, if its dispositions are not to be quite inept and monstrous. If it do not put a less value on future goods it must find that a process which promises a greater number of products in the far future is more remunerative than a process which yields a small number in the present or near future, and it must, accordingly, always turn its productive powers to remote productive ends, however remote they are, as being, technically, the most fruitful. The natural consequence would be very much as we have already pictured it [1] —misery and want in the present : and those in charge of the national economy would have no more pressing duty than to overturn this inept disposition, give the less amount of present goods the preference over the greater amount of future ones, and so prove that the difference in value between present goods and future is an elementary economic phenomenon independent of any human arrangements.

If it is now clear that, even in the Socialist state, present goods will, universally, be valued more highly, it goes without saying that, if there is an exchange between the two, it cannot be effected at par. Exactly as under the present economic organisation, present goods, as more valuable, will claim and will receive an agio. The emergence of this agio—and with it the emergence of interest in its most legitimate form— could only be repressed if every opportunity for it were repressed ; in other words, if the exchange or barter of present goods for future were removed out of the world altogether.

Now, of course, this would be attempted to a considerable extent in the Socialist state. All private ownership in the

----
[1] See above, p. 335.

means of production being banished, all production on private account would be banished also, and all opportunity of buying the future commodities, Labour, Uses of Land, and Capital, would be taken away from private individuals. Since, then, in any case the loan at interest would also be forbidden, the two chief springs, from which interest flows to private persons in the present day, would be happily stopped up. But certain opportunities would still remain open if exchange transactions between individuals were not entirely forbidden. Suppose, for instance, that free exchange were allowed in durable goods, agio and interest would immediately slip in, as it were, by a back door. Say that a good lasts one hundred years, and that its (present) year's service is worth £100, £10,000 must be the price of the good if the hundredth year's service—rendered perhaps to some grandchild or great-grandchild—is to be paid full £100. No man would be willing to pay this price. But the moment that the purchase price is calculated at less than £10,000, the owner receives, in course of time, an income greater than the purchase price, and harvests the excess as true interest.

But much more important than any such sporadic obtaining of interest by private individuals is the fact that, in the Socialist state, the commonwealth itself, as against the citizens, would make use of the principle of interest which to-day it reviles as " exploitation " and deduction from the product of labour. The Socialist state, as possessing all means of production, gets all the citizens to work in its factories, and pays them a wage. It conducts, therefore, on the largest scale the buying—forbidden to private individuals—of the future good Labour. Now, on technical grounds, various portions of the labour it buys it necessarily sets to work simultaneously towards various productive ends widely removed in point of time. One group of labourers, for instance, it sets to baking ; another it sets to sink mining shafts, which, perhaps, assist in turning out consumption goods only twenty years later ; another it sets to replant a forest. The labour directed to distant ends, for reasons with which we are now familiar, obtains a greater technical product, and that product when ripe will possess also a greater value. While, for instance, the product that a baker turns out in a day is worth, perhaps, 4s., a labourer engaged in forestry may plant one hundred oak saplings in a day, and these saplings, without added labour, may mature in a hundred years' time to strong oak trees worth 20s. apiece.

Now how much can and should the Socialist state pay as wage to those workers whose labour it directs to these far-away but productive ends?   Will it pay the foresters the whole value of their future product, say, £100 a day ?—Impossible. That would be a glaring injustice to the workers of other departments.   If the entrance to individual branches of employment were left free to all comers, everybody would be a forester and nobody would bake bread ; the country would relapse to primeval forest ; and the present, with its pressing needs, would remain unprovided for.[1]   If, on the other hand, the entrance was not free, and a very favoured minority were to be paid £100 a day, while the others received 4s. or 6s., a plutology would emerge again *in optima forma* ; only that it would not be based, as now on property, but, more fatally, on favour and protection !

But if foresters are paid exactly like bakers at 4s. per day, they are exploited just as they are by the capitalist undertakers under the present system.   In buying the future commodity, labour, an agio is put on present goods, and the labourer, instead of his future product of £100, is put off with a present wage of 4s., which represents the present value of the planted saplings.   But the surplus value which these saplings take on as they grow into oak trees ready for cutting, the Socialist commonwealth puts into its pocket as real interest.   Perhaps, —probably, it is to be hoped,—not to keep it in its pocket, but to employ it in a general bettering of the wages of its workers.   But any such supplementary common purse distribution of the interest thus pocketed does not make any difference in the fact that interest, as interest, has been received. In this the Socialist state only acts like a capitalist in the present day, who accumulates a fortune from his surplus values,

---

[1] It may, perhaps, be pointed out in reply that, owing to the increasing supply of wood, its value would be pressed down, and so, by and by, forestry would become only as remunerative as baking and such like.   I would, however, suggest that this result would only be reached when the value of hundred-year-old timber had come down to a halfpenny ; and to press down the value of wood so low, in the midst of a dense population, an enormous portion of the country would require to be turned into forest again !

and then disposes of it for purposes of the general good. A wage earned can be disposed of egoistically or altruistically, and interest received can be disposed of egoistically or altruistically, but it would be as rash to assert that a wage becomes an interest by being egoistically spent, as to assert that an interest changes its nature, and turns into wage, when it is altruistically spent !

It is, too, well worthy of remark that an equal distribution of the interest obtained by the Socialist state does not establish the same economic conditions as if the interest had not been taken at all. In this distribution it is not the persons to whose labour and product the interest was due that get the interest, but entirely different people. The forester has an amount of £99 : 16s. deducted from the value of his future product as interest. If, now, through the distribution of all the interests thus obtained, the average day's wage is raised from 4s. to 6s. per day, the forester gets a couple of shillings returned him of the £99 : 16s. taken from him; the remaining £99 : 14s. other people get, and get, indeed, just as at present, not by the title of wage, but by the title of property,—or rather of joint-property. The people who are employed in immediately remunerative production, such as baking, and create a day's product of 4s., could, as *labourers*, ask and receive a wage of only 4s. The other 2s. they receive only because they are at the same time joint owners in the national wealth, and because the Socialist state, which administers the common national wealth, as proprietor of this wealth, brings its entire right of property to bear on those workers whose labours are directed to more remote productive ends. In the Socialist state, therefore, exactly as in a capitalist society, interest is deserved by the proprietor of present goods as against those labourers who create only a · future product by their labour. The only difference is that in the capitalist society property is unequally divided, and interest falls to a few proprietors in great amounts, while in the Socialist society all are joint owners to an equal amount, and all obtain an equally small quota of the total interest.

In the above analyses I have taken my illustration from forestry because it illustrates the circumstances in question in the most striking and unambiguous way. In the most striking way, because the difference of time between the forth-putting of labour and the receiving of the mature product, and, with it, the difference in value between labour and future product, is at its maximum : in the most unambiguous way, because here no additional labour of any sort is necessary, and, consequently, the calculation of the final product produced by a definite expenditure of labour is quite simple. But it surely needs no further demonstration that exactly the same relations occur, in more or less weakened degree, in the case of all labour which is directed to more remote goals of production. They are all technically more productive than those which yield their results on the moment. Their abundant future product, too, must always have a greater future value, because it could not, economically, have been produced at all if already its present value, reduced by perspective, were not equal to the otherwise normal value of a similar amount of labour.[1]   Since, finally, the wage for similar and similarly valuable labour cannot be assessed at different levels according as the Socialist state directs its labour to a near or a remote goal of production, the wage of those labourers who are put to more remote tasks must, necessarily, be measured *under* the full value of their future product,[2] and this secures that, to a greater or less extent, there appears a surplus gain for the community which is the owner of the present goods.[3]

Nor does it require any demonstration that the phenomenon of interest must emerge to a still greater degree if the Socialist

---

[1] See above, p. 310.

[2] The levelling up of wages—that is, up to the value of the future product of the most remuneratively employed labour—is, of course, impossible, because the national product would not suffice for that.

[3] I may remark in passing that the same position holds in the case of land rent. It is obvious that, even in the Socialist state, a labourer working on a peculiarly fruitful piece of land, *e.g.* in a Rüdesheim vineyard, will produce a greater or more valuable product than one who puts forth the same exertion and skill on a common piece of land or vineyard. But it is as evident that it would be insufferable "protection" to allow the former labourers their entire greater product as wage. To avoid injustice the wage here must be levelled down ; that is to say, of the product of the more fruitful lands, the "land rent" must be first of all retained for the common purse, to be divided afterwards to all the citizens in their capacity as joint owners of the national land. Land rent, therefore, even in the Socialist state, would exist, would come into operation as against the labourers cultivating superior land, and would only be divided according to another plan than now, on account of the equal share of all in the nationalised land.

society be organised, not as one united community, but as a system of independent economic groups.[1] For in this case, at every exchange between mature and immature commodities, each group would appropriate surplus value, not only as against its own workers employed to remote productive ends, but, in a much greater degree, as against the other groups, and would divide out this surplus value to the shareholders of the wealth belonging to the group, as dividend.

Thus we come to a very remarkable and noteworthy result. Interest, which to-day the Socialists abuse as a gain got by exploitation, a robbery from the products of labour, would not disappear even in the Socialist state, but would remain, in promise and potency, as between the community organised under Socialism and its labourers, and must so remain. The new organisation of society may make some change in the persons who receive it, and in the shares into which it is divided, by altering the relations of ownership; but the fact that the owners of present commodities, in exchanging them for future commodities, obtain an agio, it neither will nor can alter. And here, again, it is shown that interest is not an accidental " historico-legal " category, which makes its appearance only in our individualist and capitalist society, and will vanish with it ; but an *economic* category, which springs from elementary economic causes, and therefore, without distinction of social organisation and legislation, makes its appearance wherever there is an exchange between present and future goods. Indeed, even the lonely economy of a Crusoe would not be without the basis of the interest phenomenon, the increasing value of goods and services preparing for the service of the future ; only, of course, that, in the absence of exchange transactions, there would be wanting the chief occasion to put exact figures on the value of goods, and therewith almost the only opportunity of calling attention and giving fixity to the phenomenon.

[1] On these forms of organisation see Anton Menger, *Das Recht auf den vollen Arbeitsertrag*, Stuttgart, 1888, pp. 104, 112.

BOOK VII

THE RATE OF INTEREST

CHAPTER I

THE RATE IN ISOLATED EXCHANGE

THE exchange of present goods for future, in which interest has its origin, is only a special case of the exchange of goods in general. It goes, then, without saying that the formation of price in this case is subject to the same laws as govern the formation of price in economical exchange generally. The question whether present goods in general obtain an agio, and also the further question of the height of that agio, are both to be answered according to the rules laid down in Book IV. as regards prices of goods in general. What remains for us here is only to amplify and vivify the colourless scheme which demonstrated that the current price of goods is the resultant of subjective valuations coming together in a market, by pointing out those concrete circumstances which in this case—the exchange of present against future commodities—influence the mutual valuation of both.

As before, it is advisable to distinguish between isolated exchange and competitive exchange.

In the exchange which takes place between an owner of a present commodity and a suitor for it, the price, according to the formula laid down on p. 199, will be fixed somewhere between the value of the present good to its owner as under limit, and its value to the suitor as upper limit. If, for instance, £100 present money are worth to their owner exactly as much as £100 of next year's money,[1] while to the suitor they are worth, on subjective grounds (say, on account of

---

[1] An assumption which, for the reasons shown on p. 315, holds very widely ; —that is to say, among all persons who own more wealth than they can or will spend in their own productive equipment.

temporarily pressing circumstances), as much as £200 of next year's money, the price of £100 present money will be fixed somewhere between £100 and £200 of next year's money, and the agio at something between nothing and 100%. The precise figure that is fixed, in the individual case, within these wide limits, depends on the skill and "staying power" displayed by both parties in conducting the negotiations. As a rule, the owner of present goods will be in a position of advantage, because he can do without the exchange and yet suffer no loss, while the suitor is often driven to pay any price for present goods. Hence the familiar cases where, in the absence of competition, usuriously high rates of 50%, 100%, even 200% and 300%, are extorted.

When we go farther, and inquire as to the deeper reasons which affect the subjective valuation of the suitors,[1] and thus affect the economic upper limit of the agio, we find them a little different in the case of the consumption loan from what they are in the production loan, to which latter the buying of labour is closely allied.

In the case of the consumption loan the determinants are; —the urgency of want at the time, the probable provision at the time when the loan is to be paid back, and, finally, the degree of the suitor's underestimate of the future. The more urgently he requires the loan, the more easily he expects to be able to replace it;[2] and the less he takes thought for the morrow, the higher the agio to which he will, in the worst case, consent and *vice versâ*.

In the production loan we find different concrete determinants. Here the important thing is the difference in productiveness between the methods open to him who gets the loan, and those open to him who has to do without it. To recur to our old illustration. If the fisher, who has no capital, and can catch only 3 fish a day by hand, gets a loan of 90 fish, and is thus put in a position to make a boat and net in the course of a month, and with these to catch 30 fish

---

[1] As regards the sellers of present goods, for simplicity's sake, we shall adhere throughout the argument to the assumption that their personal circumstances are such that they value present and future commodities alike.

[2] We may take the case, *e.g.*, of a youth standing on the brink of manhood, kept very short of cash at the moment by his tutor, but with the prospect of a great fortune coming into his absolute disposal in a few months.

a day for the remaining eleven months, the balance stands as follows :—without the loan he catches in a year $3 \times 365 =$ 1095 fish ; with the loan he catches nothing in the first month, but 30 per day for the other eleven months, that is, $335 \times 30 = 10,050$, or a surplus of 8955 fish. So long, then, as he has to give anything less than 8955 (next year's) fish for the borrowed 90 (present) fish, he gains by the transaction.

In this illustration the difference in possible return between the two productive methods, and, with it, the upper limit of the economically possible agio, is absurdly high—8955 next year's units for 90 present units is something like $10,000\%$. But there will always be a very important difference when the choice lies between capitalist production and hand-to-mouth production, as the latter is, of course, always extremely un-remunerative. The difference, again, will tend to grow less when the choice lies between two different capitalist methods ; and will become more rapidly less in proportion to the length of the process already secured without the loan. This fact is of very great importance as regards the, rate of interest, not only in isolated, but also in competitive exchange. If we put it in the clearest possible way now, it will give a good basis for what comes later.

In an earlier chapter I called attention to the well-attested fact that the lengthening of the capitalist process always leads to extra returns, but that, beyond a certain point, these extra returns are of decreasing amount. Take again the case of fishing. If what we might call the one month's production process of making of a boat and net leads to the return of the day's labour being increased from 3 to 30,—*i.e.* by 27 fish,—it is scarcely likely that the lengthening of the process to two or three months will double or treble the return. Certainly the lengthening it to 100 months will not increase the surplus by a hundredfold. The surplus return—for there will always be a surplus return—will increase by a slower progression than the production period. We may, therefore, with approximate correctness represent the increasing productivity of extending production periods by the following typical scheme.

Production Period.	Return per annum.	Surplus.
Without Capital	£15	—
1 year	35	£20
2 years	45	10
3 „	53	8
4 „	58	5
5 „	62	4
6 „	65	3
7 „	67	2
8 „	68 : 10s.	1 : 10s.
9 „	69 : 10s.	1
10 „	70	0 : 10s.

It must be understood that I do not attach any importance to these particular figures. Everybody knows that, in every branch of production and at every stage of technical knowledge, the figures will differ. In one branch the fall of surplus return may be slower, in another it may be more rapid. All I lay stress on is the fact that the figures express the general tendency of surplus returns to fall.—Assume, to complete the hypothesis, that a worker needs £30 a year to maintain him in suitable circumstances, and let us try to find out on this basis the limit of the economically possible agio which a suitor for productive credit may, in the worst case, offer for a loan of £30 a year.

If the suitor has no capital whatever, he can get a return of only £15 without the loan : with the loan, in a one year's production period he can get a return of £35. In the most extreme case he may therefore, without altering his position for the worse by the transaction, offer an agio of £20 ; that is $66\frac{2}{3}\%$. If, on the other hand, the suitor already has a capital of £30 (whence he gets it—whether it is his own or advanced from other quarters—does not affect the case), he can, without borrowing, engage in a one year's process and obtain a product of £35, and all that depends on his getting the loan is the extension of the process from one year to two, and the raising of the return from £35 to £45 ; i.e. a yearly surplus of £10.[1]   Here, then, the suitor can economically

---

[1] The total surplus return, due to the loan, figures out at £20, since, in each of the two years of the extended production period, the surplus return to labour is £10. But this surplus return is all the same divided over two years, so that only the amount of £10 is to be reckoned to one year. In more skilful disposition, however, the borrower need not take up, at the beginning of the production

offer, at the most, an agio of £10 on £30 ; *i.e.* an interest rate of $33\frac{1}{3}\%$. Similarly, if the suitor, by whatever means, is already equipped for a two years' process, the loan of £30 is now the cause of a surplus return of £8 (£53 — £45) = $26\frac{2}{3}\%$. Thus the more ample the suitor's equipment is already—the more capital he has—the lower fall the surplus returns and the ratio of agio dependent on the loan. That is to say, the surplus falls to £5, £4, £3, £2, 30s., 20s., 10s., and the rate to $16\frac{2}{3}$, $13\frac{1}{3}$, 10, $6\frac{2}{3}$, 5, $3\frac{1}{3}$, $1\frac{2}{3}$ per cent. This fall is bound to emerge unless the returns obtainable in 1, 2, 3, 4, x production periods should run, not, as we have assumed, in the progression of 35, 45, 53, 58, 62, etc., but steadily in the much sharper progression of 35, 45, 55, 65, 75.... 105.... 1005, etc. In this latter case, on every one-year extension of the production period made possible by the £30, there would depend a constant surplus return of £10, and the upper limit of the economically possible agio would remain uniform at $33\frac{1}{3}\%$. But a ratio of increase like this cannot in any case go beyond a few stages in some few productions ;[1] it cannot go on permanently and without limit in any production.

We come, then, to the important proposition that to intending producers, generally speaking, a present loan has less value in proportion to the length of the production periods already provided for from other sources. The proposition directly applies to the rate of interest in isolated exchange, inasmuch as the valuation of the borrower for productive

period, the whole amount of the loan from which he defrays his subsistence during that period : he may raise the loan by successive instalments, and this has for result that the loan is outstanding and requires to pay interest only for half the production period. If such a disposition is arranged the yearly surplus return may in the most extreme case be offered as a half-year's interest on the subsistence loan, and in this case the most extreme interest rate economically possible is double the figures given in the text. The raising of such subsistence loans by instalments thus exerts exactly the same influence on the relation between subsistence fund and surplus return, and, at the same time, on the height of the interest rate, as does a suitable "*Staffelung*" of production (see above, p. 325), with which phenomenon, as may be easily seen, it is closely and intimately connected.

[1] Up to a certain point the surplus return may now and then increase even in a greater ratio than the duration of the production period. It may, *e.g.*, happen that the transition from rod-fishing to net-fishing shows a greater advance than the transition from primitive modes of fishing to rod-fishing. But beyond a certain point this cannot be maintained, and the surplus returns show a decreasing ratio.

purposes directly gives the upper limit of the economically possible rate. It also allows us, however, to judge in what direction this proposition must . influence the rate of interest in competitive exchange, where the price is the resultant of the subjective valuations of individuals, of whom many are intending producers.

As has been said above, the case of productive credit is closely related to the case of the purchase of labour, the employment of productive labourers by the capitalists themselves. Here, however, there enter certain complications which may be as easily and briefly stated under competitive exchange. I shall not, therefore, discuss them separately, but shall go on at once to explain the rate of interest in developed competitive exchange.

CHAPTER II

THE RATE IN MARKET TRANSACTIONS

THE character of the market in which present goods are exchanged against future goods has already been described.[1] We now know the people who appear in that market as buyers and sellers. We know that the supply of present goods is represented by the community's current stock of wealth—with certain unimportant exceptions—and that the demand for them comes (1) from the suitors for productive credit who wish to equip themselves for their own work in production, (2) from the suitors for wage-paid labour, and (3) from the suitors for consumption credit. To these three categories we may add, under certain reservations, the maintenance of the landowners. Finally, it will be remembered that the resultant market price must, as a rule, be in favour of present goods, and must lead to an agio on the same. What we have now to do is to group together the causes which determine the height of this agio in one adequate and typical picture.

If we were to attempt all at once to draw a picture like this, covering, as it does, the whole area of the varied influences that cross and intersect each other on the market, we should meet with great, indeed insuperable difficulties, in the way of statement. I shall, therefore, act on the principle, *divide et impera,* and first consider how the price is determined under the assumption that, confronting the supply of present goods, there is one single branch of demand, though, in present circumstances, by far the most important branch, viz. the demand of the Wage-Earners. Once we have drawn in broad clear lines the most important and difficult part of the whole

[1] See above, p. 319, and particularly p. 330.

picture, it will be relatively easy to define the kind and measure of the share which all the remaining market factors have in forming the resultant, and so gradually to make the picture true to the full complexity of practical life. For good reasons I also retain provisionally the former assumption, that the whole supply and the whole demand for present goods meet in one single market embracing the entire community. And, finally, we shall suppose meanwhile that all branches of production show the same productiveness, and also the same increment of productiveness on each extension of the production period : that is to say, we shall assume an identical scale of surplus returns.

Suppose, then, that in our community the stock of wealth in the market, as supply, amounts to £1500,000,000, and that there are 10,000,000 of wage-earners. Following the scheme on p. 378, the annual product of each worker increases in all branches of production, in proportion to the length of the production period, from £35 (in a one year's process [1]) to £70 (in a ten years' process). The question is ;—in these circumstances of the market how high will rise the agio on present goods ?

It is quite certain, as we have already explained, that the agio will settle at that level where supply and demand exactly balance each other, and this lies between the subjective valuations of the last pair who actually exchange. But the fixing of these valuations here encounters a quite exceptional difficulty, and one which does not occur in any other exchange transaction, but has its basis in a special peculiarity of the commodity "labour." Every other commodity, that is to say, has a predetermined subjective value to the one who wishes to buy it. Labour has not, and for this reason. It is valued according to its prospective product, while the prospective product varies according as that labour is invested in a short or in a long production process. We said above that, in the subjective circumstances of the capitalist, a sum of present goods was, as a rule, worth as much as the same sum of future goods. The capitalist will, therefore, count the value of labour equal to

---

[1] The case of production carried on entirely without capital, which, according to the scheme, would return only £15, we may leave out of account as practically of no importance.

just as many present shillings as it will bring him in in
the future. But, according as this labour is invested in a
short or a roundabout process, it may bring him in £35 or
£58 or £70. At which of these figures is the capitalist to
value it ?

It may be answered : According to the product aimed at in
entering upon the method of production which is, economically,
the most reasonable. He will, therefore, value the year's labour
at £35 if, on reasonable grounds, he meditates adopting a one
year's process; at £70 if he considers a ten years' period the
most suitable. This would be very well if only it was
certain beforehand what period was the most suitable for
the undertaker. But this is not certain : on the contrary,
the length of the process is itself dependent on the rate
of wage fixed as resultant price on the labour market.
If the wage, for instance, stands at £25, a one year's process
is the most favourable for the undertaker. At £25 he
gains £10 in the year—or, to put it exactly, in the six
months, since, on the average, the advance extends over only
six months;[1] that is, 80% per annum. In a ten years' process for the £25 in wages he gets £70, and the surplus
return of £45 is, absolutely, much greater, but, when divided
as profit over an average of five years,[2] gives only £9 for one
year, or a profit of 36%. On the other hand, if the year's
wage is £50, it is quite clear that it would be as absurd to
choose a one year's process, with its product of £35, as it was
most reasonable in the previous circumstances, and only those
longer production periods which show an annual product over
£50 could be thought of.

The matter, therefore, stands as follows. Elsewhere, in
the case of other commodities, the employment for which the
buyers wish to acquire them is already determined. It is the
fixed point,—the thing which first of all helps to determine
the price offered by the buyers, and then through that the
resultant market price. Here, in the case of the commodity

---

[1] Only the wages of the first month are outstanding nearly a whole year;
those of the second month are outstanding only eleven months, and so on; all
wages of the first six months outstanding more than half a year. Against this
the wages of the second six months are outstanding for as much less than the
half-year.

[2] The calculation is exactly similar to the foregoing.

Labour on the contrary, the employment is an undetermined amount, an x, which is first determined by the resultant price. In these circumstances it is clear that the fixed point of the price transactions must be got somewhat differently from the ordinary way ; not, of course, according to different principles or laws, but with a certain casuistical modification in detail which we have now to examine.[1]

In place of the fixed point, which is not available because the employment of the labour itself is not fixed, we find a substitute in the fact that another amount, usually indetermined, is here fixed, viz. the quantities sold. It may be taken as certain that all the labour offered, like the whole sum of present goods offered, finds a market. The certainty of this is based on a peculiar circumstance. Exactly as, in the science of money, it is a familiar dogma that, in the long-run, any sum of money, be it great or small, is sufficient to do the work of circulation in a community, so is it true that any

---

[1] Perhaps one or other of my readers will take exception to my looking upon the production period, in which the work of undertaking is carried on, as not a fixed immovable amount. It will be said that each undertaker has made the arrangements for his production on a quite definite footing, and works in any case in the production period corresponding to and determined by these given arrangements. This is not the case. Even where the visible outlines of the arrangements, such as workshops, number and kind of employés, and so on, may be pretty permanent, yet, within these fixed lines, a number of little noticed alterations are possible, by which the length of the production period might be changed not inconsiderably. In the simplest shoemaking shop, e.g., the buying of a new machine-made tool, the wholesale purchase of finished uppers, or, above all, the acquiring of labour-saving instruments such as sewing-machines and the like, involves no unimportant extension of the production period. True, in the shoemaking shop itself one does not notice that the production of shoes has now become a more lengthy process. But all the more noticeable will it be in those preparatory stages of production where, on account of the shoemaker's demand—not, of course, the demand of the one shoemaker, but of many,—people must now stretch away back in time, as it were, and invest original productive powers in machine-making, founding of factories, and so on. The shoemaker, therefore, according as he covers his demand for the instruments of his business in one way or the other, may as a fact cause a lengthening or shortening of the total production period, and naturally he makes the choice which, in the circumstances, is economically the more advantageous. If, e.g., the level of wages is very high, he will prefer to buy machine-made uppers, put up a sewing-machine in his own shop, etc. ; that is to say, in entire correspondence with the statement given in the text, he will prolong the production period : while, if the level of wages is low, he will prefer directly to employ the cheap hand labour,—that is to say, so far as in him lies, to keep the production period short.

sum of present goods, be it great or small, is sufficient to buy
up the whole supply of wage labour that exists in the community, and to pay its wages.   All that requires to be done
is to contract or extend the production period.   If there are
ten million wage workers, and fifteen hundred millions of
capital, this stock is just sufficient to pay the ten million
workers £30 a year each over a ten years' production
process.[1]   If there are only five hundred millions of capital
no labourers need go idle on that account : only, of course,
they cannot have their maintenance advanced them for a
ten years' process, but (at the same wage of £30) only for
a three and a third years' process, and the average duration
of the production period must be curtailed accordingly.   Suppose there are only fifty millions of capital, all the labour
could still be bought, but now only for a four months' process,
and it must be secured, by a further shortening of the production period, that the scanty amount of present goods is renewed
after every short period by the accession of fresh returns.

It is, therefore, always *possible* for the existing stock of
wealth to buy all the labour, and there are certain reasons in
this case that work very strongly towards always making the
possible into the actual.   Between capitalists and labourers
the economic conditions are—with very few exceptions—extremely favourable to the effecting of exchange.   The labourers
urgently need present goods, and cannot, or can scarcely
turn their own labour to any account; they will, therefore,
to a man rather sell their labour cheaply than not sell it
at all.   But very much the same is true of the capitalists.
In their peculiar circumstances of want and provision for
want, their present goods—which they, in any case, would
lay up against the future—are not worth more to them
than a similar sum of future goods.   They will, therefore,
prefer any purchase of labour where there is an agio, however little it may be, rather than let their capital lie dead ;
and the consequence is that all capital, like all labour, actually
comes to a sale.   As a fact we see that, in all economic communities, although the quantitative relations between wealth

---

[1] On the assumption of a production arranged in the form of stages, whereby
(as shown on p. 328, and in Appendix I.) the initial fund need only contain subsistence for half the production period.

2 c

and number of wage-earners are extremely various, these two amounts exactly buy up each other. There are everywhere a few labourers who have no work, and a few capitals which are not employed, but this is, of course, not in contradiction to what has been said. I need scarcely point out that the presence of such unemployed is never traceable to the purchasing power of capital being insufficient to the whole number of the labourers—in a poorer country, indeed, a capital of half the amount would have to pay the same number of labourers, and actually does pay them—but always to certain frictional and temporary disturbances of organisation, such as are inevitable in a mechanism so complicated as the industrial division of labour in a great country.

We may, therefore, assume it as certain that the whole supply of labour, and the whole supply of present goods, come to mutual exchange. In this fact the length of the production period, and thus the amount of product which the undertaker may obtain through the labour he buys, obtains a certain definiteness. That is to say, we must, in any case, assume such a period of production that, during its continuance, the entire disposable fund of subsistence is required for, and is sufficient to pay for, the entire quantity of labour offering itself. If the period were to be shorter than this, some capital would remain unemployed; if longer, all the workers could not be provided for over the whole period; the result would always be a supply of unemployed economic elements urgently offering their services, and this could not fail to upset the offending arrangements.[1]

But we are not yet finished with the subject. It is not one single definite production period that harmonises with the above assumption, but a great many different periods.

[1] If, *e.g.*, the existing stock of subsistence is so great as to defray four million years' pay—in which case, as we know, where production is by stages, an initial capital amounting to two millions of wages only would be required—and if there are one million labourers in the country, then it is shown that an average four years' production period must be taken. For if, say, a three years' period were taken, the three years' payment of one million of workers would take up only a capital of one and a half millions of wage, and the rest of the capital would have to go idle. In a five years' production, again, an initial fund of two millions of wages would only defray the subsistence of 800,000 labourers for five years, and the remaining 200,000 would go starving—a position which evidently is as untenable.

Obviously, given the capital and the number of workers, a very varying number of years can be provided for according as the wage of labour is high or low. With a capital of fifteen hundred millions for instance, our ten million workers can be kept in work and wage for ten years at a wage of £30, or for five years at a wage of £60, or for six years at a wage of £50. Now which of these possible cases will be the one actually adopted ?—This will be determined, by the play of the same egoistic motives as regulate the formation of price in competition generally, in the following way.

Assume for a moment that the usual wage is £30. A capitalist then with £1000—for convenience sake we shall take this amount as the unit throughout the following discussion—may employ either 66·6 labourers in a one year's process, or 33·3 labourers in a two years' process, or 22·2 in a three years' process.[1] Naturally he will choose the process which he finds most advantageous. Which process that is will be seen from the following table, based on the former scheme of productivity on p. 378, showing how many workers can be employed by £1000 in each production period, and how much annual profit may be got from that sum.

---

[1] I here assume a well-organised production by stages, where no portion of the capital remains idle, and where, consequently, the initial fund need only contain something like half the amount of subsistence required during the course of the whole production period. I may note, however, that the correctness of the conclusions drawn in the text is quite independent of the pure question of fact whether the initial capital must be exactly half, or something more than half, or, perhaps, just so much as the amount of subsistence successively consumed by the workers during the production period. According as this is determined the figures put down in the following tables will, of course, vary—they have no value, indeed, but as illustrative—but not the laws that underlie these figures. With other figures representing the productiveness and the capital, the calculation would lead to different concrete rates of interest, but to the same laws as regards height of the interest rate, as will be shown more clearly further on.

TABLE I.[1]

WAGE £30.

Production Period in years.	Annual Product.		Annual profit per labourer.		Number of employed.	Total annual profit on the £1000.
1	£35	0	£5	0	66·66	£333·30
2	45	0	15	0	33·33	500
3	53	0	23	0	22·22	**511·11**
4	58	0	28	0	16·66	466·66
5	62	0	32	0	13·33	426·66
6	65	0	35	0	11·11	388·85
7	67	0	37	0	9·52	352·24
8	68	10	38	10	8·33	320·82
9	69	10	39	10	7·4	292·5
10	70	0	40	0	6·66	266·66

The table shows that, in the given circumstances of all the factors, it is most profitable for the undertakers to devote themselves to a three years' production period. They obtain thereby the very considerable rate of 51·1%, while both in the longer and in the shorter processes the profit is lower. In these circumstances naturally all undertakers will seek to adopt this length of process. But to what does this lead? In a three years' process £1000 can employ 22·2 workers, and therefore to employ all the available capital in the community (viz. £1,500,000,000) 33⅓ million workers would

---

[1] To be exact the figures of profit from the larger periods of production should be set down at somewhat less. They fall due, of course, all at once at the end of the total production period, and are thus less in value by the amount of the intermediate interest. In a ten years' production period, *e.g.*, the capital of £1000 realises a total profit of £2666·6, which is less favourable than £266·66 for each single year, because in the latter case the interests falling due earlier might increase by compound interest. I consider it, however, less of a mistake to give up mathematical exactness than to include involved calculations of compound interest, and make the illustration so difficult and circumstantial that, in the end, it might be perhaps more difficult to understand than the rule which I mean it to illustrate. It is not committing any blunder in principle : the neglect of compound interest leads only to the same result as if I had made the progression of the annual returns—which in any case is arbitrary and only given for purposes of illustration—a little more rapid, and then had calculated exactly.

be needed—while there are only ten millions. These ten million workers could be employed by a sum of four and a half million pounds, leaving capital to the amount of ten and a half millions lying idle. Of course these ten and a half millions of capital could not and would not remain so: they would compete for employment; attract labourers by offering higher wages; and the necessary result would be a rise of the rate of wages. The £30 rate, then, assuming the above position of the factors, cannot possibly be a permanent one.

Suppose now that the rate of wages is £60, we get the following table.

TABLE II.

WAGE £60.

Production Period in years.	Annual Product.		Annual profit per labourer.		Number of employed.	Total profit on the £1000.
1	£35	0	—£25	0	33·33	Loss
2	45	0	— 15	0	16·66	,,
3	53	0	— 7	0	11·11	,,
4	58	0	— 2	0	8·33	,,
5	62	0	2	0	6·66	£13·33
6	65	0	5	0	5·55	27·77
7	67	0	7	0	4·76	33·33
8	68	10	8	10	4·16	35·41
9	69	10	9	10	3·70	35·15
10	70	0	10	0	3·33	33·33

This table proves that, if we assume £60 as the rate of wages, production in anything *less* than a five years' period shows a positive loss, while, of the longer periods, the eight years' process is the most profitable. It yields the modest interest of 3·54%, but, relatively speaking, it is the most favourable rate that can be got. It is easy to see, however, that it is as impossible for a wage of £60, as it was for £30, to be the definite resultant price of labour. Under the assumed circumstances of productivity the eight years' period is the most profitable length of process at a £60 rate of wage. By adopting it a capital of £1000 can employ only 4·16 labourers; consequently the entire capital of £1500,000,000 can employ only six and a quarter million workers; and the remaining three and three-quarter millions must starve. This again is impossible; the unemployed will offer their services in competition with each other; and wages will be pressed below the rate of £60.

At what point, then, will this overbidding and under-bidding, which come from unemployed capital when wage is too low and from unemployed labour when wage is too high, come to an end? Obviously it will be when the most reasonable production period exactly absorbs the wage fund on the one side, and the labour offered on the other. This will be the case, as the following table shows, at a wage of £50.

TABLE III.

WAGE £50.

Production Period in years.	Annual Product.	Annual profit per labourer.	Number of employed.	Total profit on the £1000.
1	£35 0	—£15 0	40	Loss
2	45 0	— 5 0	20	„
3	53 0	3 0	13·33	£40
4	58 0	8 0	10	80
5	62 0	12 0	8	96
6	65 0	15 0	6·66	**100**
7	67 0	17 0	5·71	97·07
8	68 10	18 10	5	92·5
9	69 10	19 10	4·44	86·66
10	70 0	20 0	4	80

At a wage of £50 the six years' production period proves the most profitable. It gives an interest of 10% on the in-vested capital, while a five years' process would return only 9·6%, and a seven years', 9·7%. Moreover, as at that wage the £1000 employs 6⅔ labourers, the entire ten million workers and the entire fifteen hundred millions of capital find employ-ment; and the point is reached where the formation of price may come to rest. All who have it in their power to disturb the settlement by further over or under bidding have no inducement to do so, and all who might have an inducement have not the power, as, on economic grounds, they are already excluded from competition.   There is no idle capital which might be tempted to seek employment by overbidding, and there are no idle labourers who might be tempted to seek employment by underbidding.   And, finally, the undertakers who have placed their production on the footing which makes this favourable position of things possible are rewarded by this arrangement being at the same time the most profitable for them, and they too have no inducement to make any change. Those undertakers, on the other hand, who might have wished to engage in longer or shorter processes, and would thus have made either capital or labour insufficient, are excluded from any such disturbing competition by the fact that such methods of production show either a loss or a smaller profit.

The price of labour, then, will and must [1] settle at a wage of £50, and this involves, at the same time, an agio of 10% on present goods.   I say, it *must* do so, for, so long as this point is not reached, there are certain tendencies always at work to force the price towards it.   If, for example, the wage were only a little higher, say £51, the six years' process would still be the most profitable, but only 9,800,000 labourers could be employed by the available capital of £1.500,000,000 ; the unemployed, by the urgency of their circumstances, would exert a pressure on the price of labour, till such time as they also could be taken in, which would be the case when wage came down to £50.   If, on the contrary, the wage were a little lower, say £49, the employment of the ten million workers would take up only £1470,000,000 of capital; the unemployed remainder would attract employment through overbidding ; and the result again would be a rise of wage till such time as the point was reached at which equilibrium all round could take place.

In the assumed state of all the factors an agio of 10% is therefore the economically necessary result.   Why exactly 10% ?—The considerations hitherto presented can only answer *negatively* that the necessary equilibrium could have been

---

[1] Leaving out of account special disturbing causes, the influence of which I cannot pursue here : my business just now is to develop the fundamental law of the interest rate, just as I have already developed the fundamental law of the formation of price.   See Conrad's *Jahrbücher*, vol. xiii. p. 480.

reached at no other rate of interest.   But we may now inquire
whether our figures do not bring out some other circumstances
which may *positively* indicate a rate of 10%, and give us
matter for a precise positive law of the interest rate.

To arrive at a position of equilibrium, the capital of the
community had to be taken out of shorter processes where
full employment could not be found for the existing stock of
labour, and employed in gradually extending methods till all the
labourers were fully occupied.   This was arrived at in the six
years' process.   On the other hand, the adoption of still longer
processes, for which again the capital is *not* sufficient, had,
economically, to be prevented.   In these circumstances the
six years' producers are the last buyers, the " marginal buyers ";
the would-be seven years' producers are the most capable
excluded suitors for means of subsistence ; and, according to
our well-known law, the price that results must fall between
the subjective valuations of these two.   How does it stand
with these valuations ?

What we have to look to simply is : What is the utility
which, for those two sets of buyers, depends on the disposal over
a definite sum of means of subsistence ?   Here, first of all, it
may be put down generally that, on the disposal over each
half year's wage,—in the present case, £25,—depends one
year's extension of the production period per worker.[1]   Accordingly, with respect to the six years' producers, it specially
depends on their possession or non-possession of the £25
whether, as regards one labourer, they can embark on or
continue in the six years' process instead of the shorter five
years' process.   But according to our scheme of productivity

---

[1] Always assuming a complete arrangement of production by stages.   I may
add the mathematical proof of this somewhat paradoxical thesis.   To employ 30
labourers in a 5 years' period arranged by yearly stages, the 6 labourers of the first
stage need an advance of wage over full 5 years, that is, in all, 30 annual wages :
the 6 labourers of the second stage require an advance over 4 years, that is, 24
wages : similarly, the labourers of the third stage require 18, those of the fourth
12, those of the fifth 6 : a total of 90 wages.   To support the same 30 labourers
in a 6 years' production, the first stage, now embracing only 5 labourers, requires
the advance for 6 years, that is, 30 wages ; the second stage, 25 ; the third,
20 ; the others, respectively, 15, 10, and 5 wages : in all, 105 wages.   The
extension of the production period for 30 labourers by a whole year requires
therefore, as a fact, the augmenting of the wage fund by the amount of only
15 wages, which gives the case maintained in the text.

the year's return of one worker in a five years' process amounts to only £62, while in a six years' process it amounts to £65. What, therefore, as regards the marginal buyer, depends on his having the disposal over £25, is the obtaining of a yearly surplus product of £3. On the other hand, those would-be producers who are trying to take means of subsistence out of the market in order to extend the production period to a seventh year, could gain by their extension only a surplus return of £2 (£67 − £65). For them, therefore, all that depends on their disposal over the £25 is a surplus of £2, and they are excluded from competition inasmuch as the resultant price has established an agio which exceeds the rate of 2 on 25 (8%).

If therefore—and this is indispensable to equilibrium being reached—the extension of the production period is to halt at the limit of six years, the agio established by the fixing of the price must lie between the rate that represents the valuation of the last buyers (£3 on £25, or 12%) as upper limit, and the rate representing the valuation of the competitors first excluded (8%) as lower limit. And thus our former empirical and circumstantial demonstration of the rate of wage and the rate of interest at which equilibrium may be reached on the market, *must* point provisionally to the rate of 10%. It must at least point to the zone between 8% and 12%. The fact that, within this zone, the rate of 10% is exactly brought out, is due, of course, not to the limitations indicated by the valuations of the marginal pair, but, as described on p. 215, simply to the quantitative effect of supply and demand. We shall see immediately, however, that the wide latitude (8% to 12%) which our abstract scheme leaves for the narrowing action of supply and demand, looks considerable only on account of the figures accidentally chosen ; in practical life the latitude given is almost always vanishingly small.

Meanwhile we may put the results at which we have arrived in general form as follows :—

The rate of interest—on the assumptions already made— is limited and determined by the productiveness of the last extension of process economically permissible, and of the further extension economically not permissible ; in this way that the unit of capital, which makes this extension of process possible, must always bear an amount of interest less than the surplus return of the first-named, and more than the surplus return of the last-named extension.[1] Within these marginal limits the price may be more exactly determined by the quantitative relation between wage fund and number of workers, according to the law of supply and demand.

In practical life, however, the latter method of determining price is seldom taken. It is true that in our abstract scheme there was an unusually wide latitude to come and go on, because we had assumed a sudden decrease of the surplus return from £3 to £2 ; that is, a fall of fully one-half. But in practical life sudden differences like this scarcely ever occur. The figures which represent the productiveness of the last permissible. and the first non-permissible extension come usually very close to each other, and, consequently, they are sufficient to limit the variations of the interest rate so strictly and sharply that the theoretically more exact determination by means of the relation of supply and demand is practically unimportant.[2]   Indeed, assuming that these two marginal limits are very near each other, one of them may even be left out of account without any serious inaccuracy,[3] and the law be simply formulated thus :—The rate is determined by the surplus return of the last permissible extension of production. This coincides almost to a word with Thünen's celebrated law which makes the rate of interest depend on the productiveness of the " last applied dose of capital." [4]

[1] From this formulation it will be seen why the law now deduced does not depend, and has no need to depend, for its correctness on the concrete numerical ratio between the amount of the wage fund and the length of the production period. (See above, p. 387, note 1.) Suppose, e.g., that not a half but a whole year's wage were necessary to extend the production period by a year, all the same a capital sufficient to defray the wages of a *whole* year would require to bear something like the return of the last extension of the production period as interest. The figures may change as they will, but the typical relation holds, that the interest of that unit of capital required for a definite extension of the production period lies between the surplus return of the last permissible and the first non-permissible extension.

[2] See above, p. 217.   [3] See above, p. 221.

[4] *Der isolirte Staat*, second edition, part ii. div. i. p. 100. It is very notable that Thünen, without knowing the law of marginal utility, without any general price theory based on that law, and, finally, even without any clear insight into the origin of interest, was able to solve the special problem of the rate of interest with almost entire correctness, and in the sense of those general theories of which he had perhaps a dim presentiment.

CHAPTER III

THE RATE IN MARKET TRANSACTIONS—(*continued*)

But our task is not yet finished. Following the same lines as we took in developing the general law of the price of goods,[1] we must attempt to lay down the concrete determinants which decide the degree of productiveness of the last extension, and from our knowledge of these we must, in particular, try to get an explanation of the variations to which the interest rate is subject in practical life,—sometimes rising, sometimes falling, but with a constant tendency in the latter direction, over the whole field of economical development in historical times. This analysis too will give us a welcome opportunity of verifying our abstract theory by experience. If we find that our theory, starting with certain assumed conditions of fact, leads us, of internal necessity, to expect just that movement of interest which, in the experience of practical life and history, we see actually and always taking place when these conditions are realised, we shall be justified in taking it as a strong guarantee that our theory, although it uses such abstract machinery in the stating, is no vain imagining, but a theory obtained from the study of practical life. Moreover in what follows I shall be in much less marked opposition to old doctrines than I have been in the foregoing chapters. For certain connections between the rate of interest on the one side, and definite facts on the other, are so distinctly and unquestionably given by experience, that it was impossible for the adherents of any interest theory, however erroneous, to overlook them; and, however different the theoretical points from which they may have started, they find themselves at

[1] See above, p. 218.

one in recognising these.[1] All the same I venture to hope that what follows will give more accuracy and definiteness, as well as a new and more adequate explanation, to many a proposition long accredited by experience.

Following the line of inquiry already pursued, I shall try to investigate the concrete determinants of the rate of interest, and the manner of their working, in such a way that we can successively vary the individual assumptions in our illustrative scheme, and then see what result the variation gives us as regards the formation of the interest rate. Let us look first, then, at the influence of the amount of the national subsistence fund.

Assume that, other circumstances remaining unchanged, the available subsistence fund amounts, not to £1500,000,000 but to £2400,000,000. The repetition of the same calculation as made above leads us to the conclusion that the equilibrium of the market cannot now be attained otherwise than by an eight years' production period, a £60 rate of wages, and a corresponding interest rate of 3·54%. We may check this result from Table II. on p. 389, which is calculated on the £60 rate of wage. It shows that, where the rate of wages is £60—the rate of productivity being given—the undertaker finds an eight years' production period the most profitable; that 4·16 labourers may be employed by £1000 of capital, and, therefore, 10,000,000 of labourers by £2400,000,000; and, finally, that this (relatively) most profitable method of production yields 3·54% interest on the undertaker's capital.

As compared with the earlier ones this rate shows a

---

[1] As, e.g., in the familiar proposition that an increase of the national capital tends to reduce the interest rate. In the points here raised, I am in very thorough agreement with Walras, who, like Thünen, starts from a theory of interest which, in my opinion, is essentially wrong, and yet is able to arrive at many details correctly and with fine scientific feeling. The coming second edition of his *Éléments d'Économie Politique Pure*, the proof sheets of which, by the kindness of the author, I was permitted to see, contains many forcible and noteworthy passages on this subject. I can only regret that they are expressed in the troublesome and difficult language of mathematics. The conception of political economy as pre-eminently a mathematical science is one on which, notwithstanding what the distinguished economist has recently said (p. 191 in new edition), I fear we shall never be able to agree.

considerable decline, the reason of which is very easily explained. When the subsistence fund is increased men can only keep it fully employed by entering on further extensions of the production period, which extensions are accompanied by steadily decreasing surplus returns. Indeed the surplus return of the last extension of production economically possible (from seven to eight years) is only 30s., and the surplus return of the first non-permissible extension (from eight to nine years) is only 20s. And since the rise of the year's wage from £50 to £60 requires, for the one year's extension, not a capital of £25, but a capital of £30 per man, the marginal limits for the interest rate are 30s. or £30 (*i.e.* 5%) as upper limit, and 20s. on £30 (*i.e.* $3\frac{1}{3}$%) as lower limit. As a fact the agio of 3·54%, which we found empirically, falls between these determining marginal limits.[1]

TABLE IV.

WAGE £42.

Production Period in years.	Annual Product.		Annual profit per labourer.		Number of employed.	Total profit on the £1000.
1	£35	0	—£7	0	47·62	Loss
2	45	0	3	0	23·81	£71·43
3	53	0	11	0	15·87	174·57
4	58	0	16	0	11·905	190·48
5	62	0	20	0	9·524	190·48
6	65	0	23	0	7·93	182·39
7	67	0	25	0	6·8	170
8	68	10	26	10	5·95	157·675
9	69	10	27	10	5·29	145·475
10	70	0	28	0	4·76	133·28

Assume, conversely, that the available subsistence fund amounts only to £1000,000,000, the equilibrium, as will be seen from Table IV., is attained at a rate of wage of £42, and

---

[1] In this case it falls considerably nearer the under limit on account of the relative abundance of the capital, which would be almost sufficient for general adoption of a nine years' production period.

an agio of 19·048%. This is accompanied by some interesting circumstances which will repay a moment's attention, as they may be often enough realised in practical life, although not seen there in their full abstract purity. At a prevailing wage of £42, as it happens, two different production periods of four and five years respectively are equally profitable, and pay 19·048% interest on the capital invested in them. The result of this is that neither of them economically shuts out the other; both may be adopted simultaneously; indeed, not only may, but must, to keep the equilibrium. If the four years' period alone were adopted, only £840,000,000 of capital would find employment at a wage of £42.[1] If, again, the five years' period were exclusively adopted, the existing capital would employ only 9,524,000 labourers;[2] and in either case the unemployed elements would, as we know, disturb the equilibrium by overbidding and underbidding. The equilibrium can only be found if the two equally profitable methods of production are engaged in simultaneously, when 7,619,000 labourers will be employed by a capital of £800,000,000 in five years' production and 2,381,000 labourers by a capital of £200,000,000 in four years' production.

And, in virtue of this peculiarity, the latitude allowed in fixing the agio by the valuations of the marginal pair will be much more sharply limited in this than in the former examples. The last economically permissible extension of production is from four to five years, which brings in a surplus return of £4, that being a surplus on £21, half the year's wage. But, as it happens, the first *excluded* extension of production is also that from four to five years, inasmuch as—as shown above—the existing capital allows only a portion of the producers to take the five years' production period. Consequently the surplus return of the first excluded process—that which forms the lower limit of the interest—is also fixed at £4. The upper

---

[1] That is to say, with £1000 capital, as the table shows, 11·905 labourers could be employed in four years' production. To employ all the existing ten million labourers, therefore, a capital is required which follows this proportion :
$$1000 : x = 11\text{·}905 : 10{,}000{,}000.$$
The solution of this proportion gives :
$$x = 10{,}000{,}000{,}000 : 11\text{·}905 = 840{,}000{,}000.$$
[2] With £1000 capital 9·524 labourers are employed in five years' production ; with 1000 *millions* of capital, therefore, 9·524 millions of labourers.

and lower limit, therefore, coincide, and the interest must be determined strictly at the rate of £4 on £21; that is, at 19·048%, just as actually shown in our former scheme.[1]

Now the agio here is considerably higher than in the former cases. And our theory again explains it quite simply.

---

[1] I may call attention to the fact that now we arrive at the figure 19·048 by a quite different way, by quite different lines of thought, and by quite different calculations, than in the above table. There we sought and found empirically the figures of wage and interest at which, under the given assumptions, the equilibrium of Supply and Demand may be established. Now, applying the law of the marginal pair to the concrete case, we have deduced that the interest must lie between the surplus returns of the last extension of production still permissible, and the first excluded, and arrived thereby exactly at the same figure 19·048. In the former case we get our figures immediately by multiplication of the number of employed by the gain made per labourer (11·905 × 16 and 9·524 × 20). Here we get the same figure by dividing the dependent last surplus product by half the wage (4 : 21). I may, therefore, take this agreement as a proof that our deductive reasoning correctly expressed the results empirically established.—Here also it may be the most suitable place to point out the error into which Jevons fell as regards this question. Jevons recognises perfectly correctly that the "last surplus return" decides the interest rate ; but, owing to an oversight in principle, he makes the mistake of fixing on that other amount to which this surplus return must be put in relation, and deduces the rate of interest, not from the relation of the last surplus return to the sum of subsistence which allows the last extension of production, but from the quite different relation in which that surplus return stands to the value of the whole product which might have been obtained without the last extension of production. "The interest of capital is the rate of increase of the produce divided by the whole produce" (*Pol. Econ.* second edition, p. 267). The seriousness of this oversight will be best seen from a concrete example, which, for the sake of easier comprehension, I shall take from the case of isolated exchange spoken of above (p. 378). Remembering what was then said, let us suppose the case of an undertaker whose means would allow him to carry through an eight years' production period with a yearly return of £68 : 10s., and who, by a loan of £30, which would guarantee him subsistence for a ninth year, is put in a position to go on to a nine years' production period with a return of £69 : 10s., or a surplus return of 20s. According to Jevons this should show an interest rate of £1 on £68 : 10s., or 1·46%. But evidently there is no ground whatever why the suitor for the loan should be ready to offer £1 per year and no more as interest for a sum of £68 : 10s. It is not the amount of £68 : 10s., but that of £30, whose acquisition makes the extension of production possible, calls forth the surplus return of £1, and, consequently, may be paid, in the most extreme case, by £1, but, on the assumption noted on p. 378, note 1, by as much as £2 per year. As a fact, then, in the case of this illustration, it is not, as Jevons assumed, an interest of £1 on £68 : 10s., or 1·46%, that is economically possible, but an interest of £1 on £30, or 3½%, indeed, on the above assumption, a rate of £1 on £15, or 6⅔%. A certain very modest kernel of truth may be found, all the same, in Jevons's error ; but to point it out I should require to go still further afield into discussions in which I could not assume that the majority of my readers would find sufficient interest.

The reason is that the diminished subsistence fund allows only of comparatively short processes on the average, and consequently the " last extension of production "—that which decides the interest rate—falls in a sphere where any extension of the production periods is attended by very considerable surplus returns.

So much for the effect of an alteration in the amount of the subsistence fund: we have still to follow the effect of an alteration in number of workers. Any detailed calculation here, however, should not be necessary. It does not require much consideration to see that a change in the number of labourers must exert its influence on the rate of interest in exactly the opposite direction. Whether, for example, the number of labourers remains steady at 10,000,000, and the subsistence fund contracts from £1500,000,000 to £1000,000,000 ; or whether the subsistence fund remains at £1500,000,000 and the labourers increase from 10,000,000 to 1500,000,000 ;—in either case the subsistence fund is just sufficient to employ the existing labourers partly in four, partly in five years' periods, while the " last " and decisive surplus return is £4 on £21, and the resulting rate 19·048%. And it is as clear that, if subsistence and labourers vary simultaneously in the same direction —say that both increase—the variations will weaken the efficiency of both, and the final movement of the rate will follow that direction taken by the stronger of the varying factors ; and that, on the other hand, if both factors vary not only in the same direction but also in the same ratio, the rate will remain unchanged. Suppose, for instance, that the number of workers and the amount of the subsistence fund both double, it is evident that the doubled fund will be sufficient to provide for the doubled numbers over the same production periods as before, and that the " last " and decisive surplus, and with it the interest rate, will remain unchanged. If, again, the fund were to double while the numbers increased only by a half, it is obvious that, on the average, a longer production period could be adopted than formerly ; in which case the decisive " last " surplus return would be reduced to a lower point on the descending scale of surpluses, and the interest rate would also fall.

Finally, we might inquire, on the same lines, what will be

the effect of an alteration in a third factor, the state of productivity, assuming that subsistence fund and number of labourers remain constant. Here also we may spare ourselves any detailed tabular statement. It does not require any exact calculation to prove that if, other circumstances remaining unchanged, the scale of surplus returns constantly shows higher figures, the surplus return yielded by the last extension of production that is economically permissible—that which decides the interest rate—must be higher, and *vice versâ*. Say that subsistence fund and number of labourers stand in such a relation as to permit of an average five years' production period, the interest will be higher if the extension of the production period from four to five years is attended by a surplus return of £6 as against £4, or of £4 against £1.

We have, then, over the sphere of our investigations so far, to record three elements or factors which act as decisive determinants of the rate of interest: the Amount of the national subsistence fund, the Number of workers provided for by it, and the Degree of productivity in extending production periods. And the way in which these three factors affect the rate may be put as follows :—

In a community interest will be high in proportion as the national subsistence fund is low, as the number of labourers employed by the same is great, and as the surplus returns connected with any further extension of the production period continue high. Conversely, interest will be low the greater the subsistence fund, the fewer the labourers, and the quicker the fall of the surplus returns.

This is the way in which the interest rate should be formed, and the way in which it should alter, if our theory is correct. How is it in actual life ?—Exactly as our formula predicts, and thus experience gives that formula the most complete verification. For, first, it is one of the best accredited and recognised facts of economic history that the increase of the subsistence fund, or, to use an expression not quite so accurate but yet roughly significant, the increase of the community's capital, has a tendency to depress the rate of interest. Second, it is no less familiar and self-evident that here we do not speak of the absolute amount of the national capital, but of the relation between that capital and the numbers

2 D

of the population : in other words, we mean that an increase of population, without a simultaneous increase of capital, has a tendency to raise the interest rate.   And, thirdly, it is also an acknowledged empirical fact that the discovery of new and more productive methods of production, outlets, business opportunities, etc., which conduce to check the fall of surplus returns, tend to raise the rate of interest, while the closing of former opportunities of production or sale, or other occurrences which end in a reduction of the previous degree of productiveness, tend to lower the interest rate.   We find, therefore, that all those factors to which, on the lines of our former inquiry, we were forced to ascribe a decisive influence on the interest rate, do, as a fact, possess and exert that influence.

And now it is time to give, one by one, the features and forms of actual life to our abstract scheme.

CHAPTER IV

THE MARKET FOR CAPITAL IN ITS FULL DEVELOPMENT

Up till this point we have assumed that the annual product of
each worker, and also the annual wage, is the same in all
branches of employment. Of course, in actual life this is not
the case. But that does not in the least disturb the normal
connections and relations we have laid down, otherwise than
by acting as if there were a somewhat different number of unskilled labourers with ordinary wages and ordinary productivity.
For even if the *absolute* amount of the return to labour on the
one hand, and that of the wage of labour on the other, be ever
so various in the various branches of employment, still the ratio
between these two amounts will, in virtue of the familiar law
of equalisation of profits, remain the same all over, and this
is the essential matter in the question of Interest. If, for
instance, in one branch of production, the wage of unskilled
labour be £50, and the product of a year's labour £65, in
another branch, carried on mostly by skilled labour, the worker's
annual product may, perhaps, be double, say £130. But then
the wage of such a worker will also rise to double, say to £100.
For, if it did not rise, the undertakers in this branch of business would obtain an abnormal surplus; this would attract
stronger competition; and competition would either raise wages
by creating an active demand for workers, or press down the
price of products by increasing supply. But if the wage of
the skilled labourer were to rise higher than £100, the undertakers in question would again obtain too small a profit, and
the consequent limitation of that branch of production would
undoubtedly either press down the wage of workers, who would
now have become partly superfluous, or raise the price of

the restricted product, till such time as wage and product, here as everywhere, stand in the ratio of £50 to £65, or £100 to £130.   But if this ratio between wages and product holds, all the ratios relating to the formation of interest are exactly as they have been assumed to be in our earlier tabular statement, with the single qualification already mentioned, that the existence of better paid skilled labour has exactly the same effect as a somewhat greater number of normally paid unskilled labourers.   For, obviously, it is all the same as regards the resultant arrived at in the subsistence market, whether two labourers produce £65 each, and claim £50 each of subsistence, or one labourer produces £130 and claims £100.

Further, we have assumed up till now that, in all branches of business, the increment of annual return that accompanies the increasing extension of the production period, moves in the same rate of progression.   This also is not the case in real life.   On the .contrary, each branch of production, in virtue of its technical circumstances, has a different and often, indeed, a very different scale of productivity.   It is, for instance, quite possible that three different branches of production—call them A, B, and C—which were each turning out in a one year's process an annual product of £50, might show an exceedingly divergent return (or surplus return) if the process were extended for two to five years more.   We might have something like the following :—

Production Period.	A		B		C	
	Return.	Surplus.	Return.	Surplus.	Return.	Surplus.
1 year	£50 0	—	£50 0	—	£50 0	—
2 years	51 0	£1 0	52 0	£2 0	60 0	£10 0
3 „	51 10	0 10	53 0	1 0	65 0	5 0
4 „	51 16	0 6	53 10	0 10	67 10	2 10
5 „	52 0	0 4	53 16	0 6	69 0	1 10

Naturally this has its practical consequences.   It is the producers' interest to obtain the greatest returns or surplus returns.   They will, therefore, invest the available capital where they are tempted by the greatest returns.   If there is

capital over, or if new capital is added, they will look out for
the next best paying employments, and so on, in such a way
that they will only take a less paying employment when all
the more paying chances have been utilised.

Now if, as we have hitherto assumed, the progression of
surplus returns obtainable from similar extensions of production were the same in all branches of employment, then, in
all branches of employment, the same surplus would be reached
by the same length of process, and, consequently, an equally
long production period would prevail simultaneously over all
employments. As capital increased it would press on, with
one united front, from one to two, from two to three years'
production, and so on. But, as we have said, owing to
different technical circumstances in the various branches of
production, we actually meet the same surplus return in productive periods of different lengths. While, then, in the
investing of capital we pursue an isohypse—to borrow a
geographical term—of surplus returns, we must diverge from
an isohypse of extensions of production. Production in its
various branches must be carried on in unequally long
processes ; and, indeed, in those branches where the surplus
return sinks rapidly, it must be carried on in shorter periods.

The above scheme will illustrate this. First of all production is carried on, in all three branches, in a one year's
process with a return of £50 per labour-year. If the subsistence fund increases so much that at least a partial extension
over the one year's period is possible, people will pass first to
a two years' process in branch C, which bears a surplus return
of £10 for a half-year's payment.[1] Then the production period
will be extended in the same branch C to three years (with a
surplus return of £5), and to four years (with a surplus of
£2 : 10s.), while the other two branches of production are
all the time persisting in the comparatively unremunerative
one year's process. Only where the subsistence fund increases
still further will they pass in branch B to two years' production (with a surplus return of £2). But in branch A they
will not be able to extend the period of their production
(which only gives a surplus return of £1), until all opportunities
of production have been utilised up to the isohypse of £1

[1] See above, p. 392.

This will only be the case when in branch C the production period has been extended to five years, and in branch B to three years. Production, then, will and must be carried on simultaneously in the three different branches in two, three, and five years' periods—a conclusion which we see verified in economic practice in the familiar fact that different products are produced with very different degrees of capitalism. Food, for instance, is a much less capitalistic product than metallic goods, or clothing stuffs, or manufacturing products generally.[1]

How, then, is our law of the rate of interest affected by this complexity of actual circumstances?—It is not disturbed in the least. For all the essential circumstances on which it rests remain unchanged. It is still the case that the existent capital is employed in gradually extending processes till it is fully occupied. It is still the case that there is a certain level of these extensions, yielding a certain surplus return, which is the last economically permissible, and a succeeding level yielding a somewhat less surplus return which is economically not permissible. And, finally, it is still the case that the surplus returns of these " marginal employments " also form the marginal limits of the interest rate. The single difference —and that not an essential one—is that the isohypse of the surplus returns, and with it the line of the last permissible extensions of production, is not a straight line, but runs in an undulatory or zigzag fashion through the different branches of production, according as the same surplus return is reached by them in longer or shorter processes. But this modification gives our law a still sharper power of definition. For as, in consequence of the complexity of actual life, the scale of productivity is much more finely graduated than was our simple typical scheme, the two marginal limits, as a rule, stand much nearer each other, and consequently narrow the zone within which price is determined very much more closely than is shown in our abstract illustration.[2]

To proceed. Hitherto we have assumed that the demand for present goods comes simply from the wage-earners (either directly or through the mediation of undertakers). But this,

[1] See what was said above on p. 334 : the two passages mutually supplement each other.   [2] See above, p. 394.

again, in actual life is not correct: there are a few other competitors in the market.

There are, first, the suitors for Consumption credit. Their demand is graduated and stratified according to the urgency of their need for present goods.[1]   One class will be in such pressing need that, in the worst case, they will be glad to offer an agio of 100%: another class will only go the length of 80%: a third will offer 60%: others 50%, and so on down the scale, perhaps, to 2%.   Now these suitors join their claims to the demand which comes from the wage-earners, and each class or layer of them is satisfied concurrently with that layer of productive employments yielding a surplus return that represents the same percentage.   If, for instance, the investing of capital reaches the isohypse of a surplus of £4 on £21, all those suitors for loans will be satisfied simultaneously who, in the worst circumstances, are able to offer 19·048% or more: if it reaches the isohypse of a surplus of £2 : 10s. on £25 all suitors will be served who are willing to offer at least 10%, and so on.

It would be quite erroneous to understand this as meaning that the rate of loan interest is determined simply by the rate of interest obtained in production.   It contributes just as much to determine the latter, as it is determined by it.   Both classes of demand work in entire co-ordination.   The fact that there is a certain class of suitors for consumption loans, and that this class takes a portion of the existent means of subsistence out of the market, involves that there are fewer means at the disposal of productive investors ; investment must call a halt at a higher isohypse of surplus returns ; and this again involves a higher rate of interest in the sphere of production. Conversely the presence of the productive demand results in a considerable portion of the means of subsistence being claimed for productive purposes, and this again has the result that the wants of consumption credit are not satisfied at such low levels as would otherwise have been the case.   In the present day, of course, the productive demand is so much the more important of the two that one is apt to suppose that it alone rules the rate of interest.   But this false impression is now and then sensibly corrected by experience when some great

[1] See above, p. 376.

state-loan for consumption purposes—say for a war—makes the general interest rate fly up.   But even when the demand for consumption credit is quite insignificant, it does not fail to exert some influence on the rate ; it may always be contended that, if it were to disappear, the interest rate would be at least a fraction lower than it is now.

Another competitor in the market for capital is the Land-owner.   If owners work their own lands, and are content to maintain themselves by the fruits of their labour (whereby they lay past their rent as saving), they are no burden on the subsistence fund of the community.   If, however, they live wholly or partially on their rents, their subsistence also must be advanced out of the community's fund, for a length of time proportional to the production periods in which their land is laid down.   Suppose, for instance, that the wealthy cotton planter lives in idleness on his rents, and that the total pro-duction process of textiles, including the various stages of spinning, weaving, etc., down to the manufacture of the finished cotton stuffs, takes five years, the maintenance of the planter, just as much as that of his field-worker, must be advanced out of the subsistence fund over five years.   The advance will then, of course, be refunded out of that quota of pro-duct which—according to the law of complementary goods— is due to the co-operation of the uses of land ; but, in the meantime, the landowner lives at the expense of the sub-sistence fund.

What kind of effect has this on the rate of interest ?—Its effect is entirely similar to that of consumption credit.   The competition of landowners takes a certain amount of subsist-ence out of the market ; it thus curtails the investment of capital in production, and makes it call a halt at a higher isohypse of surplus returns ; and this, finally, keeps up the rate of interest.   In doing so, however, the claim of the land-owner on subsistence comes under a reflex influence from the height of the interest rate.   This, of course, has no reference to the *height* of the annual rents—for this is fixed by those circumstances which influence the economic value of uses of land, and need not be mentioned here—but to the *number* of annual rents for which advances of subsistence are demanded. That is to say ; if interest is high, lengthy periods of produc-

tion are not profitable;[1] the uses of land will be invested in
comparatively short processes; and, as consequence, the advances made to landowners will only be for short periods.   If,
however, the interest rate is low, then, concurrently with the
increase in production and consumption credit, increases the
subsistence advanced to the landowners; it now extends over
a greater number of annual rents according as the uses of
their land can now be invested in much longer processes.

There is one other competing party in the market, the
Capitalists themselves.   So far as they live, entirely or partially, on their interest, their maintenance also will be defrayed
from the subsistence fund, and, in so far as the fund available
for other purposes is thereby contracted, will the interest rate
tend to rise.   There is, however, one important difference
between the claims of the capitalist on subsistence, and those
of the wage-earners, the suitors for loans, and the landowners.
The claims of the latter are the cause of the agio on present
goods : the claims of the former are simply its effect.   If the
claims on subsistence presented by the wage-earners, borrowers,
and landowners did not by themselves alone exceed the existent
subsistence fund, there would be no agio on present goods, and,
as consequence, the capitalists, as such, could make no valid
claim for subsistence on the funds of the community : in
default of an income from interest they would have to support
themselves by work.   It is only because there is an agio, as
effect of the other classes of demand, that the capitalists can
claim a quota of the product as interest, and claim it indeed in
advance.   Reflexly, of course, this claim of the capitalists influences the rate of interest.   It is exactly as, for instance, in
electrical induction.   The chief current first calls out the
induction current, and then the latter reflexly influences, and
indeed strengthens, the chief current.   Just in the same way
does the demand of the other competing parties in the market,
by creating an agio, first call out the claims of the capitalists
on subsistence : but, so soon as the agio is a fact, it diverts
a portion of the subsistence fund into the income of the
capitalists; it thus contracts the disposable remainder; determines the " saturation point," in the remaining branches, at a

---

[1] Which can be quite easily calculated from our tabular examples.   See, too,
the close connection of what was said on p. 382.

higher marginal utility; and so, in the last resort, causes a rise of the agio.

Suppose we try now to unite the scattered features into one picture. In its collective stock of wealth every people possesses a greater or less fund of subsistence. This is consumed *definitively* by uneconomic persons who waste their parent wealth,[1] and by the suitors for consumption credit: it is consumed *as an advance* by landowners, capitalists, and wage-earners during the social period of production.[2] The greater the subsistence fund, the longer can the social period of production be extended, and the more completely can the demands for consumption credit be satisfied. The return of the last extensions of production still possible, and, concurrently, the valuation of the last suitors who obtain loans, determine the height of the agio on present goods.

Consequently, on the basis of our completed inquiries, the following factors emerge as the most important concrete circumstances or " determinants " which influence the rate of interest.

First come the same three factors which from our inquiry into the circumstances of the labour market in its most abstract form we were forced to recognise as decisive :—

1. The amount of the National Subsistence Fund.

2. The number of producers to be provided for out of the same.

3. The position of the scale of surplus returns connected with the increasing extensions of process.

After these come :—

4. The extent and the intensity of the desire for consumption loans.

5. The existence and the height of land rent. The higher

---

[1] See above, p. 319.

[2] Members of the community not here mentioned, as women, children, persons who occupy themselves with the performance of personal services, as artists, officials, domestics, must also, of course, get part of the subsistence fund. But they are not to be counted separately, for the reason that they are not a direct charge on the social subsistence fund, but on the portions secured by the economical classes already mentioned in the text. Violin-players, *e.g.*, receive a portion of the subsistence obtained by concert-goers ; the establishment of a rich landowner is supported and paid out of his rent, and so on.

that rent is, the more persons there are who can live on their rents without working, and the higher will be the standard of living by which they regulate their maintenance. Naturally, if the amount of subsistence which they take as advances out of the social subsistence fund goes parallel with that standard of comfort, there will be the less for other purposes, and interest will remain at a higher level. The existence of land rent, therefore, tends to enhance the rate of interest.[1]

6. The existence of a numerous capitalist class living. on their interest—for reasons which apply equally to landowners and capitalists.

7. Finally; the economical habits of the population have a great influence directly and indirectly. Indirectly, inasmuch as national thrift gathers together a greater stock of wealth : directly, inasmuch as thrifty living diminishes the claims on subsistence, whereby, if subsistence remains constant, the population is maintained for a longer period, and the investment of capital is extended till there is a lower isohypse of surplus returns. If a nation is thrifty, neither landowners nor capitalists will consume all their rents ; they will either work as undertakers, and live simply by their own labour, or at least they will save a portion of their income. The portion saved represents, as it were, a certain amount of the subsistence fund allotted but not taken up, and the amount is left free for another employment, particularly for a further extension of the production period. The same is true of savings which

---

[1] I must guard myself against a misunderstanding very apt to occur. What I maintain is that the position of land rent as a form of income—the absorption of a portion of the national product by landowners who live without working,—tends to raise the rate of interest. On the other hand, I do not say that the *causes* which call forth land rent, and raise it, raise also the rate of interest. On the contrary, the well-known law of Diminishing Returns, according to which (in the absence of technical discoveries or improvements) new additions of capital and labour in agriculture lead to a decreasing surplus return, while it exerts an upward influence on land rent, certainly exerts a depressing influence on interest (see point 3 in the text). The full bearing of my contention is best expressed in this ;—that in event of the taking away of private right to land, or heavy and confiscatory taxation of land rent, interest in that community would stand lower than it would otherwise. The *causes* of land rent, in themselves, would depress interest, but land rent, as one of the shares in the division, through its effects on the division, makes up for a portion of these influences.

the labourers, or such persons as are in possession of a secondary income, are able to make.[1]

If we pursue this line of thought a little further we shall repair an omission in our former analysis. Hitherto we have considered subsistence fund and subsistence claims as something actually existing and present: we must now consider them in the act of becoming. Hitherto we have looked at the subsistence fund as standing over against, and disputing the claims which the open market made on it: we have still to consider the noiseless but never-ceasing war waged on wealth in each individual economy by the desire of enjoyment. What follows will form both continuation and conclusion of another line of thought on the subject of the formation of capital begun on p. 124.

---

[1] It may, perhaps, have been noticed that the often-mentioned factor of Insurance or Risk, which plays so great a part in practical life, especially in determining the rate of interest on loans, is missed out in my enumeration. This factor, however, has no place here. For the surplus return which this gives the capitalist, if to all appearance it raises the rate of interest, is in truth no real interest,—no net income accruing from the possession of capital,—but only a replacement for a loss of parent stock which shows itself as unavoidable over a great average of cases.—Finally, from the whole course of my research, it will be self-evident that it was not my intention to introduce exhaustively *all* the secondary determinants of the rate of interest. I have contented myself intentionally with enumerating the most important of those determinants which come into view as typical if the economical interests of the market are followed without let and hindrance. On the other hand, the influence of motives such as generosity, national prejudice, vanity, etc. (see Conrad's *Jahrbücher*, vol. xiii. p. 486) I have purposely left out of account here. See also below.

CHAPTER V

EVERY man has the power of disposal over a certain amount
of goods, small or great, partly delivered him as "parent
wealth" by the past, partly obtained by him as "income"
in the present, and these two together form his "wealth"
(*Vermögen*). The natural destination of this wealth is to
satisfy his wants. It may be said wealth exists for wants.
But many wants compete with each other and put in rival
claims. On the one hand, wants of different kinds compete
at the same point of time; on the other hand, wants of
different times—wants of the present and wants of the future
—compete with each other. How are these various claims to
be adjusted?

In a good economical system they will be adjusted in
accordance with the principle of "economical conduct," which
prescribes that the goods available should secure the highest
possible personal utility. And since even the richest man's
wealth is not sufficient to satisfy all his wants and wishes,
this again demands that he make a wise selection among his
wants so that he may procure satisfaction, as his available
means will allow, to the most important, and leave the unimportant unsatisfied. Applied to the competition of different
classes of wants this leads to the principle of harmonious
satisfaction; by which is meant that, in all branches of want,
satisfaction reaches down to the same level of importance, so
that, over the whole field, the unit of goods procures the same
marginal utility. For if in one department of want a man were
to break off the satisfaction he gets at a high level, in order to

seek for satisfaction in another department at a lower level, it would mean that he deliberately renounced a greater utility for a less one, and this would be to run counter to economical principles.[1]

But we employ the very same principle of harmonious satisfaction, and for the same reasons, to regulate the competition between the wants of various times. In the economical furtherance of our life we reach the highest possible point, when we distribute the means of satisfaction, which we have at our disposal, over the various periods of time in such a way that the last unit of goods procures the same marginal utility at all points of time. For, so long as this is not the case, we shall, obviously, be able to increase the amount of our gain by withdrawing units of goods from those times in which they procure a smaller marginal utility, and applying them to the provision of those times in which they are fitted to procure a greater marginal utility.[2]

Rationally speaking, therefore, of the presently existing stock of goods we should only consume so much in the present that the satisfaction of present wants is broken off at the same level as the satisfaction of wants will be broken off in future economic periods—considering the then state of wants and satisfactions: everything over that should be preserved for the service of the future. In terms of this rule " parent wealth " should, economically, almost always be saved. For, if it were consumed in the present along with income, the present would be, relatively, over-provided, and provision

---

[1] The possibility of a complete harmony of satisfaction is only now and then prevented through an imperfect divisibility of wants on the one side, and of units of goods on the other. See my *Grundzüge* in Conrad's *Jahrbücher*, vol. xiii. p. 68, and in particular Wieser's *Ursprung und Hauptgesetze*, p. 148.

[2] It must not be thought that this equilibrium of provision is reached if the available sum of goods is divided over the various periods of time in entirely equal amounts, so that each period obtains, allotted to its consumption, exactly the same quantity of goods. The position of wants also changes. A bachelor has to provide for fewer wants than the father of a family ; a healthy man has to make much less expenditure on the preservation of his health than an invalid and frail old man, and so on. Now, obviously, any one would make a very unsymmetrical provision for his wants, who proposed to consume mechanically the same amount of goods during all periods of his life, whether as bachelor, father of a family, or old man. To secure anything like harmonious provision a man must anticipate a probable increase of wants, and meet it by an increase of provision.

would be made for unimportant classes of want; while, in the following years, only the current income, and that in decreased amount, would be available, and the consequence would be a loss of satisfaction affecting even important classes of want. In exceptional cases, on the other hand, it is directly on the lines of rational economic management to lay hands on this parent wealth: at such times, say, as the income of the present is abnormally small, or want is abnormally urgent, while the prospects are that the future will bring a more favourable state of provision.

As regards the employment of the current *income*, the standard law of harmonious satisfaction of present and future will lead to a very different method of treatment in different cases. People whose future is secured by safe permanent income, and who, at the same time, do not expect any essential increase of their wants, may, quite reasonably, consume their entire current income in the current period,—such people, for instance, as rich landowners who have not a very large family, or who have no wish to secure each of their children in a similarly comfortable life. People, again, whose future income is uncertain or decreasing, or people whose future wants—either their own or their families'—will rise while their income is likely to remain unchanged, must, economically, retain a portion of their present income against the more poorly provided for wants of the future: they must "save," and must save enough to put the present and the future on a level as regards provision.

To be exact: something more should be saved, and the provision be made a gradually augmenting one. The reason for this lies indeed in the existence of interest. Interest on capital being a fact, what we have to choose between is not whether £100 worth of wealth gives us more utility according as we consume it to-day, or consume it next year, or consume it in two years. The £100 saved to-day increases in the next year, through interest, to £105; in the next again to £110, and so on; and the choice now is whether it is more useful to us to consume £100 to-day, or £105 next year, or £110 the next again. And we shall increase the total amount of our utility by withdrawing more and more goods from the present so long as, with £105 in next year, or £110 in next again, and so on, we can secure a greater marginal utility than by £100 in the present year. Thus while, if there were no interest, the limit of rational saving would be the point at which the utility obtainable with just £100 now, and with £100 obtainable at various future periods, is exactly the same, that limit, when interest is a fact, is the point where the provision for the various periods is so adjusted that £100 to-day are as useful as £105 next year, £110 in two years, and so on. But if an *increasing* expenditure in the future only gives the same amount of utility, it presupposes that, as time goes on, wants of less and less urgency are satisfied—in other words, that the provision for future periods is becoming progressively more ample.[1]

Thus it would be if the principle of " economical conduct " were followed with mathematical exactitude. But one might almost say that there is no point where it would be so difficult for men to act up to the claims of this principle as here. To divide their stock of goods adequately between present and future, they would require to know exactly both the future's want and the future's provision—the provision which the future periods when they come will make for themselves. But men have merely vague conjectures as to both amounts. Even as to the momentous question of how many future periods should in general be provided for, the uncertainty of human life makes them grope about completely in the dark—an uncertainty which, it must be said, has no disturbing influence on the economical transactions of that very large class who are anxious to provide, not only for themselves, but, with as much or even more devotion, for their heirs. All the more sensibly, however, is economical conduct disturbed by the familiar psychological fact that almost all men, in greater or less degree, underestimate the future and its wants.

Under the influence of the circumstances just described the economical conduct of human affairs suffers a twofold deviation from the ideal of economical provision. First : men provide for the future, on the average, more insufficiently than they should. They do not distribute their goods between present and future in such a way, that the marginal utility of

---

[1] That is to say ;—the utility of £105 in the future is equal to the utility of £100 now, only on the condition that the community's wealth is increasing.

the unit of goods allotted to the present is equal to the effective marginal utilities of those units allotted to future periods and increased by the intermediate interest. They distribute them in such a way that the marginal utility of the present unit of goods is equal to the marginal utility of the units assigned to the future, as that marginal utility is *perspectively reduced.* They save something for the future only in so far as it is clear that, if they did not, they would have to do without future satisfactions whose urgency, even as partially underestimated by them, still appears as great as the urgency of the last present wants which are satisfied, while its real urgency is, to a more or less degree, greater. Since the partial undervaluation of the future varies excessively in different individuals, classes, and nations, the divergence from the ideal of economic provision caused by it is, naturally, very different in degree. Among prudent and savingly disposed peoples its influence will be almost nil; in others it will show itself only in an insufficient percentage of saving; in others, again, in the absence of all saving, or even in light-hearted squandering of parent wealth. Second : economical deliberation on the claims of present and future is not often a finely worked-out piece of economic calculation. For the most part it is only a rough and ready reckoning of tendencies. For exact action, before deciding whether to "spend" or "save" a particular sum of goods, one would always have to be making an accurate picture of want, provision, and marginal utility for the current period, and another picture of want, provision, and marginal utility for all future periods. But this is a piece of work which is somewhat difficult, always troublesome, and one that, in spite of all care, offers no guarantee of any correct result; for, in dealing with the future, one is always compelled to work with very uncertain and conjectural data. In these circumstances not only is it easily explained, but, from the point of view of economical conduct, it is even commendable [1] that the majority of men, instead of repeating from one case to another, or from one year to another, the troublesome and yet deceptive calculation of the claims of present and future, should, once for all, accept the guidance of an economic tendency which suits their circumstances fairly well, and only make a revision on

[1] See my *Grundzüge* in Conrad's *Jahrbücher*, vol. xiii. p. 74.

occasion of great changes in their economical position, such as a marriage, receiving a legacy, and the like.

Very often this rough and ready way of economic deliberation takes this form;—that persons, to whom the exact application of the principal rules of economical conduct is too troublesome, make a secondary rule for their circumstances, and for the time live up to it. One man, for example, makes it an inviolable rule to keep his parent wealth intact: another, to leave his cumbered estate free to his children: a third, to put past so much that he may leave each child a farm: a fourth, to save enough to yield himself £500 a year, and so on. Secondary rules like these will generally coincide, more or less, for those who adopt them, with the demands of the true principle of economic conduct. Sometimes, however, they do not thus coincide, with the result that the people who faithfully follow their secondary rule sin grievously against the primary law. For instance, it is grossly uneconomic conduct in any one to cling doggedly to his resolution of not breaking on his parent wealth, and refuse the costly treatment necessary to restore his health; it is uneconomic not to make some sacrifice for the education of one's children; and so on. Finally, a great deal of uneconomic conduct arises from the fact that people who have once got into a definite habit of saving, quite reasonable at the time when it was commenced, persist in it, in a wooden sort of way, when their economic position has entirely altered. How often do we see people on the very brink of the grave, who have become rich through great saving, still grudging everything to themselves and others, and continuing to scrape and hoard mechanically for love of it. They begin with saving for love, and they end with love for saving

Of these two deviations from the ideal economic conduct, the first mentioned is the more important and the more pernicious. The neglect of exact calculations prevents people from following closely the guidance of economic conduct, but it very seldom prevents them from being more or less true to it; while the psychological undervaluation of the future forces men positively—and often far—off the lines of economic conduct. In the undervaluation of the future, we have thus to notice a factor of interest and of the interest rate which, economically, is not at all a pleasing one, but, practically, is a very active one.   In an earlier chapter we saw that it co-operates in the origin of the phenomenon of interest, in so far as it assists to give a foundation for an undervaluation of future as against present goods : now we come to recognise it also as an exceedingly active indirect determinant of the rate of interest.   The stronger its action in a community, the higher will interest rise in that community.   For the partial undervaluation of the future leads to curtailing the claims of the future as against those of the present ; to assigning too many instruments of satisfaction to present wants and too few to future.   But this leads, on the one hand, to an increase of the present claims on subsistence, and, on the other hand, to a wasteful nibbling at the stock, or, at least, to an inadequate renewal and increase of it through saving : and thus emerges the situation favourable to a high rate of interest, viz. that a (relatively) small subsistence fund is eaten up by (relatively) heavy claims on subsistence, and so suffices only to defray these claims for a relatively short period.

The theory I have put forward has a certain resemblance to the noted, or perhaps I should say notorious, " Wage Fund theory " of the older English school.   Like it I maintain the existence of a certain Subsistence Fund, from which the wages of labour in any country are defrayed, and, like it, I attribute to the amount of the subsistence fund an important influence on the reciprocal height of wage and interest.   But here the resemblance ends.   All the other features, and, among them, the most essential features of both theories, are widely divergent. The Wage Fund of English economists, although considered by them a given and fixed amount, is really a fluctuating indefinite amount ; an amount which, consequently, cannot give any secure point of support on which to base any conclusion as to the height of wage.   I mean that the " amount of capital destined by capitalists to pay wages " is neither equivalent to the total national capital, nor to the total " circulating capital," nor yet to any one fixed quota of the national capital.   It represents a *variable* portion of the community's wealth, and a portion the extent of which *varies directly*, among other things, with the height of wages : it is greater when and because wages have risen, smaller when and because wages have fallen. In explaining, then, the rate of wages by an amount which itself is conditioned by the rate of wages, the Wage Fund theory describes a circle.[1] My Subsistence Fund, on the other hand, starts with a fixed given amount—the stock of wealth accumulated in a community. Of course that amount of goods which specially serves as subsistence for labourers, and which *I* might call the "Wage Fund," forms a part of the total subsistence fund. But the amount of this portion does not hang in the air, as it does in the English theory : in exactly analysing what parties share in the total subsistence fund, and according to what laws, my "wage fund" becomes—at least relatively—fixed and definite.

But the most important difference is the following. The English theory has it that the rate of wages is simply got by dividing the wage fund by the number of existing workers. This is entirely wrong. In any case the labourers get the wage fund wholly and entirely as wage : but that does not say wage for what time ;—for one year, or two years, or three years, or more. The increasing of the subsistence fund has not at all the result, assumed by the English school, that, the number of labourers remaining constant, the rate of wage rises in the same proportion as the amount of the fund increases. The increase of the subsistence fund is, in the first instance and principally, used up in lengthening the production period ; and it is only in so far as the lengthening of the production period leads, at the same time, to a decrease of the surplus returns (according to the diminishing scale of surplus returns which accompanies successive extensions of production) that it leads to a curtailment of the capitalist's share, and to a proportionate rise in the wages of labour ; the rise too being in a much weaker ratio than the increase of the subsistence fund. The English Wage Fund theory has thus a core of truth, but it is wrapped up in a quite overpowering mass of error.[2]

[1] See the short and clear statement by Mithoff in Schönberg's *Handbuch*, second edition, vol. i. p. 643, particularly note 53.

[2] I do not at all pretend, in the somewhat sketchy suggestions which this chapter contains on the subject of wage, to have given a perfect theory of that matter. In particular, my occasional remarks have only dealt—in a half-complete sort of way—with one of the sides that comes into consideration as regards wages ; viz. the relation of wage and interest. On the other hand, I have given

And now we may dispense with one last abstraction which has served us as scaffolding in our work of explanation.   Hitherto we have represented the total supply and the total demand for present goods as concentrated in one single great market.   Instead of this, the commerce in present and future commodities is split up into innumerable part markets.   First it is divided into certain great groups, such as the Loan market, the Labour market, the Land market, the market for Concrete Capital.   And each of these markets is divided up again and again, partly according to branches, partly according to districts of business.   There is one market for mortgages, another for business credit in connection with large undertakings, and still another for business credit in connection with small. There are different loan markets for the peasant and for the citizen, for men of position and for the poor artisan or factory hand, and so on.   And, again, within each of these subdivisions there are as many distinct local markets as there are natural or artificial districts devoted to that particular department of economic life.   The Labour market, too, is as much split up as the Loan market ; first, there are as many groups as there are branches of labour, and then each group is divided up into as many part markets as there are local districts.   And so on through all the chief groups above named.

What results from this division and subdivision ? — As there is not *one* market only for present goods, neither is there only one price for them, but many and diverging market prices, as these arise directly out of the relation of supply and demand ruling in each of the individual part markets.   There are in the community at the same moment perhaps a hundred different agios on present goods, and, accordingly, a hundred different rates of interest.   But the hundreds or thousands of part markets are not hermetically sealed against one another. They are all in communication, and constantly engaged in

no express consideration to another side which is at least as important, — the question as to the influence exerted on the rate of wages by the difficulty that exists, in consonance with the law of diminishing returns, for an increased number of people to obtain the necessary subsistence from the earth.   All the same, the attentive reader may find in this book, if in scattered form yet tolerably completely, the foundation-stones on which the principles of a theory of wage might be built ; partly in the theory of complementary goods (p. 170), partly in my explanation of the law of costs (p. 223), partly in the present chapter.

arbitrating each other's prices. If in one part market the
agio on present goods is for the time abnormally high, new
amounts of capital quickly press into it to get the advantage,
and thus reduce the advantage again to zero. If, conversely,
in one part market the agio is for the moment abnormally low,
the fact is sufficient to prevent any further accession of capital,
and even to convey a part of the capital employed in it to
other and more favourable part markets, till such time as the
unfavourable difference of price again disappears.

It is, therefore, quite right to say that the price which
obtains in each part market is, indeed, *first* determined by the
relation of supply and demand as it exists in the special part
market, while this local condition of the market itself, and
with it the local price also, is determined indirectly by the
immensely more powerful pressure exerted by the *totality* of
supply and demand over the whole community. The vast
mass of the national supply, acting under the influence of those
tendencies to equalisation with which we are familiar, forces
itself into all part markets in proportional amounts. Part
markets, where there is not sufficient capital, it hurries from
other quarters to supply : from part markets over-supplied
it flows off to other communicating part markets. And
if there is neither inflowing nor outflowing, and if, therefore, the local market seems to form its local price purely of
its own power, it is then that it is really least independent : it
does not require to yield to any foreign market influences at
the moment just because it has so completely yielded to them
already. It is for the moment at rest only because it is.
supplied, in exactly the proportion which is required and
effected, by the pressure coming from the total relation of
supply and demand over the community.

It was then no empty abstraction when we spoke of one
united gigantic market for present goods, and of the laws of
its united market price. The circumstances of the whole
decide on the average amount of supply given to the part
markets. Local influences may, for long or for short periods,
raise the supply above the average level in one place, and
depress it below the level in another, but these are only
secondary phenomena, showing themselves, as it were, on the
surface of the principal movement, and carried up or down

with it—just as the surface of a great wave is furrowed and ridged by smaller wavelets that rise and fall with it.

If the mobility of capital were perfect, the particular divergences from the normal rate of interest could not have any considerable strength, and still less any considerable duration.   But as matter of fact there are numerous hindrances, little and great, which check the levelling ebb and flow of capital like weirs on a stream, and these raise or depress local prices.   People do not so easily change their employments of capital.   If sugar-refining yields one per cent more than cloth-making, a powerloom weaver does not become a refiner on a snap of the fingers, and it may be a pretty long time before so many people have put capital in sugar-refining that the rate of profit is pressed down to the normal level.   Indeed, in specially favourable circumstances, one special branch of industry may retain *permanently* an abnormal rate of agio. The disinclination of a great many affluent people to lend their capital, in small amounts and without security, to necessitous persons, from whom it is difficult to get it back without strong personal effort and supervision—or, it may be, lengthy pro-cesses and processes of distraint which are painful to one's own feelings,—almost universally keeps the supply in this particular loan market permanently and abnormally low, and the agio permanently and abnormally high—even disregarding the deduc-tion which must, of course, be made in this case for premium against risk.   And, similarly, the discount market may enjoy a permanently and abnormally low rate of interest, owing to the frequent inflow of large amounts of capital seeking short temporary employments, and, naturally, not finding such either in the mortgage market, or in agricultural loans, or in industrial investments.   The great security of the investment, again, and the prospect of future rise in value, keeps the rate of interest in immovables always low ; and considerations closely akin to this account for the present lower return of interest on state bonds, preferences, etc., payable in gold as compared with those payable in silver or paper.

It is not my intention to pursue the fate of the rate of interest into all these much-tangled bypaths, where special circumstances and special considerations by the thousand may drive it.   The divergences from the normal rate—temporary divergences even more than permanent—are, in truth, in their totality a highly important phenomenon. In them lies the soul and the source of the greater part of "undertakers' profit"; that profit which falls to the undertakers as fruit of their prosperous arbitrage transactions in present goods. But to work this out in detail is a task by itself; an important and grateful task, but one which in importance comes behind the developing of the great law of the rate of interest. In any case it is a task much too troublesome and much too lengthy to tempt me to a new effort, when I am in sight of home after a long and difficult journey. I have stated the way in which the particular abnormalities are connected with the chief law, and for the moment enough has been done towards understanding the theory of them.

And now to finish. On a former occasion, at the end of the historical part of my work, I laid down the programme for my positive theory in the following words :—" To find for the vexed problem a solution which invents nothing and assumes nothing, but simply and truly attempts to deduce the phenomena of the formation of interest from the simplest natural and psychological principles of our science." I cannot wish more than the recognition that, in the carrying out of the work, I have been true to my programme. For if, through logically developing the elementary theory of value, I have succeeded in obtaining the explanation of interest, it will give the strongest security that could be wished that we are moving on the right lines with *two* theories, that of value and that of capital. It can be nothing but a support for my theory of capital, if that theory can assert its existence as the legitimate and natural outcome of a value theory which has already given so many fair proofs of its correctness, and which is now receiving adherence among all systematic schools and in all countries that have shared in the advance of economical theory. And for the value theory, again, it will be a new proof and, perhaps, the most powerful one, if, by its instrumentality, a problem is solved which all theoretical systems hitherto have attempted in vain.

APPENDIX TO PAGE 327

AMOUNT OF SUBSISTENCE FUND NECESSARY BEFORE ENTERING
ON A PRODUCTION PERIOD OF GIVEN LENGTH

IF one year be the period of the production process and the stage period also be one year, so that no new goods, finished and ready for consumption, are turned out under a year's time, then, obviously, before beginning such a process, there must be on hand a fund of subsistence containing sufficient to cover the entire wants of the workers for one year, and that in a finished state. If we call the Subsistence Fund S, and the year's Want Y, then, in this case, $S = Y$.

If two years be the production period, and the stage period, as before, be annual, it is necessary that, at the beginning of the production period, there should be on hand one year's supply finished, and a second year's supply half finished. In each year the finished year's supply is consumed by the workers, while the half-finished is finished by the workers of the second stage—thus securing the subsistence for the next year—and a fresh year's supply is put in hands by the workers of the first stage, and, in turn, half finished. Here, therefore, if we call the half-finished year's supply a half year's supply, $S = 1\frac{1}{2} Y$.

Similarly for a three years' production process, with annual stages, we require one year's want entirely covered, another $\frac{2}{3}$ covered, and another $\frac{1}{3}$ covered: or, one year's supply finished, another $\frac{2}{3}$ finished, another $\frac{1}{3}$ finished. In each year, then, the finished year's supply is consumed, the $\frac{2}{3}$ finished is finished by the workers of the third stage, the $\frac{1}{3}$ finished becomes $\frac{2}{3}$ finished by the workers of the second stage, and a further year's supply is newly created by the workers of the first stage, and is finished to the extent of $\frac{1}{3}$—whereby, at the end of the year, the *status quo* is restored, and continuous provision is guaranteed. S, therefore, here $= 1 \; Y \times \frac{2}{3} Y \times \frac{1}{3} Y = 2 \; Y$.

Similarly, if the stage is still one year, then in a four years' process $S = (1 + \frac{3}{4} + \frac{1}{2} + \frac{1}{4})Y = 2\frac{1}{2} Y$:

in a five years' process $S = (1 + \frac{4}{5} + \frac{3}{5} + \frac{2}{5} + \frac{1}{5})Y = 3 \ Y$:

in a six years' process $S = (1 + \frac{5}{6} + \frac{4}{6} + \frac{3}{6} + \frac{2}{6} + \frac{1}{6})Y = 3\frac{1}{2} Y$:

in a seven years' process $S = (1 + \frac{6}{7} + \frac{5}{7} + \frac{4}{7} + \frac{3}{7} + \frac{2}{7} + \frac{1}{7})Y = 4 \ Y$:

in a ten years' process $S = (1 + \frac{9}{10} + \frac{8}{10} + \frac{7}{10} + \frac{6}{10} + \frac{5}{10} + \frac{4}{10} + \frac{3}{10} + \frac{2}{10} + \frac{1}{10})Y = 5\frac{1}{2} Y$.

If we look closely into these figures we shall easily discover the law that underlies them : Every production period requires a fund of subsistence containing sufficient to cover half a year more than half the production period.

Suppose we continue our inquiry under the assumption of a different stage period, say, half a year. Here it is quite the same whether the stage period occurs under the division of labour or not, the only thing essential being that, every half-year, finished consumption goods are turned out from the total process. To enter upon a one year's process, with half-yearly stages, what we require is a finished supply for one half-year—during which no fresh consumption goods are turned out—and half-finished supply for the second half-year. During each six months, then, the finished supply is consumed; the half-finished is finished by the workers of the second stage; and a new six months' supply is begun and half finished by the workers of the first stage, whereby the *status quo* is restored. S here $= \frac{1}{2} Y + \frac{1}{2} \times \frac{1}{2} Y = \frac{1}{2} Y + \frac{1}{4} Y = \frac{3}{4} Y$.

Similarly in a two years' production process, with half-yearly stages, we require $\frac{1}{2} Y + \frac{1}{2} \times \frac{3}{4} Y + \frac{1}{2} \times \frac{1}{2} Y + \frac{1}{2} \times \frac{1}{4} Y = (\frac{1}{2} + \frac{3}{8} + \frac{1}{4} + \frac{1}{8}) Y = 1\frac{1}{4} Y$, while in a three years' period we require $\frac{1}{2} + \frac{1}{2} \times \frac{5}{6} + \frac{1}{2} \times \frac{4}{6} + \frac{1}{2} \times \frac{3}{6} + \frac{1}{2} \times \frac{2}{6} + \frac{1}{2} \times \frac{1}{6} = \frac{1}{2} + \frac{5}{12} + \frac{4}{12} + \frac{3}{12} + \frac{2}{12} + \frac{1}{12} = 1\frac{3}{4} Y$.

Here, again, the underlying law is plain : If the stage period be six months the fund necessary contains subsistence for three months longer than half the production period.

If we were to carry out our inquiry still further we should find, similarly, that, where the stage is three months, the fund must contain six weeks' more subsistence, where it is one month, must contain two weeks' more subsistence, than half the production period. And thus we arrive at the general formula of p. 327, that the fund of means of subsistence must be sufficient for half the production period plus half the usual stage period.

INDEX OF AUTHORS MENTIONED

THE END